WORST.
EUROVISION.
EVER.

ROY D. HACKSAW

Published by Earth Island Books
Pickforde Lodge
Pickforde Lane
Ticehurst
TN5 7BN

www.earthisland.co.uk
© Copyright Earth Island Publishing Ltd

First published by Earth Island Publishing 2022

First edition printed March 2022

ISBN 9781739795535

Printed and bound by IngramSpark

Cover art – Kylie Wilson

A note from the author

This story takes place in an alternative timeline where Lys Assia didn't win the first Eurovision Song Contest in 1956. This set off a completely different chain of events where the only two things that still exist from the Eurovision canon that we know and love today are the contest itself, and the bloke with the inflatable hammer who always gets in the way of the cameras in the crowd shots. In this Eurovision universe even the real show's organisers, the European Broadcasting Union, were bought out by a fictional organisation called the Continental Television Federation at some point in the early sixties – partly for fanciful narrative reasons, and partly in the hope that the actual EBU don't get the hump over some of the entirely fictional events that take place in this torrid tale of showbiz shenanigans and televisual topsy turvy and start asking us for money.

With that in mind, you can also be assured that none of the characters in this book represent real life people from the real life Eurovision world – however thinly-veiled or well disguised. There might be a few that are broad composite amalgams of people I've met and worked alongside in more than twenty years of covering the contest as a journalist, but none of them wholly represent actual living people who really exist and breathe air and eat dinners and stuff. So if you think you might have spotted yourself or someone you know in here, you really haven't. Honest.

However, many of the events that take place across the following pages are occasionally similar to things that have happened at actual Eurovision in some shape or form along the way, whether they be on-stage excess, backstage misbehaviour, or scandalous delegation party frolics. But even more of it is just made up comedy nonsense – so it's up to you to work out what is vaguely real and what is not. Although trust me, in my days of going to the contest I've witnessed tomfoolery that would put even the most rock and roll of musical artists to shame.

But when it boils down to it, this is just a silly bundle of vaguely entertaining fluff, all wrapped up in the casings of an international festival of top quality song – much like the real contest itself. So turn your brain off and dive in for a look at what really goes on – kind of – behind the scenes at the world's most loved, and loathed, televised musical event!

I dedicate this book to all the amazing people that I've met at this contest over the years, many of who have gone on to become my closest friends and confidants, but very few of which I have ever actually met in their own countries. You're all beauties, the lot of you. Well, most of you...

PS I finished writing this story in December 2020, long before any of the songs or artists for the 2021 or 2022 contests had been chosen, so any similarity to anything that has happened since is so ludicrously coincidental that I must be some kind of a seer. Or maybe a wizard.

THE RUN UP
1

"And with the results of the public telephone vote now complete, Michi Rotari is leading Maxim Munteanu by a staggering 24 points as we move on to the scores of the juries."

Michi Rotari could barely believe he was hearing those words. They rang around his brain in a confused blur of muffled sound, and his vision began to develop a strange blue haze. Was this really, actually happening he wondered?

This was the fifteenth time that Michi had entered O Melodie Pentru Europa, Moldova's selection show for the Eurovision Song Contest. But on every one of his fourteen previous attempts he'd failed to get even as far as the big showbizzy studio finals in March, instead going no further the live-streamed audition process every time. These auditions were a brutal affair, where each act lined up to sing their chosen song into an unchecked microphone, and with no hint of the backing musicians or flashy stage production that they could expect if they made it onto the proper show. Michi would be the first to admit that he didn't have as strong a voice as some of the other performers, but he made up for that with enthusiasm and stagecraft – as well as what some might describe as extreme strangeness. He'd become a cult figure amongst Eurovision fans worldwide for his repeated fruitless efforts, but he just couldn't break into the line up for the final show. Until this year, that is.

Quite to an entire continent's surprise, Moldova had won last year's Eurovision with a slick dance number that turned out to be incredibly memeworthy. It had become an international TikTok sensation during the weeks running up to the contest, which gave it something of a victor's edge. Their win, in turn, gave the nation the right to have first refusal at hosting the following year's contest, which they grabbed boldly with both hands before they could check whether they had an arena big enough to actually hold the thing. And within minutes of the confirmation that they would most definitely be holding the show in twelve months' time, Moldova's most popular and all-time best-selling performing artist Maxim Munteanu announced that he was very much interested in being his nation's representative in their hosting year. And that was a pretty big deal. However, he insisted that he didn't just want to be handed the golden ticket to Eurovision glory without a fight, insisting that he put it to the people like the national hero that he was, and let them decide whether he was worthy or not.

Of course, this led to much fear and consternation within the Moldovan music industry. Who was going to dare to pit themselves against the mighty Maxim? Who was likely to risk all the time and effort of writing and recording a song and devising a killer stage routine for it, only to be tossed aside on Mr Munteanu's inevitable path to glory? Nobody in their right mind would even consider such a thing, surely? Fortunately, the Moldovan music scene is well populated with people who fit that description pretty well, and who were more than happy to give it a go. But where around eighty bands and singers would try their hand in any given year, this time only four plucky souls dared the shame and humiliation of being battered into meek submission by the all-conquering Maxim Munteanu on national prime time television. And these were:

Mikael Doibani: a car park attendant from the tiny city of Comrat in the south of the country whose mother sent in a tape – an actual cassette tape – of him barking out a repetitive folksy little number while he was troweling about in the garden one Spring afternoon.

Iulia Cucerenco: a junior school teacher from Moldova's second city of Balti, in the north. She liked to make up pretty little songs for her pupils to sing along to, and thought that it might be nice for them to see her singing one of their favourites on the TV.

Viktor Golban: a pensioner from the capital Chişinău who had been entering long rambling half- spoken tales about his childhood for almost as many years as Michi had been trying to get onto the show.

And finally, Michi Rotari. Michi was also from the capital and worked in a greeting card shop in a mall in the centre of the city. He'd also long harboured the ambition to become an international rock star. But he had to work out how to get his songs released first, and figured that his best chance of finding quick fame was via Eurovision. Although it had taken him fifteen years to get even this far.

This unlikely foursome were up against the aforementioned Maxim Munteanu. Born in the self- proclaimed breakaway state of Transnistria, which sits grumpily along the easternmost edge of the country, he was a veteran of fifty-five album releases and endless television specials. He was also the only person ever to be awarded Moldova's highest honour, the Order of the Republic, on two separate occasions. Now thought to be in his late sixties, he first became a singing star back when the country was still part of the Soviet Union in the early 1970s, and so holds a massive place in the hearts of not only the country's sizeable Russian population, but also those who still looked

back upon the old Communist days with a dewy-eyed nostalgia. He was also one of the very few Moldovans who'd had major hits outside of his country's borders, and still toured regularly, playing to packed crowds at massive arenas in Russia, Belarus, Kazakhstan, Ukraine and Romania. Oh, and Namibia, weirdly, but no one had ever quite worked out why. So surely the four hopeful singers who dared to stand against him in this year's show were nothing more than sacrificial lambs, there simply to make up the numbers and give the impression of a fair competition – which in turn would make the old master appear even more popular than he already was.

However, there were a few people who'd taken against the virtual anointing of this year's musical messiah and had decided to try and do something about it. The Anarchist Song League Of Moldova, or ASLOM for short, claimed that the veteran songsmith was nothing more than a cipher for the state, and feared that this level of nostalgia for the old days was dangerous in a country whose people, in the main, desperately wanted to be considered as a modern European democracy. Then there was another, more politically motivated group called Moldova For The People, who were deeply suspicious of Transnistria. They'd noticed that seven of the last ten songs to represent Moldova at Eurovision had hailed from that region and wanted to stop it from happening again this year. On top of those two belligerent organisations, a popular late night TV talkshow host called Ruslan Rusu had begun to pour a little mischief into the ether by suggesting to his viewers how funny it would be to give old man Munteanu a bit of a scare, and had encouraged them to all vote for one of the lesser-known artists in the the national final just for the fun of it. And quite by chance, each of the three groups of people backing this idea had decided to pick Michi Rotari as their stalking horse candidate – the one they would pile their support behind to give the establishment a bit of a scare.

All of this had given the people at Moldova Smash something of a headache. It was a relatively new independent TV station, but through insistent lobbying they had quickly attained full membership status of the Continental Television Federation. This, in turn, gave them full rights to broadcast the Eurovision Song Contest, which they very soon did. That success encouraged the new company to put in a massive bid to buy the rights to the long running O Melodie Pentru Europa competiton, and this was now the third time that they'd organised the show. The winner of their first attempt, a shimmering and powerful ballad called Why Do We Pretend, came second at Eurovision proper, while last year's banger won the thing by a mile. So Moldova Smash now had a reputation to uphold, and didn't want any old ordinary Joe off the streets embarrassing both the station and the nation come that Saturday night in May. Moldova had by right of being the reigning champions automatically qualified for the Eurovision final on the Saturday night, so whatever they picked to represent them would have the eyes of a quarter of the world upon them, so they really didn't want to mess it up.

The ideal contestant that a host nation should have representing them on their home turf needs to be an absolutely safe pair of hands – one that the home crowd would adore, the jury panels would give a respectable number of points to, and that the folks at home in TV land would enjoy just enough to get them onto the top half of the scoreboard without ever really challenging the contenders. Because although every competing nation at Eurovision dearly yearned for the honour of both winning and hosting the contest one day, there was always the nagging fear of having to run this expensive and complicated old bandwagon for two years in succession. So Maxim Munteanu was absolutely perfect for this role. He was experienced and likeable, and his song had a beautifully warm everyman tone about it that should just about see him right when it came to the tallying of votes at the end of the evening. It was the perfect option. The last thing the execs at Moldova Smash needed was some rank amateur from the musical hinterland stamping about clumsily on stage when they were trying to showcase the very best that their young and lesser- known country had to offer, and the coincidental tripartite campaign from the three very different agencies that had chosen Michi as their favoured candidate had made them very nervous indeed. So they figured that they'd give themselves a couple of insurance policies to ensure that the worst didn't indeed happen.

First of all they reversed the standard format of the voting element of the show and announced the televoting first. This would be followed followed by a short musical interlude from last year's winners, before moving onto the points decided by the juries – a scheme that gave them breathing room to work out exactly what they had to do to help things along should the results not be going their way. Next, they selected a jury who were either of pensionable age, or residents of

Transnistria, just to give their favoured artist a bit of a helping hand if the scores were against them. The musical interlude, of course, gave them just enough time to decide exactly how many points Maxim needed to win the show by a believable margin, and they could then, for want of a better word, suggest to the jurors how they might like to think about voting in order to get the result that they wanted. They hoped then that this strategy should get them over the line with the only credible act on their show, while taking every possible potential pitfall into consideration. After all, he was the odds-on favourite at the bookmakers, the Eurovision fansites all had him winning by a distance, and the opinion polls in Moldova suggested he would win with more points than the other four artists combined.

Stefan Smolenko and Dumi Enache were the two executives at Moldova Smash with the most to lose if things didn't go their way. Stefan was the executive producer of O Melodie Pentru Europa, while Dumi was the head of light entertainment programming. They were certain that lovely old Maxim was a shoe-in to take the win, but they both still had nagging fears at the back of their minds that something was going to go terribly wrong, and had done everything that they possibly could to set the odds in the old man's favour. Maxim, however, knew nothing of this. Despite his immense fame and popularity in the country he was a warm and gentle soul, and that perhaps was a big part of his charm. His insistence that he stood in open competition with his countrymen wasn't done through any kind of vain pride, but for a genuine love of the music and the people of his nation. And if he ever found out that Stefan and Dumi were trying to fix the circumstances in his favour there was a very big chance that he would pull out of the competition altogether. So the pair had to be incredibly careful how they went about it.

They'd hatched up their emergency plan after watching the equivalent Eurovision qualifying show from Belarus. Every year one song would soar ahead in the first section of the voting, only for there to be a long, awkward break while some local pop star sang a medley of songs that were considerably more interesting than any that the competing artists had just offered. While all this was going on, it was heavily rumoured that the show's producers rang the President to ask him which song he would prefer from the list of potential winners. Then, after they'd got the nod from him upstairs, the points were arranged to give his favoured song just enough points to sneak over the line and win. Stefan and Dumi were keen not to make it look quite that obvious however, although with only five contestants in the show it would be tricky to make any tweaking of the results look entirely believable. So as the chairman of the 20 person jury passed them the envelope holding the tally of their votes, they each held their breath in fear as they opened it.

"Oh man!" they said in unison, not entirely believing what they were seeing.

On stage, the show's two glamorous hosts Elina Gospodinova and Bobby Odobescu were patiently filling dead air with inane chatter while the show's producers argued in their ear pieces about how they were going to present the results. Elina was a seasoned professional, well used to hosting high profile TV events. But Bobby was something of a newcomer, having been plucked from a life as a popular local YouTube influencer by Moldova Smash in the hope that he'd bring some of his younger followers back to television. But where he was great with off-the-cuff online presenting from his own living room, he wasn't terribly comfortable with standing on a big stage in front of a crowd of people while working to a loose script with someone that he hardly knew. And this made their conversation come over as perhaps just a little bit stilted.

"So Bobby," Elina asked, hoping to wring a bit of personality out of the newcomer, "how was your first time?"

Bobby looked sheepish. "Erm, well, I don't think I should really talk about that on live television," he said nervously. "He was a priest after all, and I was very young..."

"No no no!" Elina shrieked, pretending to laugh in a way that suggested Bobby was joking when she clearly knew that he very much wasn't. "I meant, how was your first time presenting O Melodie Pentru Europa?"

"Of course!" blustered Bobby. "Just my little joke! Yes, it's been absolutely great! There's been some absolutely great songs, and some absolutely great singers! And I'm hoping for an absolutely great result tonight!"

An angry voice came into both of their ear pieces. "Get that idiot off the mic, Elina," barked the director from the gallery. "You do the fills from now on. And don't – DON'T – ask that babbling lunk any more questions!"

"OK!" said Elina out loud, talking to both the director and the viewing public at the same time. "We are nearly here with the results. In the meantime ladies and gentlemen of the audience, who do you want to win?"

She opened her arms and beckoned to the crowd to shout out the name of their favourites. Then chaos ensued. About sixty percent of the audience immediately shouted for Maxim, while almost everybody else screamed for Michi, only just that little bit louder. Somewhere at the back a loud, shrill voice was shrieking Mikael Doibani's name at the top of her lungs, and it sounded a lot like his mum. But then things began to get agitated between the two most vocal sections of the crowd, and they started to push and jostle each other until security filed in to separate them. Despite how massive it looked on TV, the studio was surprisingly small in real life, and with so many people crammed into such a tiny space the atmosphere was now febrile and pretty much ready to blow.

"Calm them the bloody hell down, Elina would you," the director bellowed loudly in her ear. "We don't want a riot kicking off on live TV... Again!"

"OK!" she said again, raising her hands into the air once more, before slowly lowering them as she wiggled her fingers in a soothing motion. The crowd quelled at her showbiz power. "People, we are nearly there. We've got the message that the votes are on their way. We just want to count them twice to make sure that we're extra certain they're correct. This is a big decision, after all. And while we're all here, let's have a big portion of your applause for Bobby Odobescu. Didn't he do a great job tonight?"

The crowd half-heartedly clapped for the terrible new host for no more than a couple of seconds, but it still gave Elina a moment to think of her next move.

"Right, they're here," she said, putting her finger to her ear in that manner that suggested she was listening to the gallery – when in actual fact she was making it all up as she went along.

"No they're not!" came three voices from the gallery at once, each as panicked as the others. "Yes, yes, here they are," she continued.

"Shit!" cried Stefan. "We'd better give her what we've got or things are going to get really awkward for her."

"Not half as awkward as they're going to be if a full-blown riot kicks off out there!" Dumi shouted back.

"This is it, we've got to do it. Let's just announce them and be damned!" Stefan announced.

"It's your head on the block, mate," Dumi conceded, absolving himself of any blame. "You go for it!"

"OK, Elina luvvy," Stefan whispered into his gallery mic. "I'm going to give you the results in reverse order. When we get to the last two, I'm going to pause, you're going to ad lib a little fill about the songs that are still in it – you know, to build up the tension –

and then you're going to announce the runner-up, give his points, then announce the winner... but whatever happens do not tell the punters how many points he got. And for Christ's sake don't let Bobby say anything!"

"Right!" Elina affirmed. "Here we go, the results..."

She paused for a couple of seconds, looking to Bobby to try and increase the tension. But Bobby just stared back at her blankly.

"In fifth place, with seven jury votes, giving him a total of... seven votes... is..."

She paused again for a couple of beats to try and give things just a hint of tension when the whole country knew exactly who was going to be last.

"Mikael Doibani!"

The crowd all gave a polite round of applause and a collective sigh of commiseration, while Mikael Doibani's mum went berserk at the back of the audience, screaming all kinds of abuse at the two presenters for the measley votes they'd just given her son. Elina graciously ignored her.

"In fourth place, with fourteen votes, giving him a grand total of 36 votes... is... Viktor Golban!"

The crowd were a little more appreciative of Viktor's positioning, as he'd practically become a fixture on this show over the years, and fourth was his highest ever placing by some way. Even if it was also second from last.

"Well done Viktor," the host said warmly, as she gave him a very professional peck on the cheek. "See you again next year!"

There was a brief pause, as the tension music got just a little bit louder. The TV screen for the folks back home had split three ways to show the faces of Michi, Maxim and Iulia Cucerenco.

"And in third place…" Elina announced, "with 26 votes… giving her…"

Iulia's shoulders slumped at the mention of the word 'her', while Michi's face was smeared with absolute confusion.

"… a total of 45 votes… is…"

But there was next to no tension, either in the audience or on the stage, as everybody had already worked it out.

"Iulia Cucerenco!"

Elina went over and gave the deeply disappointed schoolteacher a big friendly hug, but Iulia barely responded in her disappointment.

"So!" Elina announced, putting her finger to her ear once more." We have two left… Maxim… And Michi. Maxim and Michi. Who's it going to be, audience?"

"For God's sake don't wind them up any more, Elina!" the director screamed down the mic. But it was too late. Each rival faction in the crowd had begun to chant their favoured artist's name, and with both sets of fans coming from vastly different ideological viewpoints things began to get just a little bit edgy.

"OK! OK!" she shouted above the rabble, "I have the scores…"

Stefan fed the numbers down her earpiece, and Elina stopped for a moment, took a big deep breath – followed by a hard swallow – and continued to build up the tension.

"In second place... with 18 votes..."

The crowd gasped, then began to work out all the possible scenarios in their heads, as did the good people of Moldova watching at home and the many thousands of Eurovision fans tuning in on the internet right across the world.

"So hang about," said one of Michi's fans wearing a bright yellow ASLOM t-shirt, in clear earshot of the Maxim faction. "Doing the maths quickly in my head, this either means that Maxim's got a ridiculously low score with the juries and Michi has won by a mile... OR... Michi's been done over by the juries and Maxim has stolen this by a couple of points. And I know which version of the story I'm suspecting."

This led to much angry muttering as the theory began to spread like falling dominoes through the crowd. Elina could sense the rising tension in front of her and sped up her delivery, hoping to distract them a little.

"...giving him a total of 78 votes... IS..."

The crowd fell silent. The nation fell silent. A scattering of national final spotters from around the globe staring at their laptops fell silent. The tension was so thick that you couldn't spoon it out of a cup.

"...Michi Rotari! Which means that you, Maxim Munteanu will be representing Moldova as we host our very first Eurovision Song Contest in May! Congratulations Maxim sir!"

As the gold and silver ticker tape began to tumble in wads from the sky, Michi stood silently in the middle of it all looking as though the very soul had been ripped out of him. He may have been surrounded by the mad joy and excitement of Maxim's win, but he felt terribly alone all of a sudden. It as if he was watching it all on a VR headset rather than being at the heart of the action. Suddenly a voice from the crowd ripped him out of his internalised gloom.

"Michi! Michi!" came the insistent voice. Michi looked down to see one of the more burly men in an ASLOM t-shirt shouting his name.

He crouched down at the front of the stage, and politely replied "I'm so sorry I didn't win. I tried my very best for you."

"You did brilliantly, Michi," came the voice again, "but do you know how much he beat you by?" "Ooh I don't know," the disappointed singer answered. "I don't think they announced it.

The show's co-host Bobby Odobescu suddenly slid into view. The audience had almost forgotten that he was there, but he had some information that he'd heard in his earpiece that would literally stop the show.

"One point, mate," Bobby blundered. "He won by one, single point!"

Michi's heart sank. Would he ever get that close to his biggest dream again? But as he began to wallow in his sadness once more, the news of the scores began to ripple through the crowd, and the Michi faction became even more angry and restless.

"Shit Bobby, what did you have to say that for?!" screamed a voice in his headset. "Elina, close this thing down... quickly."

"OK!" she said. "So we have a winner. Maxim, come here for a moment. How does it feel to be representing your country at its most important Eurovision ever?"

"You're going off piste, Elina," shouted the director. "Close this thing down fast... NOW!"

The contest's elderly victor offered a big, warm smile to the camera, before walking over to Michi and putting a friendly arm around him.

"I want to thank this gentleman here for giving me such a good fight," Maxim warmly proclaimed. "Michi Rotari embodies all that is great about this beautiful country of ours. Strength, commitment, and that most intrinsically Moldovan quality of never, ever giving up. Sir, I hope that it's finally your year next year. And if anything happens to me between now and May, I want the TV company to honour my wishes and make you our Eurovision representative. I honestly think you deserve it."

Michi just stood there, looking at this great national hero with a tear in his eye. That was probably the most incredible thing that anybody has ever said to him, and so he swung around and gave Maxim a massive embrace. While he was hugging him, the veteran singer whispered into Michi's ear.

"And if you ever want anything, anything at all – from advice, to help with your music – just give me a call. I will make it my duty to be your mentor from this day on, young sir!"

It was all that Michi could do to whisper the words 'Thank you!' back to Maxim, as his mouth was dry and his legs were starting to buckle beneath him. But as he gave his thanks an enormous hubbub suddenly kicked off in the crowd behind him. With tensions already high in the audience, Mikael Doibani's mother had grabbed a fold-up chair and thrown it in disgust across the audience, hitting a member of ASLOM square in the face. Once he'd picked himself up from the ground, the ASLOM member shouted at the top of his lungs – "Right, they've been asking for it! Let's get 'em!" – and led a charge at the Maxim faction on the other side of the studio floor. The two sides met in the centre of the room with a crunching thud and started to scrap it out there and then, on live TV. Shoes were flying everywhere as security began to usher the contestants and presenters off the stage to safety.

"Right cut, cut now!" bellowed the panicked voice of the director from the gallery. "Let's go straight to the video of the winning song and get the cameras away from the rioting! What the hell did you have to tell them that for, Bobby? Your television days are numbered, son!"

As they were bundled away to the safety of their dressing rooms, Maxim caught up with Michi again and grabbed him warmly by the hand.

"That wasn't just for the camera, Michi my lad," he said. "I really mean it. I see the same spark in you that I saw in myself in the early days. Your music may not be exactly to the taste of an old man like me, but your spirit is bold, and that excites me. Let me get you a few singing lessons and then I'll introduce you to some reliable faces in the music industry and we can work on getting you back even bigger and better for next year! Now let's go and hide away safely in our dressing rooms until all of this excitement is over."

And with that, Maxim placed one of his business cards into Michi's quivering hands, cracked a massive friendly smile, gave a military style salute, and waved the younger singer a hearty goodbye before he passed through his dressing room door.

Michi stood open-mouthed as he thought about what had just happened over the last ten minutes or so. He really couldn't believe that any of it was true. Surely he was dreaming a big weird dream, and he'd wake up in his tower block apartment any second now. But no, it was all true. Every last bit of it, and he wasn't entirely sure how his life could ever quite be the same again. He opened the door to his dressing room and just sat there until well after the noise of the riot outside had subsided, half-crying, half-laughing at the events of this strangest of days.

2

Once the riot had finally quelled, the artists had been sent home, and the studios were all locked up safely, Stefan and Dumi went back to the offices of Moldova Smash to try to work out what had just happened, and to get their story straight for their audience with the TV company's senior management the next morning. The meeting had originally been booked to work out a plan of attack for presenting the winning song at Eurovision proper. But they now feared it would take a more serious turn and they'd have to explain away the more unexpected events that happened during the live broadcast.

The headquarters of the Moldova Smash organisation were laid out in a curious arrangement on the most distant outskirts of Chişinău. The studios were nothing like you'd imagine for a major European broadcaster, resembling a cluttered collection of army buildings and light industrial units that had been converted at speed into something more televisual as soon as Moldova Smash got their broadcasting licence. At the highest point of the compound sat a massive metal TV aerial that looked more like a converted electricity pylon than any kind of traditional broadcast equipment. The rumour around the offices was that Smash's owners bought it cheap from a disused satellite tracking station in Azerbaijan, painted it red and white, then took an omnidirectional broadcast transmitter that they'd bartered from Chişinău's biggest cab company and bolted it roughly to the top. But however Heath Robinson it may have looked it certainly did the job, and still managed to broadcast the station's content not just across the whole of Moldova, but also for a significant distance into their neighbouring countries of Ukraine and Romania too. Although it did tend to struggle a bit if the weather was too windy. Or foggy.

The company offices, though, were in a squat twelve story tower block a good hundred yards away on the other side of a busy duel carriageway. There were no official crossing points or lights at the most direct route, so anyone who needed to travel from one building to the other would have to either take an eight-minute walk up the hill to a relatively safe crossing point, or run the gauntlet of the city's notoriously aggressive drivers and dash through any rare gaps in the oncoming traffic, then hop over the crash barrier and wait on the central reservation until the lights changed at the top of the road, before using that small window of opportunity to scamper across the remaining stretch of road while hoping that nobody had jumped the lights. Which quite often they had. It was a dangerous business, and a member of the station's staff was hospitalised on average every three months while trying to take the quick route.

The building itself was a bleak affair. Built in the Soviet era, it was a big and cheerless chunk of concrete thrown up on what looked like a traffic island. Inside it was everything that you'd imagine an office block built at the heart of the seventies would look like around those parts. The first thing that you met as you walked in through the stiff metal doors was a massive dark foyer that was swathed in deep brown wood panelling and formica everywhere you looked. The whole place was lit naturally in the daytime from a big window in the roof of the central atrium, although the glass had become almost opaque with algae, moss and dead pigeons over the years, so now an eerie green tinge was cast across the centre of the building. Its lighting was set to the same light meter as the street lights outside, so in the hour or so before full darkness it was almost impossible to get any work done unless you'd brought in your own torch. And everywhere you looked, no matter what time of day it was, there were middle-aged women in blue checked aprons and headscarves mopping the floors in a surly manner. Heaven forbid if you ever happened to step through a bit they'd just wiped with their dark and grimy looking water, as you'd quickly receive a deeply disappointed tut, and a scowl that could melt through three-inch steel plate armour. The grim building didn't give off an atmosphere that was conducive to creative work at the best of times, but after what had just happened across the road, Stefan and Dumi were in no great frame of mind to think about anything outside of saving their own backsides.

"So you're really, actually, telling me that Maxim won fair and square by a single bloody measly point?" Dumi cried in exasperation, as he plopped himself into his big office chair and scattered some papers that recorded the final voting across his enormous leather-topped desk.

"Seriously Dumi, he did," said Stefan, still barely believing it himself.

"But it just looks so dodgy, mate. Especially after the jury decided to give that idiot fool Doibani seven points! I mean, what were they thinking there? This looks like a fit up from start to end. We definitely didn't fix it though, did we, Stefan? Please tell me we didn't."

"Absolutely not – well, unless of course you count our careful selection of the jurors. These numbers are straight up, as bad for the company as they might look?" Stefan explained.

"What are the fan press saying?" Dumi asked. "You grab your phone and I'll grab mine and we'll have a look."

Both men fired up their social media accounts, and their shoulders sank in unison. "Worst fit up in years," said one message. "Anyone would think this was Belarus!"

"How bloody obvious was it THAT was going to happen?" said another. "This is a Euro scandal of the highest order!"

"Same old Moldova, always cheating!" said a third.

"This isn't good," Stefan said, with a deeply worried look on his face. "I know it's only the Eurovision fansites having a bit of a jibber, and they always hate everything anyway. But the grown up papers often monitor what they're saying, and if they pick up on any suggestion of us cheating before we put on the big contest then we're going to get terrible international press before we even start the rehearsals – and that's not exactly the best way to showcase our beautiful country to the world, is it now, Dumi. What do you reckon we should do?"

"I guess we'll just have to be honest and declare all the voting results and numbers, and maybe get a few comments from some of the jurors on the breakfast show tomorrow. Get a quick press release knocked up, Stefan, then I'll give it the eye over and get it sent out to the papers before we leave. We've really got to hit this head on and get in there before they grab us by the throats and wave us about like rabbits in the jaws of wolves."

"Of course it didn't help matters any when Maxim promised the Eurovision slot to that goth freak if anything happened to him. Who gave him the authority to say that, Dumi?"

"You know Maxim – he's an authority unto himself. And what he says unfortunately goes. If we act against his word we'll have the government on us like a ton of bricks, and you know how precariously we're gripping onto our licence at the minute. They're watching our every move now that the eyes of the world are on us, so everything's got to appear to be above board and bang on message. Going against the explicit word of our biggest living national treasure would be exactly the opposite of that, so sadly I think we're stuck with it. Let's just hope nothing happens to the old goat between now and then, eh!"

"Yes, Dumi," said Stefan, "I'll make sure that we've got full medical insurance for him, and double the premiums between now and May. As far as I know he's not got any underlying health conditions, but I'll make sure that we give him a full medical and overhaul next week, and then plan a promotional regime that's not too taxing for a man of his age." Stefan stopped and pondered for a moment. "Hold on, how old exactly IS he? I genuinely don't know."

"Well the official story is that he's in his late sixties," Dumi explained.

"But I seem to remember my old grandma telling me stories about him from when they were both much younger, and she's well into her eighties now. So unless her memory is on the blink, he could be a lot older than he claims. We've got to keep an eye on him and give him the very best care."

"Well at least the contest is taking place in his home town," said Stefan, "so he can stay in comfort at his own ranch, rather than at some dodgy hotel with the younger artists shouting about down the corridors all day and night. There had to be some benefit to going to that godforsaken sink hole in bandit country."

"Ah yes, Tiraspol," Dumi replied, shaking his head in dismay. "I'd almost forgotten Tiraspol for a moment there."

When Moldova had unexpectedly won Eurovision nine short months earlier, most people had assumed that the next year's contest would be held in the country's capital, Chişinău. It wasn't perhaps Europe's prettiest or most exciting city, but it did have a certain old world charm to it, and was just about the best the country had to offer. But to spread the Eurovision narrative out across the whole year, the CTF always liked to hold a bidding process where different towns and cities from all over the hosting nation could put in a tender explaining exactly why they should be holding it there – and then after all that has happened, the city you first thought of usually wins. It always seemed like a bit of pretence, as in most cases the most appropriate arena was usually located in any given country's capital. There was also the issue of accommodation, and although fairly light on hotels compared to most other major European cities, the vast majority of Moldova's reasonably decent rooms were in Chişinău.

However, there was one small problem with the capital, as the city's main arena was only big enough to hold an estimated 5000 people for gigs at a push – and that's before you factor in the traditionally massive Eurovision stage which usually knocks a few hundred off the final audience numbers. And if that wasn't quite bad enough, the building had been nearing final completion for some years now, and had never quite been fully finished. The next most popular option is usually to put some kind of a roof on the host city's biggest football ground. But the Zimbru Stadium, despite holding a good ten thousand punters, didn't have continuous stands and had massive open gaps in two corners of the ground, so it didn't match the official CTF venue criteria. Even the city's main exhibition centre, the delightfully named MoldExpo, was no bigger than your average Aldi store, and most definitely didn't have the height clearance or roof strength for all those heavy lights and staging equipment. So the city burghers of Chișinău had got themselves into something of a panic trying to work out quite where they could hold it. And just as they were considering how they were going to build something big enough in the pitifully short space of time that was available to them, their worst nightmare happened. And that nightmare came in the shape of a man called Timur Turgenev.

Turgenev was the de facto king of Transnistria in everything but name. A massively wealthy businessman, the official story was that he'd made his fortune first in local corner shops and chemists, and then in property, before he got involved in the international oil trade and joined the ranks of the super rich. But there were stories that he'd actually made his first pot of cash by smuggling cheap Moldovan booze and cigarettes into Ukraine, and then helping to launder money from the Russian ganglords in exchange for political influence. Indeed, Russian agitation had always been suspected in Transnistria, and there were many in the rest of Moldova who believed that the breakaway republic was just a vassal satellite state that was being used to nip away at Moldova's new positioning as a part of modern Europe, and to act as a remote staging post for some of the Kremlin's more dubious international actions. There was never any solid evidence for of this, of course, but those rumours never quite seemed to die – although people who tried to question Turgenev's power very often did. And often in highly suspicious circumstances.

He'd piled absolutely millions of his own money into improving Transnistria's infrastructure, trying to turn its capital, Tiraspol, into a flourishing Eurasian trading city. Pretty much any major capital project that was ever proposed in the small breakaway pseudo state got designed, built and completed in a matter of months. And nearly always on Turgenev's say so.

Transnistria was the strangest of places even before it attempted to break away from Moldova. A narrow strip of land between the Dniester river and the Ukranian border, and only 24 miles wide at its broadest stretch, it had been at the centre of a geographic tug of war between the Romanian, Russian and Ukrainian states, as well as the full might of the Ottoman Empire, for centuries. But even before Moldova broke away from the Soviet Union and became its own independent nation in 1991, Transnistria had declared itself fully independent and completely separate to any other country. There had been numerous scraps and skirmishes over the area in recent years, with many people losing their lives over this tiny patch of unremarkable yet contentious land. The two sides of the argument currently sat in an uneasy truce, although close observers suggest that if the wrong kind of thing was said at the wrong kind of time it could all kick off again. And kick off big time.

For such a small place, Transnistria had an awful lot of money passing through it, and harboured some pretty big ambitions. And so it was that, upon hearing of Chișinău's difficultly at finding an adequate venue to hold the following year's Eurovision Song Contest, Timur Turgenev stepped in and declared that he would personally bankroll the entire project, just so long as it took place in the Transnistrian capital, Tiraspol. Jaws dropped the continent over, as people started to check it out on maps, then wonder how such a small and obscure city would be able to hold such a major event.

"What about the arena?" the world's press asked.

"I will build one in eight months," came Turgenev's reply. "If they could do it in Azerbaijan then we can most certainly do it here!"

"But what about the hotels? Surely you don't have enough rooms to accommodate an entire Eurovision – not only for the performers, but the crew, the press, and the paying fans, too?" came the next question.

"Then we shall build them as well," came the oligarch's instant reply. "Not only will we construct thirty world class hotels in the city before next February, but we will bring in fifty hotel boats to moor on the banks of the Dniester, our nation's most defining and beautiful river, to offer more reasonable accommodation to the fans and tourists."

"But, but, the airport?" was the next big query. "That's nowhere near big enough, surely? And there are no scheduled flights from most of the rest of Europe. Will people have to travel in from Chişinău?"

"No, not at all!" came the assured response. "We are currently in the process of building a multi- million dollar new terminal at our own airport, and I will personally charter flights from every major European city to get people directly to Tiraspol. It is absolutely no problem."

For every question that people asked of him, Timur Turgenev had an instant, and to be frank pretty believable answer. It almost sounded as if he had been planning this out thoroughly for many years. The people at the CTF were forced to agree, and awarded the contest to Tiraspol as they appeared to be the only city with both a detailed, and doable, plan.

However, the little matter of how they were actually going to broadcast the contest was a different matter. Tele Transnistria still hadn't been accepted as a national broadcaster by the CTF, as up to this point the tiny wannabe nation had only been recognised as an actual country by the fellow ex- Soviet breakaway states of Abkhazia, Artsakh, and South Ossetia. And to be fair, at this early stage

in their development they didn't have the experience or the expertise to broadcast this kind of massive international event. So Turgenev was grudgingly forced to do a deal with Moldova Smash and commission them to put the televised element of the show together. Neither side was greatly happy about it, but the wealthy Transnistrian had promised to pump an awful lot of cash the way of Moldova Smash in order to produce the best show possible, so Smash just bit their tongue and got on with it, despite the constant interference from Turgenev's advisors.

And now, with three months to go, the oligarch had been true to his word. Everything that he had promised had been built in double quick time. The flights had been commissioned and booked, and the hotel boats had been brought in an positioned perfectly along the river. And despite the CTF's fears that none of this would have been completed in time, they had been pleasantly surprised at quite how professional and efficient the whole process had been – especially when they thought back to how some of the preparations had gone in supposedly more stable Western countries in the recent past – and they really had very little to complain about with the way this one was going.

But they could never in their wildest dreams have imagined quite how the next few weeks were going to turn out...

3

The day after the strangeness of the O Melodie Pentru Europa show, Michi Rotari was at home in his apartment on the eleventh floor of a tower block in the Sectorul Ciocana neighbourhood at the very easternmost edge of Chișinău. It's an area typical of cities in the former Soviet Union, populated with massive stretches of tall apartment buildings scattered around a single broad boulevard where all the shops and bars and restaurants are located. And despite it being a majority Moldovan neighbourhood, the local Russian element are especially proud of their heritage, and insist on writing everything in their businesses in the cyrillic alphabet, which has led to a weird self-imposed apartheid where each side of the population keep themselves to themselves in distinct corners of the suburb. It was cut off from the main centre of Chișinău by the massive and bleak Parcul Râșcani, ostensibly a city park, but in reality a huge wedge of dirty woods where people went to drink, shoot up, and dump their household waste. It was never a surprise if the odd dead body suddenly appeared amongst the scrubby trees, and the parents of Sectorul Ciocana did everything they could to keep their children from playing down there. This led to the residents of the neighbourhood considering themselves as coming from an almost separate town to the rest of Chișinău, and their only means of escape was via the unreliable little white marshrutka buses that beetled infrequently around the outer fringes of the sector.

All of this only added to Michi's sense of otherness, and was a massive factor in his decades long attempt to find some kind of salvation in the world of rock'n'roll. As a teenager he played in a succession of short lived metal bands, at first as a bass player, but later as the lead singer. He had a strange, awkward charisma that set him aside from the other neighbourhood rock kids. While they wanted nothing more than to rock out at a local bar in front a few of their mates, Michi had his sights set on much higher things, and harboured an ambition to become Moldova's first big international heavy metal star. The main problem, however, was that despite his quite unique stage presence, his singing voice was thin and willowy and never seemed to match the music of the bands he was playing in. His big epiphany came when he was sixteen and met a bunch of local goths called Glory Of The Crow, whose singer had recently committed suicide. They hailed from the Durleşti neighbourhood right on the other side of the city, but they'd seen him play in a metal band called Dirty Brew about a year or so earlier, and had him earmarked as a replacement for their rapidly deteriorating lead singer if the worst came to the worst. Which indeed it eventually sadly did. After a couple of early disastrous gigs in some of the dark and dingy cellar bars that nestled at the foot of tower blocks across the city, they finally clicked into place and got to play a couple of dozen shows across the country, once even travelling down to Odessa on the south coast of Ukraine to play at a fairly substantial goth festival. Michi soon realised that this was his music, as not only did it speak to the darkness of his inner soul, but it also totally matched his strange and awkward on-stage persona. The band even got to put out a self-released album called Journey's End. Full of dark caterwauling songs about death, loneliness and the end of days, it still remains highly collectable to aficionados of gothic music the world over. However, as is often the way with teenage bands they didn't last too long. A couple of them grew out of playing in bands and joined the army, while the drummer and the keyboard player had children and couldn't afford either the time or the money to keep going. The only members that remained were Michi and a guitarist who preferred to call himself Deep Loneliness, and together they hatched upon an idea to get this most dark of all music genres onto the TV.

At this point Moldova had only just begun to take part in the Eurovision Song Contest, and the pair of spooky kids realised that this could be an opportunity to get their music heard outside of the confines of their national borders. So together they wrote a song that they were convinced would be ideal for Europe's favourite music show. But unfortunately for them, Moldova wasn't quite ready for a gloomy noise ballad called The Perfect Corpse, and so began an obsessional fifteen year quest to get onto Eurovision. Their next three attempts were no more successful. I Only Love You Now You're Dead was deemed unsuitable for Saturday night prime time television, while both Fuck Buddy and You Beautiful Children met a similar fate, being far less people friendly than the pair had anticipated.

It was around this point that the two friends had split, somewhat acrimoniously. Michi had accused Deep of not being committed enough to the Glory Of The Crow project, while Deep accused Michi of syphoning the almost non-existent royalties from the band into his own bank account without spreading any of the cash his way. Neither claim had any basis in reality, but there was no way of telling the two hot-headed young men, and they both went their separate ways.

But while Deep Loneliness went back to his job as a mechanic at a local truck garage, Michi just couldn't shake off his rock star ambitions and went it alone, employing a succession of local bands to provide the backing tracks, while he overlaid the vocals in a self-built home studio in his tower block bedroom. His first two solo attempts were as unsuccessful as his work with the band. Both Mary's Breasts and Smoking Your Eyes were considered a little too esoteric to get to the televised stages of O Melodie Pentru, and lacked the subtle musical touches that Deep Loneliness had brought to their earlier work. But it was an unexpected quirk of fate that brought him to a much wider audience beyond the borders of his nation.

Michi had been a minor cult figure among the more rabid collectors of Eurovision national selection show oddities since Perfect Corpse first found its way onto the fandom's underground grapevine. But up to this point no official video had ever been put up on YouTube – mainly because he'd never made one. So the good people of Eurovisionia had never actually seen what he looked like when he was performing. But one year an old school friend was taking an evening course in film production and asked Michi if he'd be up for letting him do a video of his next song. Michi jumped at the chance, and together they produced a weird and unsettling clip for a song called Virgin's Tears that featured the singer lip-synching a succession of incredibly creepy rhyming couplets while standing pensively on the many bridges spanning Chişinău's two-lane highways as if he were about to jump into the traffic below. And while blatant suicide songs about a prospective lover spurned by an innocent teenage girl weren't exactly typical Eurovision fare, the darker, more militant corners of its fandom were absolutely blown away by this disturbing little film, and lobbied for him to be accepted to the semi-final stages of O Melodie Pentru at the very least. But sadly to no avail.

From that year on though, and through successively dark and unsettling songs and videos, Michi built himself something of a niche popularity amongst the Eurovision press of the west, who looked upon him as a beautiful outsider artist who displayed a deep and wonky wisdom far beyond his knowing. He even took part in a number of interviews with foreign journalists, but never fully understood that they were treating him more as a figure of mild fun and derision than the serious gothic rock star that that he truly believed he was. But this had still built him just enough of an international cache that the producers at Moldova's other major broadcaster TRM had begun to give him a serious look. Sadly a short succession of appearances on the country's most popular breakfast TV show, Happy Morning, did much to destroy his briefly rising star. Performing four of his unsuccessful Eurovision songs every other week on a Thursday morning, he made the mistake of doing a Michael Jackson style crotch grab on his first appearance, swearing in Romanian on his second, and just being unspeakably creepy on his third and fourth – especially the fourth, as he mimed along to his song while wearing the uniform of the popular greeting card shop where he worked. Many people thought that this was some kind of weird and threatening performance art, or perhaps even a wry commentary on commercialism in music, but it was actually because he had to dash straight off to open up the shop immediately after his appearance.

With that, TRM put a black mark by his name, and swore never to let him near their studios again. However, a couple of years later they began an open audition process that was streamed live on the internet, and they just couldn't keep him away. His first audition, with the song Murderous Intentions, was so dreadfully performed that it was stopped by the show's producers no more than a minute in. His next couple of attempts were slightly more successful, as both The Smell Of Your Legs and Touch Me Down There at least got to the end of their respective performances before he was booted unceremoniously out of the studios. But quite unexpectedly he actually, genuinely, turned heads with his thirteenth attempt. A pair of Swiss composers had penned the song Sad Bird specifically for him. It was a thinly veiled allegory about a man considering self-immolation after a disastrous relationship, but it hit an unexpected nerve with the nation, who called upon it to be selected for at least a berth in the O Melodie Pentru semi-finals. But it was the first year that Moldova were running the contest and they didn't want to take any risks with an artistic outlier, so it was again consigned to the dustbin of audition failures. Sadly he was unable to capitalise on that unexpected interest the following year when he reverted to type with a haunting tune called My Grandmother's Ghost, where he painted a verbal picture of an old lady flying over modern Moldova and cursing everything that she could see. He wasn't allowed to get much more than two minutes into his audition performance before he was gonged off.

But this year was different. He'd teamed up with an American production outfit called Warp Control who figured that he'd be the perfect vehicle for a song they'd composed called The Wisdom Of The Times. It was a slow, dark, imposing number that didn't stretch Michi's vocal limitations too harshly, but still enabled him to emit his maximum stage presence as he emoted and over-annunciated the tortured lyric. Of course, with there only being four other acts who had applied to enter this year's contest he was always likely to get a slot on the show, but there were those amongst Moldova's intelligentsia who firmly believed that this would have been his year – finally – however many people had applied. And more importantly, Warp Control believed in him, and stumped up for a glossy video with some pretty high production values (for Moldova) that got showed in regular rotation on the local music television shows. Michi suddenly dared to believe that his lifelong dream was finally possible, and when those lobbying groups and Ruslan Rusu from the Late Night Tonight TV show had got behind him, he started to let himself think that maybe, just maybe, he had a chance of getting to Eurovision this time. Maxim Munteanu or no Maxim Munteanu.

But as we have all learned in life, it's the hope that kills you, and this morning, as he sat staring out of his eleventh floor window across Parcul Râşcani and down to the main city centre in the distance below, he began to dream of what could have been and what he might have lost. This could so very nearly have been his ticket out of this grey and impersonal tower block and onto a wider music scene that would have taken him across borders way beyond his own. Had it not been for that single point – that one measly decision taken by a juror to place him below another, less- accomplished song on their voting card – he could be sitting in a production office somewhere at this very minute, trying to work out a staging treatment for The Wisdom Of The Times instead of peering into the smog and gloom of a Spring Sunday morning from his bedroom window, while wondering whether he had the nerve to go back into the shop on Monday morning. After all, how would his regular customers react? Would they hug him in sad consolation, or mock him mercilessly for his brutal public failure after leading the voting table for so long. He was almost dreading the consolation more, as he found pity a much more uncomfortable emotion than derision. It was then that he remembered the business card the kindly Maxim Munteanu had stuffed into his hand while the riot was raging around them last evening. He reached into the pocket of his dark black combat trousers and fished it out. He stared long and hard at the mobile phone number printed on the card. Should he ring it? Would Maxim even answer his call? He took a deep breath, stared at the card for a little while more, and reached for his phone.

Meanwhile, across the city at the headquarters of Moldova Smash, Stefan and Dumi were pacing around Dumi's office waiting to be called into an emergency meeting with the broadcasting company's senior management. This unusual Sunday morning gathering had always been pencilled in, but after the less than savoury ending to last night's show the two men suspected that they were in for an ear-bashing – and possibly even worse. The morning papers were scattered with headlines like 'Scandal At The Studio' and 'Euro-Riot!', and they were struggling to see how this could possibly end well for either of them. Especially as the company's flamboyant owner Lucian Dobre was expected to be there.

No one was entirely sure how Lucian Dobre had made his fortune. A tall, imposing figure, he first came to the public eye playing basketball to a decent level for his home town club Basco Balti.

Never quite making it to the national team, he still built up a cult following for his flashy and extravagant playing style, and even more showbizzy off-court demeanour. After a knee injury put an early stop to his playing career, he moved onto coaching, then club management, and then club ownership, before he started buying up companies all over the country, developing a small but successful business empire. Some claimed that it was entirely down to an acute acumen for buying and selling businesses at exactly the right time. But there were others who doubted that his success was entirely down to his own talents, and suspected that he was just a high profile front for a much darker kind of businessmen who were happy to hang in the shadows while Lucian did all the more rock'n'roll stuff in front of the cameras, with his fast cars and his flashy suits.

He'd first had the idea for Moldova Smash four years ago. Named after his signature slam dunk on the basketball court, it began as a radio station famous for its uncompromising presenters and stern criticism of the government. So it was a surprise to everyone when he was granted a licence to extend the station's reach to a television channel. Moldova Smash TV quickly became the most popular station in the country, mixing flashy gameshows and dour soap operas with hard hitting news programmes and discussion panels. It still came as a shock, though, when they bought out the rights to O Melodie Pentru Europa, as the station was still untested with big live events. But Lucian's can-do attitude combined with the massive wad of cash in his back pocket reinvigorated the competition, which soon became one of the new highlights of the Eurovision calendar, taking bold risks with the most unlikely genre artists.

It was one of these artists, Bessarabian Turbo Squad, who brought the nation their unexpected Eurovision success. Up until then a wholly underground act who mainly played at warehouse raves and semi-legal outdoor festivals across the country, their unlikely mash up of ancient Moldovan folk music and some absolutely banging techno hit a happy nerve with the whole continent, and had nans and school kids and Eurofans from Reykjavik to Baku dancing with unabashed joy on their sofas. And despite a middling jury score at the previous year's Eurovision final, they absolutely hammered the televote and won by a distance, going on to be a chart smash in sixty countries across the world and launching them into something of an unexpected international pop career.

So this fresh new channel now had a reputation to uphold, and Stefan and Dumi both feared that there was a good chance this could be their last morning on the job. Dumi's phone rang. It was Lucian's secretary inviting them to his office on the top floor. The two TV executives slowly climbed the six flights of stairs like condemned men. They could have used the lift, but it was never advisable in this building. You took your life into your own hands in those lifts. Seven journeys out of ten they would either break down, the lights would go out, or they'd make terrifying deep screaming noises as if the cables were about to snap. And on the few rare occasions when they did work perfectly there was always a deeply strange smell and weird bits of detritus mounting up in the corners, as even the building's surly cleaners rarely dared to venture into them. But the long haul up the mock marble staircases gave the pair the chance to get their stories straight before they entered the potentially fateful meeting.

They got to Lucian's deep brown door in the darkened hallway, paused for a moment, and knocked.

"Come! Come!" bellowed a theatrical voice from within. "Ah, it's you two," Lucian cried with joy at seeing their sweaty faces. "I assume you didn't take the lift then?"

Stefan and Dumi both replied with an awkward half laugh, before Lucian took in a massive deep breath.

"Bloody good job last night, boys!" he proclaimed.

Stefan and Dumi cast each other confused and surprised looks as the big man behind the enormous desk continued.

"We got the result we wanted, but still had a bit of excitement at the end. Just how we like it!" he shouted with a jolly lilt in his voice. "I feared it was going to be a bit of a boring cakewalk for dear old Maxim, but that gothicky laddie with the dark eyes – what was his name? Michi? Yes! Michi! He gave the old fella a right scare there didn't he! And that riot at the end! Perfect television. I've had TV stations from all over the world ringing in to try and licence that clip for their news programmes. I'm going to get a massive Moldova Smash logo slapped all over it and charge them through the arse for rights. It'll get our name about perfectly! Whose genius idea was that fight though? It was bloody priceless!"

"Erm, it kind of happened all by itself, Lucian," Dumi anxiously explained. "We had a couple of rival factions in there, and they wound each other up until they blew!"

"Even better!" the big businessman yelled! "We've got to use that energy going forward. Build up some jeopardy for the big show. Make it more exciting!"

"Ooh, I'm not sure that the CTF are going to like that, sir," Stefan meekly suggested. "There's already stories going around in TV circles that we fixed the vote last night. And while we might have made things easier for Maxim with the selection of the judges, those numbers at the end were the genuine real scores. And then there's the fan press…"

"Sod 'em!" Lucian butted in. "Sod the CTF and sod the fan press! This is our show now, and we'll do it our way. The Moldovan way, with noise and chaos and sunshine and stupid dancing! They gave us the show and now it's ours to tinker with."

"Ahem, Lucian sir…?" came a voice from the back of the room.

Stefan and Dumi had barely noticed three of the station's most senior producers sitting at the back end of the big oval meeting table in the centre of the room. The man who interjected was the station director Iurie Mirea, a former head of programming at TRM, and a man who knew a little bit about how these things worked.

"What's that, Iurie?" the big man asked.

"We do have to pay at least a little mind to what the CTF wants, Lucian," he said nervously. "They can still take the contest off us at this late stage if they think we're going to sully its reputation… and they're anxious enough as it is. Sweden are poised, waiting to lap this thing up if we start looking too dodgy. They're so bloody keen and experienced that they could set one of these things up at a fortnight's notice if they had to."

Lucian put on his best thinking face for a moment, leaned forward at his desk and tilted his head to one side.

"As boring as your point is, Iurie, unfortunately it's a pretty sound one. Yes, I guess we'd better go a bit easy on the rock'n'roll for a bit. We can stir up some ire and angst locally, behind the scenes, but we'll keep it all on the QT front of house. We don't want to give those bastards at the CTF the opportunity to take this thing off us, after all. That lot in Tiraspol might think we did it on purpose to spite them and it could start another bloody civil war. And as good as that might be for the TV ratings, even I don't want that!"

Everyone in the room looked around at each other and nodded approvingly for a few moments, before Lucian leapt from his chair purposefully, and slammed both hands on the desk.

"Right!" He shouted enthusiastically. "Let's get this thing done! Stefan! You talk to Maxim over the next couple of days and liaise with him about what he wants to do with the song on stage. Then we'll ship in the best creative designers that we can find to try and snazzy him up a bit. Dumi! You get hold of that Michi lad. I liked him and all his funny mannerisms. We can use him in the run up to this thing. Get him a slot on Ruslan's talk show, and maybe sort out a little solo special for him to go out afterwards. The kids are going to love him. Iurie! Keep me in the loop on your discussions with Turgenev and his people, and let's just keep the ideas flowing here. And you two at the back! I can never remember exactly what it is that you do. You just keep on doing it, whatever that is, and report back to Iurie if anything important happens. We've got this, gentlemen. We're going to make this the best Eurovision Song Contest that there's ever been!"

And with that he grabbed his big, sturdy military-style coat from the hatstand, swung it over his shoulder, and bounded out of the room.

All five men that remained in the room sat in silence for a

moment, as if they'd just escaped from a whirlwind, before Stefan turned to Dumi.

"Well that went a whole lot better than I was fearing. I think?" he said, with an air of mild confusion in his voice.

"Yeah, at least we didn't lose our jobs," Dumi replied. "We've still got a whole heap of firefighting left to do after last night, whatever Lucian says. But we appear to have somehow pulled that out of the flames. Although I'm not entirely sure how."

"Right then, the first job we've got to do tomorrow is ring the CTF and tell them how our plans are going," said Iurie. "Do you want to do that, Dumi?"

"Oh yes, I suppose I'd better," he replied.

"But for God's sake, Dumi," Iurie added anxiously, "Don't tell them about the riot unless they bring it up first!"

4

It was Monday morning at the headquarters of the Continental Television Federation in Lucerne. Filip Ivanović, the new Executive Supervisor of the Eurovision Song Contest was sitting at his desk and shaking his head.

"Did you see that debacle in Moldova on Saturday night, Terry?" he asked. "Absolute bloody nightmare. The whole thing descended into chaos at the end, and the result looked well dodgy."

Terry van Boom, the Eurovision organisation's head of communications, looked up from his papers and replied.

"Ooh, I missed that one Filip. I was watching the Norwegian final. There were some cracking tunes in that one, but then something horrible won. So what happened in Moldova, then?"

"Oh it was utter nonsense from start to finish. They had one massive star, and four rank amateurs up against him. Proper local town hall talent contest fare, they were. It looked like it was a coronation in waiting. But then the public inexplicably took to this creepy looking kid and he was leading by some distance at the halfway point. But then when it came to the juries, the old guy ended up winning and it all kicked off in the crowd. There were chairs and shoes flying about and all sorts. Then they quickly cut to the credits rolling over a video of the old fella's song. I tell you, Terry, that voting at the end looked really dodgy. It was the kind of stunt that Belarus are always pulling. It really makes you wonder if we made the right choice by letting them hold it. It could end up as a right mess of a show. Why can't normal countries ever win this damn thing any more?"

"Ooh yes, that does all sound rather unseemly," Terry replied. "How do you want us to play this on the website?"

"Just straight up, Terry. Results and points, a little bit about the winner's biography, and Moldova's history in the contest. Any more than that and we'll go off message, and we don't want to give the fansites any excuse to have a pop."

"Right you are, Filip," Terry replied. "I'll get the writing team on it."

Filip had only been in the executive supervisor role since just before Christmas. His predecessor, a Swede called Cory Kjellberg, had been caught in a compromising position late last Autumn. A Dutch news channel had set up a sting where a reporter pretended to be an oil-rich prince from Qatar who wanted to buy his country onto the show. Kjellberg protested his innocence, of course, and claimed that he was just humouring the pretend royal. But the CTF weren't up for any kind of a long-term scandal and relieved him from his contract as soon as they were legally able.

Filip had been one of his assistants. He'd been working mainly on the production of Junior Eurovision and the Young Musician shows, and was considered a safe pair of hands to take over in the interim, with a view to getting the job long term if his first go at it went well. There had long been disquiet among the ranks of the participating nations that the top job always seemed to go to Scandinavians, so it was a great PR coup for the organisation to give the reins to a highly experienced Serbian TV producer, and he'd slipped into the role like a smooth hand into a very comfortable glove.

However, he'd also inherited the chaos of the whole Moldovan issue, and he wasn't terribly happy about it. Had it been down to him, this year's show would have been an entirely CTF-led affair, using all their regular production crew and a temporary arena built using a specialist CTF construction team. But there had long been suspicions that Kjellberg was in the pocket of some of the more unscrupulous Eastern European businessmen when it came to tendering for the show, and it was now too late now to renege on the deal that the Swede had made with Timur Turgenev. The other big issue was that the CTF had to be seen to be visibly helping out the smaller nations if they happened to fluke a win at the contest. Most of the richer countries had no trouble in putting together a decent show proposal, but many of the less wealthy European states were always going to have trouble producing the show on their own. So the CTF had to at least give the impression that the minnows weren't just there to make up the numbers and increase the advertising revenue, but had an equal chance of hosting the thing if they ever won it. Up to now Moldova had always been a competition outsider, with a couple of respectable near misses. But no one had expected that they'd ever take a victory, let alone by a record score. Thankfully the CTF had set up what was covertly known as The Moldovan Emergency Fund, just in case the unlikely scenario ever happened. But now that it had, everyone was in a bit of a flap about it.

Filip's sidekick, Terry, had come to the organisation by a different route. Originally the editor of the fansite Eurovision Explosion, he had proved to have a keen eye for PR and was an excellent mobiliser of volunteers. Soon his site was getting more page views than the CTF's official Eurovision site, and together with his deep knowledge of how to work all kinds of social media to his best advantage, the organisation figured that his was the kind of expertise that they could use, and offered him a job running their Twitter feed throughout the national final season. He quickly worked his way up through the PR department, and when Kjellberg got the boot just before Christmas, the people at the top table thought that it was perhaps best to move most of his closest staff and advisors off to different roles away from the contest, and so promoted Terry to head of communications. This had proved useful, as his understanding of how the competition worked from a fan's point of view was invaluable in helping the new team quickly gain trust from both the international delegations and those that closely followed the contest via the fan press. But the two men knew that they had a big job on their hands with their first Eurovision, and they had to ensure that it all went as smoothly as possible if they wanted to be invited back to have another run at it next year.

"Do you think we should be worried too much about that Moldovan mess at the weekend, Terry?" Filip asked his colleague.

"I mean, I won't say that it's not worrying, Filip," the younger man replied. "But that was solely a local production. And that studio they held it in is a pokey little rathole, anyway. I went there for their final a couple of years back, and it didn't encourage the best of atmospheres. When we get to Tiraspol we'll have a lot of our own people on the ground supervising and running the desks, and we've got time now to make contingency plans for if the worst does come to the worst. Barring any localised unrest in the run up to the contest I think we should be OK."

"That's exactly what I'm worried about, Terry," Filip said anxiously. "That part of the world is like a tinderbox right now. And you know what the Kremlin's like. They'd be happy to mess things up just for the hell of it. Which reminds me. Do we even know what their song is going to be yet?"

"No boss, not yet," Terry replied. "They're keeping their cards close to their chest, as usual. But you can bet your life that it's going to be one of those laser cut spectaculars that's being hand-tooled in some terrifying showbiz laboratory as we speak. They're still busting for another win, so I can't see them encouraging it to all kick off in Moldova if they reckon they're in with a shout."

"True enough, Terry," said Filip, "But they're just as likely to send a bit of thinly veiled political agitation all dressed up as a happy disco song that will swoop right over the heads of Western Europe, but strike the fear of God into the East and all their old republics. They've got an awful lot of form in this, after all."

"Oh yes, I'd not looked at it that way, Filip. While they're never exactly flouting the rules, they're skating very closely to the edges, and on some very thin ice. I just hope they send some charming old folk nans again. The people always like them."

"Yes, but you can never tell with that lot. And you just don't know what they'll have up their sleeves." Filip paused for a moment, tried to shake the potential for Russian mischief out of his head, and got all businesslike again.

"Right then, what's our plan of action for today? We've got calls scheduled with Moldova this morning, plus Norway, Portugal, Iceland and Lithuania, who I believe all chose their songs at the weekend. Is there anything that I need to know about any of them, Terry?"

"Not unduly Filip. They're mostly solid and decent Eurovision songs, Norway excepted. Iceland is, of course, a little batshit. But the delegation is always friendly and helpful so we can easily work with that."

"Great, what else will you be doing today?"

"I've not got too much else on, to be honest, Filip. I'll just start building the story about that Maxim fella on the website, and start doing a little back reading on the people who are in charge over there so we can put together a dossier for the folks upstairs about what we can expect in the run in."

"Fantastic idea, Terry. Just don't make it too scary though, mate. We don't want to put them off the whole Moldovan idea when there's still a chance they could switch it to Gothenburg. And I really don't want to be going back to Sweden any time soon..."

*

Back in Chişinău, Michi was on a marshrutka heading off to Maxim's place. He was struggling to believe that any of this was actually happening. He took the risk of calling the the veteran singer the previous evening to thank him for his kind words at the Moldova Smash studios, and was amazed to receive an invitation to his palatial house on the edge of the city for coffee and a chat. As lovely as the old guy was on the night, Michi feared that it was just the usual showbiz platitudes and empty promises, but it turned out that Maxim was a 100% bona fide gentleman away from the stage as well, and had insisted that he popped over for a catch up.

Maxim lived just outside a small suburb called Vatra on the banks of the Ghidighici Reservoir, right on the north-westernmost fringes of the capital. Michi had to make three changes of minibus from his home in Sectorul Ciocana, and the journey had already taken him well over an hour. The reservoir was the largest body of water for at least fifty miles in any given direction, and so many of the country's great and good had built homes overlooking it. The neighbourhood was close enough to the centre of the capital to get in and out easily for work, but just far enough away to enjoy a little bit of the countryside. Michi, though, had never been out this way before, and was peering through the dusty bus window like a wide-eyed tourist. Well, this kind of place wasn't for the likes of him, he reasoned with himself, and he wasn't sure if he was ever likely to visit it again, so he was taking it all in while he still could.

When he got to his stop he had another couple of hundred yards to walk down a broad but broken lane before arriving at the big gold gates outside Maxim's house. He pressed the intercom and a stern voice muttered. "Yes. Mr Munteanu is expecting you. Come in through the gate and walk up towards the house, then I'll give you a security check. If all is good, then you can see him."

The gates buzzed, automatically opening a tiny crack for Michi to squeeze though. But then he stopped in his tracks. He had never seen anything like it in his life. The plush green gardens were bursting with exotic plants, and flowers in hues that he'd never imagined had existed. A winding path in front of him zigzagged though the plumes to a broad, one-storey building that seemed to be made entirely of glass. The security guard beckoned him over and ran a metal detector all around his body.

"Now clear out your pockets and take off your shoes," he said, gruffly, before closely examining all the items that had been placed in the small dish and giving them back to Michi. "Is good. Now you go down there. Thank you, sir."

The burly man had close-cropped hair and crumpled flesh at the back of his head that made it look as if his brain was pressing through his skull. He pointed his large, fight-beaten hand towards a set of steps that led down to the building. Michi skulked nervously down them and through the big glass door into this most amazing house.

"Michi! Michi sir! I'm so glad you could make it," came a voice from behind a book case. "Sit down and I shall make you a drink! Do you like tea?"

"I'm not sure that I've ever had it," Michi said nervously. "But I'll try most things once!"

"That's the spirit boy!" replied the warm, friendly, familiar voice, as the man attached to it walked fully into his view.

Maxim was wearing a deep red velvet dressing gown with gold brocade lapels. Beneath it he was still in his pyjamas, made of gloriously multi-coloured paisley silk. On his head he was wearing a small, red circular hat with a golden tassel on the top. He looked every bit like one of those wizards from the fantasy comics that Michi used to read as a child.

"Sorry about the attire, Michi lad," the old man said. "I've only just got up. Shows like that one on Saturday take it out of you when you get to my age. Heavens knows how I'm going to get through Eurovision itself."

He let out a big, warm smile as he passed Michi his cup of tea, and the younger man was instantly enveloped in its rich and unfamiliar aroma.

"It's Earl Grey," Maxim proudly announced. "The English can't get enough of it. It's the bergamot in it that makes it smell so delightful, apparently."

Michi took a sip and the drink's complex flavours exploded across his tongue.

"That... that's a wonderful flavour, thank you Maxim," he said. I'll really have to try that again some day."

"Oh, we drink it all the time here, Michi. You can have it whenever you come and visit. Now, if you'll excuse me for a moment, I've just got to pop to my bedroom to get my day wear on. Have a look around if you like."

Michi cast his eyes around the massive room. There were framed pictures of Maxim with famous Moldovan singers and artists and sports players and politicians on every available inch of wallspace, and in one corner sat a tall glass case absolutely brimming with awards statuettes. The room was split in two by a pair of bookcases just groaning with titles in Romanian, Russian and English, and at one end of the left-hand section of the room was a huge fireplace. Above the hearth, sitting on dark blue velvet in specially made glass cases were Maxim's two Order of the Republic medals. At their centre sat the crest of the republic, surrounded by a large white enamel circle. Around that was a stylised gold and silver sunburst, and each medal was suspended by an ornately carved chain, showing stars, sheaths of wheat and a more simple representation of the national crest, all rendered in gold. He'd never witnessed anything so incredible with his own eyes, and had only ever seen them before on the news when they were being awarded to some famous scientist or politician.

"You like those then, Michi?" said Maxim as he returned to the room wearing more appropriate day clothes.

"Why yes, Mr Munteanu," Michi spluttered nervously. "They really are quite beautiful." Maxim walked towards Michi and leant in conspiratorially.

"To let you into a little secret, I suspect they only gave me the second one because I'm not dead yet!"

Both men laughed a hearty, honest laugh.

"Seriously though, they'd run out of honours to give me, so I guess they either had to make a new one up or give me that one again! But I'm just a simple farm boy from the country. I'm not used to such gaudy baubles. Hey Michi! Maybe you might win one for yourself one day!"

"Oh I don't know, Mr Munteanu..." Michi stuttered. "Call me Maxim, sir!"

"Erm, yes, Maxim. Sir. I'm not anywhere as near as popular as you, so I can't begin to imagine I'll even have a hit record, let alone get any kind of awards."

"Nonsense lad!" Maxim guffawed. "From what I saw the other night you've got an incredible spirit, and if guided in the right direction I still think you could go a long way. How old are you now?"

"Thirty-three," said Maxim, slightly embarrassed about his age, as he still tried to cultivate the image of an awkward goth teenager.

"Thirty-three? Thirty-three!!! I didn't know who I was when I was thirty-three! You still have plenty of time to build your career, and I shall help you wherever I can. You did a great job on Saturday, and although I can't say that I entirely understand your music, you've got something in you that I want to see more of!"

"Oh, thank you for saying so, Mr... erm, Maxim," Michi mumbled, scarcely believing what he was hearing.

"And that leads me to why I've brought you here today, young man."

Michi was suddenly concerned. What was about to happen, he wondered? This sounded as though it was about to lead into some kind of proposition, but he wasn't entirely sure of what shape it was about to take. He suddenly realised that in his keenness to impress the veteran singer he may have naively put himself into a potentially dangerous situation. He'd heard a lot of nasty stories about showbiz people in the West, and he started to worry about whether it was an endemic issue in the industry. He held his breath and anxiously waited for Maxim to move onto his next sentence.

"Now, I still think that you've got a lot to learn in this business, so I'd like to make you a proposition..."

"Oh here we go!" thought Michi to himself as he desperately tried to work out what was about to happen.

"I'd like you to be my personal assistant for the duration of the Eurovision fortnight," the old man said with a little smile crinkling at the corner of his lips.

"Oh!" thought Michi to himself with a start. "Of all of the possible scenarios there, both positive and less so, I'd never have imagined that this was going to be one of them."

"That way you can follow me around, see all the things that I have to contend with on a big show like that, and see if it really is for you,"

Maxim explained. "It also means that you'll get to meet an awful lot of important TV and music businesses people from around the world, and hopefully make something of an impression on them, too. I think it would be the perfect little job for you. Now, does this sound like the kind of thing that would interest you, sir?"

"It does," Michi reasoned in his inner voice. "It very much does. But surely it's too good to be true. Surely there must be some catch?"

"And there's no catch, either," Maxim laughed, obviously reading Michi's confused face. "I don't expect anything from you, except your assistance and your friendship. And in return you'll get a rare experience that very few people in the world have ever had. How does that sound to you?"

"That sounds perfect, Maxim," Michi heard himself saying, still in something of a daze.

"Great!" Maxim replied. "Now if it's OK with you, I've got to go off and make a few business calls and do a few interviews. Everybody wants a piece of you when you've just won something. You can finish your tea, and then I'll get Evgeny on the door to drive you back into town, if that's OK."

"Yes, yes, that would be perfect," said Michi, still utterly bewildered by the chain of events that had transpired over the last few days.

"Right then Michi, I'll give you a call next weekend, and we can start going over some plans for what we might be doing over in Tiraspol. Talk to you then!"

"Yes! Let's do that!" said Michi, as the old man left the living room and walked into a room down the long corridor.

Michi finished his Earl Grey, carefully set the cup down on a coaster on the glass table in front of him, and walked back up the stairs to where the security guard was stationed.

"Yes?" the guard asked Michi as he walked towards him. "Erm, yes, hello, erm, Evgeny is it?"
"Yes."

"Maxim said that it might be OK if you drove me back into town," Michi asked nervously. "Yes, that will be fine," said Evgeny, coldly. "You don't have to take me all the way back to Ciocana though. Cathedral Square will do me just fine," Michi offered meekly.

Evgeny's face cracked into an unexpectedly broad beaming smile.

"Oh, you're a Ciocana boy are you. My dear mother lives in Ciocana! I'll be happy to take you, then I can pop in and visit her while I'm there! And I know the short way around the back too. It'll be much quicker than taking you into town. Jump into the car and I'll get my keys."

And with that Michi climbed nervously into the back of the big black Mercedes, and began to wonder if this day could possibly get any stranger.

5

Across the city at Moldova Smash HQ, Dumi is running over what he's going to tell the CTF about Saturday night's shenanigans.

"Just be honest," he said to himself. "Tell them the scoring was accurate and offer to email them the scorecards. Then be a tad economical with the truth about the riot. That should just about do it. We've got the artist that everybody wanted, after all, so that should sweeten the pie just a little bit. Right, here goes."

Dumi picked up his big office phone and called the Lucerne number.

"Hello, is that the CTF ? Yes. Yes, I'd like to speak to Filip Ivanović, please. Yes, he's expecting me. My name? Oh yes, Dumi Enache from Moldova Smash. Thank you. Yes, I'll wait."

The receptionist put Dumi on hold and the call waiting music was a rather grand version of Charpentier's Te Deum – better known to the rest of us as the Eurovision theme tune.

"Oh that's all I bloody need!" Dumi grumbled to himself. "I'll be glad when this whole sorry charade is over."

The music suddenly cut out and he could hear the phone being grabbed, then dropped, then picked up again at the other end.

"Hello Dumi!" said the voice. "Filip Ivanović here. How's it going? Sorry about all that noise, I just dropped the phone as I picked it up. Chucked the darned thing halfway across the office in my eagerness to answer."

Filip's bumbling followed by his light-hearted apology set Dumi a little more at ease than he was before the call.

"Hey yes, Filip. I'm good sir. And you?"

"It's all going swimingly, Dumi," said the man from the CTF. "So, I hear you've got a song for us?"

"Yes, yes," said Dumi. "And as expected it's from our revered national hero Maxim Munteanu. It's a sweet and nostalgic song about a life well lived. The local audience are going to go crazy for it, and it'll look amazing on television. I can't tell you how much stage presence the old guy has got."

"As I saw, Dumi. I watched the whole thing live at home on Saturday night. It was a great song, but I gather the show didn't entirely go as planned?"

"How do you mean, Filip?" Dumi anxiously replied, trying to buy himself a couple more seconds to think.

"Well it looked like it all got a bit, how shall we say, lively at the end there?"

"Oh that!" Dumi laughed, trying to deflect a little from the situation. "That's just Moldova for you. We're a hot headed bunch, and it was the pure passion and emotion of the evening spilling out. Our TV is like that all the time. You ought to see what they get up to on Moldova's Got Talent. It's totally normal for here, Filip."

"Well, I hope that nobody's going to be throwing any chairs on our big night, Dumi. I don't want to have to nail them all down to the floor, now!"

Dumi detected a hint of mirth in Filip's voice, so thought it right to assume that he was perhaps joking with him a little. All the same, he proceeded cautiously.

"Oh there'll be no trouble with that, Filip," he said, not entirely confident of his own words. "Eurovision is an entirely different animal to O Melodie Pentru, and there'll be people from dozens of different countries mixing in together, so it will be very unlikely that anything of that kind is going to happen again. And anyway, our selection show is recorded in a tiny tiny studio, and everyone in the crowd was related to one of the acts in some way or another, so tensions are bound to run high."

"Well just as long as you can assure to me that nothing of the kind is going to happen again, and that we can still trust you to get the show on without there being threats of violence from any corner of the audience who might happen to feel agitated for any reason," Filip asked, now with a little more steel in his voice.

"Oh don't you worry, Filip," said Dumi, trying to quell some of Filip's obvious fears, "the security team that we'll be using on the night are all former special forces operatives, and they're trained to spot any kind of trouble bubbling up before it gets fully brewed and then put a quick stop to it in the calmest manner possible."

"Ooh, that all sounds a bit serious, Dumi. Just as long as they don't steam in there swinging batons at people on live international television. We wouldn't really want that now, would we."

"Oh no need to worry about that, Filip, they've all been fully briefed not to hurt anyone until they're out of the arena..." Dumi stopped himself for a moment and realised quite how bad that particular wording might sound if taken out of context. "Ahh, yes, sorry, I meant to say for them not to be too conspicuous inside the arena."

"Hahahaha!" Filip laughed, heartily. "I get exactly what you mean. I am Serbian after all. We have plenty of experience of this kind of thing."

"That's a relief," said Dumi with a loud and obvious exhalation of distress. "It was just my use of English. Sometimes it lets me down a little."

"No worries at all, Dumi," Filip reassured, "I fully understood what you meant. Now, I have another question, just between you and me."

"What's that, Filip?" Dumi asked, now becoming a little bit anxious again.

Filip's voice quietened a little as he asked his next question. "Did you actually fix that result last night?"

Dumi's world began to spin around him as he grasped the air for a satisfactory answer. He stalled. "How do you mean, Filip?"

"Well it did all look a bit suspect from where I was sitting. National hero trailing by miles on the public vote, then suddenly storming back to win it at the death, which in turn caused a riot to kick off. It's what we quietly call The Minsk Gambit in our offices. You've got see it from our point of view."

"Oh very much so, Filip. Very much so. We couldn't believe the scores ourselves. We had to check then double check them just to be sure, and I think that long wait is what caused all the tension in the crowd. We've got all the numbers here, if you want to see them. They were officially audited by our most prestigious company of accountants. It all rings true when you have the figures in front of you."

"No, don't worry Dumi mate, we trust you," Filip said in a reassuring voice. "And to be honest, we were all glad that the old boy won. That spooky kid who came second would probably have been just a bit too weird to be a home entry. He'd have easily seen you in the bottom three at the very best, and nobody wants to see that."

"Yes, but that mostly came about through a local late night talk show host causing a bit of mischief and trying to get everyone to vote for that Michi fellow as a comedy protest vote against the government. He was never going to win the jury vote in a million years. Michi's a bit of a standing joke over here, as he's had more attempts at qualifying for Eurovision than most people have had hot pies. And as luck would have it, the jury did their job. It was a bit too close for our comfort though!"

"You're telling me, Dumi. Well, I think you dodged a bullet there! Aside from all that, how are the preparations going in Tiraspol? Has everything been built yet?"

"Yes, Filip, indeed. All the infrastructure has gone up and the charter flights have been booked. They've just got to add the final touches to the inside of the arena and put the cabling in the press centre and it'll all be done!"

"Damn that's efficient, Dumi!" Filip said, pleasantly surprised. "Some years even the Scandi countries are still painting the floors as the audience is walking in! That's a ridiculously good job! I'll be coming over for the Heads Of Delegation meeting in a couple of weeks, so I'll be able to see for myself – and it'll be great to see you again."

"And you, Filip sir," Dumi replied.

"Right, I've got to get off. Busy day. I've got to talk to Norway now, and we're expecting a reveal from Azerbaijan any minute! It's all go, eh! Anyway, keep me posted if there's any developments at your end, and we'll speak soon, OK?"

"Yeah, OK Filip. Nice speaking. See you!" "Bye, Dumi!" "Yes bye!"

Dumi put the phone down and slumped into his chair, relieved.

"Well that went a whole lot better than I could ever have imagined!" he said out loud to himself in the mirror over by the door. "I think he bought it. This whole mad Moldovan Eurovision adventure is still on track!"

Meanwhile, in Lucerne, Filip put his phone down on the table, turned to his head of communications in the corner of the room and shook his head.

"Bollocks!" he exclaimed. "Put the kettle on Terry mate, I need an industrial strength coffee fast!" "What's up, Filip?" Terry asked with concern in his voice.

"It's Moldova Smash," he replied with a hint of anguish. "I fear they're going rogue on us. I could scarcely believe a word that Dumi Enache just told me there."

"Oh shit," said Terry. "What are we going to do about that, do you think? It's too late to crank up the Gothenburg option, surely? It's only a fortnight until the heads of delegations meeting."

"Exactly, Terry," Filip replied with a steely look in his eye. "But I have a plan. Firstly we're going to have to break out The Moldova Emergency Fund. And secondly, we'll need a big chunk of it to get The Sparkle Crew in and try to quietly take over the running of this darned thing before it's too late. Them Moldovans aren't going to like it, but if we do it subtly and make them think that it's their idea then we might just about get away with it. The other option, that we leave it entirely to Moldova and they mess it up in front of three hundred million people, just doesn't bear thinking about. Get me Håkan's home phone number. We're going to need all the help we can get."

*

Håkan Jakobson was a big burly man, with a shock of dark curly hair and a voice made entirely out

of whisky and cigarettes. He ran a production outfit called The Sparkle

Crew who were the CTF's go to guys for any major international event that needed a stern, experienced hand on the controls.

Ordinarily they'd be the people who'd do the technical set up for your standard Eurovision show. But every nation who wins has first dibs on using their own local crew, and Moldova insisted on the whole production being staged entirely by Moldovans. Filip at the CTF had suggested that they do it in tandem with their regular preferred suppliers, seeing as the biggest event they'd ever televised up to this point was the Water Polo World Cup, but they were having none of it. For good and for bad, Moldova is a country steeped in masculine national pride, and they understandably didn't want to be patronised by outsiders during their big moment.

However, there were a number of technical tasks that were completely beyond the Moldovans – not through any lack of willing or good intentions, more that the requisite kit had never made its way that far across Europe yet. It's all well and good hiring in the biggest plasma screen on the planet, but if you haven't got someone with a good few years experience in operating the thing it's highly likely that you're going to be left with nothing but the blue screen of death at a very awkward moment on live television.

So slowly, one by one, Filip had been placing his own experts into the Moldovan production crew by wont of necessity. But the locals hadn't been entirely happy about it, and there had been some tense stand offs. Well, until they tried fruitlessly to operate the kit, that was, and they came sheepishly back to the CTF for help. It was a tactic that was working very well in an organic kind of way, but what Filip was now proposing was a slow coup, whereby he injected Håkan and his team into the arena after what he would describe as a necessary technical innovation regarding the way television signals were now being broadcast in the West. He'd try to bamboozle the local tekkies with big science words and diagrams and hope that they'd fall for it. However, the locals were no suckers when it came to tech. Most of them had trained in France or Germany, and were used to rigging big one-off travelling arena shows. But none of them had worked on a production of this magnitude that involved performance and broadcasting and an audience. So Filip had to work The Sparkle Crew in carefully, not just to keep the on site techies sweet, but also the people at Moldova Smash, and indeed Timur Turgenov's own advisors, who seemed to spend much of their day at the future Eurovision area just watching and taking notes. So Filip had to find a way of getting Håkan onto the show's technical crew in an advisory capacity, and then gradually bring in more and more of his own people on the pretence of this as yet unknown technological advance. It was going to be a tough job, but after what he'd just heard on the phone from Dumi, he feared that it was a risk that he would have to take.

When Filip called Håkan, the Swede was still barely awake. When the Eurovision Moldova gig fell through, he'd signed up to run the stage production for the Swedish power metal band Frosty Witch Kult on their massive stadium tour around Europe. It was no ordinary show, as it featured fire and explosions and dozens of costume changes, and even tonnes of realistic snow made of real ice crystals that coated the first 100 rows in a chilly white blanket. It was quite a task managing the many different elements of stage business on a travelling tour, but one that Håkan was easily the measure of. The tour was just coming to an end, and the technical genius sounded as though he'd been partying for two or three days without sleep when he answered the phone.

"Yes? Who is this?" his voice rasped like an earthquake on a sandy mountain. "And why are you calling so goddam early?"

"It's Filip, Håkan. And it's nearly three o'clock in the afternoon!"
"That is bloody early on a tour day off," he barked. "Whadaya want?"
"It's that Moldovan lot. They proving to be a little more complicated than we feared. How are you fixed for transferring over once your tour's finished? Y'know, to tidy up some of the mess they've been making for themselves?"

"Shit man, I was going to sleep for the whole month of May! But now that you bring it up, it would be a bit weird going a whole year without my Eurovision fix. Count me in! But how are we going to play it, though? Those Moldovans are solid, proud bastards, and they wouldn't want some loud grumpy asshole like me piling in and telling them they've been doing it wrong. Even if they have been. Do you have a plan?"

"Well I've kind of got a plan," explained Filip. "I propose that we tell them there's some new European broadcasting stipulation that means we have to use a very particular piece of kit to get the show onto the new breed of super smart TVs that they've not yet had the access to over there. Then you could sidle into town in an advisory capacity and slowly take over... in your own traditionally subtle way. Is there anything you can think of that could pull the wool over their eyes just enough so that they don't suspect we're taking the piss, Håkan?"

"I'll sleep on it, Filip. I'll call you back Wednesday when I've woken up properly." And with that Håkan clicked the phone off without so much as a cheery goodbye.

"He's a rum old sort that Håkan fella, Terry, but he certainly gets the job done," said Filip.

"Yeah Filip. But we've just got to trust that he doesn't wind those Moldovans up," warned Terry. "You know how much he enjoys a scrap, and I don't reckon the locals are going to stand for it!"

"Yeah, but if anyone can get through to them it's him and The Sparkle Crew. Now I'd better get back to the Norwegians. I've had them on hold for bloody ages."

6

Two weeks later, and it's time for the traditional Heads of Delegation Meeting. It's here that the CTF invite representatives from the 42 participating countries to the host city – in this instance Tiraspol – along with senior members of the production crew, in order to show them the facilities at the arena, give them a tour of where all the principal hotels, clubs and meeting places will be, and have presentations on the technical spec of the production. It's also where the delegations all get to officially present their chosen songs, and ask questions about what they can expect while they are there in May. After all, up to two weeks in a strange new city can be a very long time when you only have to rehearse once every three or four days, and so it's important for each competing nation's representatives to have a broad view of what their singers and dancers and costumiers and choreographers and hair dressers and so on will be able to do during their down time.

And of course, it's also a great excuse for a jolly good piss up amongst old friends from around the continent.

The biggest bone of contention at this year's HoD meeting was the inclusion of Kazakhstan. Nobody there had any issue with the song or performer in themselves, however. It was more the way that they were suddenly parachuted into the show at the last minute. It had been no secret that the Kazakhs had been trying to get into the contest for some years now, but a succession of executive supervisors had turned them down – partly because there were now so many countries who wanted to take part that the contest was becoming a bit cumbersome, and partly because if they ever actually won the thing, the four hour time difference between the major cities of the Eurasian nation and Central European time would have meant that the show would have to start at 1am, which would have been something of a tricky ask for both the performers and the local transport links. There were also less publicised fears that, as amazing as Kazahki music is, it was perhaps just that little bit too 'other' for a more conservative European palate to digest.

However, one of Cory Kjellberg's first moves when he took the rudder of the contest was to formally invite the desert state to join. This is partially what led to the sting operation by the Norwegian press, as there were quiet fears that he had taken a massive bung from the oil rich nation to guarantee their participation. Others suspected that it was merely an ego-fuelled legacy project by the new incumbent, so that people would look back at his reign in years to come and remember his bold move. So while everybody was being nice to the delegation from Kazakhstan to their faces, there were many mutterings of disquiet behind their backs.

But that was the least of Filip Ivanović's problems. With a population of less than 135,000 people, Tiraspol was one of the smallest settlements ever to have hosted a Eurovision, and as such there was pitifully little to do outside of the contest. Timur Turgenev had got his people to convert a disused warehouse into a massive Euroclub party venue, and they were planning a Eurovillage of sorts along the length of 25th October Street in the city centre. This would feature large screens at each end, so that those locals not able to afford the punishingly expensive show tickets would be able to watch the contest all together in one place. And while there were many drinking haunts across the city, they were mainly of the type where old guys in sturdy hats perched themselves up against the bar and bedded themselves in for the evening slugging endless shots of local vodka rather than the kind that the more happy-go-lucky Eurofan would be likely to enjoy. And what nightclubs there were seemed divided into two main categories: either cheap and cheerful old time local discos, with sticky floors and a DJ playing an endless stream of local dancy folk pop, or incredibly high end glamour haunts, where muscular men in leather coats and 24 hour sunglasses scuttled out of their enormous blacked out jeeps with impossibly tall stick thin models on their arms to sit grimly in private booths around the dancefloor. It was generally suspected that these places were reserved for the more criminally inclined elements of local society, but most regular residents of the city never quite mustered the nerve to find out.

Filip also had deep fears about the possibilities of serious homophobia from the locals during Eurovision fortnight. While Moldova wasn't noted for any kind of modern views on a gay lifestyle, Transnistria leaned even more towards a Russian point of view on the matter, which led to grave concerns about the safety of both delegates and audience members over the duration of the Eurovision period. The local government had given wholehearted assurances that this wouldn't be an issue at all, and that anyone who was caught harassing song contest visitors in a homophobic manner would be severely dealt with. But there was still an underlying fear by plenty of people within Eurovision circles, and many high profile members of the fan press had already very publicly boycotted this year's event.

And if all that wasn't enough, there was a constant concern about the very fragile state of relations between Transnistria and Moldova as a whole. There had been something of an unsettled truce over the last few years, where, despite no major skirmishes having taken place in decades, the atmosphere was often tense and complicated. So considering that the city burghers in Tiraspol liked nothing more than flashing their cash about and embarrassing their neighbours to the west by buying in all the bigger events, it always felt like the grudge match could have kicked off again at any minute under the slightest of provocations. And having a bloody great international song contest on that side of the Dneister had already put a few noses out of joint in Chişinău.

But for now things seemed to be going surprisingly smoothly, and the delegates were all sitting down in what would become the press centre just outside of the newly built arena to receive a presentation from the local organising committee. Dumi Enache talked at length about each of the venues for the Eurovision period. The venue itself looked sturdy and well-equipped for a building constructed at such a rapid rate, and all the press, broadcasting and dressing room facilities appeared top notch, too. The Eurovillage on 25th October Street was being sold as a massive two week long street party, with ample opportunities for all of this year's artists to perform their songs in front of the locals. And the reveal of the Euroclub, which was set to be held in a vast warehouse around the back of the city's biggest vodka distillery, gained an impressed ripple of applause from those in attendance. But it was the announcement of the venue for the closing party that led this up-to-now pretty businesslike meeting to descend into chaos.

"And now, the jewel in our crown," Dumi proudly announced, puffing his chest out before the big reveal. "The venue for our grand aftershow party will be... the historic... Bender Fortress!"

Immediately the delegations from the United Kingdom, Ireland and Australia let out massive hoots of ribald laughter.

"What is it? What is so funny about this?" Dumi asked with a confused look on his face?

"You're kidding us, right?" came a loud Australian voice from the centre of the room. "Bender Fortress? Really?!!"

"I don't see what the problem is here," Dumi said, now more confused than ever. "Bender Fortress is the most important historical building in Moldova. It signifies the centuries-long struggle to be recognised in our own right, and it is a building that many people hold dearly in their hearts. It's on the postage stamps and everything."

"That may well be so, Dumi mate" came the Australian voice again, "but do you know what the word Bender means in the English speaking countries here?"

"It is some kind of tent, I believe?" Dumi asked hopefully.

"Well it's that too," bellowed the Australian, "but it's also a bit of a nasty slang term for gay men. And considering that the two weeks of Eurovision are going to see the biggest annual congregation of gay men on the planet, our local press are going to have a field day with this. Seriously, mate. And the delegations are going to find it hilarious!"

"Well, that will be really disrespectful to our local history, sir," said Dumi, now looking a little cross. "That's as maybe, mate. But it's going to happen, so you'd better prepare yourself for it."

A slow ripple of laughter started to work its way around the big room as the delegates from the other nations had begun to work out what it was that the Australian was suggesting, and the laughter soon magnified into loud guffaws. Dumi stood at the plinth looking hurt and disappointed, while a little way along the top table, Filip Ivanović just sat there with his head in his hands, slowly shaking his head.

"It's going to be an almighty bloody disaster," he muttered to himself. "I just know it is".

7

It was now early April, about a month before the delegations started to arrive, and the technical crew were well under way with their plans to build the massive stage, as well as the huge tonnage of lights and sound rigging that are required for a production of this scale. The television people were also just starting to arrive, building their camera gantries and pulling miles and miles of cabling to an ad hoc gallery at the back of the arena.

True to his word, Håkan had begun to quietly inveigle his way into the production hierarchy. Over the course of the last few weeks, he and Filip had hatched up a plan about a new EU broadcasting regulation – completely made up of course – that needed a very special bit of kit that was required to beam their pictures to the new Extra Extra Ultra HD televisions that were making their way to the living rooms of the West. Håkan had knocked up a believable looking bit of kit he called the MacGuffin that all the television feeds had to run through. He'd told the local engineers it was there to convert the signal to the EU's EEU-HD standard. In actual fact, he'd contrived a complicated box of tricks that reverse engineered the signal to a much lower form of HD if it was turned off, which had tricked the Moldovan crew into believing that it actually really did have to be there. Of course with Håkan being the only person there trained in its use, and holding the only legal certificate to be able to officially operate it (Filip had one of those knocked up by the graphic designers back at CTF HQ), the people at Moldova Smash conceded that he was a useful asset to have in the production office, and were thankful of the broader experience that he'd brought to the build.

By turn, Håkan was then slowly bringing more and more of his regular crew in to supervise matters. The locals didn't notice at first, but when they gradually came to realise that everywhere they looked there was a Swede or a German or a Dane poking their nose into their business, they started to get a little more difficult to work with. Things came to a head when Håkan's curt Finnish chief of lighting, Ari Heikkinen, got into a heated exchange about the correct way to hang an ellipsoidal reflector spotlight, and the entire Moldovan crew downed tools and refused to do any more work until all the outsiders had been removed – or at least until they stopped bossing them around and let them get on with their own jobs in hand. At first Håkan suggested that they just ship The Sparkle Crew in wholesale and get the job done themselves, but the local crew had got the security staff onside, and they had quite plainly stated that they would refuse to let any more foreign infiltrators into the building. This angry stand-off lasted for just over two-and-a-half days, before an exasperated Filip managed to appease both sides with a compromise. Håkan had to stay, that was a given. But the rest of the foreign technical engineers would have to promise to sit back in their own Portakabins out in the service yard just monitoring the build, and they could only come out to work when requested by the local production staff.

As it turned out this was a pretty decent compromise for both sides, as The Sparkle Crew got to goof about with each other and work on some of their own projects on company time, while the Moldovan crew gained the benefit of the abroadians' years of experience in putting together a show of this size and called on their help and advice frequently and often. But as long as they always thought that this was their own idea, Filip reasoned, it might just work. The fact remained though that they'd lost a big chunk of the build schedule, and the time was now getting tight. Filip began to worry that all of the necessary equipment wouldn't be in place before the stand-in camera rehearsals. This is where local singers take the place of the official Eurovision artists in order for the production crew to have a full run though of the visual presentations requested by each national delegation. And while corners were most definitely not to be cut, some elements of the production build would have to be prioritised over others, which wasn't an ideal situation at all. This would mean that a few long late nights would have to be worked, but Håkan was impressed by the dogged determination of the Moldovan crew to get the job done despite the many hurdles they faced, and was happy to dig in with them and do any task they asked of him, whether it was well below his pay grade or not.

"These locals are fantastic people," Håkan explained to Filip in one of their secret hotel meetings. "They might not work in the same way that you or I are used to, but they'll bust a kidney to get this thing completed in time, which is more than I can say for some of the other countries we've run this show in lately. I'm more than willing to get stuck in alongside them. And boy do they know how to drink. I was off around the old boy bars with a few of them last night after we'd knocked off, and I tell you, they can pile it away without even seeming even the tiniest bit wonky. Must be something in the genes over here."

While Filip was heartened to learn of the Moldovan workers' strength and efficiency, he was a little concerned that Håkan had started to go native again. He had history at this, and the longer he worked in a country, the more he began to absorb the cultural foibles of its people. This, of course, was a good thing when it came to liaising with production folk from unfamiliar nations, but it could lead to the occasional problem if he began to veer too far off the racing line. There was absolutely no one on the planet who could do the job like Håkan, but he could be a complicated character at the best of times and needed careful managing. So Filip had to play this very carefully over the next month or so. Very carefully indeed.

*

As the stage was being built over in Tiraspol, Maxim Munteanu was beginning his final preparations for the big contest at his house by the reservoir on the edge of Chişinău. Although Transnistrian by birth, he'd lived in Moldova's capital for the last twenty years, as it had become an easier hub for him to work from now that he was getting a bit older. He still retained a fairly sizeable ranch on the outskirts of Tiraspol, though, where he spent most of his summers, and employed his brothers and their children and their grandchildren to look after the horses and cattle when he wasn't there.

Michi had now given up his job in the card shop and was working for Maxim full-time, helping him with whatever the old singer needed in the run up to his Eurovision performance. He still had his tower block flat in Ciocana, but Maxim had let him stay in the summerhouse down by the water's edge on evenings when they were both working late. He was beginning to become accustomed to this new way of living, and travelled back to his regular home less frequently as time went on. He'd also struck up a great friendship with Maxim's driver and security man Evgeny, who was a much warmer and funnier human being than Michi had initially thought. Quite often the unlikely pair sat on a big bench overlooking the reservoir, drinking local plum brandy and exchanging the stories of their lives. Evegeny still thought that Michi was a bit of an odd character, but he enjoyed his company on those balmy Spring evenings, and was beginning to feel like something of a big brother figure to the skinny and haunted looking singer.

Maxim's plans for his song were simple. It was called Moldova's Landscape, and was a figurative tale explaining the ebbs and flows of all the different people and cultures who had passed through this geographical crossroads over the centuries. But he was singing through the metaphorical eyes of the mountains and the grasslands that had witnessed it. He performed it in his traditional deep folksy baritone, with the added nostalgic edge of a voice that was just starting to gently crumble with age. And he was to have no dancers or flashy stage act. Just five backing singers, stood in a rank at the back in traditional regional costume, filling the song with warm vocal harmonies at all the most emotional points of the songs. Meanwhile, on the giant LCD screens in the background, they were to show images of the Moldovan scenery and the occasional eagle sweeping in front of them. It was pretty simple stuff, but a song with this much heart, when sung in front an audience chiefly made up of adoring Moldovans, would cause the arena to melt with old time joy. If done correctly there wouldn't be a dry eye in the house, and it was surely bound to reap in a whole cartload of respectable scores on the big night – if not quite enough to trouble the top five. The perfect home entry indeed.

Maxim had asked Michi if he wanted to be one of the backing singers, but the younger man had politely refused. Partly because he honestly didn't feel that his voice was up to portraying the kind of rich emotion that this song required, but also partly because he didn't want to damage his reputation as a singer of darkened Gothic tales about the fringes of Moldovan society. He did give it some serious thought though, but felt that, for this project at least, the time wasn't quite right for him. But he was still happy to help Maxim with whatever he needed to get the project completed in time, and was acting as a go-between for the singer and his costume designers, and well as letting the backing choir know when they were needed for rehearsals, and liaising with Dumi at Moldova Smash, which he had to admit didn't come naturally to him.

Over the last few weeks that he had been working with Maxim, Michi had begun to notice the old man getting more and more tired and pale looking, and he was starting to get a little concerned about his new friend. One evening, after they had finished an especially long rehearsal session, Michi caught the old man alone to ask him if everything was OK.

"Maxim sir?" Michi asked nervously.

"Yes, young fellow?" Maxim replied with the caring warmth of a grandfather. "What is it that you'd like to know?"

"Well, I'm a little bit worried about you, I have to confess," Michi admitted. "More than a little, actually. You just seem to be more and more tired every time we have a run though of the song. Do you think it's a good idea to work quite so hard in the run up to Eurovision? That whole process is going to be ten times more punishing than these rehearsals could ever be, so I want you to be in full fitness by the time we get to Tiraspol. Seriously, Maxim. I think you need to look after yourself."

Maxim cracked a big beaming smile and laughed a little. "Nonsense, young Michi. I've been doing this since I was younger than you, and I still have the strength to do a full tour of Russia every couple of years. This silly little thing will be a walk in the park. I'm only singing the one song, after all."

"Yes, but don't forget that it won't just be the one song. There will be dress rehearsals and costume calls, interview sessions and personal appearances. And of course every TV station from here to Sydney is going to want a chat. And that's before the Eurofans get their claws into you. Seriously, Maxim. I think you should rest up for a little while."

"You've got a good point there, little Michi. I have been feeling a bit under the weather for the last few days. I've got no engagements for the next week or so. Maybe I should take to my bed and let myself recuperate. You're so good to me, Michi. You're like the grandson I never had."

"Awww thanks, Maxim," said Michi with a self-effacing shrug. "I'm just, you know, doing whatever I can to help you on this project. I know I'm not experienced in very much – apart from selling greetings cards and being a failure on televised singing shows. But I try my best, and being your assistant has been just about the most important thing that's ever happened to me!"

"Well you deserve it, young Michi. If there's one thing that I regard highly it's a trier. And I can't think of anybody who's tried more steadfastly at this competition than you. You are an inspiration to us all – even to an old man like me."

Michi stopped for a moment and began to look thoughtful. Maxim noticed the faraway look in his eyes.

"What is it, young lad? You look as though you have something to ask me."

"Well I do, kind of. But I really don't want you to think that I'm being rude," Michi said, shyly. "Oh go on then, boy! Spit it out! When you get to an age it's almost impossible to be offended!"

"Well, Maxim. It's just that." There was a long pause before Michi asked the question that had been troubling him for several weeks now. "How old actually are you? I've always wondered, and I really have no idea!"

Maxim let out a hearty roar of laughter and slapped his hands on his thighs.

"Why you cheeky young fella!" he yelled with delight! "Only my own mother knows that for sure, and she's long gone from this world!"

"Oh I'm sorry to have asked, Maxim," Michi quickly apologised.

"No, no, not at all! In fact I'm really rather glad that somebody has finally asked me to my face! And the actual answer is that I'm not entirely sure myself. Like I told you, I grew up on a farm on the outskirts of Tiraspol. It was a much smaller place back then. Barely a city at all. And no one really bothered keeping records in those days. But as you probably know, the official story has it that I'm 68."

"Yes," said Michi, "I've heard that. But some times you seem much younger than that, and other times you feel a little bit older. So I just don't know!"

"Oh you little charmer, Michi," Maxim laughed. "But do you know what, I think you're right. By my reckoning I must be at least, oooh, 81 years young!"

That number flashed through Michi's mind's eye like the price indicator on a wonky petrol pump.

"Could Maxim really be quite that old?" he thought. "I mean, I know show business can keep you looking younger and everything, with all its make up and its flashy clothes, but I'd never imagined that he was quite that long in the tooth. How is he even going to cope with the pressures of getting through Eurovision? The whole thing could see him off!"

"But!" said Maxim, now with a serious edge in his voice. "You must never, ever tell anyone what I've just told you. Especially the people at Moldova Smash – and what a silly bloody name that is for a TV channel. Anyway, it'll play havoc with my insurance if anyone finds out. They'll start treating me like a frail old dodderer, and my pride just won't allow it. It's for the people of Moldova, too. They still think that I'm a virile, dynamic younger man, and I wouldn't want to damage their ideals when they think so highly of me. Maybe when I retire in a couple of years, but not now. Not just yet. So perhaps that's why I'm looking just a little bit tired to you, young fella. And I think you're right, I will need some rest. Cancel my rehearsal plans for the rest of the week and I'll go and have a lie down with a nice cup of tea. What a fine and caring young man you truly are."

And with that, Maxim stood up on unsteady legs and tottered off to his bedroom, closing the door gently behind him.

For a long while after the old man had gone off to bed, Michi just sat there on the big white sofa with a million different options running through his head. What if was all too much for Maxim? What if his ever more frail old body just couldn't take the pressure of such a long and intense process at Eurovision? And what would happen if he wasn't able to perform? Michi had become very fond of the old man and had started to care deeply about his welfare. But he was now terrified that he might lose his new friend before his time. Should he tell anyone about what he'd just learned? Or should he keep his word to the old man? It was such a terrible dilemma.

WEEK ONE

8

It was the Saturday before the start of the rehearsals and the delegations from the competing nations were beginning to arrive in Tiraspol. True to his word, Timur Turgenev had arranged travel for the delegations via his own Pridnestrovian Airlines, but rather unusually each plane acted more like a rural bus service, stopping in one country to pick up a delegation, before heading off to the next to pick up theirs. The poor souls who got on first had taken off and landed a good eight or nine times before they arrived at Tiraspol's shiny new airport, and were exhausted before they'd even got off the plane. The Australians, though, had to make their own way, which involved a tiring three stop journey via Doha, Athens and Bucharest, followed by the short journey from Chișinău to Tiraspol by liveried Eurovision bus. But Turgenev still reimbursed them for the full price of their airfare, which they were terribly grateful for.

It was different too for the press and the fans. Each day at 10am a free shuttle plane would set off from the fifteen largest capital cities on the continent. Anyone from outside of those cities would have to either get themselves to their nearest major transport hub, or make their way to Tiraspol at their own expense. Needless to say the demand for these free flights was enormous, and Pridnestrovian Airlines were already looking into running a second service later in the evening.

Preparations for the big show at the new arena were now back on course after a number of punishing late nights by the crew. The building had been rather unsnappily named The Tiraspol European Palace Of Culture, although people on the ground were all calling it The Teapot, in part because of its unusual rounded shape, but also because the initials of the building's new name almost spelled that, and Teapot was much funnier than TEPOC – well, to the crew at least. There had been a few concerns that the roof wasn't strong enough to support the weight of the massive lighting rigs that were to be suspended from it, particularly as many of them would be moving up and down frequently throughout the show. But Håkan managed to source some enormous roof props at ridiculously short notice, and managed to integrate them into the design of the arena so that it looked as though they were always meant to be there, which rather enamoured him to the local production staff. They were now starting to come round to having him there, and saw him as an important asset rather than an intrusive inconvenience, which, in turn, meant that he was more able to bring his regular Sparkle Crew experts in to advise and oversee all the works. This meant that they were able to execute all the vital tests and trials much more easily. Håkan's giant props did however mean that there would now be a couple of sections of the crowd with slightly impaired views. But if they put up a couple of extra screens in the affected areas and knocked a couple of quid off their tickets he was was sure that the punters wouldn't complain all that much. This was Eurovision, after all. For most people just being in the hall and bathing in all that heady atmosphere was enough. In fact, there was a strange sub-cult of Eurovision fandom who always specifically asked for seats that had more complicated views so that they could witness all the goings on of the production rather than what was going on up on the big stage with the performers, so some of the more rabid fan types would be quick to snap up a seat that was stuck behind a massive great column if it meant they could watch the backstage action more easily.

As the first delegation plane landed at the spartan aerodrome they were met personally by Timur Turgenev, who shook each of their hands as they descended down the ladder to the tarmac, while a folk band in regional dress hammered out some traditional local music in the background – all of course streamed live onto the Transnistrian national news website. They were then directed to a fleet of buses, all decked out in the livery of this year's contest with one each for every delegation, and were driven to their hotels. The journey wasn't too long though, as Turgenev had built a couple of his big new luxury hotels about a half mile to the west of the airport, within easy walking distance of the Teapot Arena, and part of a new sports and events complex that he was having built. Nearly all of the delegations would be staying there, although a few countries who had more complicated security arrangements, like Israel, Russia, and rather unexpectedly San Marino would be staying elsewhere. The crew, the production staff and the CTF officials had their own purpose-built hotel right behind the arena that was packed with all the state-of-the-art conference and media facilities that they would need over this busy few weeks, while the audience for the show would either be staying in the cheaper hotels and Air B'n'B rooms in town, or on the fleets of hotel boats on the Dniester River around a mile-and-a-half from the arena. These boats had the most splendid views of Bender Fortress – although after the unfortunate events at the Heads of Delegation meeting a few weeks previously, all literature now referred to the place by its medieval Moldavian name of Tighina rather than its more giggle-inducing Ottoman appellation. The local townspeople were a little bit put out by that at first, but when Filip and Terry from the CTF explained what was likely to happen everybody soon realised that it was probably for the best.

Even this year's Euroclub was in relatively easy reach, as it was located in that disused warehouse at the side of the massive Yahontov Vodka distillery complex just by the airport, while the Eurovillage in the city centre was just being finished off as the visitors began to arrive. It ran a full quarter mile along 25th October Street in the beating heart of the city, and spilled out into Suvorov Square and its surrounding parklands too. It was to include big screens at each end of the closed off section of road, and a massive stage in the park where many of the performers at this year's contest would be performing throughout the week. The Embassies of each competing country were also invited to build themselves stalls along 25th October Street, and many of them were using it as both an opportunity to show off their nations to the locals, and to sell a bit of their local cuisine while they were at it. Alongside those stalls there would be tents and caravans and buses representing all of Moldova and Transnistria's biggest companies to give out samples of their wares.

Filip Ivanović from the CTF just couldn't believe how efficient and well-organised the whole thing was turning out to be. For as long as he'd been working for the organisation he'd heard mutterings of fear in the darkened corridors of the CTF HQ about how much of a disaster a Moldova-hosted

competition was likely to be, but he had to confess that it was all flying along surprisingly well, even despite that early blip with the local crew walk out. He was well aware that his organisation were in a slightly awkward moral position, considering what everybody suspected about the business practices of Timur Turgenev, not to mention the historically difficult stand off between Transnistria and Moldova proper, but he reasoned that most of the people watching at home wouldn't have a clue where Moldova actually was, let alone all the socio-political implications of holding it in this corner of the country. Having said that though, the eyes of the world's media were still on the organisation after the Cory Kjellberg affair, so they had to ensure that absolutely every last thing that was happening in Tiraspol over the next fortnight was completely transparent and utterly above board. But as it stood, things were going well. Perhaps a bit too well for Filip's liking.

"It's all running too smoothly, Terry," said Filip to his head of communications as they stood awaiting the second of the Pridnestrovian Airlines delegation sky ferries to arrive at the airport. "It's making me anxious."

"I know what you mean, Filip," his sideman agreed. "There's usually been at least one major snafu by now in even the most reliable of countries, and yet, here we all are, waving in the delegations, with absolutely nothing to trouble the suits back in Lucerne. It can't be this easy, surely?"

"Well perhaps this is what happens when you effectively give the contest to an oligarch with a bottomless well of money," Filip replied. "It doesn't entirely sit well, I'll have to confess, but everything is getting done exactly as it should be. It really has been a remarkable feat, but, y'know, I can't help feeling just a little bit on edge, like something big and nasty is about to happen."

"Totally. Absolutely," said Terry. "We've just got to keep our eyes and ears open and try to ward off any weirdnesses and misdeeds before they happen."

"Have you been keeping an eye on the weather forecasts though, Terry? I keep forgetting to have a look."

"It all seems pretty good at the moment, Filip. There's a little rain scheduled towards the end of the second week, but I reckon we'll be good for the big night if it all continues like this."

"Let's hope so, Terry. Let's hope so."

9

By Sunday morning, all of the competing delegations (shy of the Big Five of France, Germany, Italy, Spain and the United Kingdom, who'd all be turning up later in the week), had arrived in the country, received their handshake from Comrade Turgenev, and were cosily ensconced in the brand spanking new hotels, enjoying the glorious smell of new carpet and the pristine never- before-used bathroom suites. The full 42-song line up of contenders for the two semi-finals and the big final show were as follows...

Albania
Xhyljeta – Why Do I Cry?
A traditionally dark and dramatic ballad about the difficulties ethnic Albanians have suffered in neighbouring countries over the last few decades. The singer's name is pronounced pretty much the same as Julietta would be in English, but the Albanian spelling of it has already been giving reporters and sub-editors nightmares.

Armenia
Takouhi Vardanyan – Bounce
A trite but entertaining dance number with a deep Caucasian edge. The stage show is reported to be something pretty spectacular.

Australia
Space Truckers – Ten More Beers
This veteran Aussie punk band might look older than your granddads, but they still pack a mighty punch and can drink just about anyone at this contest under the table. They only entered their national selection show, Australia Decides, for a laugh, and because they thought there might be a free bar. But the country took them to their hearts after many years of nice-but-dull solo contestants, and voted for something that would most accurately represent the true Australia.

Austria
Danny B – Dance Dance With Me
Kind of like an extremely watered down Justin Timberlake, this boy has certainly got the looks, and the song itself has one of the most infectious choruses in the entire contest. But the lad is unproven on a big stage, and there are doubts whether his voice, and indeed his temperament, are up to it.

Azerbaijan
Murad Orujov – I Sleep With The Stars
While the song is a stirring anthem about spending your nights out in the wild mountains of Western Azerbaijan and becoming at one with the nature of your nation, there are many observers who have taken the awkward English of the title to mean that the fella is nothing more than a groupie, and that he'll have a go on anyone with a whiff of fame about them. He's had all this explained to him and apparently he's not terribly happy about it.

Belarus
Kirill Kisly – My Mother My Soul
A mawkish ballad about family ties by a tiny, terrified looking young lad. Very few people give this a chance of escaping from its semi-final – as well meaning as it may be – because it's just a little too sickly sweet for the wider European palate.

Belgium
Gladys – Lonely Nightclub
A bit of a dark horse, this one. Gladys might be a bit of a new name on the Belgian music scene, but her deep, haunting voice and glacial delivery layer perfectly over the song's sparse arrangement. It's the kind of thing that the juries go loopy for.

Croatia
Marta Marić – Heart Cold As Stone
Another mid tempo plodder. And while the singer has the most

terrific, emotive voice, the song itself is a little flimsy and anonymous. Might just scrape through on her merits as a performer, but it's got a fight on its hands.

Cyprus
Thea Evangeline – Sweat
Another in a long line of Cypriot bops that sees a slight blonde girl wave her hair around in the middle of the song instead of there actually being a chorus. A massive favourite amongst Eurovision fans, but many experts fear that it'll be a case of diminishing returns.

Czechia
Jolana Nováková – Strong
The first of a trio of very similar female empowerment anthems with the same name. This version is perhaps the best of the three, as the performer has a long history in musical theatre and can deliver the heck out of a song.

Denmark
Happy Band – Your Smile
The traditional slice of schmaltzy Danish shuffle pop. Lots of banjos and waistcoats and people sitting on benches. Almost impossible to hate, but very little to make you love it either.

Estonia
Kaspar Kikkas – Torm Minu Hinges (The Storm In My Soul)
An impossibly handsome man with a jaw so strong and angular that you could bend metal bars on it. His song is a stock tortured love ballad, but his steely grey eyes will hypnotise you into believing every last word, even if he is singing it in the Estonian language.

Finland
Troll – Helvetti Paskiainen (Hell Bastard)
The Finns go back to what they're best at with some extravagant fantasy metal. Expect swords, leather, pointy noses and an awful lot

of chanting. The CTF let the song's contentious title through, by the way, because they figured that hardly anybody outside of Finland understands the Finnish language, and the words lend themselves to one heck of a rousing chant.

France
Zuzi – Je Peux Vivre Sans Toi (I Can Live Without You)
Don't be fooled by Zuzi's innocent looks, because what sounds like a frothy bit of jazz pop to those unfamiliar with the French language is actually a wickedly naughty break up revenge song, where the singer tells the pig of a guy that she's just dumped everything she dislikes about him. He might protest "I can't live without you!", but she proudly proclaims "But I can live without you!" Strongly tipped to be France's highest finisher in years.

Georgia
Kutaisis Mamak'atsta Gundi – Chveni Mits'a (Our Land)
The act's name literally translates as Men's Choir Of Kutaisi, and their song is a spectacular display of polyphonic singing that will tear the living hearts out of an audience all set for a nice dance and a singalong. The lyric is also thought to be a sly dig at their Russian neighbours, who the Georgians fear have been looking a bit too covetously over the garden fence of late.

Germany
Sissi And Sal – Strong
A duet about female empowerment between two very different looking women who clearly don't get on. There are many who are tipping this for a last place finish, and a few crueller commentators who state that they'd be surprised if it even finished that high.

Greece
Adonis – Fight Night
A swarthy brute of a lad with a big bouncy dance song about having a great night out. The lyric isn't necessarily about actual fighting, but it

gives him the opportunity to show off his pecs with a few boxing moves between the choruses. It's as dumb as all hell, but still loads of fun.

Iceland
Vikingur The Dog Boy – Howl
A bit of an oddity this one. Our performer here dresses in a plushie dog costume and howls plaintively over a minimal techno beat for two minutes and fifty three seconds. And that's it. The bulk of Eurovision fandom are up in arms about it, claiming that it's nothing but a joke and making a mockery of the contest. But it turns out that Vikingur is a very serious man, and has won awards at numerous performing arts festivals across the world. He absolutely doesn't understand why people are finding his act so funny. The good people of Iceland though, to their eternal credit, thought it would be hilarious to send a bloke so devoid of a sense of humour – who also happened to be dressed as a dog – to Eurovision, and for that we must applaud them.

Ireland
Billy McNamara – Lonely Girl
You pretty much know what you're getting with an Irish song these days. A chirpy looking lad in a denim jacket with a face that only his mother could love waving his hands about in front of a guitar and singing a dewy-eyed song about a lost love, despite looking barely old enough to have actually met a girl in real life.

Israel
Uriella Shemesh – Why Do We Have To Fight?
On the outset this emotional ballad appears to be about a relationship on the rocks, with lyric lines suggesting "our only fight should the fight to keep us together". But there are a few commentators who suspect that it is a little less literal than that, and that it's actually a thinly-veiled story about the political situation in Israel. But whatever it's really about, it's perhaps a little too dull to progress all that far in the contest.

Italy

Explodo – Grande Boom Bang

The Italian tradition of talk-singing lends itself well to the world of rap, and this flamboyant local superstar of Salsa Grime won Sanremo by an absolute mile with this wicked takedown of the Italian government. This is perhaps a little too bold and left field to win the whole thing, but it's certainly going to turn a lot of heads.

Kazakhstan

Rayana Bayzhanova – Meniñ Ädemi Ayğırım (My Beautiful Stallion)

The debut nation had to put forward nothing short of a show stopper in order to justify their controversial inclusion into the Eurovision fold. And boy have they done that in heaps. Beginning with a dark moody first verse, it soon explodes into a giant great Eurasian groove with unfamiliar local instruments tootling along to the vocal line, before it builds to a huge crescendo and explodes with joyful dancing. It surely had to be a contender to win the contest this year, and was skirting just behind the favourites in the betting. However, some wag pointed out that the song's title was perhaps a bit too similar to the parody Eurovision song My Lovely Horse off Father Ted, and now that's all anyone in the West of Europe can think of when they hear it. Although it's almost impossible to explain why it's quite so funny to the Kazakhs with their long and proud tradition of horsemanship.

Latvia

Laumina Balodis – Stop That Beat

An artist who'd finally got her chance after eleven near misses in the Latvian qualifying contests, her songs have got increasingly more loud and unhinged with each passing attempt. And just when everybody thought that she'd recorded something that was too wild even for Latvia to send – boom, there she goes and wins her local Supernova competition. She's also notorious for being something of a handful to work with, so the sparks are likely to fly during her rehearsals and press conferences.

Lithuania
Four Peace – Song To The Future
Two girls and two boys, straight out of drama school it seems, sing a sad message to our future selves apologising for the things we've done to the planet. The contest seem to get at least one of these every year, but this is by far the dullest version there's been in some time.

Malta
Lia Maria – Strong
The third song of this title in this year's contest, and while not quite as impressive as the Czech version, it's considerably better than the Germans. But despite being a little more down tempo than the other two, its lyric is almost identical to the Czech song, even though it has a completely different songwriting team.

Moldova
Maxim Munteanu – Moldova's Landscape
We know all about this one, and if the old boy is on form on the night it could easily crawl its way into the top ten. The reception in the hall for this national hero of song will be utterly immense.

Montenegro
Steam Engine – All The Days
Another unlikely entry. This five-piece band are all dressed up in steam punk Victoriana, and prowl their way through through a dark technopop banger with a heavily Gothic tinge, while a dancer dressed as a stone angel creeps about behind them. Quite unexpected stuff from the Balkan state, but the band have been having a few moderate-sized hits at home, so the Montenegrin delegation decided to pick them internally.

Netherlands
Lieke Roos – On Top
After a run of pretty interesting songs, the Dutch have gone back to their old form and sent a woman of a certain age singing a mid-tempo major-

key plodder about how men will never get the better of her. Incidentally, she's bang in the middle of her third acrimonious divorce, so her mind might not entirely be on the game.

North Macedonia
He/She – You
Another duet, only this time it's from the brother and sister act Dusana and Jovan Marković. The pair also played siblings in the popular Macedonian soap opera, Our Street, and were selected because of their popularity at home – which is never perhaps the best idea when your song is as anonymous as this one.

Norway
Stormgiver – Ride The Skies
The Norwegians have finally relented and done what the rest of the world have been wishing they would for years by sending a proper black metal band to Eurovision. They've got the full works – corpse paint on their faces, a massive amount of studs on their scant leather outfits, and a logo that looks like an untidy bonfire. It's as yet unclear as to whether they've burned any churches, but the song's lyric does talk a lot about ancient Norse mythology, so there's a decent chance that they might have.

Poland
Hold Tight – It's Party Time
A good old-fashioned hands-in-the-air, glow sticks out and poppers at the ready party belter. The act consists of a gurning DJ, and old fella strumming on a curious stringed instrument, a rapper in terrible sportswear and a pneumatic blonde who sings the risqué lyric directly down the camera in a way that makes your granddad feel uncomfortable. Already a respectable chart hit right across Europe, the juries will hammer it, of course, but it's a locked in fave with the punters at home.

Portugal
Rodrigo Braga – O Que Era Uma Vez (What Once Was)
A throughly beautiful little number. The singer sits perched on a stool

and lovingly caresses his acoustic guitar as his quiet and fragile voice recounts a past love lost, and how it makes him stronger for the future. There's no telling how this could do on the big night, but if he taps into the mood of the continent this could be causing big trouble on the scoreboard. It only weighs in at two minutes fifteen long, but its brevity is its strength as it leaves you aching for more.

Romania
Ruxandra xXx – I'm Incredible!
Exactly the kind of song the casual Eurovision viewer back home loves to sing along to on their sofa, and an instant Euroclub floor-filler too. Its singer has been the biggest hit at all of the preview parties, too, and the fans have taken this larger-than-life character completely to their hearts. Expect to see this one topping many of the fan polls, only to struggle for points a little on the night.

Russia
Gennady – Like The Wind
This lad was only announced as the Russian artist on the morning of the Heads Of Delegation meeting, and is so beautiful to look at that there are many who suspect that he is actually a hologram. However, there are mutterings from the Russian music press that he was a last minute choice after a major Russian artist with a string of international hits behind them pulled out of the contest at the very last minute following an argument over contracts and payments. The delegation haven't revealed any details of the stage show yet, but three massive container lorries with Russian number plates have been parked up behind the arena for a couple of days now, so everybody is suspecting that it's going to be spectacular.

San Marino
Mohammad bin Faisal – Barak Aismuh (Bless His Name)
The Sammarinese have long provided something of a flag of convenience for anyone with enough money to buy a spot on the Eurovision playbill. But this is perhaps their strangest paymaster yet.

The artist is a minor Saudi prince, and he sings a repetitive nasal chant in traditional white garb, while five identically dressed men holding riding crops stand in close rank behind him, smiling sweetly and joining in with every fifth word. Having said all that, it's got one hell of a groove behind it, but it might be just a little too far off the Eurovision message to garner much in the way of votes. This does, however, explain why San Marino's hotel was so far out of town. The security issues must be immense with this one.

Serbia
Zivko Bodrožić – Dajem Ti Sve Moje Srce (I Give You All My Heart)
Classic Serbian fare here. The incredibly tall Zivko starts by walking swiftly towards the front of the stage, almost breathing out a delicate minor-key ballad accompanied only by a regional flute. As the song begins to build, the backing singers walk to the front to join him, before they all raise their hands in the air and power out the last few notes to the beat of a huge great drum. Always a crowd pleaser, this kind of song, if not a little from the old days of the Serbian playbook.

Slovenia
Crate – Ljubezen Ljubezen Ljubezen (Love Love Love)
It's not entirely clear whether the name of this three-piece girl group has any deeper meaning, or if they just picked an English word that they liked the sound of. But what is clear though, is that this is the kind of song that everybody enjoys on the night, but that hardly anyone gets around to voting for. Which is a shame, because it's got a lot of potential, despite its somewhat unimaginative title.

Spain
Emiliano Ganador – Hablemos Mañana (Let's Talk Tomorrow)
Every year the Spanish fans are convinced that this is finally going to be the big one, and every year they go home sorely disappointed with a lower mid-table finish. But this time they reckon it's written in the stars – especially so as their performer's last name literally translates as 'Winner'. The song itself is instantly recognisable as hailing from

Spain, although behind the jangly flamenco guitars and the Latin groove there's not really a whole lot to it. You might have to be changing your name rather soon, Señor Emiliano.

Sweden
Ebba Green – Swing
The Swedes have been past masters at the identikit Eurovision contender over the past few years. But as time has passed they've slowly begun to slide down the table. They always finish in the top ten, mind, but have been a couple of points off the pace for a few years running now. And after what most observers declared was an unusually weak array of songs in their Melodifestivalen selection competition, there are fears that this sweet little pop tune could get lost in the crowd and struggle to qualify.

Switzerland
Carly Carly – Deep
This kind of fractious electroclash was all the rage a few years back. But whether or not it can still grab the attention of a Saturday night TV audience is a bit of a worry, no matter how much she looks and dresses like Lady Gaga.

Ukraine
Bohdana – Holy Cow
Giving Switzerland a massive lesson in how to manage excess, this is a big, beaty mess of a song with a pounding techno thump, loads of farty trumpets, and a rank of oiled-up muscle men writhing about behind her. At one point she even starts beating the heck out of an actual kitchen sink with some metal pipes at the back of the stage. She knows exactly who she is, and what she's for, and doesn't care what anybody thinks of her. Absolutely maximum Eurovision fodder, and destined to crop up on clip shows for many years to come.

United Kingdom
Jason Brown – Time Has Come

After losing out to a comedy dog act on Britain's Got Talent, Glaswegian Jason has been doing personal appearances at small town nightclubs right across Scotland for the last couple of years. However, there are concerns that the BBC only picked what is the first Scottish artist to sing for the UK in decades because they were trying to appease the SNP, who have been lobbying for a separate Scottish act at Eurovision via BBC Alba. Already on a bit of a hiding to nothing, the British press have rather unkindly dubbed him Jason Beige. He's a smashing young lad, but there's the feeling within television circles that he's something of a sacrificial lamb, which to be honest he really doesn't deserve.

In two weeks time one of these acts was going to go on and win Eurovision, dragging the whole merry charabanc off to their own country the following May. But who was it going to be?

10

It's the morning of the first day of rehearsals, and a long queue was snaking out of the accreditation centre and around the back of the arena. To the regular attendees this was considered to be the first day of Eurovision proper, as the artists began to take their first faltering steps on the big stage, and the early adopters amongst the fan sites and local papers started to claim their tables in the press centre with every intention of camping out there for the next fortnight. But for the organisers at both the CTF and Moldova Smash it was the day when things began to get demonstrably real, as everything that happened from here on in would be played out in the gaze of hundreds of pairs of eyes with a connection to the internet and a lust to report every single last thing that was being said and done. And to the crew, all these people were just an annoyance as they went about their daily business of making everything look and sound amazing.

However, the really keen members of the press had done this all many times before, and arrived a day or two earlier so that they could familiarise themselves with the surroundings and pick up their accreditation the night before rehearsals began, so they could get straight into the press centre without let or hindrance and bed into their preferred corners of the room the minute the doors opened on day one. The largest proportion of the press corps at this stage of proceedings were made up of the fan sites, who seemed to swell in number and professionalism with each passing year. Some of them operate like swish media organisations, with different reporters delegated for specific tasks tasks and all wearing matching outfits, while others are more ad hoc affairs who potter along reporting on what they see as they go along. In among them are the odd smattering of national and international press from around the globe, who occasionally embed reporters in for the long run, and a strange little subgroup of the Eurovision world, the professional gamblers, who always bag a table with the best view of the screens in the press hall, and rarely leave their seats in case they miss a morsel of information that might give them a benefit on the betting exchanges. It's this little corner of the room that sees the most traffic over the fortnight, as information about the songs and the artists is bought and exchanged like a currency of its own.

Lastly there were the local press. Some years, especially if it was a nation new to the hosting duties, the room would already be packed with them, each one eager to report every last nut and bolt of the production to a readership who had never witnessed this kind of thing before. Other times, and usually when it was being held in a Western European country with a more cynical approach to the contest, they would be few and far between. But this year it was somewhere in the middle. Moldova didn't have an enormous amount of indigenous media, but what it did have seemed to be crowding around anything and anybody that moved, ramming microphones into surprised faces and constantly asking the more international elements in the room what they thought of Moldova, and Transnistria, and especially the "beautiful new complex" that they'd found themselves working in. This was a moderate nuisance to all the regulars who'd been to this thing on multiple occasions in the past, but nobody could really begrudge them their excitement, as this was a pretty substantial and unusual thing to be happening in their oft-overlooked country.

Already billeted into the press room were the rival factions of EuroStorm and ESC Cargo. Both highly popular fansites ran tight ships, with a dozen journalists each reporting on practically anything that happened as the rehearsals went on. EuroStorm tended to favour the more sensationalist showbiz tittle tattle and appeared to act as a vehicle for its ebullient owner Michael Storm – a loud New Zealander who liked nothing more than to make himself the centre of the site's reportage, and who would sell his own Auntie's teeth if it meant he was going to get more air time and more clicks online. This, of course, had put a great many noses out of joint among the wider fandom, but you couldn't deny the sheer volume of traffic that the operation was pulling in on a daily basis – although these days those numbers were starting to noticeably dwindle.

ESC Cargo, on the other hand, was more of a collaborative affair between citizen journalists from a dozen or more countries who preferred to concentrate strictly on the cold hard facts of the news. It tended to lean a little towards the serious and dry side, but they were famous for breaking news and being the most trusted info source amongst the specialist sites. They'd only been going for three short years, but had grown enormously in stature and range since they were first formed by a freelance Luxembourgish journalist called Radouane Thill. So popular had the site become that that Thill had taken the leap to cut back on his regular work as a court reporter for his local news agency to go full-time on Cargo, and he had a willing tribe of loyal volunteers to do all the hard graft for him.

But the most important thing that you have to know about Michael Storm and Radouane Thill is that they absolutely hated each other. And with a passion that knew little bounds. Storm thought Thill was nothing more than a dull young upstart who was coming into the Eurovision fanpress word expressly to steal his readers, while Thill considered Storm to be a brash charlatan who was only in the game to increase his own media profile and use the contest as a stepping stone to further fame. And both men would stop at nothing to make the other one look bad – whether by fair means or foul.

Each group was set up at opposite ends of the cavernous press hall, and although they weren't in direct earshot, they could definitely see each other – with their liveried flags and colourful uniforms garishly apparent – and were constantly keeping one observant eye on the opposing faction just to be sure that their rivals were neither misbehaving, nor bagging some scoop that they hadn't themselves been party to. But one thing was sure – both factions were primed with arch schemes to discredit each other. Something was going to blow between the two men. It was just a case of when, and what, and why.

*

Over in the arena, the first few acts were preparing for the morning's session of rehearsals. Although the majority of television viewers at home simply imagine that the Eurovision Song Contest is a one night affair some time in Spring, there's actually an awful lot of preparation to get through before the acts take to the stage. There's the two midweek semi-finals to get through first, on the previous Tuesday and Thursday, where those acts who don't automatically qualify for the final have to battle it out to earn a berth on the big show. Each semi-final usually has around eighteen songs fighting to be one of the lucky ten who make it through, and these shows are generally more closely contested that the final itself. Each of the three big shows has at least three full dress rehearsals, where the songs are all performed in their competitive order, with the hosts and interval acts and some manner of dummy scoring – and usually in front of a crowd of locals.

But before they even get to that point, each song has to go through two sessions of individual rehearsals, where they sort out the soundchecks, camera marks, lighting, choreography, backdrops and pyro cues – if they have any. They tend to get around four or five full run throughs of their song in each session – depending on how much time they spent messing about with their choreography – before dashing off to check the footage in an editing suite to see if everything was to their approval. After that they face a barrage of mundane questions in a press conference, with many acts also electing to take part in individual interviews with the press afterwards, which can go on for quite some time and usually involves them answering the same five questions over and over again, before posing for awkward selfies with everybody and anybody that each successive journalist managed to cram into the interview room. So when combined with the pre-rehearsal costume and make up calls, and waiting in line for the previous act to finish their rehearsal stint, a simple one-song practise session can go on for the best part of the day – although thankfully, once it was out of the way, they wouldn't have to go through the whole thing again for another four days, upon which they had a much shorter second rehearsal day.

Each semi-final was divided into two halves, which were drawn at random at the head of delegation meeting, and the eventual running order was built around those halves. So the first half of semi-final one rehearsed on the first day of rehearsals, the second half of semi-final two rehearsed on the second day, and so on. Things got bunched up a little more later in the week when the Big Five turned up and they had less time with their run throughs, but this was essentially the way things panned out over the first few days of rehearsals. This tight schedule was managed with military precision by the stage manager – a stern German woman called Hanna Enkelhart.

She ran the day's timetable with a rod of iron. If anybody was late, for whatever reason, they would still have to finish at the time that was written on the schedule. And she didn't allow for any sort of pop star behaviour or messing about. With only the occasional break when a host country insisted on bringing in their own local crew, she'd been doing this job at Eurovision for a good twelve years now, and there was no human alive who could get the acts on and off with such precision.

For ten of those twelve years she'd been working alongside the crew ganger Linnea Bergstrand, and the pair had developed an almost telepathic method of collaborating, where each could tell what was required of them next by a shrug, gesture or inflection of voice. It was Linnea's job to organise the crews of stage hands that got one act off the performance area, and the next one on to replace them. And the chief aim was to get that changeover done within the 45 seconds of film between the songs that have come to be rather sweetly refered to as the postcards. Her crew was split in two. One to bring the act and all their equipment and staging onto the stage, and another to drag it all back off again, and place all the bits and pieces into the correct spot in the backstage storage area. A further, smaller crew were poised with brooms and polishers to get any remnants and residue from the previous act off the stage, so that the next lot could have a nice, clean and safe space to perform, where they could play out their three minutes in the most stress-free and unhindered manner possible. Such residue could include anything from stray feathers from a boa, to confetti, glitter (and there's a lot of glitter), skidmarks from the soles of the performers' shoes, bits of leftover fireworks, and the more visceral leftovers of sweat, spit and discarded hair.

Some acts were a dream to get on and off. Just a simple singer and perhaps an unplugged guitar, or maybe a pop act with a few dancers or a small rank of backing singers. But then there were the others. The show offs with giant props, enormous costumes and several pounds of high explosives for their pyro show. The existing bands who were already used to putting on this kind of a spectacle were usually no trouble. It was the acts where the TV companies had decided to spunk a whole load of money on some elaborate show with giant climbing frames and moving screens, alongside circus performers on stilts and high flying trapezes that were the biggest trouble. The singing talent usually didn't have the slightest idea what was involved in getting all those props on stage, and so more often than not became something of a diva while all around them was getting assembled or dissembled. However, Linnea knew how to handle them all with her calming manner and warm, helpful face. She was known as Ice in the trade. In part because her last name began with Berg, but also because she was famous for keeping a calm head while everything around her was getting cluttered and insane. Of course she always had a few choice words about any prima donnas that she had to deal with, but only once they were well out of earshot. So together with Hanna's stern presence, they made quite a formidable team, and could be trusted upon to quickly and simply sort out even the most testing of on stage situations.

However, none of the crew were quite prepared for what was about to happen with the very first rehearsal of the day.

11

The first act due to do their turn were the Montenegrin band Steam Engine. When they were planning the running order, Filip and Terry wanted something exciting and unusual to open the show, so picked the Balkan steam punk act as something that would catch the public's eye and encourage any casual viewers to stay on and watch at least a few more songs. They had also been told by Montenegro's head of delegation that they were planning a significant stage show, and once they'd seen the production video that suggested the staging that they required, everyone on the team agreed that it would be a good idea to get this one out of the way first, so that they had a little more time to get everything in position while the hosts were explaining the voting procedures in English and French. Now this all seemed like the perfect idea until it was 9am on the first morning of rehearsals. Steam Engine had already been up for five hours – three of them in make up and costume putting together their elaborate visual appearance. The band's singer Bobby Victoria needed around a kilo of prosthetics applied to his face alone, and was to be lowered onto the stage from the roof by a wire, appearing to be flying in on stone wings. After such an early start the act were already tired and grumpy, and they hadn't even made it to the stage yet.

Meanwhile, things were getting a bit panicky towards the back of the hall. The guy in charge of all the sound equipment, Skunk Torsvald, was pulling out cables and plugging them into different holes whilst giving off a cloud of the most creative swears. His Moldovan counterparts, by this point maybe a little bit terrified of him, were standing back and looking at each other with puzzled shrugs, while the tiny, angry Swede was scrambling around on his knees beneath the desk.

"OK, which one of you dozy fuckers tripped the off switch?" he said, casting a vicious stare at the three members of local crew who were within his gaze. All three men slowly paced back until they could no longer see his eyes. They weren't, however, safe. The Skunk, living up to his name with a broad white stripe running through the middle of his jet black hair, darted up and began to prod his finger into the chest of the nearest person – a startled looking volunteer called Bogdan who'd only popped by to top up the production fridge with fresh bottles of water.

"I'm sorry sir, I've only just got here," said Bogdan, calmly. "What seems to be the problem?"

"What seems to be the problem?!" Skunk bellowed. "I've got no fucking sound coming off that desk and I've got a gaggle of powdered clockwork morons coming on stage in precisely four minutes. Some stinking piece of toilet has either unplugged us, tripped over a wire, or pressed the killswitch

with their elbow while they were picking their nose, and now it's left us with a major bloody problem." He pointed his heavily tattooed arm at the local crew and flicked it around with utter distain. "Which one of you dopey arse nuts has done this then? Come on, own up to it. It must have been one of yous?"

They all looked at each other utterly puzzled, before the bravest one of their number stuttered forth. "We genuinely have no idea what has happened here, Mr Skunk sir," he mumbled. "We've just been sitting behind you all this time, taking your direction and doing exactly what you've asked of us. I'm not sure what else we can say."

Skunk calmed his rage a little and began to pull a grudgingly reasonable face. "I hate to say it, but you're right chaps. Sorry for having a dig at you all. But I just don't know what has happened here. Twenty minutes ago I was running the sound test lovely and nice, but now it's gone. All gone.

Nothing. Any of you boys got any clue as to what we can do next?"

Out of the corner of his one good eye, Skunk could see the first act shuffling onto the stage dragging their big outfits along with them, as Linnea's crew scuttled around them like worker ants putting all the props and pyro into place. He could hear Hanna's voice booming in the distance. "Check. Check. Sound please? Can somebody patch me in to the hall monitors please?"

"Oh bollocks," Skunk said with a worried look on his face. "Now we're in the shit. Has anybody got fifty cents for the meter?" he nervously joked, before Hanna's voice came bursting out of his crackling radio.

"Skunk! Hey Skunk! Do you have any sound for me?" she boomed, with her naturally hoarse voice already of the verge of decay. "We got nothing down here mate. No hall sound, no monitors.

Nothing. Can you fix it for me?"

"We're trying, Hanna. We're trying," Skunk anxiously replied as he fiddled with a few more knobs. But not so much as a light was flickering on the desk.

Back in the press hall, the ranks of journalists were staring at the screens a little confused.

"The band have messed up," shouted a small ginger Austrian lad on the EuroStorm table. "Look, they just stand there like lemons. They have no idea what to do!" he mocked.

From the other side of the hall came a more reasoned theory. "This looks more like a technical issue," said a bearded and bespectacled man from the ESC Cargo benches. "You're bound to get this on the first day. It happens in some form every year. They just need to sort out the early teething difficulties. It's no big panic."

"Yes, but look," came a third voice, a woman with a heavy Slavic accent. "Look at the time. They are already three minutes over their allotted rehearsal slot. This is cutting into the Serbian rehearsal now, and I'm quite sure that my country won't get the time to catch up and they'll rush us. It's always the same. There's always a conspiracy against us!"

"Shut up you old moaner," came another voice from the depths of the hall. "It'll all clean itself up in time. Just chill yourself, girl!" And with that the conspiratorial muttering in the room began to swell like the sea on a gusty day, with rumours and doom-laden predictions fluttering about like malevolent leaves on the wind.

Back in the hall, Skunk was beginning to get into a bit of a panic. Not only was Hanna screaming at him down the radio, but Håkan and Artiom Balan, the head of the local Moldovan crew, could be seen marching towards the sound console with concerned scowls. And in the distance on a far balcony, Filip and Terry from the CTF could be seen shaking their heads in woe.

"What seems to be the problem here, Skunk?" shouted Håkan across the gloom.

"The sound's fucked, Hawk Man. Nothing. Nada. Nilch," Skunk replied, before correcting himself to "Zilch!".

"I've tried bloody everything," he continued, "but I just can't see what the problem is."

"Excuse me Mr Skunk sir," came a quiet voice from the back of the gaggle of local crew. It was Bogdan the runner. "It might seem a stupid question, but have you tried turning it off and on again?"

"Of course I tried bloody turning it off and on again, you stupid little turd... LOOK!"

Skunk began to hammer his stumpy thumb into the on-off switch like it was an ancient arcade game.

"See! Piss all!"

"I don't mean there," Bogdan calmly continued. "I meant at the plug socket on the wall." "You mean this thing isn't plumbed directly into the mains," Skunk replied, a little puzzled.

"Oh no, our safety regulations would not allow it," Artiom Balan affirmed as he reached the console area. "Just follow the lead out of the back and see where it takes you."

Skunk pulled the kind of face that dogs in cartoons make when they know they've done something stupid and clambered to the back of the desk, tugging the power cable as he went.

"Jesus, the bloody thing goes down ten rows of seats. That's not ideal!"

He hurdled hectically over each tier of fresh new seats before he came to the end of the cable, and stood there angrily with an unsocketed plug in his hand."

"Who the shatbags has pulled this out?!" he shouted angrily.

"He looked up at the now considerable crowd behind the sound desk as they collectively turned their heads to the left and laughed. One row forward and about ten seats across, a Moldovan lady in a head scarf and house coat was busily cleaning the floor with an old-fashioned stand up hoover.

"Check the plug socket by her!" Håkan yelled down at Skunk. He skipped over the last row of seats to see a single plug socket below one of the seats. And following the cable that was plugged into it took his eyes directly to the oblivious cleaning lady.

"You're bloody telling me that the main source of power for the whole sound desk... for this entire show... is wedged between a couple of random seats where anybody can prat around with it?!" shouted Skunk, utterly bewildered. "I'm going to go over there and give her a good talking to!"

"Nooooo!" shouted pretty much everybody in the hall who had ever worked with Skunk before, knowing how easily he could fly off the handle.

"It's not her fault, Skunk," shouted Håkan. "She wasn't to know. Let's get you plugged in there again for now, and we'll plant a guard by the chair to stop any further disruption today. Then we can get on with this morning's rehearsals, while Artiom here sorts us out a more appropriate power supply."

"Oh... alright," conceded Skunk, disappointed that he'd been done out of a good argument. "Right," he warned, "make sure that it's turned off at the console before I plug it in, or there's going to be an almighty pop!"

One of the Moldovan crew ensured that the switch was firmly set to Off, before sliding every volume control on the desk to zero. Skunk plugged the cable back in and turned it back on at the wall, before the local crew member slid the volume back up to a reasonable level. But as he did this, the voice of an angry German woman began to get incrementally louder.

"...and if somebody doesn't tell me what's going on soon I'M GOING TO STAMP ALL OVER THEIR NUTS... Ah... so... I see that the sound is working now. You there, Steam Engine. Get on with your show now."

Over in the distance on the CTF's observation balcony, Filip had his head in his hands and was trembling with anxiety.

"We're fucked, Terry. It's all fucked. This is song one of day one

102

and it's all turned to shit already. What more can go wrong, Terry. What more?"

*

The rest of that day's rehearsals went relatively well considering the rather challenging start. Most of the remaining artists were delightfully helpful in trying to speed things along, and pretty soon they'd caught up the time lost at the start of the day without having to eat too deeply into the crew's much needed break times. The only real difficulty came when they first attempted to wheel Poland's massive DJ booth structure up the production ramps at the back of the stage, as it was a bit too top heavy to safely roll up that level of incline with the DJ still in it. So the poor fella had to hop out and then shin up a hastily arranged step ladder around the back once the cumbersome structure had been put in place. Clearly they wouldn't have the time to do this in the live situation, so the more technically minded members of the props crew were already trying to sort out a means of counter-balancing the whole thing for the next rehearsal.

Aside from that, it was plain sailing, shy of when the little Belarussian lad lost his stage shoes and refused to go on without them, claiming they were his lucky omen. Hanna the stage manager wasn't going to stand for any of that nonsense on her tight schedule, though, and practically dragged him on by is ear to do the entire first run though in his socks, which led to a bit of ungainly sliding about on the shiny stage. But fortunately his flimsy little ballad didn't require too much in the way of movement, so he wasn't in any real physical danger. The stage hands, however, weren't terribly pleased at having to sweep his sweaty footprints off their nice clean stage afterwards.

At the end of the day, and with all the necessary songs rehearsed, Filip and Terry from the CTF and Stefan and Dumi from Moldova Smash had the first of their scheduled debriefing meetings about how the day had gone in one of the conference suites behind the main arena.

"Well gentlemen," said Filip. "After a bumpy start things got flowing along quite smoothly. I guess we were lucky that everybody today bar Montenegro and Poland had pretty simple mid-tempo songs and we didn't have to get too panicky about too many of the changeovers. It'll make for a bit of a dull first half hour of the show, but I'll take that over any major dramas and explosions," he laughed.

"Is that thing with the sound that happened this morning usual in this game?" Dumi asked. "It seemed to us like quite a major issue there."

"Par for the course," Filip assured him. "We always factor space for a couple of minor teething issues on the first couple of days. Once we've got past them we're flying. We'll be running the thing on rails and finishing early each day by the time we get to the last few rehearsals. Which reminds me – have you got someone sorting out that power supply for the sound desk? If we were to keep it plugged in where it is we'd have to lose a good hundred seats, and at this late stage we can't afford to mess about with the punters' tickets. There'd be hell to pay if that's where they'd ended up putting someone like the Australian fan club and then they found out they couldn't get into the arena!"

"A very good point there, Filip," said Stefan. "I've got someone from works onto that now. They're chasing a new cable up to the sound area as we speak, so that should be all set and dried and safe by the morning. Now then, what do we have to expect on tomorrow's timetable?"

"Ahh," said Terry, a little anxiously. "Tomorrow won't be quite as simple as today, I'm afraid. We've got the Norwegian black metallers third song on, and they look like they look like they could be a bit of a handful. Turns out that the singer is a bit of an unreconstructed sunwheel pagan, and he's prone to unexpected bouts of racism and homophobia. And seeing as we've got them on between the Saudi Prince and that sweet little Danish band, who are half-black and three-quarters gay, we might be in for a spot of bother when it comes to the press conferences. We didn't really know all that much about those Norwegians before they won their national final. We just thought they were another knockabout comedy horror metal band in funny masks. But it turns out that they're deeply serious about their old Norse ways and are edging a little too near to the extreme right in their attitudes for my liking. I've read some horrible interviews with them in the specialist metal magazines over the last few weeks. And it doesn't help that they're trying to cram more flames and fireworks into a three minute performance than a six month Rammstein world tour. So I fear that we're going to have to do a lot of careful image management with the press on this one."

"I'll alert Hanna and Ice on the crew to try and shooshy them along a bit quicksmart," said Filip, looking a bit serious over his glasses. "We don't want to start an international incident or anything!"

"I must confess," Dumi said, looking a little concerned, "this kind of thing is all a bit new to us. So we'll have to trust to your experience here. Anything else that we should need to worry about?"

"Well, we're hearing reports that the Lithuanian drama school kiddies all throughly hate each other and are on the verge of splitting up," said Terry. "So we'll need to keep an eye on that one and carefully massage their egos to get them all on stage at the same time. And the Latvian girl we've got on last is a bit of a diva – but that's why we put her there. We only have to worry about her fitting in with one other act, so I'm sure it'll all be fine."

"Duly noted, Terry," Dumi replied.

"How's the press looking today?" Stefan enquired.

"Oh it's all the usual stuff," Terry replied. "The locals are excitedly showing pictures of all the artists on stage and explaining what a wonderful thing it is to have such a big show in their country. The internationals haven't really got going yet, shy of the odd little filler paragraph stating that it has all started today, and that nothing much else has happened yet."

"How about the fan press," Stefan asked.

"Well it's pretty much the same as usual," Terry sighed. "It's mainly page after page of forensic dissection of how run through two of any given song was significantly different to run through three, when all that actually happened was that one of the dancers happened to scratch their nose at the one minute twenty three second mark. That and endless interviews all asking what they think of Tiraspol, who their favourite singers are, and who they think is going to win the competition this year. Same as it's ever been."

"EuroStorm are on one of their traditional warpaths though, Terry," Filip added, with a smirk on his face. "Did you see?"

"Oh dear," shrugged Terry, knowingly. "What are they on about now?"

"Well, they reckon that this morning's delay was a sure sign that the CTF don't know what they're doing, and that our people are battling with the local crew at every turn," Filip chuckled. "How did they even come up with that dumb-assed story? We're not letting the press into the main hall until Thursday, so they couldn't possibly know that!"

"They're just doing what they always do and jumping on the tail of anything that looks lumpy and putting all the blame on us," Terry laughed. "There's no point in even dignifying that story with a response. Everybody knows what they're like. Surely nobody takes them seriously any more? I don't know why we keep granting them accreditation?"

"Numbers, Terry. Numbers." Filip replied. "If it was down to me I wouldn't let them in the country. But they're still getting some pretty decent figures on their site, and they always manage to ensure that they're near the top of every web search. So the people upstairs seem to think that this is good business, as they're keeping the property's name in the chatter zone and they're doing it for free. Even if pretty much everything they say is a load of old cobblers."

"Erm, actually Terry," Dumi nervously cut in. "We've had word from some of the sound crew that Mr Skunk has been treating them pretty badly."

"Ah, that's just his way," Filip assured the anxious Moldovan TV executive. "He's not as scary as he looks, and he can take it just as well as he gives it out."

"Yes, but that's not the way we do things around here, Filip," Dumi replied, now looking a little more serious in his response. "If he keeps talking to the people around him like that we might very well end up with a walk out. And if one section of the local crew walks out, they all will. But as much as you lot at the CTF might like that, I can't see Timur Turgenev being quite so happy. Around here he's got the power to have all of your people marched off site in an instant, and that's not going to be a good result for anybody."

"Hmm yes," Filip replied, now realising the seriousness of Dumi's point. "I'll get Håkan to have a word with him tonight, and hopefully we can get someone a little more level-headed working alongside him tomorrow to keep him from being quite so hair trigger."

"Good good," said Stefan. "Right then, any other business?" "Don't forget that Euroclub is opening tonight," added Dumi.

"Oh yes, I'd almost forgotten about that," Stefan replied. "Filip. Terry. I trust that you'll be joining us? We've got a gala night with lots of local DJs playing Eurovision classics. Everyone's invited!"

Filip and Terry cut each other a crafty side-eyed glance. They knew that every year's Euroclub opening party featured local DJs playing Eurovision classics, and they were beginning to get a little tired of it. But they didn't want to dampen the Moldovan pair's excitement in what was admittedly a big night for them.

"Oh yes, I think we'll pop in for a little while, just to check how things are going," Filip answered while nudging Terry's foot conspiratorially under the table. "They're usually a little quiet at the start of the week, and we've still got a lot to plan for tomorrow, so we might have to dash out early. But we'll definitely be there."

"Great! great!" said Stefan as he rubbed his hands with glee. "We'll look forward to seeing. We've got lots of spectacular things planned!"

"I would imagine that you have," Filip replied. And with that, the four men shook hands, and the Moldovan half of the meeting quickly dashed out, almost certainly to get their party garb on for the big night.

"Ten minutes? Just to show our faces and appear to be willing?" said Terry under his breath. "Ten minutes, Terry mate,' Filip replied. "At a push..."

12

It's now just before 10pm that same evening, and Filip and Terry are on their way to Euroclub in one of the courtesy cars provided by the host broadcaster. There was a whole fleet of brand new Mercedes-Benz E Class limos darting around the city, all festooned with that year's Eurovision livery – a bright design based around local embroidery patterns. Every time one of them went through a neighbourhood, the local kids stopped and waved in some excitement, squinting in through the darkened glass to try and catch a look at whoever might be riding in them, just in case they were famous.

"We haven't had this kind of reception anywhere else ever, Terry," Filip noted with a smile. "Some of the places these shows have visited lately we've been lucky that they haven't thrown rocks at us!"

"Oh yes!" Terry replied. "The locals have really embraced this competition. Look, there's a Eurovision-branded flag hanging from every lamp post and traffic light. I love it when a country takes the contest to its heart like this. It makes all the hassles and complications worthwhile."

"Excuse me sirs," came the voice of the driver from the front of the car. "We are nearly at the Euroclub venue. As we enter the complex, you might like to look at the brewery building on the right. It is very beautiful!"

"Thank you for your advice, Vasile," said Terry. "We'll be sure to."
"Here it is now! Look! Look!" said the driver, excitedly.

The two men in the back of the car lowered their heads to peer out of the darkened windows. Vasile was right, as before them stood the one of the most breathtaking examples of Stalinist industrial architecture that either of them could ever remember seeing. The stark white constructivist walls were ribbed with art deco pillars, each topped with bright red stars. Above every tall, narrow window sat impossibly colourful mosaics, each describing a different part of the vodka distilling process, and every person depicted had the distinct and powerful jutting jawlines that were common signifiers in Soviet heroic worker art. And it was enormous, stretching out for almost as far as they could see, with giant silos and tubes towering above the building from behind.

"So this building is still in use then, Vasile?" Terry enquired.

"Yes Terry sir. It produces millions of litres of Tiraspol's Finest every year. It's one of our biggest exports. That's what the name means – Luchshiye... Finest."

"Oh, I wondered what that stood for. I just assumed that it was the name of one of the owners," Filip noted.

"We are all owners, Filip sir. It belongs to the state. The state of Transnistria. We all have a stake in it."

"Very nice indeed, Vasile!" Filip smiled.

"So Vasile, I have a question," asked Terry. "If this factory is still in operation, how come they've allowed us to to take over a massive chunk of it to host our Euroclub?"

"Now there is quite a story," Vasile replied, readying himself to spin a bit of a yarn. "This big engineering company asked Luchshiye if they could rent out this warehouse space for a couple of years. It was a slight inconvenience to the distillery, but they reasoned that they could temporarily keep their vodka secure in a local lock up while charging the engineers an enormous rent for their warehouse, which the engineers were more than happy to pay. The vodka people asked no questions, and the engineers told no lies."

"So what were they making, these engineers?" asked Terry, now thoroughly hooked by Vasile's tale.

"Well my friend, you would have never have believed it," the driver replied. "They were six months into their contract and one day the police came charging in, with swat teams and snipers and all kinds of riot equipment. Hundreds of cars and buses and policemen were shipped in for a dawn raid. Nobody in the vodka factory had any idea what was happening. But it turns out that these engineers were making bootleg helicopters for the international market..."

"Stop! Hang on?" said Terry, looking all confused. "Bootleg helicopters? How in the name of heck do you bootleg a helicopter?"

"Very easily, Terry my friend. They bought a cheap old second-hand Kamov KA-26 from Russia, carefully took it apart piece by piece, then replicated every single part using cheaper materials. Of course it was highly illegal, and incredibly dangerous. But someone at the factory must have developed a conscience and tipped off the authorities, because they were just about to start shipping the things out."

"Where in the name of heaven to?" asked Terry, now rather concerned.

"Oh, mainly to the old Soviet states, like all the Stans in Central Asia, plus a few of the poorer countries in the middle of Africa. They had a dozen all ready to go, and the investigators found order books for at least twenty more. There could have been a terrible tragedy if any of them had ever made it to the skies. Terrible."

"So how long ago did all of this happen?" Filip asked.

"Oh, about three months back. A lot of the massive tools and helicopter parts are still lying around in the warehouse. I'm told that they've made decorative features out of them to give the warehouse an industrial feel. When the space suddenly became available Moldova

Smash were on it inside a day. I believe they'd originally been looking to put up some kind of a giant tent alongside the banks of the river. But this is much much better."

Filip and Terry looked at each other in utter disbelief as the car finally rounded the corner of the factory and they got their first view of the Euroclub. This building too was absolutely massive. Not nearly as big as the factory that stood in front of it, but still pretty substantial. Outside it there were giant balloons on metal cables jostling about in the light wind, huge spotlights flickered across the clouds as if this was a 1930s Hollywood premiere, and the outside of the building was swathed in plush fabric that made up the colours of the flags of all the competing countries.

"Wow, they really have made some effort here," said Filip. "I don't know why we didn't come down and inspect it sooner. We've had a few of these things in old breweries and warehouses in the past, and they've always been, well, a little bit boring to be honest with you. But this all looks

absolutely splendid. It's just a shame that there won't be too many people in there to fill it out this early in the process."

"Erm Filip," said Terry with a surprised voice. "You may want to take a look at that queue..."

"Man alive, that's bloody enormous!" proclaimed Filip! "I'm not waiting at the end of that to get in. We'll be here all bloody night."

"Have no fear, Filip sir. You don't have to," said Vasile. "There are three queues. One for the locals. These people have all bought rather expensive tickets to be here, and to be honest with you, I'm not sure they'll all get in. Then there's one for people with press and crew and volunteer staff accreditations. That still looks reasonably long, as there's nothing much else to do in Tiraspol on a Sunday night after ten. And then there's one for the national delegations and TV executives. That's in the middle, and it'll get you straight in. I'll take you right to the gate and give security the nod, then they'll usher you forwards."

"Thank you so much, Vasile," said Filip, earnestly. "Do you want to pop your head around the door with us, just to have a look at what it's all like inside?"

"You are too kind, Filip sir, and I thank you for your offer. But I've had a long day. So I'm just going to park up around the front of the factory away from the noise and have a little sleep in the car until you want to go back to the hotel. Give me a call when you're just about to leave the party and I'll have the car waiting for you exactly where I dropped you off."

"We'll definitely have to get you in another night though Vasile," said Terry, warmly.

"Another night. Yes, that would be most welcome," the driver replied, as he pulled up to the middle of the queue, right outside the main entrance to the vast building. "Oh and sirs, there's one more thing. The local press don't yet know who any of the artists are, apart from our most revered Maxim Munteanu, so they are highly likely to start snapping your picture the moment you step out of the car just in case you're famous. Don't be alarmed. Just go with it and act like rockstars as you walk down the red carpet!"

"Thank you for the warning, Vasile," said Filip. "And we'll give you a shout when we're leaving. We probably won't be terribly long anyway."

"Right you are good sirs. And good luck!"

Just as Vasile predicted, a sea of flash guns began firing off the moment the two men from the CTF opened their car door and stepped onto the red carpet outside the massive warehouse.

"Erm, Filip?" Terry said anxiously. "It's all just a little bit awkward this, isn't it? I mean, they have no idea who we are, yet they're snapping us like The Kardashians. Who knows where these shots are going to end up – or indeed how we're going to be captioned?"

Filip surveyed the gawping people in the queue and the massed ranks of photographers crouched in front of them, and considered the situation for a moment.

"I must concede, Terry, that it does feel a little bit odd. But sod it, we put all the work into this thing with so little regard or even notice from the world at large. Let's milk it for a moment. We bloody deserve it!"

"Oh I'm not sure that I feel comfortable doing this, Filip," Terry spluttered, nervously. "If anyone back home sees this they'll never let me forget it!"

"Nonsense, lad. I mean, when is this ever likely to happen again? Chin up and stride boldly forward!"

"Oh OK, Filip. If you insist..."

The two men bounced a little on their toes, then sprung forward towards the tightly packed queues, which parted neatly in front of them. The photographers were hectically snapping away, while at the same time thumbing through print outs that featured the faces of all this year's artists as they tried to work out who it was that they were actually snapping, then just randomly shouting 'Hey! You!' at the two men to try and gain their attention.

"Actually, it is a bit good, this" Terry whispered into Filip's ear. "I can see why so many artists want to come back year after year."

"Especially as half of them are shop workers and backing singers who had a bit of luck on a local televised singing competition," Filip laughed.

"Ha, yeah, I can see that!" Terry chuckled in reply, as he was bustled through the fog of snappers by a burly security guard.

As the red velvet rope was unhooked and the doors to the venue were opened in front of them, the two men just stood and gasped. Before them stretched out the most enormous cavern of delights. Circus performers were flying about on trapezes in the roof space above them, and women on stilts were circulating amongst the crowd distributing drinks and nibbles in long dangly baskets. At one end of the room, a DJ on a regal looking plinth was pumping out some of the more danceable Eurovision sounds, while at the other, some roadies were setting up a selection of instruments on a stage built in the form of a Greek temple. All around the floor of the room were the frames of the knock-off helicopters left behind after the recent sting operation. Each was beautifully lit, and surrounded by bars crammed ten deep with revellers trying to stock up on the free booze before the happy hour ran out. Out of the mist a volunteer approached the pair and assertively demanded "Please. Please sirs. This way to the VIP lounge".

Filip and Terry looked at each other and both gave one of those little shrugs that suggest "No, I don't know what he said either", and followed the young man as he bounded through the swelling crowd with some purpose. He took them up a few short flights of industrial stairs, and onto a large, plush balcony packed with the comfiest looking soft furnishings, a considerably less busy bar, and a handful of dead-eyed girls dancing in cages in their underwear. Terry pointed over to them with a bit of a wince.

"Ooh, as incredible as this place is, I'm not sure that I like all that caged dancer business. It's not terribly in keeping with the image of Eurovision, is it!" Terry suggested.

"And they're playing to completely the wrong crowd too!" Filip replied with a wry wink. "I'll have a word with Dumi tomorrow and see if he can get them replaced with something a little more tasteful. I don't really want Instagram to be full of pictures of the artists posing in front of caged women all week. You're right, it's not terribly becoming – especially as most of them look like they really don't want to be there."

Suddenly a voice came from out of nowhere. "Drinks sirs?" it asked.

Filip and Terry looked at each other, and then down to where the sound was coming from. There stood a very short woman decked out in full Regency garb. Powdered wig, epaulettes, tight breeches, the lot. She was standing there holding a tray packed with drinks.

"These are mostly vodkas or G&Ts, gentlemen. But I can get you something more special mixed up at the bar if you'd like. We have an array of 30-year-old whiskies too if you'd prefer?"

"No no, gin will be fine. Thank you," said Filip. "Terry?" "Oh, yes. Erm, I'll have a G&T too, thanks."

"Here you are gentlemen," said the waitress as she handed the two men their drinks. "And if you need anything more, just give me a wave."

"Erm, yes. Yes, we will. Thank you. Thank you so much," Terry replied. As the waitress walked off, Filip looked up and stepped back with a start. "There's bloody dozens of them, milling their way around the tables like worker ants! It all feels a little, a little... well, icky," he said.

"How do you mean, Filip?" asked Terry. "They're just people, like you and I, doing their jobs." "Well yes," Filip replied with a pained expression on his face, "But it all seems a little bit exploitative. I mean. They've not been hired despite being dwarves. They've been hired because of it. It all seems a bit decadent and unseemly to me. No offence to the actual waiting staff, mind. She seemed very nice and helpful. But, y'know, it just doesn't sit right."

"Hmm yes, now that you put it that way, I can see what you mean," said Terry. "But, a girl's got to work, and why should she not be in on some of this."

"I totally see that side of it too," said Filip. "But all the same..."

Then, from the corner of the VIP lounge powered a big, booming voice. "FILIP!!! TERRY!!! Come over here with me and the girls for a proper drink!" "Håkan!" the two men chirped as one.

"Oh shit, you know how this goes, don't you Terry. We could be here all bloody night now! Remember Junior Eurovision last year?"

"Only just!" laughed Terry. "And that was only the hotel bar – not this enormous bacchanalia!" "We'd best go over for a bit though, to keep the crew sweet and all that."

As they approached the bar, Håkan rushed forward and put one of his big tattooed arms around each of the CTF executives.

"What do you think of this place, then? Bloody great, eh!" Håkan bellowed in their ears. "And what's even better is that up here it's all free, all night, for the next fourteen days! I think I'm in heaven!"

Filip and Terry cast each other a worried and knowing side-glance from beneath each of Håkan's workmanlike armpits, as he turned to drag them towards his drinking buddies.

"You know Hanna and Ice from the stage detail, of course..." he shouted. "Yes, yes, hello ladies..." Filip sputtered.

"And Skunk from the audio desk..."

"Hey Skunk," Terry chirpily replied. "Glad you got the sound thing sorted in the end..."

Skunk cocked him a serious scowl, before his face cracked into a broad beaming smile.

"And these two gentlemen are my new best friends. The little one is Dananau, head of the local Moldovan gangers..."

"Hello Dananau," Filip politely offered.

"Call me Dan," the small, balding man replied. "It's easier." "OK Dan," Filip smiled.

"...and this big meaty fellow is their head of security... The Ox!" Håkan continued. "Hey, erm, The Ox!" Terry smiled.

"Actually it's Aurochs," big man replied, towering above even Håkan. "I was named after the creature at the heart of our state flag. But The Hawk here likes to call me The Ox. So that will do."

"It's a world of beasts around here, don't you know!" Skunk laughed.

Filip affected a more serious voice. "Er, Håkan. Do you mind, you know, letting us go now?"

"Oh shit, I'm sorry. Got caught up in the moment there a little," Håkan snorted. "Here you are... free!"

"I'm not really digging these girls in cages," Hanna confessed. "It's all feels a little sexist to me. And they all look about 14 as well."

"It is a common sight at the more luxurious parties this side of the river," The Ox explained. "It shows that the hosts have put a lot of thought and effort into the night. They don't get paid too much, but they make an enormous amount in tips from the more, how shall I say, refreshed gentlemen in the room. It helps get them through university."

"Yes, but I'm still not sure that I like it, Ox," Hanna continued. "Filip, can you do something about them?"

"I'll have a word with Dumi in the morning," he replied.

"It's not as if they're going to make an awful lot of tips anyway," Hanna added.

"Why's that?" The Ox asked. "Is this not an event full of red-blooded men and heightened passions?"

"Well yes and no," Håkan butted in. "Let's just say that those girls won't be quite the right flavour for most of the men who'll be coming to this party."

The Ox looked puzzled for a moment before the cogs clicked into place and he shouted out "Oh! You mean they're all homos? Ah ha ha ha ha!"

Every Western European around the bar looked momentarily panicked, and their eyes darted towards each other, hoping that somebody else would be brave enough to speak out first.

It was Filip.

"Yes, Ox. They are. But I mean no. No. We don't use that term at this contest. Or anywhere, for that matter. Any more talk like that and you could get your security crew taken off the job."

"Oh! Oh! I'm so sorry," said Ox, looking a little flustered. "We're not used to these kinds of things around here. I will promise to be more careful, just in case any of them hear me!"

"I heard you, Ox," said Terry, looking a little more emboldened than usual. "How do you mean, Terry?" said Ox, now even more confused.

"I'm one of those, 'homos', as you called them, and we don't take kindly to that kind of homophobic language. If I hear any more of it I'll personally make sure you're off the production."

"Oh oh, I'm so sorry Terry sir," said The Ox with some genuine contrition. "But that's the only word we have for them... erm, you... erm, you know what I mean... around here. I will have to change my language. But what should I call them? Erm, you?"

"People, Ox. Just people," Terry stated coldly but assertively. "You'll be seeing more and more of us as the weeks go on. So many in fact that we will easily become the majority. And Eurovision is famous for being a safe space for the gay community, so you'll have to do your utmost to protect everyone and make sure that they are free from harm. Can you do that for us, Ox?"

"I will be sure to, Terry sir," said Ox, looking fully chastised. "It is just my cultural ignorance. I haven't got anything against anybody, really I don't, so I'll do my very best to make sure that everybody is safe and comfortable. And I'm so sorry for any offence I may have caused here. I'll tell my team at the briefing first thing in the morning, and if any of them don't comply with this order they'll be out of here."

"Good, good," said Terry. "I hope I didn't get off on the wrong foot." "Not at all, Terry sir," The Ox replied. "I'm just glad that I know now!"

There was a long awkward silence, before Ice cut in with an unexpected comment. "And what about those dwarf waitresses? Surely that's a little bit disablist, too?"

"Ahhh, no, in this case it's not," Dan replied. "It's actually a practical measure. We have a trend in this country for very low and comfortable seating in our VIP lounges. So it can get a little awkward if the serving staff are all tall and stringy. There's also a much greater risk of spilled drinks ruining some very expensive garments. So we hire these smaller people so that they can easily dart between the sofas and serve people at face height. It's really a practical solution to a specifically local problem. And the money's great for them too. So far from them being exploited, they're actually doing pretty well out of it."

"Well that's a ridiculously smart solution," Ice replied. "Suddenly it's not half as iffy as I first thought. Fair play to you all!"

"Right, can I get anyone any more drinks?" Håkan barked. "They're on me!" "They're all free anyway, you great idiot!" Skunk sneered!

"I KNOW! It's great, isn't it!" Håkan replied. "You boys good?" he continued, gesturing his glass towards Filip and Terry.

"No, we're fine," Filip replied. "We're just going to have a lean on the balcony and watch all the revelry downstairs for a bit. It's been a long day – a long week in fact. Good job to all of you though for getting through it!"

They all raised a glass towards him in thanks. "Next one's on me," he added, with a wry smirk.

13

Fifty miles away in Chişinău, Michi Rotari was helping his mentor, Maxim Munteanu, prepare for the short journey to his ranch on the outskirts of Tiraspol. But he had grave concerns that the old man wouldn't be up to the trip – let alone the vigorous programme of events and performances he had scheduled for the next two weeks.

"Are you sure that you're feeling OK, Maxim?" Michi asked. "You've been looking a little pale and tired all week."

"Nonsense, young man!" chirped the elderly singer, "I've never felt better. When you've done as many shows in the depths of a Siberian winter as I have, a silly little pop show like this will be a walk in the park."

"But that's just it, Maxim," the younger man added. "It's not just the pop show. You know you've got all sorts of press responsibilities and photo opportunities and social events to attend to. And that's not to mention all that waiting around when it comes to the final shows."

"Don't worry yourself, little Michi," Maxim replied, this time with a softer, more caring voice. "I'll be fine. I'll take it slowly and get plenty of sleep. It's easy for me to just pop back home to the ranch if I'm getting a little tired. Moldova Smash will understand. I've got unspecified relaxation breaks written into my contract. They know that they have to treat me delicately."

"All the same, Maxim," Michi countered, "I know what you're like. You'll just soldier on, not wanting to let anyone down, when really you're on the verge of exhaustion. Are you quite sure that everything's alright?"

"Quite quite sure, little Michi. I've just got that little Spring bug that's going round. It'll be gone by morning. And with that, I shall bid you goodnight. I want to be up bright and early in the morning. We're having our first tour of the arena at one, followed by a bit of a press conference once we're done. I've got to get my beauty sleep – although with a face this devilishly handsome, I don't know why I even have to bother!" Maxim laughed warmly at his own little joke, and Michi smiled for the first time that evening. But he still had his concerns.

"Seriously, don't worry about me, I'll be fine. And remember, if anything does happen to me – and fingers crossed that it won't – you'll be taking my place, alright!" And with that the old man darted off to his bedroom and closed the door.

"Wait! What?" Michi said to himself. "He really wasn't joking all those times that he said I'd be covering for him if he fell ill, was he? Was he??? This can't be right, surely? I'm sure that Moldova Smash would have a few things to say about that. And the CTF too, at the very least. Heck, I'd better start learning the words to the song, just in case. The chances are that the better prepared I am for the worst, the less likely it is to happen. Oh my good heavens, I hope this isn't true, and I hope he isn't as frail and poorly as I fear he is."

Still slightly alarmed by what the old man had just told him, he tottered down the marbled corridor to Evgeny's room at the other end of the house and tapped on the door.

"Come in!" came the gruff voice from within. Michi gently pushed the door open.

"Ah Michi lad! How are you?" Maxim's right-hand man asked kindly. "And more importantly, how is your mother? Is she keeping well?"

"Yes Evgeny," Michi nervously replied. "Very well. The both of us."

"What is it, lad? You're looking worried," Evgeny asked. "Something troubling you?"

"It's Maxim," came the reply. "I'm beginning to fear that he's not up to all this excitement. I mean, I know he's got plenty of experience at this kind of thing, but I really don't think that he's looking terribly well."

"Yes, Michi, I know what you mean," said Evgeny. "I've been thinking that myself. He always seems to go into his shell a little bit before a big tour or a grand engagement, but I've never seen him quite this frail before, I must confess. But I'm sure that he's just tired and a bit overwhelmed at all the excitement. He'll be as right as rain in the morning, you see."

"Well, you've known him a lot longer than I have, Evgeny, so I'll take your word for it," said Michi. "But I'm sure you can understand my concerns."

"Absolutely, Michi lad. We've got a national treasure in our hands here, and we don't want him losing his shine before the big night. I'll be sure to keep very good care of him. Now you go and get a good night's sleep too, and don't fret too much about all this. It'll all turn out just fine, I'm sure of it."

"Yes. Yes," Michi replied. "I'm sure it will. Good night then, Evgeny."
"Good night, Michi lad!"

And with that, Michi closed the door and walked slowly towards his summer house out in the garden. He sat on the bench overlooking the lake for a little while, just pondering all the problems that could arise over the next couple of weeks, and getting himself all het up about the ones that nobody else had even thought of yet.

"What if Maxim gets so ill or tired that he can't make it? What if he passes out on stage? What if I pass out on stage? What if I let down my country? What then? I'll be a laughing stock, and I'll never be able to show my face in public again. Oh my, this could all go terribly wrong. I never expected any of this to happen when I called Maxim that Sunday morning back in March. It's become almost too much to bear for a fragile soul like me!"

Michi knew that his life was likely to change beyond recognition over the next two weeks. It already had since he became the runner-up at O Melodie Pentru, but this was taking things to a whole new level. And he just wasn't sure that he was up to any of it.

"We'll just see how he is in the morning," he reassured himself. "Evgeny's right, I'm sure everything's going to be just fine."

"And with that, he took himself to the summer house and went to bed.

14

"I must say, Terry, you impressed me greatly taking on The Ox last night," Filip said to his friend as they sat on the CTF balcony waiting for that morning's second act to begin their rehearsal. "I didn't know you had it in you!"

"Cheers mate... I think?" Terry japed back. "I thought I'd better just nip that kind of behaviour in the bud before it took hold. You know how these ex-Soviets are reputed to be with their homophobia. I figured that it was best to confront it there and then so that we could just move on with the show business."

"He was mightily impressed with your nerve, I have to tell you," Filip revealed. "He sent me an email this morning apologising for his misstep, and explaining how he'd briefed his team that this kind of language was in no way acceptable amongst his team going forward, and that anyone who transgressed this rule would be marched off site without pay and have their accreditation cut up with scissors in front of them. They don't mess about around here!"

"So that Dan fellow said last night," Terry replied. "He reckons that everybody is usually too scared to stand up to The Ox, because of his size and presence. I think we've accidentally done ourselves some favours amongst the local crew here. They know that we're not to be messed with, but they're also aware that we're approachable and aren't scared to go out for a drink and socialise with them. And that seems to count for a lot around here."

"It certainly seems to," laughed Filip, "Although I'm not sure if I've got the strength to get away with it too often over the next fortnight. I've not got the constitution of Håkan. But fair play to him for inviting us over. I think that move paid dividends."

"Yes, as did that fourth G&T he insisted I down. I really didn't think I was going to make it in for the first song this morning," Terry sighed. "Thank heavens the hotel is only next door."

"Ooh yes, what was the first act like?" asked Filip, a late riser himself.

"The Czechs? Easy as, Filip. The girl's a pro, and she was on and off in a flash. The song's a bit dull though. I'm more concerned about the next little run of performances."

"Yes mate, that's why I'm here," said Filip. "We've got to make sure this Saudi chap is well looked after without pandering to his every whim, and then do our best to keep him away from the Norwegians. That's a potential flashpoint in the making there, and of course, we don't want to cause any international incidents. Again."

"That's a good point, Filip. Where is he? He's due on right about now, and I can't see hide nor hair of him."

Down in the backstage area, Ice was starting to get a little concerned. "Yep. Yep. So where is he?" she mumbled into her radio.

"His people are saying that he doesn't need to rehearse," came the disembodied voice at the other end, "and he's refusing to leave his hotel. He's sent all the other laddies in the background to do the warm up for him."

"The little shitbag!" Ice said to herself under her breath, before clicking the talk button on her communication device. "Right then. First of all, tell him – or his people – that this first rehearsal isn't for him, it's for us. And next up, get hold of that kiddie who did the stand in rehearsal last week, if he's about. But we've got to turn this over quickly."

"He's here," replied the voice. "He's one of the volunteers in the press centre. I'll radio the head of press and get him over to you."

"Nice one!" Ice affirmed, before signing off the call. "Right, you lot…" she shouted at the Saudi Prince's terrified backing singers. "You all shuffle onto the stage and take your places while we get your props sorted out. You can do you mic checks up there while you're at it!"

They dutifully ran onto the stage as the stage hands carted some enormous living palm trees in giant flowerpots onto the back of the performance area.

"Everything OK back there?" asked Hanna, who had been prowling about the stage, calling for the Sammarinese delegation.

"Yep, Hanna, we're on it. We're missing the lead singer for this run through. But we've got the kiddie that did the stand-in hotfooting it to the stage as we speak."

"Great work, girl! Are you after my job?" Hanna laughed. "Let's get them in place and get the music rolling for a backing singer check".

Thus followed the strange spectacle of a row of five men in traditional Saudi Arabian garb, standing in line, doing a quaint little two-step dance while waving their riding crops about and gleefully enunciating every fifth word.

"I'm not entirely sure what's going on here, Terry, but I kind of like it," Filip quipped from deep within the bowels of the hall. "Get on the radio to Hanna to see what's happening, though, because none of them especially looks like that Prince to me."

There was a brief pause before Terry came back with the reply.

"She says that the Prince doesn't fancy turning up today, but that they're getting the stand-in to do the last run through."

"Oh that's all we need, isn't it. A bloody prima donna Prince. Oh well, let's get this one over and done with as quickly as possible. We've got more on our plates with those damn pagans up next!"

And with that, the stand-in came running to the side of the stage, quickly jumped into the Prince's stage costume, and began the final run through, still slightly out of breath.

"He's good this lad," said Filip. "And singing in Arabic too. That can't have been easy to learn."

"Yeah, and I have to confess that this song is starting to get under my skin, Filip. That constant repetitive groove is like nothing we've ever had before, and I've been finding myself shuffling around my room to it. It's terrible, of course, but it's beautiful at the same time, and I reckon it could be the dark horse of the tournament."

"Oh don't say that, Terry," said Filip, with an exasperated look on his face, "Let's save that kind of thing for Asiavision. If it ever bloody happens!"

Both men let out a knowing chuckle, before their attentions were once more drawn to the big stage.

"Right then, let's see what these black metallists have got for us, eh," said Filip, now looking more worried than ever. "Hanna was telling me that they've got a lot of fire planned."

"And awful lot of fire," Terry replied. "We've had to get extra fire stewards in just for this lot..."

Terry stopped in his tracks and his jaw dropped to the floor. He turned to Filip, who was frozen rigid with exactly the same expression.

"It's our worst possible nightmare," Filip said aghast. "They're bringing a bloody wooden church onto the stage. A great big bloody wooden church! Why did nobody warn us about this, Terry?"

"Well Håkan kind of did last night, but I think you'd started on the cocktails by then," said Terry, nervously.

"They're going to burn the bastard thing, aren't they Terry," Filip said with a dark resignation written all over his face. "They're going to burn a bastard wooden church on live international television. We're bloody doomed, Terry. I tell you. Doomed!"

Filip and Terry were both crouched forwards on their seats as Stormgiver confidently strode onto the stage and began their first rehearsal. The mic checks were as to be expected – lots of guttural roars and spooky, demonic growling. But the voices were so affected in their signature snarl that even Terry, who had a degree in Scandinavian languages, couldn't quite pick out what they were saying.

"There's the odd bit about Gods and snow and trees and fire, as they've got in their lyric sheet in the programme," he said, relieved. "But nothing that would have anybody writing in to the papers."

"We hope. There's bound to be some thinly-veiled allusion to something dubious, I'm sure. I'll go through the words with a fine tooth comb tonight, just to be sure," Filip replied. "And there's something about the band themselves that I just don't trust. They're used to being more spontaneous in the live gig sphere. I've got serious concerns that the singer might start freestyling and we'll all be in the mire!"

"Ooh, they're starting the song," said Terry. "This could get interesting!" "Depends what you mean by interesting, Terry mate," Filip laughed.

The backing track kicked in and everybody in The Teapot took two steps backwards. A massive wall of guitar noise flooded out of the speakers, and the double kick pedal on the bass drums beat out a furious angry throb. The band's lead singer, Hermóðr Heimdall, stepped to the mic and let out the fiercest, most gravelly roar you ever heard, before he started chopping up the syllables like a possessed wraith.

"OK, so it's unlike anything ever heard on a Eurovision stage before, but I think we're just about getting away with it. And best of all, that church is remaining intact! The juries will hammer it for his voice alone, and I can't see it picking up too many votes from the Nans out East, so there's no way it's getting to the final, surely?" said Filip, visibly exhaling his stresses. "I think we're safe here – but I'll hang around to the end, just in case!"

The two following run throughs went by without anything untoward happening, although Hermóðr did appear to strike up a rather animated discussion with some people in a row of camp chairs just in front of the stage directly before they embarked on their final performance. Then, out of the darkness, the stage manager Hanna uttered four words that struck the fear of God into the men from the CTF.

"Once more, with pyro..."

As she spoke she was dashing down the equipment ramp way faster than anybody was used to seeing her move, and a pregnant three seconds of silence filled the expansive hall.

The moment the music kicked in the stage was awash with fire. And not just the usual rank of delicate burners along the stage fringes, but massive, terrifying walls of flame, like an Iraqi oilfield in the nineties. The people in camp chairs down the front were picking them up and running towards the back of the room as fast as they could, the heat was so intense. Indeed, both Filip and Terry could feel the fire on their faces from their elevated positions at the side of the hall.

"It's just for the start of the song, right Terry?" Filip asked. "They're

not going to do this for the whole bloody performance, are they?"
"I have my fears," his friend replied. "I really have my fears."

The song had reached the two-minute mark, and the on stage inferno had yet to abate. "At least the church hasn't gone up yet," Terry said, hopefully.

But the very moment those fateful words left his lips, tiny gas burners all around the edges of the huge wooden prop kicked in, and the scale model of a Norwegian stave church slowly began to burn.

"Oh Jesus, oh Lord, we're fucked," said Filip, looking like he wanted to pack it all in there and then.

"Don't worry Filip, mate," said Terry reassuringly, "This is bound to contravene about a dozen health and safety regulations. We just can't let it continue in this form. I mean, with the amount of polyester in the mosh pit, the front ten rows will have spontaneously combusted by the second chorus."

"Well if they melt that dipshit's inflatable hammer I won't be entirely unhappy," Filip joked, and the two men let out a little anxious laugh as their eyebrows were gently singeing.

But just as the music had ended, Hermóðr let out one last almighty yell.

"Death to the darkened Eastern invaders!" he yelled, holding his fist in the air with a single finger pointing to the skies. "And death to the ladymen from the South!"

Both Filip and Terry froze in their tracks, their mouths agape. Nervously they turned to face each other, their eyes open as wide as they could possibly go.

"Did he just say what I think he said?" asked Filip, incredulously.
"Erm, I think he just did," Terry replied. "Shit..."

"Right. That's it. Get onto the invigilator. We're cancelling their press conference," said Filip, urgently. "Put out a release about there being some technical issue and someone in the band getting burned by all that fire. That should cover it for now. I'll get hold of the Norwegian head of delegation and give them an official warning, and then hopefully we can get them on again with no further incidents. I don't want to have to kick them off the show – we don't need that kind of scandal. But, y'know, we can't be letting them get away with this shit, even if it was some arcane allegory or another."

Suddenly Terry sat bolt upright, and a deeply haunted look etched itself onto his face. "What? What is it Terry?" Filip asked.

"The press hall. The bloody press hall. They've all seen that on the screens down there, haven't they. Oh man, we're done for."

A hundred yards away in the press hall, every last person stared at the big screens in stunned silence for what seemed like an eternity. Radouane Thill was the first to crack the air with a comment as he turned to one of his reporters and asked "Erm, did he just say what I THOUGHT he said? I think he did, didn't he?"

A few panicked phone calls later, Filip and Terry were just about to leave the viewing balcony and get down and do some firefighting of their own when they noticed a commotion on stage.

"What's happening down there, Terry?" Filip asked, puzzled. "One moment, I'll get Hanna on the radio and find out." Hanna quickly answered with a world weary sigh.

"What is it, Hanna?" Terry asked gently, "What's up?"

"It's the Danish kids," she replied, "They're hiding under the stage. They say they're refusing to come out and do their rehearsal until the nasty devil men have left the building. Apparently Mr Heimdall was saying some pretty horrible things to them as they were all waiting in line to go on stage."

"Oh heavens, that's all we need," said Terry. "Tell them it's all safe now, and they can get on with their rehearsal."

"I'll try Terry mate, but they look absolutely terrified," Hanna answered. "We might have to fish them out of there with big hooks!"

"Well do the best you can, Hanna," Terry affirmed. "We're bang on time right now, so we've got a bit of leeway."

"Right you are, sir!" And with that Terry could see her take her finger out of her ear and lean down over the edge of the stage to try to coax the frightened Danish pop kids out of their hiding place.

"Right then Terry, plan of action," Filip said assertively. "I'll go grab Håkan and get down to the Norwegian dressing room to lay down the law with them, and you get back to the press hall and try to calm things down a bit."

"The Twittersphere's already gone berserk with this," Filip, so I'll do the best I can. I've had one of the lads in the office draft that release about their lack of a press conference, too. I'll try to nip this one in the bud before it gets out of hand."

"Good luck with that, fella!" Filip joked. And with that he was off on his motorised scooter to the backstage area.

Somewhere in the distance, Terry thought he could hear the sound of crying in a Danish accent. As he sped through the cavernous entrance halls of the giant arena, Filip gave Håkan a quick call. "Hey, Hawk, are you in the building?"

"Yeah man, just in the canteen having my breakfast. Did you see that

Norwegian lot? They were bloody amaaaazing!" Håkan replied.

"Well that's exactly the problem, Hawk man," Filip answered. "Not only was it just a tad sacrilegious with all that church burning business, but it sounded to me like he was was being a little bit racist and homophobic at the end there, too."

"Ooh yes, I see your point," Håkan conceded. "I was just looking at it with my heavy metal head on. In this sphere, that kind of thing just doesn't wash."

"Exactly, Hawk. I'm going down to their dressing room to have a word with them after they've done their stint in the viewing room. Do you want to come down with me, mate? You speak their language, after all, musically, I mean."

"I'd love to, Filip. Love to. Let me just hoover up this plate of fine Moldovan cheeses and I'll meet you in the production office. Then we can formulate a plan before we confront them. Oh I do love a good confrontation, me!"

"Right you are! See you in ten, Hawk."

*

On the other side of the building, Terry was on the way to the press hall. Everyone he passed had a shocked and bewildered look on their face. The more pop-orientated Eurovision press corps may have seen a few scattered noisy acts in their time, but this was something else. With every new step he took, people were looking more and more traumatised. As he entered the big doors of the press hall, there was suddenly an explosion of sound. The usual low hum of the chattering was now a loud hubbub, with people furiously typing to try and get the news out first. All of a sudden a group of journalists spotted him and began to call out his name.

"Terry! Terry!!! Can we have a comment about that vile performance we just saw?" shouted one member of the EuroStorm crew.

"Not just yet," Terry diplomatically answered. "We've just got to establish the facts first, and we'll get back to you with a full statement later."

"Oh, don't cop out on us man," the reporter asked. "Surely you have a position on this?" "I'll get back to you on the half-hour, ma'am," Terry stalled.

"Will we be seeing you in the Norwegian press conference though? I think a statement needs to be made."

"The conference is off," Terry declared. "I'll get back to you in a bit."

And with that he ducked behind the big counter at reception and took the back corridor to his office.

"Did you hear that, everyone?" shouted the EuroStorm scribe. "The conference is off. The CTF are trying to cover this all up!"

A loud muttering passed through the room, like a wind through bullrushes. Pretty quickly it reached the press conference hall, which was unusually packed for this early in the rehearsal cycle. People were crammed into every crevasse, waiting to confront the Norwegians. The poor delegation from San Marino were just finishing their stint, but unfortunately for them nobody was much interested in what a bunch of backing singers had to say.

"We're not leaving until those Stormgiver hounds come out and make a formal statement!" shouted a voice from the back of the room. The conference invigilator Anastasia Popov, rose to her feet to try and calm the baying mob down a little.

"People, people. Can we just let the Sammarinese delegation finish their chat and then we can address any issues with the Norwegian song."

Another, angrier voice from the middle of the room yelled out "Scab!" before the whole room began to chant the word over and over again.

"Scab! Scab! Scab! Scab!"

The cries were getting louder, and Ms Popov had no choice but to bring the conference of San Marino to an end and get everybody off stage in a safe and seemly manner.

"Hello, People," Ms Popov stated firmly into her microphone. "In the interests of safety, for both myself and the San Marino delegation, as well as for the people at the front of the hall, we are cancelling these press conferences until further notice. The Sammarinese photo op is also postponed. Would you all now kindly leave the room in an orderly manner."

Ms Popov was used to handling unruly crowds as the host of a sensationalist daytime talk show. But this lot were beyond even her capabilities. The chanting got louder and louder, and things began to get thrown around the room. At first it was free delegation bags and promotional CDs, followed by the fold up chairs that were laid out in neat rows on the conference room floor. But soon the plant pots that were decorating the outer aisles of the room began to fly stageward, and they looked pretty heavy.

Ms Popov made one last call out over the microphone. "Security! Press Conference Hall, now! Please!" before she ducked behind the curtain to safety.

The Ox and his boys swiftly blocked all the exits in a near military style operation and began to slowly move into the room, kettling off the miscreants from the wider press hall. The chaos soon began to quell, as the angry mob could see that it wasn't likely to end well for them if they continued their angry protests. The room quickly subdued to silence, before a voice at the front loudly yelled "Bollocks! I only came in here to get a kiss off a Saudi Prince!"

Over in the main press office, Terry was watching the events in the conference hall unfold on a big screen on the back wall.

"This is bad. This is very bad!" he fretted, as his staff were quickly answering calls from major press organisations about the events that had just occurred.

"How are we going to make this any better? How? If we let Stormgiver go on we're going to risk further debacles like this. But if we kick them off the show, we're going to risk upsetting our Norwegian partners, who have been very good to us in the past. Either way we're risking the reputation of the whole contest, and in a way that I'm not sure it can easily recover from. I hope Filip's hatching a useful plan somewhere. I hope to God that he is!"

*

Filip was waiting anxiously outside the Norwegian dressing room with Håkan at his side, waiting for the nod to come in from their head of delegation. Suddenly his phone throbbed in his pocket. It was Egil Boberg, the Norwegian HoD.

"Come in, it's safe. But be warned, they're not happy!" read the message.

"THEY'RE not happy?" Filip said angrily to Håkan. "They have the temerity to be unhappy after what they've done to MY show? Why I oughta..."

"Easy now, Filip," said Håkan, calmly. "You don't want to go in there all guns blazing and make things worse before you've begun. Just take a breather for a second and then we'll go in."

"Coming from you, Håkan, that's a serious piece of advice!"

Pausing to calm his blood for a moment, he rapped on the door with a fast, irritable rhythm. There was a short pause, before a deep, imperious voice boomed out through the plywood.

"ENTER!" it rang, with a deep, regal tone.

Filip slowly opened the door, but was stopped dumbfounded in his tracks. Where all the other dressing rooms were an insipid shade of magnolia, with maybe a trestle table along one wall holding complementary drinks and an apologetic plastic bowl that was half full of crisps, this was a much more terrifying sight to behold. Black emulsion had been daubed from floor to ceiling, with coarse Nordic runes etched in white paint all around the walls. In the centre of the room sat Hermóðr Heimdall on an enormous carved wooden throne, and at each side were the rest of his band mates, two abreast and seated on smaller, but equally elaborate chairs. On the other side of the room sat a worried looking backing singer in a monk's habit clutching a complimentary bottle of fizzy water.

The place was lit, not by the unforgiving strip lights that glowed harshly in all the other dressing rooms, but by huge candles, held at face height in tall bronze candlesticks – they too etched with mystic runes. The band were still wearing their corpse paint and studded leather outfits, and each of them had their hands on their knees with their heads tilted to one side.

"Are you the minion from the CTF?" roared the lead singer, as if he was in a heritage production of some lesser known medieval play.

"Erm, erm, yes, I suppose I am," Filip answered, still a little confused by the curious scene that he'd walked into. "And we need to have a serious word about your show, Mr Heimdall..."

"Silence!" the angry looking singer howled, as he cut Filip off mid-stream. "I'd like to put in a formal complaint. You are very clearly mocking us with this running order!"

"I-I-I don't entirely understand what you mean, Mr Heimdall," Filip stuttered, now utterly at a loss to make any sense out of it all."

"Nonsense!" the black metaller bellowed. "You've put us on in between some brown infidels from the desert and a gaggle of ladymen, born of those traitorous Danes who sold their birthright to the Teutonic scum in the South! You truly mock the purity and majesty of the Norsemen."

Filip could see that this wasn't going to be an easy task, but if left to fester this was a wound that could infect the whole production, and he had to put his foot down before things got out of hand. He quickly decided that he was going to fight fire with fire, so took a deep breath, and in his finest Shakespearean voice he boomed out his wrath.

"Now listen here, Mr Heimdall. This is MY show. You and your underlings here are mere players in it, and you are ultimately expendable. The church burning we can just about get away with for comedy value. But if I hear any more of this racist and homophobic bullshit from you, then you're off the show, Norway are out of the contest for the next five years, and you'll have to pay for not only your entire production budget – and that's a lot of gas – but the fees for the satellite and crew time too. You will be personally ruined, and the nation you claim to care about will be a laughing stock for at least the next decade. So which is it to be, eh? Heroic ignominy or eternal financial damnation?"

Hermóðr Heimdall arched his eyebrows in surprise and nodded regally. He beckoned his tour manager forward with two inward flicks of his upturned palm and whispered in his ear for a few seconds. The tour manger absorbed everything the deathly singer was telling him, before he stood upright and made a proclamation.

"Mr Heimdall, demon lord of all he surveys, says that on this occasion you offer an acceptable compromise. If you make sure that he is kept away from all of the unsavoury and distinctly un- Norse elements, he will keep his side of the bargain. Mr Heimdall is a reasonable man. But if these agreements are not upheld, he cannot guarantee that he will not rain forth brimstone and damnation upon your organisation. To prove his willingness to serve, he will make a blood offering to you."

Upon this, Hermóðr pulled a long curved blade out of his chair and gestured that he was about to pull it across his hand.

"No, no, that's really not necessary, Mr Heimdall," said Filip in a panic. "Your word is good enough for me."

"So be it!" said Hermóðr, now in a much calmer voice. "You may leave."

Somewhat startled at this abrupt cut off from the pompous Pagan, Filip turned his head towards Egil Boberg and mouthed the words "Outside. Now!", while Håkan bellowed a hearty laugh.

"Good to see you again, Tim," Håkan said to the singer as he walked towards the door with a chuckle.

Hermóðr dismissed him with an impatient wave, and the three men left the room.

"I used to knock about with his Mum, you know," Håkan laughed. "I've known him since he was about five years old."

"Well why didn't you say anything, you great lump?" Filip angrily barked.

"I was having too much fun watching you get all cross and assertive. I've never seen that side of you before," Håkan replied.

"Well you'll be seeing it more often if you keep on with that kind of behaviour," Filip snapped. "And as for you, Egil," he continued. "What the hell did you think you were doing sending that assortment of sideshow freaks to the contest? Didn't you know what they were like?"

"Not until it was too late, Filip sir?" Egil anxiously replied. "We just thought that it was all a comedy jape. We didn't know that they lived the whole paganry thing 24-7."

"I must confess," added Håkan, "Tim has changed considerably since I last saw him. He seems to have gone full Varg Vikernes!"

"Varg Vikernes?" Filip enquired, sounding puzzled. "Who's that?"

"Oh he's a Norwegian black metal singer who got put away for burning churches and murdering a rival," Håkan explained. "This new breed of bands that have come after him seem to worship the very ground that he walks on. All the historic wooden churches around Norway had to have 24- hour guards placed on them just in case any of these metal kids take their spiritual leader too seriously."

"But why would they want to burn churches?" Filip asked, now even more bewildered.

"Well, they reckon that to be a true Norseman you must renounce the ways of the invading Judeo Christian religions that they claim have stained the Northern lands, and devote your life to the Pagan ways. And that involves getting rid the churches that were built on ancient sacred places," Håkan continued. "The most worrying thing though is that it all got a bit right-wing along the way, and all the usual political agitators are happily fanning the flames and letting the metallers do their dirty work for them."

"Then how in the name of hell did we let such people onto our safey nicey happy pop show?" Filip spat, incredulously. "Didn't you have any idea what they were like, Egil?"

"Well, like I say, we just thought it was a bunch of overgrown schoolboys larking about in make up,"

Egil replied. "And the good people of Norway, in their wisdom, thought that it would be funny to send them, just to wind us up. We only really, truly found out what they were like when we were recording the official video back in April, and by then it was too late to pull out without incurring a massive fine and a ban from you lot. So we just kept our heads down and hoped for the best!"

"Oh you great big tit!" Filip shouted. "You know that we're reasonable people at the organisation, and we'd have made allowances in these difficult circumstance. I'm sure we could have arranged for you to ship in some bland-but-safe balladeer to fill their slot?"

"Well, you could," Egil replied. "But the people of Norway are 110% invested in this lot. Like ridiculously so. Our national final got the biggest ratings we've had since the seventies. We'd have lost a ridiculous amount of cred if we'd have binned them off at the last minute."

"Not as much as we're going to lose if they let loose with some racist tirade on live international television next Tuesday, Egil. You try and keep a lead on them, while we try to sort out the mess they've left behind after this morning's incident. We're going to have to do some very creative reputation management with this one over the next couple of hours, I tell you!"

Back in the press office, Terry was doing his best to ignore the constant banging on the door.

"Don't answer it Jeff," he barked at one of his assistants. "We're not ready for them yet. We'll go out to them once I've finished crafting this press release about this morning's sorry farrago."

Terry continued to type for all he was worth, frantically hammering the backspace key every few seconds, until he was finally happy with what he'd produced.

"People, let's try this approach. Have a listen and see if we've got this on the money." He cleared his throat and started to read.

"Accident curtails Norwegian contribution to Day Two of Eurovision Rehearsals." "Sounds pretty good to me so far," said Jeff.
Terry continued with the body of the release.

"Monday morning's rehearsal with the Norwegian Black Metal band Stormgiver came to an abrupt end when their lead singer, Hermóðr Heimdall, ventured too close to the wall of flame that surrounded his band, and breathed in some of the hot vapour, damaging his throat in the process. The band have now cancelled all engagements until further notice as Mr Heimdall rests his voice in the hope that he will have recovered by the band's scheduled second rehearsal in four days time. With this in mind, all interview requests with the band have been cancelled until we learn more about his health situation.

Mr Heimdall would also like to apologise for comments that he made during his performance that may have been misconstrued as both racist and homophobic. In a statement to the CTF's press office, Mr Heimdall's tour manager has explained that Stormgiver are a concept band who are steeped in the ways of a pre-Christian pagan North, and that some of the language of those times may appear archaic and out of place when listened to with twenty-first century ears. With that in mind, the band has promised to review any further language that may be deemed offensive, and intend to be fully compliant with CTF rules from here on in.

The band also accept that it is against the rules to change any lines of a song's lyric once it has been printed in the official event programme, and state that they intend never to utter another misplaced word on the Eurovision stage from this day forth.

All further developments will be reported to the press corps in due course."

Terry took in a deep breath and looked over his glasses to the rest of his colleagues. "So, what do you reckon?" he asked the room. "Do you think we've got it covered?"

"Just about," Jeff replied. "But are all those scandal ghouls out there are going to believe it? That's the bigger question?"

"Not for a minute, Jeff. Not for a minute," Terry answered. "But they'll be so busy trying to fill the gaps and look for conspiracies within conspiracies that they'll start posting all kinds of pie-in-the- sky guff, and we'll have them over a barrel. The only ones we've got to watch out for are that ESC Cargo bunch. They tend to take a more measured approach, the bastards. I'm sure they'll fish something out of the mire, but I reckon this release will cover us for at least another couple of days – much as it pains me to cover for the homophobic dickheads. But you've always got to think about the greater good and help save the reputation of this competition, god dammit. I'm sure that we'll find other ways to throw them under the bus somewhere further down the line."

"Amen to that!" Jeff sang, and everybody in the room gave out a polite little clap.

"Right then you lot, let's get this thing printed out and distributed amongst that rabble out there," said Terry. "I'll go make the first contact, and then you lot go out placing them on all the desks. And if anybody asks you about anything – anything at all – just plead ignorance and say that you're just doing your job. That should shut them up for a bit. Right, let's go..."

Terry was stopped in his tracks by Hanna's urgent sounding voice coming out of his radio.

"Filip? Terry? Dumi? Is anybody there? It's all kicked off again on stage and I'm not sure how we're going to calm this one down!"

"Oh shit," said Terry as he slumped into his chair. "What is it this time?"

Filip and Håkan also heard Hanna's call for help on the radio, and seeing as they were in the immediate vicinity, quickly skipped over to the stage area. As they approached the production ramp they could see Ice laughing like a drain.

"You really want to see this, lads!" she spluttered, trying to stifle her guffaws. "It's a completely new one on me – and I thought I'd seen it all!"

They dashed up the ramp to see two dark-haired women – one in a shimmering gown and the other in jeans and a t-shirt – tearing absolute chunks out of each other. All around them were backing singers anxiously trying to prise them apart, and overseeing the whole thing was Hanna the stage manager, telling the woman in the stage gear that she had only six minutes left of her rehearsal.

Håkan looked at Filip with a massive cheeky grin and chuckled. "Oh the day you're having Filip – I hope they're still filming this for the crew's after party showreel!"

Filip just stood there, staring at the vicious cat fight for a couple of moments, before he took a deep breath and let out a yell in a low, booming voice.

"STOP!" he bellowed.

Everybody fell silent as his voice echoed around the cavernous hall.

The two women put pause to their fighting mid-punch and stopped and stared at him. The one in the expensive dress had a small line of blood trickling out of the corner of her mouth, while the lady in her day gear was

gripping a hair-piece that was clearly wrenched out of the back of the other woman's head.

"OK, what's going on here then?" Filip asked. But immediately the two women started angrily shouting, each trying to explain their side of the argument.

"ENOUGH!" Filip yelled, beginning to lose his patience. "Hanna, can you explain to me what has just happened here?"

"Well Filip," she began. "The Maltese girl Lia Maria had just started her first run though when a voice started heckling her from the darkness. I couldn't quite work out what it was saying, but then Lia stopped mid song and calmly said: 'It's YOU that's the plagiat, sister!' With that, the angry voice came charging on to the stage and swung a tasty left-hook, completely flooring Lia. It was then that I recognised the stage invader was the Czech singer, Jolana Nováková. Apparently she's got a grievance about Lia having ripped off her song. To be honest, I'm not sure what she's worried about, because hers is drawn first and is considerably better sung..."

"Hey!" The Maltese singer shouted from the shiny stage floor "Are you trying to start something too, you cheeky witch?"

"You see our problem, Filip." said Hanna. He nodded.

"They've been at it for a full ten minutes now, and neither of them want to concede an inch. And what's more, I suspect that Jolana has been drinking."

"Oh that's just what I need!" Filip sighed. "Right! You two! Stop this nonsense immediately. You must remember that I have the power to disqualify you both from the competition right here and right now for unseemly behaviour. Each of you stand up and step away from the other."

"Oh, you won't DQ a bunch of Homophobic Norwegian racist men, but you'll kick two women out for having a bit of a disagreement will you?" slurred Jolana.

"It doesn't have to come to that if everybody acts calmly," Filip reasoned. "And by the way, where did you hear that?"

"It's all over EuroStorm," she replied. "They're claiming that you're too chickenshit to kick out the Nazi Pagans because you're taking bribes from Norway. But little countries like ours don't stand a chance up against all the usual rich buddy buddy Scandi mafia. Not a chance!"

Filip added a quiet chat with Michael Storm to his mental to do list, before he changed his tone and addressed the subject at hand.

"So, putting aside all that other stuff, what seems to be the problem here, ladies? Jolana, you first?"

"Bitch stole my song – plain and simple," the Czech singer replied.

"Hey! I'll slap you again if you keep this trash talk up," yelled Lia. "And I'll hit you so hard this time that you won't feel it until Wednesday!"

The two women started to square up to each other again, but Hanna wisely got between them.

"And you, Lia," asked Filip. "What's your response to all this? And if we can do it calmly, then all the better."

"If anyone stole the song, it was that rancid drunken Czech cow," the Maltese singer replied. "We've had this song since late January – publicly declared and everything. She just ships up in March with a suspiciously similar song, and now she's calling me the copy!"

"I've been working on my song with my team of Swedish writers since last July, I'll have you know, you rude bitch!" Jolana cut in. "If anyone's the copyist it's her!"

"Right then, I can see the issue here," Filip suggested. "You both have Swedish songwriting teams, yes?"

"YES!" came the response from both women.

"But neither of your teams are the usual big names, right?" "Erm, well," Jolana muttered "I suppose not."

"Mine are!" barked Lia, crossly. "Well, they're on their way up at least!"

"We feared that there was going to be an issue with this, which is why we kept your songs as far away from each other as we possibly could in the draw once we knew which half you were going to perform in," Filip explained. "And this doesn't have to be an issue. Lia. Jolana. I'm going to have a word with both of your heads of delegation, as well as your respective songwriters, and we'll see if we can sort this out. There doesn't need to be any more violence. Your position on the show relies on that. What I need from you, Jolana, is to go back to your hotel and chill out for the rest of the day. And you, Lia. Just finish off here right now and we'll come back to you at the end of the day. We'll restart the clock on your rehearsal, and you can do it all cleanly and calmly. That OK with you, Hanna?"

"That's fine by me, Filip," Hanna replied. "There's not much to this one..." Lia growled again, casting Hanna the most evil of stares.

"... production wise. We've only got that Georgian choir left to come today, and they don't need any props or showbiz. So I reckon we can spare the odd quarter hour. That good with you, Lia?"

"'Spose," grumbled the bedraggled Maltese singer. "And that good with you, Jolana?" Filip added.

"Yeah, alright," she spat. "But you've got to keep me away from that bitch, for her own safety!" "Easy now, Jolana," said Filip in a low gentle voice. "You're in different hotels right?"

"Yes," both women replied more quietly than before.

"Well both keep to your own accommodation for the next couple of days, and we'll contact the social crew to make sure that the pair of you aren't booked on any kind of day trips together. We don't want anybody falling off a turret or down a deep ancient well or anything, do we now?"

Both women nodded, grudgingly.

"Right, we're done here," said Filip. "Håkan, you escort Ms Nováková off the premises and back to her hotel..."

"Why me?" the burly Swede asked, somewhat surprised.

"Well one, because you're here. And two, because you've been taking the piss all day and need to work off your bad juju points!"

"Ahh yeah, I suppose you've got a point," he conceded. "Come on, Jolana, grab an arm and I'll take you home."

"Ooh, that'll be lovely," said Jolana. "Lead me to my bed!"

"I'm taking you to the door and no further, alright?" said Håkan with a smile. "Spoil sport!" Ms Nováková replied, as they both headed for the exit. "OK, so Lia. Are you in any fit state to continue for a quick run through while you're here?" asked Filip.

"You betcha Phil!" the Maltese singer confidently replied.

Lia's backing singers took their positions, Hanna counted down the backing track, and the first Maltese rehearsal continued, despite their singer looking like she'd been dragged through a pine forest by an angry bear.

"And relax!" Filip said to himself as he walked back to his office, before grabbing his radio and giving a callout to his senior press man.

"Erm, Terry," he quietly asked, "I think you need to prep another press release..."

15

The rest of the dress rehearsals went by without a hitch, and an hour later, Filip and Terry were in their daily debriefing meeting with their Moldovan counterparts.

"So, another successful day then!" said Stefan with eager excitement. "Day two passed without a hitch!"

"Have you two actually been here today?" Filip responded with an incredulous squint.

"Well for parts of it," Stefan replied. "We had meetings with Lucian Dobre, our station owner this morning, and then we've had a conference call with Timur Turgenev's financial people this afternoon. Just boring office stuff. We'll be back in amongst the nitty gritty tomorrow. Anything much happen today? I heard from our crew that it was a quiet one."

"A quiet one?" Filip snorted. "I'm not sure what it's like working in Moldovan TV on a day-to-day basis, but I've possibly had the most difficult single day of my entire television career!"

"Ooh, how so?" Dumi enquired. "We heard those Scandinavian Satanists were a bit flamey, but that's about all we really know."

"Flamey? Flamey???" snapped Filip. "They damn nearly burned the whole arena down, then made some very unsavoury comments, on mic, at the end of their rehearsal. And the press are having a field day with it?"

"Oh dear," said Dumi, now looking more concerned. "That's not good at all, you're right! How have you left it with them?"

"Well we've told them that they're on their final warning, and that they'll have to pay their whole delegation's costs if they transgress again," Filip explained. "It seemed like they agreed, but to be honest it's difficult to tell under all that spooky make up. But I get a horrible feeling that they're up to something."

"The fan press are on our backs, too," added Terry. "EuroStorm published a piece about how we were being bribed by Norway to keep it all quiet, which I have to underline isn't the case at all!"

"I wasn't going to ask," said Stefan, with a wink "We keep these things to ourselves over here."

"No, seriously, we haven't," asserted Terry. "Our lawyers have served them with a cease and desist, but they're calling out press freedom and all that. When I told them we'd rescind their accreditations they soon took it down, but I don't trust them. And enough people have read it that it's all over Twitter! That's the sort of muttering that just doesn't go away."

"And that's not all," added Filip. "Tell them about the name thing."

"Oh yes, the name thing," said Terry, rolling his eyes. "Well the news people on the ESC Cargo site have been doing a little digging into the singer of that Norwegian lot. Turns out that his name is a deliberate indicator of his political intentions to those in the know!"

"How do you mean, Terry?" asked Dumi, looking a little confused.

"Well, he's named after two different Norse Gods," Terry explained. "The first one you could kind of expect. Hermóðr is a war spirit in old Norse mythology. It's the usual kind of cosmic macho bullshit that you'd expect from these kinds of bands. But it's his last name that puts a totally different complexion on it, so to speak."

"Why so?" said Dumi, now looking even more lost.

"Well it's Heimdall. It might sound like a common or garden Nordic family name to you or I, but it refers to his reputation as the Shining God, or the God with the whitest skin of them all. His name, it could be read, is essentially telling his followers that he is the war bringer of white supremacy.

And now that Cargo lot have exposed this we could be on the verge of some deep deep shit."

"Oh no!" said Stefan. "That really isn't good. I mean, we're used to a bit of casual racism around here – people just aren't used to seeing that many dark faces in this part of the world. But full-on white supremacy is taking it just a little bit further than our management would like. I'm going to have to raise it with them to see what they think about it all. But they're just kids messing about with creepy devil shit, right?"

"That's what we thought at first, but I think they've fully bought into it now," Terry replied. "We're really going to have to keep a close watch on them from here on in. If they step over any more lines before the end of their next rehearsal they're out of here!"

"And you would get the full support of Moldova Smash in this development, too!" agreed Stefan. "Right then, on to any other business then is it?" Dumi hopefully asked.

"Ha! You'll be lucky!" Filip laughed with a sarcastic edge. "We've not got on to the catfight yet!" "You had cats on stage?" asked Dumi. "I don't quite understand."

"Oh no, sorry Dumi," Filip apologised. "Your English is so good that I sometimes forget that it's none of our first languages. No, we had two rival contestants having a full on fist fight – on stage, no less – about who ripped the song off who!"

"And are these traditionally violent men?" Dumi asked, innocently.

"Men? Ha no!" Filip laughed. "It was the women from Malta and Czechia. They were having a right old scrap over the fact that both of their songs sound almost identical. They each reckon that they were the first ones to commission it. But it turns out that they've both just gone to the same cheap Swedish rent-a-tune mob, and they've slapped out two very similar songs featuring all the lowest common denominators of pop songwriting. They are both distinct and different songs in their own right, but they're both so by-the-numbers that they're crammed full of all the same old tired cliches from start to end. I mean, they both ticked the old 'fire/desire' rhyming gambit off in the first verse they were that unimaginative. I knew this kind of thing was going to happen one day. We've just got to keep them apart and hope that they both fail to qualify for the final. And to be fair, they're both so crushingly ordinary that this is almost certain to happen."

"Ooh, that reminds me," said Terry. "I've had a quiet word with Juri, the Czech head of Delegation. He reckons that Jolana is usually the sweetest, quietest and most gentle women he's ever worked with..."

"Well I had that impression, Terry," Filip cut in. "She seemed like a dream to work with during her rehearsal."

"Quite," Terry replied. "But he also told me that if you get her anywhere near alcohol she turns into some kind of screaming demon after no more than a couple of sniffs. And with the amount of complimentary booze we've got sloshing about at this contest, we could end up with a big problem."

"Oh yes, I see what you mean," said Filip. "We've got to encourage Juri to keep her away from the sauce as much as possible – and for heavens sake, keep her on a leash at the official opening party!"

"Oh my," said Stefan, "It sounds like you've had quite a day.

Tomorrow's going to be a much quieter one, I assume?"

"Ooh, I don't know, Stefan," Filip replied with a worried look on his face. "We've got another bloody Scandi metal band that are going to sing about Lord knows what, that Icelandic freak who howls like a dog, a Latvian diva, and the Kazakhs, who are just a complete unknown quantity. It's going to be a long day, I can feel it in my water. So it's no Euroclub for me tonight."

"Or me, Filip," said Terry. "And yes, that's a point, where were you boys last night? You practically dragged us out, and yet you were nowhere to be seen."

Ah. Yes," said Stefan, awkwardly. "We WERE all set to go. But then we got a late call from our overlords demanding that we go into meetings with them all day today, and we just had to bail. There's no way you want to go into a five hour financial discussion with Timur's people after a couple of hours' sleep. And you've not met our boss Lucian Dobre yet, have you?"

"Not yet," said Filip.

"Oh you will," laughed Dumi. "And you're in for an absolute treat!"

16

At Maxim Munteanu's ranch to the North of Tiraspol, Michi Rotari was getting even more concerned about his elderly friend. They'd set off late from Chişinău last night after Moldova Smash called and asked if they could interview him in his living room as part of their pre-show coverage. Of course, the old man agreed, as he never wanted to let anyone down. But it meant that by the time they got to the Bicioc Bridge to cross the river into Transnistria the traffic was backed up for miles. The stop-starty journey clearly took it out of the old man, and he didn't get up until way past noon. But he was still insisting that he wanted to make it to the Romanian garden party that evening: "You know, just to show my face and shake hands with a few old associates," he insisted.

But Evgeny the driver knew that Maxim could never just show his face anywhere in this country, and he was likely to be kept there until long after midnight.

"It's not good," Evgeny said to Michi. "He's going to put himself in hospital again, like he did the last time he was in Moscow."

"Wait?" said Michi, "He's been as bad as this before?"

"Oh a few times now," Evgeny replied. "But I can't ever remember seeing him looking this weak and pale. We've got to do everything we can to keep him home tonight."

Michi had only known Maxim for two short months, but he was beginning to understand that making Maxim do anything against his will was going to be a hard task.

"What can we do to make him stay in, Evgeny?" Michi asked

hopefully. "Surely you must have developed some tactics over all the years that you've worked with him?"

"Oh I have, young Michi," Evgeny replied, "I have. And we're in exactly the right place to do it." "How do you mean?" Michi asked, puzzled.

"Well, Maxim's three brothers tend the ranch for him when he's away. They're all pretty elderly themselves now, but some of their sons work here too. So if we can encourage them to bring a few of their children over to the cabin we could keep him distracted until it's just too late to set out to the party."

"Great idea, Evgeny!" Michi replied! "But won't having all those kids running around make him even more tired than a party?"

"Ha!" said Evgeny with a bold snort. "You misunderstand me! His grand nephews and nieces are all in their mid-twenties to early thirties. And some of them work on the ranch too. But he's not seen many of them for a year or more, and considering that a few of them are coming back to Transnistria especially for Eurovision, I reckon a discrete little family gathering could do the old fella the world of good. I'll tell them all to leave all the littlest great-grandchildren at home, though. We can do that party another day."

"Oh! Yes! I see what you mean," said Michi. "That actually sounds like a decent plan."

"Doesn't it though," said Evgeny, looking a little pleased with himself. "I'll get the brothers on the phone and see who I can rustle up. You slip the hint to Maxim that some of his family might be coming round, and I'll make all the more practical arrangements. He's a sucker for family, that man. It's one of his great charms."

"Actually, that's something that I've always wondered about. If he's so much into family, why did he never have one of his own?"

"Well the official answer that he always tells reporters is that he's married to his music," said Evgeny. "He says that if he ever got entangled with a family of his own it would detract from the emotion he portrays on stage. He claims that his songs are his children, and the people of Moldova are all the family he needs."

"Oh that's terribly sweet of him," said Michi. "But have there never been rumours that he's gay?"

"A few," said Evgeny. "But none that ever amounted to anything. And to be honest, in all the years that I've worked at his houses I've never seen him with man, woman or child."

"Child?" Michi asked, with a start.

"Well yes, you know what some of these showbizzy types can be like," Evgeny answered. "But there's never been so much as a single unsupervised lady come though his doors over all these years."

"Well why do you think that is?" said Michi.

"Well partly I believe his story," explained Evgeny. "I've never once seen him even the tiniest bit lonely in the big house. He seems really content with his own company. But there was this other story that one of his brothers once hinted at. But you must never tell another soul, OK?"

"Oh I'm so terribly fond of Maxim that I'd never want to let him down!" asserted Michi, before adding more nervously, "Unless the story is too ghastly, that is?"

"Oh no, it's nothing like that, Michi," Evgeny reassured the younger man. "It goes back to his days in the army. The story has it that he was on a training exercise in the woods up in the North, near Briceni. He'd lost pace with his unit and was racing to catch up with the rest of the troops when his rifle got caught in some low branches. He ended up getting tangled in the trees just a few feet off the ground by all the straps and webbing on his kit, but with all the weight on – how shall we say this delicately – his important manly regions. It took them four hours to find him, and they say that he was never the same again."

"Oh my," said Michi, "That's terrible. Has he ever spoken to you about it?"

"Never. Not one single word. But his brothers claim that his injury is the reason he's retained his boyish good looks, even into his eighties, and it's why his voice has always been so sweet and clear and angelic. It kind of makes sense to me – but like I say, that's between me, you and his doctor. This story must never leave these four walls. Are we good with that?"

"Oh definitely, Evegeny," Michi assured him. "It kind of makes me love him all the more now."

*

TV executives Stefan Smolenko and Dumi Enache were in deep conversation in Moldova Smash's suite of offices just behind the arena in Tiraspol.

"You know what, Dumi," said Stefan. "Things all seem to be going pretty well on stage at the moment."

"Well, apart from all that Nazi Viking business," Dumi joked.

"Yes, apart from that," Stefan answered. "But that's more of a worry for the CTF. They're the ones who approved it. But I'm still feeling a little uneasy."

"Why's that, Stefan?" Dumi asked.

"Well partly it's the crew. Our friends from Lucerne have been slowly sneaking more and more of their people in, and our very capable workers are starting to have their noses put out of joint by it all. That Skunk fella is doing his very best to piss off everyone on the sound gantry, and that Ari guy in the lights seems to be able to wind up anyone he comes into contact with without even trying. And as much as I appreciate that Filip and Terry are doing their very best to keep everything on an even keel, they can be a bit snooty and aloof at times. It's only really Håkan that's managing to keep the two sides together, and to be quite frank he absolutely terrifies me. What's worse though is that Lucian Dobre told me he's planning on popping down for a tour of the site at some point over the next couple of days... and he might be bringing Timur along with him. And the last thing those two are going to want to see is a load of pasty Northern Europeans doing all the good jobs, while our lot are all bullied about like skivvies. That's not what either of them put their money into this thing for."

"Do we know when they're due to arrive?" said Dumi.

"Not a clue, Dumi. You know what Lucian's like. He just does things on a whim, so he could be walking into the building right now as far as we know."

Suddenly there was a knock at the door, and a familiar booming voice bled though from the corridor.

"Come out little pigs," came the voice. "I know you're in there!"

"Oh shit, Dumi, it's him. I made that happen, didn't I. I said his name and he appeared, like an extra tall Candyman with less bees. What are we going to do?"

"Well I'd let him in first, or he's going to blow that door down, by the sound of it," Dumi laughed.

"Now is not the time for levity," said Stefan with a stern look on his face. "I'll stall him for a while, and you go out and warn Filip that Elvis is in the building and that we've got a lumbering great complication to our day."

"Right you are, Stefan. I'll skip out now and pretend I never heard the knock." Dumi opened the door, and was greeted by a massive bear hug from the big man.

"Mister Enache! My man! You weren't leaving already, were you?" he boomed as he lifted Dumi a good couple of feet off the floor.

"Lucian! Good to see you sir!" panted Dumi, his ribs being crushed into his lungs by the pressure of Lucian's unwelcome embrace. "No, I was just off running some errands. I've got to get this information down to the press centre," he said, waving a few random papers that he'd grabbed off his desk, hoping to dear God that his boss didn't want to see what was on them.

"Oh! OK then, I don't want to keep you!" said Lucian, as he weakened his grip and let Dumi fall to the floor.

Dumi stood there, panting for breath for a few seconds, before he dashed off down the corridor shouting "Byeee!" and then coughing a deep booming lung-damaged cough.

"So Stefan!" The big man proclaimed! "What have you got to show me? I've come to have a little look around my little investment."

"Are you alone?" Stefan asked, checking that he had no other high profile local guests with him.

"Oh no. Timur couldn't make it. I think he's polishing one of his yachts or something. He says he'll be down in the week."

"Oh great!" said Stefan, though his teeth, sarcastically.

"What was that, Stefan?" Lucian enquired, unsure as to whether he was being mocked.

"Great!" bluffed Stefan. "It's great that you're here, and great that Mr Turgenev is due a visit too. It's just a shame that you couldn't have come together."

"I know, I know. But at least this way you can show me all the secret stuff, and let me in on some of the things that you'd never have had the nerve to tell him!"

"Oh Mr Dobre, there's nothing of that kind going on here," Stefan assured him. "Because this is a co-production with the CTF, everything has got to be above board. We're an absolutely open book here. Do you want to see some figures?"

"Oh no, I don't need to see the boring shit like that!" Lucien replied, dismissively. "I've come here to see explosions and showgirls and show business! And actually, where is that guy from the CTF?

What is his name? Phillips?" "Filip," Stefan corrected.

"Ah yes, Filip. I'd like to meet the man and ask what he thinks of our beautiful competition this year, and how much better it is than all the other ones his organisation have worked on."

"Well funny you should say that, sir, because I'm due a meeting with him in a couple of hours, just to check over how are preparations are going. You can sit in on that one, if you like?"

"Yes! YES! I'd love to, thanks! Pencil me in for that. And in the meantime take me to the stage. I want to see a little of that rock'n'roll music!"

"Of course, Lucien, follow me!" said Stefan as he led his station's owner out of the door and down towards the big hall, praying that Dumi hadn't got waylaid somewhere down the corridor and was warning Filip this very minute of what was about to befall him.

"Mister Filip! Mister Filip! Are you about?" Dumi frantically spat into his radio. "It's a bit urgent. Do you have a minute? It's Dumi."

There was a long, empty pause before Filip replied.

"Yes, Dumi! Where are you?" Filip's crackly radio voice replied.

"I'm just on my way into the arena, Filip," Dumi panted. "We've got a visitor!" "Timur Turgenev?" Filip asked, with a worried edge to his voice.

"No, it's differently difficult," Dumi replied. "It's Lucien Dobre, and he really wants to see you?"

"Oh gawd," Filip sighed. "I'm just with the Finns at the moment. "See you at the CTF balcony in ten?"

"I'm heading there now," said Dumi.

"Right, sorry about that chaps," Filip said to the Finnish folk metallers. "Just a spot of TV business. So, I've popped in to find out what you're going to be doing on stage today. You may have heard about that awkward bit of business that we had with the Norwegians yesterday, and I don't really understand metal music and all its myriad sub-genres. So I'm just after a little reassurance that there's nothing dubious or distinctly un-Eurovisiony that you're going to try to cram into your three minutes today. It's nothing personal of course, chaps. I'm sure that everything is going to be completely above board, but you can understand my concerns."

"Oh perfectly," said Troll's lead singer, a man in a rubber mask who went by the name of Uggg. "We've played at a lot of the same festivals as that Stormgiver mob, and everybody tries to give them a wide berth. They're notoriously unhinged, and they really believe what they're singing about. We're just a bunch of dumb rock kids jumping about in make up and singing songs of the woods and the weather. You've got nothing to fear with us... and you won't even have to make a blood oath to Lucifer if you want us to change anything. You can just ask, and we'll be happy to help."

"Oh that's terribly reassuring, erm, Uggg," said Filip sounding quite relieved. "You can't imagine how weird and complicated it was trying to get that other lot to agree to anything. We had to threaten them with fines and sanctions to get them to tone it all down. At least I think they agreed."

"Oh that sounds just like Tim," laughed Uggg."He's always been a pompous little bastard, and I think he's starting to believe his own press. Don't you worry though Filip, there's nothing political or quasi-intellectual about us Trolls. We just like to rock out and have a laugh!"

"That's good to hear, fellas," Filip replied. "Right then, good luck with it all today. The press lot are going to love you. Prepare to be mobbed for selfies for the next ten hours!"

"Oh we're used to it, boss," Uggg laughed. "You don't look like this for a living and get to walk to the toilet without being stopped for a few quick snaps! I hope the rest of your day goes OK too!"

"Oh I'm hoping for a really really quiet one – as if I should be that lucky," Filip smiled. "Cheers chaps!"

And with that he left the dressing room to a flotilla of cheery waves from the men in the knobbly prosthetics.

"He's gone, lads," said Ugg, conspiratorially, "I can hear him going down the corridor. Right then, get Jimmy The Midget out of the washing basket. We've still got some work to do on him..."

*

Dumi was already at the viewing balcony when Filip arrived, and he was looking a little fretful. "Hey Dumi!" said Filip cheerily. "How's it going? All good I hope. So what's this about Lucien?" "Yes, I'm great, thanks," said Dumi, "but your day's about to get double complicated."

"How do you mean, Dumi?" Filip enquired. "I thought Lucien was a cheery sort of chap?"

"Well he is, but he's also pretty hard going at the best of times. He's a sportsman, so he's from a world of locker room banter and practical jokery, which means you never entirely know where you are with him. And he's also larger than life – in every sense of the term. He's well over two-and-a- quarter metres high, with a personality to match. He's going to want to see every single last thing in the arena and its surrounds... and he wants you to show him. No one else will do."

"Oh crap," said Filip. "He's going to be hard work, isn't he!"

"Yeah, a little," Dumi nodded. "But he's easily swayed by shiny things, so just give him the bare bones of a tour, let him watch a couple of rehearsals, and we should be alright."

"Yeah, that should be OK," reasoned Filip. "I've got a conference call with Lucerne at three, but I've got no solid plans until then, outside of overseeing and trouble shooting. Bring him on!"

"He's on his way now, sir. Stefan's bringing him over, the speed he walks at he should be here any min..."

"FILIP!" shouted a deep, booming voice as it burst through the double doors at the back of the balcony. "So nice to finally meet you!"

Before Filip could say a word, the big man had picked him up in both arms and was squeezing him to the verge of a nasty rib injury.

"Lucien, I assume," Filip panted through the bear hug.

"Yeah man, it's good to be here," said Lucien, before dropping Filip to the floor and giving him a massive slap on the back. "I've come to see how my little investment is going, and I have to say that it looks bloody brilliant."

He stood at the edge of the balcony and waved his long, heavy arms in a gesture reminiscent of a medieval King casting an eye over his domain from a castle's ramparts.

"And that stage! Shit man, that's unbelievable! Did our people do that, Filip?"

"A co-production, Lucien," Filip proudly proclaimed. "Moldovan design, CTF technology, international manpower. It's what Eurovision is all about!"

"Yes, yes, I see," said the big man, his eyes darting everywhere excitedly. "When does the music start?"

"You've arrived just in time to see the Slovenians make their final rehearsal, and then the Finns are on. And I'm expecting them to be quite something," Filip explained.

"Ooh, ooh, those Slovenian chicks looked pretty hot in the video," Lucien enthused, "I can't wait to see what they're like in real life!"

"Well you're about to get a look see right now," said Filip.

The lights dimmed, Hanna counted down the backing track, and a single spotlight pointed at a big wooden box on the stage.

"Where are the girls?" Lucien asked.

"Not terribly sure at this point," said Filip. "I've not see this one yet."

Suddenly muffled voices could be heard singing along to the music, but none of the three girls could be seen anywhere. Filip's eyes snapped to the big screens above the stage, and could just about see the girls' faces between the slats of the massive wooden box.

"So THAT'S what the name's all about!" he laughed. "They're singing the song from within a massive great wooden crate! Oh, I've seen it all now!"

"They're going to come out at some point though, aren't they?" questioned Dumi. "You know, like a big reveal for the last chorus, or something?"

"Well you'd like to think so, Dumi," said Filip, hopefully. "The song's so pedestrian that they need something a little out of the ordinary to happen, otherwise it's a classic case of death by staging!"

"This is bullshit," said Lucien, angrily. "I want to see some girls, not a big lump of wood on stage!"

On stage, two steady-cam operators circled the crate as the women within sang. Every now and again you could catch a glimpse of one of the singer's eyes on the big screen, or maybe a few fingers poking out teasingly. But it was looking increasingly like nothing much else was going to be happening.

"Nope, they're onto the last chorus now," laughed Dumi. "This is going to be it now, I fear, unless the whole crate explodes or something at the end!"

All three men let out hearty laughs at the very thought of it, before the song petered to a finish, and a big banner fell from the front of the crate bearing the words for love in every possible Eurovision language. "Was that it?" shouted Lucien "Really? What a waste of pure sex power!"

"Well I don't know about that, sir," said Filip, "But it was just a little bit of a let down, wasn't it." "Too right, mate!" the big man replied. Once the song had finished and all appropriate checks had been made, Hanna the stage manager said "Thank you Slovenia. See you later in the week." And upon that instruction, three sets of hands came out of the cracks in the crate's slats, picked the box up from within, and scuttled off down the exit ramp like some kind of awkward tortoise.

Everybody in the hall exploded with laughter, from the cleaners to the tech guys – and even Slovenia's own delegation. Filip was doing his best to stifle a giggle, but had to let it free. This was the first proper laugh that he'd had in days, and it was a welcome release.

"Who ever thought that would be a good idea?" he bellowed, as the three men on the balcony rolled around in their seats, wracked with the happy pain of mirth.

"Welcome to Eurovision, Lucien!" Dumi gurgled through the guffaws. "This is how it rolls around here!"

"That was the worst... and the best... most stupid thing... I've ever seen in my life!" said Lucien, struggling to breathe between the sentence fragments. "I want to see some more!"

"And I'd like to welcome Finland to the Eurovision stage!" Hana's voice cheerily announced over the sound system. Ice's crew burst onto the performance area like worker ants, putting all of Troll's instruments into the right positions, and bringing a forest of artificial trees and massive great fibreglass turrets to surround the band as they played.

"It's getting even more mental now," Lucien spluttered!

"You just wait until the band come on…" said Dumi, just as five small Finnish men filed onto the stage, with big rubber troll heads and torn brown leather outfits.

At the site of this, Lucien went up three gears in his comedy convulsions and swung back into his seat, cracking the back of his head on the seat behind him with such force that it let out a massive 'THUCK!" The three men fell silent for a long moment before they all burst into even more uncontrollable fits of laughter. Even Filip had tears streaming down his eyes as the band completed their mic checks and began to pile into their song. Loud guitars filled the empty arena, and an insistent folksy whistle tooted out an infectious jig.

Lucien began to punch his fist into the air, shouting "This is more like it! Yeah man, yeaaaaah!" before nodding his big mop of greying hair like a teenage metal kid. It was around three quarters of the way through the song before Filip noticed the rope being lowered from the ceiling.

"Erm, what's that for, Dumi? he asked, still clucking slightly with laughter. "Is that supposed to be happening, or is it just a crew thing?"

"I really don't know, Filip," Dumi replied. "I'll keep an eye on it, then get back to Hanna if it's an issue."

The rope slowly lowered behind the trees at the back of the stage, before it started to rise again. Now tied into a noose, they could see that it was wrapped around the neck of a tiny man in a monk's outfit.

"It's a dwarf!" shouted Lucien in abject delight. "They're hanging a fucking dwarf! Man, this is better than Spinal Tap!"

Filip's mirth though came to a slamming halt.

"Those little shits just told me that everything was OK and above board and that we had nothing to worry about," he snapped angrily. "You wait until the next time I see them!"

"Right, I think I've seen enough of the singing now," shouted Lucien above the noise. "I want to save some of the surprises for showtime! But can you show me around backstage now please Filip? And if you can, take me where the girls are!"

"Certainly Lucien," said Filip, as Dumi rolled his eyes dismissively from behind the big man. "Come this way…"

The rest of the third day of rehearsals passed with little incident. Iceland's Vikingur The Dog Boy might have been incredibly odd, but his ambient doggy howling proved strangely soothing after the noise of some of the earlier acts, while Latvia's Laumina Balodis was almost disappointingly professional and relaxed, and nothing like as much of a diva as her reputation suggested. Indeed, pretty much everybody else scheduled to rehearse that afternoon just drifted along like clockwork, with hardly a foot stepped out of place or a minute dropped from the schedule. It was almost too perfect as the stage crews prepared for the last song of the day – Rayana Bayzhanova with Kazakhstan's debut performance in the contest.

"Anyone know what she's supposed to be like?" Ice asked her crew and colleagues through the backstage radios.

"I met her at the hotel last night," Hanna replied. "She seemed a little pop starry, but I guess she is as big as Mariah Carey back home. But, you know, she was quite pleasant to talk to, and the song's an absolute blinder. I reckon we'll be alright."

"Good to know, Hanna, good to know."

"Any sign of her yet, Ice?" asked Hanna. "Is she running a little late?"

"Yep, she's here," Ice replied, "And that horse thing is with her."

The horse thing that Ice was referring to was a large mechanical horse puppet, operated by four puppeteers who were standing around the big prop with long sticks controlling its movement. It was like a cross between the equine marionette from the stage version of War Horse, and something you'd see at a panto – although this was much more stunning to look at than either of them. The puppeteers brought the horse up the ramp into its position on stage, and a slight young dancer followed, her outfit reminiscent of Kazakh national dress. In the background the visuals crew were test running images of beautiful grasslands on the big screens. The elements were all aligning for this to be a pretty interesting performance.

And then Rayana Bayzhanova herself strode purposefully onto the stage. She cut a stunning presence. Well over six feet plus boots, her massive shock of black hair was stacked up behind an elaborate golden headband encrusted with jewels and gems of many colours. She wore a tunic reminiscent of a 15th century warrior princess, while her skirt and sleeves were tinted in the same sky blue hue of the Kazakh flag. She may have been well into her forties now, but her striking Eurasian features radiated under the bright stage lights, as if some minor goddess from an unknown religion has just descended from the firmament in order to bestow some unearthly treasures upon us mere underdeveloped humans.

"She's... she's... absolutely bloody perfect!" Hanna stuttered through her radio.

"I know, right," Ice replied. "At least three of my crew swooned when she walked into the backstage area. I have never seen anything like her. She'll be visiting me in my dreams long after we get out of here, I reckon!"

"I guess we've got to get her going with the rehearsal now though," said Hanna. "I'm almost scared to ask her to do anything in case she smites me with her steely gaze. How's her English, do we know?"

"No idea," said Ice. "She didn't say a word to any of us when she came in. Even the mic monkeys." "I'll go over and talk to her now, then," the stage manager replied, excitedly. "Wish me luck!"

Hanna walked the few steps across the stage to the spot where the singer was peering out into the darkened hall, radiating.

"Everything alright with you there, Ms Bayzhanova?" she nervously asked. "Are you almost ready to start your rehearsal now?"

Ms Bayzhanova stared out into the darkness for a few more seconds, before she turned to Hanna, gazed upon her with her deep brown eyes, and answered in a deep and smokey voice... "Yes!" before gracefully turning away again.

"Erm, OK," Hanna thought to herself. "A woman of few words. Perhaps it's stage fright. Or perhaps she's just getting herself into character. I'll leave her be."

Hanna took a few steps towards the back of the stage, before whispering into her head mic "OK now, music in three, two, one..."

A gentle wistful melody tinged with unfamiliar Eastern flavours wafted around the stage, as two spotlights lit the big puppet horse as it grazed on a projection of grass beamed onto the stage floor. Another spot appeared on the opposite side of the stage, illuminating the dancer, who was twirling and swirling around in a blur of graceful yet complicated movements. The horse looked up, the girl ran towards it, the music suddenly kicked in to a banging complex groove, and the whole stage was awash with light. Rayana Bayzhanova, her head first pointing down towards the stage, looked up with a start and peered straight down the camera. Hanna could imagine viewers across the continent melting into their sofas with unabashed awe at the very sight of her. She slowly raised the mic to her mouth, pulled in a deep breath, and let out the most dreadful flat drone that you could ever possibly imagine.

Everyone watching back in the press centre, until then drawn into the deeply compelling drama playing out on stage, let out a massive communal gasp of shock.

"She can't sing for shit!" shouted one voice at the back, which encouraged around half of the room into embarrassed laughter.

"Shhh! Wait!" said another towards the middle of the room. "It might be an art thing. Give her a minute or so and then we'll know if it's just local colour."

But it wasn't. For the full three minutes she drably crooned on, the deep bass elements in her voice rattling the fixtures and fittings in the arena.

"The song itself is incredible," remarked Radouane Thill from the ESC Cargo website to his colleagues, "And the staging is absolutely out of this world. She even looks like a beautiful angel. It's just that when she sings it sounds like a rusty old foghorn! She'd have had a chance of winning if only she could sing. It's an absolute crying shame!"

The young journalist had a point. It was if all the ingredients to make the finest cake you ever eaten were right there on stage before them, only the eggs had gone off and were making the whole thing taste a little grim.

"I wonder what's happening in the odds?" said Radouane. "Quick, Olivia, run over to the betting table and see what they're are making of this."

Radouane's eager sidekick skipped over to the darkest corner of the room, where the professional gamblers were in a frenzy of activity.

"Hey Olivia!" said one of their number. "Can't speak for a minute. I'm laying this one like an absolute mofo before the market get wind of how awful she is. God, I had a grand on her at 70/1 to win the whole damn thing before she was even confirmed. Now I'm not sure if they're even going to qualify. She's had an absolute shocker there."

"Can I use that as a quote, sir?" Olivia asked tentatively.

"Sail away ma'am, it's all yours," said the gambler happily, before interrupting himself mid- sentence. "Look, she's plummeting down the ranks before our very eyes. We're going to make a mint out of laying this!"

In the background, Hanna's voice came through the PA in the press room. "OK, are we ready for the second rehearsal? Yes? In three-two-one..."
A loud plaintive cry rang out amongst the whole of the press corps. "Nooooooooo! Not again! Please...!"

17

Over in the press office, the CTF's head of communications Terry van Boom had called Michael Storm, owner and chief writer of the fansite EuroStorm, in for a little chat. The site had long been notorious for printing whatever fell out of their heads, and ripping off news stories from other fan publications word for word – even omitting to edit out the typos when they posted them. Their abrasive nature was part of the attraction, but they'd been putting important noses out of joint for just a little too long now, and people were starting to get tired of their schtick.

They'd already invoked the ire of the people upstairs at their CTF with their corruption allegations following the Norwegian act's unsavoury on-stage utterances. But the final straw had come in their reporting of the Icelandic performer after his first run through that afternoon. The act himself had strongly objected to EuroStorm's headline after his performance – "Dog? Shit!" it read. But when he discovered that Storm himself had frequently referred to him as looking like a child molester in one of their reaction videos on YouTube, he made a formal complaint to the CTF, and stated that he was seriously considering legal action against both EuroStorm and the CTF for defamation. The former for doing it, the latter for failing to do anything about it. So the people in Lucerne had demanded that Terry haul the website's editor into the office for a final warning.

"Seriously Michael, you just can't get away with insulting the acts like this," said Terry, sternly. "Remember when you called that poor Bosnian girl fat and ugly to her face at Junior, and then got surprised when we suspended you for the rest of the year?"

"Well she was!" sneered Michael Storm as if Terry had just said the most stupid thing in the world ever.

"That may or may not be so," said Terry, at the edge of his patience. "But you don't go saying that to a vulnerable nine-year-old that we have a duty of care over."

"Why not?" Storm spat once more. "It's the only way these precious little chubbers learn!"

"Likewise with your comments this afternoon, Michael," Terry continued. "Vikingur has contacted his lawyers, and says that he's on the verge of taking legal action against us both if we don't make moves to curb your behaviour."

"Let him! Let the little freak sue me if he wants!" shouted Storm, now getting increasingly agitated. "I've got the sanctity of the press on my side. He can't subdue my freedom of speech!"

"Well actually he can, Michael," said Terry. "You've made some very serious allegations against the man in a publicly broadcast video that has been seen by many thousands of people – and none of which you have any legal proof for. You're liable to a sizable fine if you don't immediately retract your video and then issue a sincere written apology. Libel and slander have nothing to do with freedom of speech."

"Fuck him!" said Michael, "Fuck him and the kids he sleeps with. He hasn't got the nerve to sue me, of all people. I'll be just fine! Doesn't he know who I am?"

Terry was getting increasingly frustrated with the stuck up quasi-journalist and his delusions of grandeur, but was biting his tongue in case Michael had a recording device on him, all set for his angry words to turn up on some dismissive video in the near future. So as difficult as it was, he kept his calm and continued with his ticking off.

"It doesn't matter who you may or may not be, Michael," he said.

"There are strict libel laws in pretty much every country in Europe about saying these kinds of things in the public sphere without solid and incontrovertible evidence that this is a cast iron solid fact. And do you have that evidence?"

"Oh I don't need evidence," the New Zealander sniffed, haughtily. "Just look at him. Everybody can see that he's a paedo. I'll bet he's got a basket of young Moldovan children locked up in his hotel room as we speak!"

"Michael mate," said Terry, clenching his hands so tightly with the stress that his fingernails were cutting into his palms, "That's not good enough. And I don't think you realise the gravity of this situation. You can't just go around saying whatever you think of. You've got to take a bit of responsibility for your actions and not keep printing these wild and unfounded allegations just because you've decided that they're true."

"Well I've got away with it so far?" Storm said with a huff. "So why wouldn't I just keep at it? No one seems to mind, and the readers just lap it up."

"I mind," said Terry. "The CTF minds. And Vikingur and his lawyers very much mind. You're bringing the good name of this competition into disrepute, and you're putting us in a very difficult legal position..."

"Oh that's just it, isn't it!" Storm yelled as he leapt up from the table, tipping his chair roughly onto the floor behind him. "You're only interested in covering your own sweet ass! Now the truth is coming out into the open."

"No Michael, it's the law," said Terry. "And you're getting perilously close to having to deal with them very soon."

"No Terry, no. You know what NWA said? Fuck tha police! Comin' straight from the underground! I ain't afraid of no Law! Let them come at me!"

Terry took off his glasses, rubbed his face and sighed. "Well in that case I've got no alternative than to issue you and your writers with a final warning. Any more transgressions this week and I'm afraid I'm going to have to ban you from Eurovision. For life. We'll have you marched off site unceremoniously by local security – and you know how rough handed they look – and we'll take steps to keep you out of the arena during the shows, whether you've got expensively bought tickets for them or not. So what is it to be? Are you going to behave, and stick to the rules and regulations of the press at this competition that were written in the box you ticked when you applied for your accreditation? Are you? One more incident like this and you're out on your ear, I tell you!"

"Well Terry," Michael replied, his nose in the air and looking all superior. "If that's what you want, that's what you shall get. But I'll still decide what does and doesn't go onto my site. So if something's true to the best of my knowledge, then that's exactly what I'm going to publish."

"I do wish you could be a little more co-operative," said Terry, now looking a little less stern. "You did amazing things for Eurovision reporting when you first got going. You helped change the way people looked at the contest, and to be absolutely honest, you did a lot of the heavy lifting for us on the internet a few years back. I think that's one of the reasons that the suits upstairs have held their patience with you for so long. But you let it go to your head, and now you give the very clear impression that you think you're bigger than the competition. And nobody is. Not me, not you, not anybody. The good name of Eurovision is the most precious thing of all, and if anyone insists on continually dragging it through the dirt then I'm sorry, they're going to have to go."

Michael Storm looked temporarily taken aback by Terry's little speech. He seemed genuinely moved by some of the kind words that had just been offered to him, but his ego wouldn't allow him to acknowledge that. So quickly he snapped out of his vulnerable moment, stood up straight and snapped out "Right, is that it then Terry? I'm a busy man. I've got words to write, videos to make, and trouble to find. I trust we'll be seeing you at the Israeli party tonight then?"

Terry was momentarily startled by this sudden gear change in the conversation.

"What? What?" he foundered. "Oh! Oh yes. Well it will all depend on how the video meeting goes with Vikingur's lawyers in the next hour or so. If I tell him that you're on your final warning and that you've promised to be on your best behaviour, then I think we might have just about gotten away with it. Just don't go calling him any other bad names – at least on record that is."

"Oh you can trust me, Terry," Michael sneered. "You can always trust me. What else am I likely to say about the dog-sucking paedo freak?!"

And with that he turned on his heels and dashed out of the door.

"I think that went OK there," Terry said to himself. "But I'm still not 100% sure that we can trust him to behave. I've got to keep a close eye on his site between now and the end of the contest, because I can sense that they've got something up their sleeve..."

18

That evening saw the first of the major party nights of the competition fortnight. Each year, many of the delegations hold little shindigs to help promote their song and stave off some of the boredom that comes from waiting around for their next rehearsals. These range from classy little soirees at the host city's embassies, to drunken bacchanals at the major local nightclubs. But seeing as Tiraspol was a little short of both of those sorts of venues, the delegations had got a little more creative this year, holding their parties at theatres, bars, boats, and even a nearby cattle farm, which the Icelanders who dreamed it up seemed to think was a hilarious idea at the time. But now that everybody had discovered quite how humourless Vikingur The Dog Boy actually was, people were starting to wonder if it was actually going to be all that much fun. Some of these parties are free-for-alls to anyone with accreditation, and some are more select, invite-only events, and it has become something of an art amongst delegates to not only find out where all the parties are going to be held, but also to trade information for invites and plot the most efficient routes around the city to squeeze in as much revelry as possible.

After a couple of low key and polite events at private houses in the near suburbs, and the ever- present offer of Euroclub on the edge of town, tonight was the first of the super party nights, where nations who had already had their first rehearsal and still had a bit of hanging about to do tried to outclass each other with the biggest, most bonkers shindig that their budgets would allow.

Tonight saw five gatherings. These kicked off with Ireland, who traditionally hold their party in the best Irish pub in town. But when they learned that the nearest venue with even the slightest sniff of a shamrock was a two-hour drive away in Chişinău, they decided to hold it in a local a venue called the Soviet Garage Pub instead. Then there was Greece, who were having a private do at a Greek restaurant in the city centre. This overlapped by an hour with Ukraine, who were having a big old blowout for all-comers on a giant party boat on the river. Then came Finland, and their full blown gig at Big Rock Heaven – the city's one reasonably sized music venue, and the night was topped off with the traditionally extravagant Israeli party at Euroclub that was expected to go on until the wee small hours.

News of these events creeps out by word of mouth or personal invitation, and already the press corps, delegations and other accredited hangers on were working out where they were all geographically located so they could sort out their travel arrangements, while at the same time establishing which events were worth missing and which were the definite must dos. The Irish party was always an early starter, as their ageing commentator could rarely manage a late night out these days, so the massed ranks of party goers were piling into the lines of opportunist local cabs hanging around outside the city's hotels and sped off to the Oktyabrsky neighbourhood in the far East of the city to find the Soviet Garage Pub.

What most of the revellers hadn't reckoned with was that Oktyabrsky was one of those old tower block neighbourhoods that were common in the former Soviet nations which, while being perfectly safe, looked dark and foreboding to people from the more gentile Western creases of Europe.

Terry van Boom had decided that this was going to be his one big party night out of the year, and after the couple of days at work he'd just had he really needed to let his hair down and have a bit of a blow out. He'd jumped into a cab with four of his friends from the press office, but as the tiny cramped Lada got further out from the centre of the city, he was beginning to get a little anxious.

"Erm, I'm not sure that I like the look of this neighbourhood," said

Terry as he peered up at mile after mile of weather-beaten tower blocks. "Are you kids sure that you really want to go to this?"

"Yeah man!" said Sunny, a big, brash Cypriot lad who was crammed into the back seat with his three colleagues. "The Irish parties are always a hoot, and you're never likely to be coming to an area like this again, so just soak it up while you can and live a little!"

"Yes, but is it safe?" Terry enquired.

The cab driver turned towards Terry with a scowl, cracked a giant smile, and in broken English said: "Is safe sir. Is very safe. My mother, grandmother, she live here. You be fine!"

"There you go," said Jeff, Terry's English sideman, with his face pressed up against the car's right window. "The man said it himself... is safe!"

"Oh, well I'll take your word for it just this once, Jeff," Terry laughed. "But if it's a shithole, I'm out of there!"

"No shithole!" said the driver with a twinkle in his eye. "Very good pub!" "See Terry," said Jeff, "Our cabbie wouldn't let us down! He knows!"

"Yeah, but what's good for here isn't necessarily good for anywhere else," said Terry seriously. "I'll reserve judgement until I see it for myself."

The cabbie cut off the main road, down into a side lane, and then turned again into a narrow, pot- holed alley, flanked by two rows of family car garages.

"Oh this can't be it, can it?" said the Swedish IT manager Jan, "Surely not?"

"They certainly weren't wrong when they said Garage, were they," Sunny laughed. "Is here," said the driver. "Soviet Garage Pub. Very good place."

"You're kidding us, right?" said Terry in the front seat. "Is here. You listen for music," the driver replied.

Jeff rolled down the window, and indeed he could hear traditional Irish music coming from behind one of the garage doors.

"I think this is the place," said Jeff. "Look, there's the hammer and sickle painted on one of the doors, and a whole lot of cyrillic writing underneath it."

"Oh yes," said Dean, an Australian intern, who was the fourth person squeezed into the back, "And there's some green and orange balloons gaffa taped to one of the doors. I reckon we're here! Let's get out!"

"But how are we going to get back to the city afterwards" Terry fretted. "We're never going to be able to flag a cab down from out here."

"You OK," said the driver, "I wait. I will be your drive for the night. You safe 100% with me!" "Oh you don't have to," said Terry, "You must have other fares to take."

"No, I wait. Happy to wait," the driver replied.

"Oh you're such a love," said Terry. "What's your name sir – we can't just keep calling you driver."

"Call me Elvis," the driver said with a smile. "Rock and roll!"

"Then Elvis it is!" said Terry, shaking his hand furiously. "Meet you outside in about half an hour?" "No, I come too. I know owner," Elvis answered. "He good guy!"

"Great!" said Sunny. "Then show us the way!"

The doors of the cab opened, and the six men spilled out onto the broken lane between the two rows of garages.

"But how do we get in, Elvis?" Dean asked.

"Watch!" said Elvis. The driver gripped his freshly lit cigarette between his teeth, walked up to the garage with the coarsely painted hammer and sickle, and kicked the bottom of the door. Instantly it opened, and dry ice and colourful lights began to tumble out.

"This is already quite brilliant!" said Sunny with a massive grin on his face. "I live for this kind of shit!"

As the smoke cleared, they could see that rather than just being the one garage, four had been knocked together to make a quite significant space. The walls were festooned with Soviet era memorabilia, and the furniture looked as though as if it had been pilfered directly from a babushka's tenth floor flat.

"Gentlemen!" came a familiar voice from the gloom. "So glad you could make it!"

"Ice?" said Terry, uncertainly through the mist. It was indeed Ice, and before he knew it the crew ganger came bounding through the smoke to give him an almighty hug.

"What are you doing here, Ice? The parties aren't usually your scene are they?" "Oh no," she replied eagerly, "they're usually too full of bullshit and bad trousers..."

Each of the five party goers instantly looked down to see if their strides would pass Ice's muster.

"But this place is great," she continued. "It's where the crew have been drinking since we started setting up the stage a month ago! Everything's so damn cheap, and anything goes! And I mean absolutely anything. I have to say though, we were all a bit surprised when we heard there was going to be a delegation party here."

"Well now that we've found it, where are the Irish," Sunny asked.

"It's that lot in the corner, looking a bit scared," she laughed. "I think they've bitten off a bit more than they can chew, to be honest with you."

"I'll go and have a word," said Terry.

He walked towards the back of the stage area in the second garage to find the Irish singer Billy McNamara and his five backing singers cowering terrified behind their equipment.

"Everything alright, Billy?" he asked. "You've found yourself quite a place here."

"Yes Terry, but it wasn't my doing," he said with a little tremble in his voice. "Brendan the HoD looked in the local listings magazine and saw that it was the only place in the city with the word pub in its name. But I really don't think he looked too much into it after that. We're absolutely bricking it.

Everyone here looks so scary."

"Half of them are our stage crew," Sunny laughed. "They're nothing to be scared of – unless you turn up late for rehearsals!"

"Yeah, and our driver Elvis tells us that it's as safe as houses," added Terry. "You'll be alright mate." "Erm, is Elvis the old boy in the flat cap at the bar necking shots with the landlord?" asked Billy.

"Oh, shit, yes!" said Terry. "Could this night get any more weird and wonky than it already is? We're only at the first venue! I hope he's going to be alright to drive?"

"All the cabbies here drive drunk," Ice cut in. "It's like a badge of honour for them. There's never any crashes either – at least none that I've seen."

"That's terribly reassuring," said Terry, looking far from reassured. "I shall rest easy in my thoughts for the rest of the night now."

After about ten minutes, another thirty or so people with accreditation hanging around their necks stepped anxiously into the garage, and Brendan gave the nod for Billy and his singers to start the show. The young Irish singer stepped up to the microphone and nervously uttered a few introductory words.

"Hello to you all, and thank you for coming all the way out here to see us when there's so many other things you could be doing tonight. How do you like the venue?"

He swished his hand regally at the spartan surroundings and received a huge ironic cheer from everyone in the room. By now some of the locals from the nearby blocks had heard that there was a Eurovision performer in the area, and had crammed into the tiny venue to have a look at what was going on.

"Right then, first of all me and the girls are going to sing this year's Irish Eurosong entry, Lonely Girl, and then we're going to do a small selection of traditional ballads from the Emerald Isle. I hope we can all have a bit of a sing-song."

His hands were shaking as he tightly gripped the microphone, before Brendan pressed play on the backing track and the song's intro began.

"By the way," Billy said before his singing bits kicked in, "there's one free drink for everyone. No Guinness I'm afraid, but plenty of local brews."

Upon those words there was a stampede towards the bar at the back of the room, and only a small few people remained by the stage to watch his song.

"He could have timed that announcement better!" Dean said loudly into Terry's ear. "Too right he could," chuckled Terry. "Anyway, here's the song".

Billy breathed in, and what could only be described as the voice of an angel flew from his lips. Suddenly the clamour at the bar subsided and everyone turned to face the frightened lad. His confidence visibly swelled, and by the time he'd got to the end of his sweet, uncomplicated little song, the whole place was utterly silent, with many a surly local secretly wiping away an unexpected tear. The song finished, Billy said "Thank you!" and there was an awkward moment of silence. Suddenly, Elvis the driver began a loud, slow round of applause, before the volume swelled and every single person in the room was going wild with appreciation. The young Irish lad looked genuinely surprised and overwhelmed as he thanked this most unexpected audience.

"Thank you, thank you, you really are too kind," Billy said, himself on the verge of tears. "And now some songs from the old country."

From here on in the night became quite the bash. The accredited delegates had begun to melt away as soon as the Irish-branded goodie bags were given out, but the locals and the crew stayed, and drunkenly sang along to every word of every old Irish standard that Billy warbled out.

"Looks as though this town really could do with an Irish bar," Dean joked.

"Looks like they've finally found themselves one," Jeff replied. "I think poor Brendan's going to have a heck of a time getting young Billy out of here!"

"Oh! Damn!" said Terry with a start. "I didn't see what the time was, I was enjoying myself so much. We're going to miss the Ukrainian boat if we don't get going!"

"What about the Greek party though?" Jan asked hopefully.

"I think we're going to have to miss that one this year, Jan," said Terry. "It's only a polite one in a restaurant anyway. I'm sure we won't be missing much."

"Oh, OK..." Jan sulked, before Terry piped up: "Where's Elvis?"

"It's fine Terry," said Jeff, "I've kept my eye on him all night. He's still propped up at the bar!" "Elvis!" Terry shouted across the room. "We're ready to go!"

Elvis got off his stool and stumbled a little. "Is OK," he said. "Not drunk, just tired."

"Good good!" said Terry, "Well can you get us across town to the riverboat pier? We've got to catch a ferry in about twenty minutes!"

"I get you there in ten!" Elvis proudly boasted. "I know quick way."

It turned out that Elvis didn't know the quick way, and the cab only just made it to the pier as the boat's captain was tooting his final launching horn and the crew were about to pull up the gangplank.

"Wait! Wait!" Terry yelled to the crew as he ran towards the boat. "You got room for six more?"

"Five," said Sunny, dashing along behind him. "Elvis says he doesn't like boats, so he's going to sleep this one off."

"That's one less thing to worry about then," said Terry. "I hope he's still there when we get back.

The crew held off their final gangplank toils until the fivesome got onboard, and then the boat began to slowly pull out from the jetty.

"Damn that was close," said Dean. "I didn't think we were going to make it for a minute there."

"Yes, but we're here now,' Terry replied. "So let's get our breath back, find the bar, and see who's here."

As they picked their way through the packed bar, they were greeted with a roar from the depths! "Gentlemen! So glad you could make it!"

"Ice?" said Terry, puzzled. "What are you doing here? I really didn't think that this was your kind of thing?"

"Long story, Terry," she said, leaning in to whisper the words into his ear among the mad throng. "But some guys from one of those websites – what is it...? Storm Child?"

"EuroStorm," asked Terry, anxiously.

"Yes, that's the one, EuroStorm. I got chatting to them at the Irish party, and they said they'd bring me down here for a laugh. So I thought, why not!"

"Ooh, you've got to be careful with them, Ice," Terry warned his friend. "They'll do everything they can to try and drag some dirt out of you so they can run a scurrilous story tomorrow morning."

Ice grabbed Terry by the lapels and leaned in close again.

"I know!" she said, unsurprised. "I know exactly what they're trying, and it ain't going to work. When have you ever known me give away a single secret."

"Never, Ice, it's true!" he replied.

"Damn right!" she laughed, pointing at her temple. "I've got so much locked up here that I could write a book about all the goings on. But I'm not gonna. I'm gonna stay zipped up!"

She pulled her clenched thumb and finger across her lips in a zipping motion, before continuing. "And besides, I can drink all those little boys under the table and then go around at least once more. They're never going to get the better of me!"

"Well you just watch out, they're tricky bastards!" said Terry, "Especially that Michael!"

"What, that Aussie guy?" she asked, her face all scrumpled up in confusion? "He's just a darling. We left him at the Greek party."

"Wait! What?" said Jan, jealously. "You went to the Greek party too?"

"Yeah, kinda," Ice laughed. "But it was a bit shit really. Just a lot of eating and Greek music. Nothing special."

"See Jan," said Terry, "You'd rather have been here than there, wouldn't you?" "I suppose," Jan replied, grudgingly.

"But it did pick up when that Czech girl arrived," Ice continued. "She seemed to get absolutely batshit blotto in about sixty seconds, and started smashing up all the plates. Somebody had to tell her that the owners weren't actually Greek – they were just locals who liked Greek food – and they didn't do things like that around here. But she wasn't having any of it. She had to get carried out of there by her HoD kicking and screaming after she punched the poor Greek singer right in the mouth. It was bloody hilarious!"

"See, I told you we missed a good one!" said Jan in a grump.

"But how did you get between them all so quickly?" asked Terry, puzzled.

"Well we left the Irish do just after that tiny little man child started singing," she explained. "The EuroStorm lot have got their own driver and an executive minibus, and so they took us straight to the Greek bash. But we were only there maybe twenty minutes – if that – and got here about five minutes before this old tub launched. Handy friends to have, eh!"

"I don't know where that little shit Storm gets his money from!" said Terry. "This must all be costing him a mint!"

"What, the Aussie guy?" Ice asked again.

"Actually he's from New Zealand," Terry laughed. "But keep calling him an Aussie, because he'll absolutely hate it!"

"Oh you silly little petty man," said Ice, smoothing down Terry's hair, "I love it!"

"Right, we've got to circulate and mingle now Ice," said Terry, "we'll see you on the next lap! Have you got any idea where anything is?"

"No clue," said Ice with a shrug. "Not one idea. I'm only here for the free bar and a little bit of fresh air!"

"Well don't you get too blitzed, girl," said Terry. "We've got an early start in the morning." "And precisely how long have you known me Terry?" said Ice with comedy disapproval. "Too long, Ice. Too long!" Terry surveyed the party mayhem before him, then made an announcement to his four fellow revellers "Right chaps, I'm off to show some face and slap some hand. Occupational hazard, isn't it. If any of you want to tag along, you're most welcome. Otherwise, if we get split up we can meet at the end of the gangplank when we disembark and hope that Elvis hasn't died in the night!"

"I'm game to come with," said Dean. "You can introduce me to a few important people along the way!"

"Oh, you're such a gold digger, boy," Terry laughed. "You three? You hanging or splitting?"

"I reckon I'll just stop here with Ice for a bit," said Sunny, "and then have a bit of a wander about when the entertainment starts."

"That sounds fine to me, Sunny," said Jeff. "You up for that too, Jan?"
"Yeah, I'm happy with whatever," said the Swede.

"OK then, see you all in a bit," said Terry, as he started to nudge his way into the throng.

"See that boy?" Ice whispered conspiratorially to the three remaining press lads, while thrusting a thumb in Terry's direction. "Great guy, but he just can't switch off the work mode. Stick with me and I'll show you the real party!"

As Terry and Dean pushed their way through the crowds, they were starting to get an idea of just how vast this party barge was. The upper deck was entirely devoted to an underlit dance floor with a stage at one end. The Ukrainian Eurovision performer Bohdana was due to give a full set of her stadium show up there in about a half hour, but there were already people dancing to wild Ukrainian turbo folk. On the second level it was mainly bars and a seated restaurant area, with a busy casino to one end, while below the water level was a full on night club playing nothing but Eurovision bangers. The whole vessel must have been getting on for a hundred feet long, and was absolutely throbbing with people.

Every few steps that Terry took he was met with handshakes by high ranking members of delegations, reporters, television people and other randoms who wanted to come along and say hello.

"Wow, you're quite the popular guy," said Dean, slightly in awe of his boss.

"Well, you say that, but most of them just want to keep in my good books in case they want anything from me in the future," Terry replied wearily. "But it's good to do this run around at least once every Eurovision to keep up a presence, and so that we don't look too aloof to the great unwashed."

"True," said Dean, "But it must feel nice knowing that everybody here knows who you are and what you do?"

"Blessing and a curse, Deano," said Terry. "About half of the people are genuine, and it's really great to see them once a year. But the other half are just looking for an angle and trying to work out what they can get out of you. You'll start noticing it soon, mate. Now that they've seen you out with me they'll be trying to work out who you are and whether you're important enough to talk to. Have you seen those crafty little flickers of their eyes as they look down to your accreditation pass to see who you are and what you work on?"

"Yeah, now that you mention it, they're all at it, aren't they, boss."

"Welcome to the club, young man. You're one of us now!" said Terry with a smirk at the corner of his mouth.

A loud voice came over the tannoy. "Miss Bohdana will begin her performance in ten minutes. If you could make your way to the top deck, she will soon be ready to entertain you."

"Jesus," said Dean. "If everyone rushes to the top all at once this thing could topple over!"

"Don't you worry Dean," Terry reassured his fresh young friend. "Most of the people here are only on the boat for the freebies and to be seen to be seen. They'll all make their way up eventually, but there'll be no big stampede. Having said that, we've got to work our way up there somehow as I've still got say my hellos to the Ukrainian delegation. I've not managed to see them yet this week, and they're good people."

And with that the two men began to slowly ease their way to the upper deck through the bobbing heads of the happy revellers.

To the surprise of no one, Bohdana pulled off an absolutely immense set. Cramming her entire stadium show onto a small stage on the top of a moving boat, she performed hits from throughout her entire eight album catalogue for a good hour, making use of flamethrowers, troops of Cossack dancers, holographic projections, stilt walkers, giant hamster balls, motorised pogo sticks, and of course the kitchen sink that everybody was waiting to see. And when she eventually performed her Eurovision entry Holy Cow, it was so immense and intense that many of the fans crammed up to the front of the stage passed out in sheer delight. And even as she played, people were ringing their bookies and getting on the exchanges on their smartphones to lump a tasty sum on her to win the whole contest – she was that darned good.

Terry and Dean didn't manage to push their way to the upper deck before the performance began, as so many people had wanted to shake Terry's hand and have a little chat, so the pair were waiting in the wings to receive Bohdana as she finally dragged herself off stage.

"Terry! Darling!" she cried, gently steaming in the night air after her long and energetic set. "I've not seen you since the preview party in Tel Aviv! How are you my darling?"

She dashed forward and wrapped her sweaty arms around Terry, planting a big wet kiss on both of his cheeks.

"I'm great, Bohdana. And I have to say, that was an absolutely stunning set! You're going to slay them on Thursday night. I think you're sailing through to the final with no worries."

"Oh do you think, darling?" the singer said with a gently furrowed brow. "Do you not think that maybe it's a bit too much? There's a lot of good songs in my show – and especially at the end. I'm too scared to predict what's going to happen."

"Me too," Terry replied. "But whatever the jurors think of you – and they might be divided, if I'm absolutely honest – the folks at home are going to absolutely lap you up. I reckon you're going to finish top three in that semi at the very worst. Although obviously I'm not allowed to express that kind of opinion, what with the job I'm in and all. But, y'know, I think you're safe."

"Why thank you Terry darling," Bohdana replied, looking quaintly humbled. "That's so good of you to say. I will keep my fingers crossed and the hope in my heart for Thursday then. But wait just a minute... who's your handsome friend here?"

"This fella?" said Terry, casually gesturing at Dean. "Oh he's one of my assistants. I'm just showing him the ropes with all this backstage schmoozing business. Say hello Dean."

"Hello Dean," came the reply, as the dumbstruck newcomer was bowled over by the Ukrainian performer's presence. He shook his head and continued, "Erm, I mean Bohdana! It's a pleasure to meet you. You were just amazing up there!"

"Well you're just as darling a young boy as Terry here," said Bohdana with a warm smile. "We'll have to meet up for a drink at my hotel some time!"

"Now you hold on BoBo girl," said Terry in an exaggerated voice. "Dean here bats for the same side as me. Don't you go getting too excited now!"

"Oh no, my illusions are shattered again!" the singer laughed. "One day my prince will come!"

"Not at this show he won't Bohdana," Terry chuckled, as the

Ukrainian singer made a comedy crying gesture by wringing her hands at the corners of her eyes.

"One day, Terry," she said, jokingly. "One day I'll make you mine! Right, I've got to get myself hosed down and dried off. I've got to meet the Ukrainian ambassador in a minute, and I don't want to do that smelling like a horse. See you boys! And nice to meet you Dean!"

And with that she leaned forward and planted a big sloppy kiss on Dean's forehead.

"Erm, thanks Bohdana," he stuttered, as the singer dashed off to her dressing room like a tiny whirlwind.

"Can you see why they prefer having us lot working here now, Dean?" said Terry. "Those straight lads would be falling aimlessly in love at the slightest sniff of a backing singer's perfumed sleeve."

"Oh, I don't know, Terry," Dean laughed. "I think she's got me on the turn!"

Suddenly there was a commotion over towards the back of the dance floor. Jolana Nováková, the Czech singer, had climbed onto the roof of the boat's bridge, and was loudly singing her own competing song. Below her were a small crowd of people throwing beermats at her, and a member of the captain's crew was trying to coax her down before she hurt herself.

"I'm better than any of you!" she yelled, as her HoD stood beneath her with his head in his hands, looking like this was the worst day of his life. Again. "And I'll fight every last one of you!"

At this precise moment, the boat had started to pass the floating hotels that many of the press and fans were staying in. The window of one of the rooms flew open and an angry voice blasted out of the darkness.

"Shut up you screeching Czech whore," it yelled gracelessly. "Your song's shit, you're shit, and I'm trying to get some sleep. Thank God you're going home on Tuesday!"

Jolana was briefly stunned to silence. Her jaw jutted out defensively and she began to breath heavily as if in distress.

"Why you dirty little nobody bastard," she yelled. "I'm coming over there to teach you a lesson. A lesson in pain!"

And with that she ran the short three or four steps to the edge of the bridge's roof, took a massive leap, and sprung right off the boat and into the river, effecting a perfect swan dive as she went. She hit the water leaving hardly a spash, and everyone watching held their breath for a terrifyingly long seven or eight seconds until she appeared again at the surface of the water, some yards away.

"Oh thank heavens for that," sighed Terry. "We've never lost one before. I thought we were going to break our duck there!"

"There's still time," said Dean. "She's wearing a pretty elaborate frock and some massive boots, after all. And she was really, really hammered."

"I believe that she trained as an Olympic standard swimmer when she was a girl," said a nerdy voice from behind. "I think that she will be quite alright."

And sure enough she was. She swam the short distance to the hotel boat with consummate ease, but it was only when she attempted to scale the side of the floatel that she started to get into difficulties. The captain hammered his fist into the emergency warning siren and yelled to his crew to get the lifeboat out. It probably took a full twenty minutes to get the lifeboat into the water and prise Jolana's vice-like grip from the bottom of the lowest balcony of the accommodation boat.

"Don't touch me!" she shouted angrily, as one of the disco boat's crew tried to help her into the boat, before she loosened her grip and fell flat on her back into the rescue vessel. "And don't think that I don't know who you are, scum!" she shouted, pointing roughly to where the mocking voice had come from on the hotel boat. "I'm coming to get you as soon as I get out of this fix!" And with that, she fell soundly asleep in the arms of one of the crew men.

"Every bloody night," sighed the Czech head of delegation. "Every bloody night!"

"You're going to have to keep her off the pop, mate," said Terry to the beleaguered television executive.

"We've tried, Terry. Really we've tried. But she just keeps finding it somewhere. It's a damn shame, because when she's sober she's one of the most delightful human beings that I've ever worked with. But give her the sniff of a bottle and it's like pulling the demon's tail. I'm not sure how we're going to get through this, really I don't."

"Well best of luck with it all," said Terry, sympathetically.

"I'm going to need it," said the tired looking Czech. "I'm really going to need it."

"The problem we have now, Dean," Terry explained, "is that the Israeli party is due to start right about now, but nearly everybody who's likely to be going is currently trapped on this boat, and after the delay we've just had, it could be at least an hour until we all get there. I tell you mate, the people who run it are not going to be best pleased..."

A couple of miles up river, the organisers of the Israeli delegation party were standing at the big doors to the venue, anxiously looking at their watches.

"They're usually queuing around the block by now," said Shani Applebaum as she urgently checked her social media for updates. "I don't know where they could all be?"

"It beats the hell out of me," replied her business partner David Boim as he turned to look back in the hall. "The place is still practically empty, Shani. They're usually swinging from the rafters by now. All we've got in the so far are the local Jewish dignitaries – which to be honest is a much smaller group than we're used to – then half-a-dozen bored-looking Mossad agents trying to blend in, and a lot of heavy looking Russian guys just staring at the food counter, waiting for it to open.

Shall we let them have a nibble?"

"No, there'll be none left for the artists!" snapped Shani. "You know what that lot can be like at a free buffet. They just hoover it up!"

"Do we have any idea where everyone is though?" David asked. "This is an unprecedented occurrence."

Shani and David had been organising the Israeli delegation party for the last five years, and they were usually the hottest ticket in the Eurovision schedule. Great ambience, incredible food, untold freebies and goodie bags, and a flood of performances from that given year's competing artists, and well as a few guest appearances from Israeli performers of the past. But the only one of this year's acts that was anywhere to be seen right now was Vikingur from Iceland sitting by himself on a chair at the back of the room, still in his dog costume, and looking like he'd been abandoned by his delegation.

The Israeli broadcaster always threw a lot of money at their party every year, and it was always a resounding success in the main. But they were generally cursed by one major incident each time, be it exploding electricity generators plunging the room into soundless darkness for forty minutes, or the rogue DJ who decided to start mixing all the Eurovision songs into one messy bootleg session that nearly caused a riot last year. There was even a time when all the security locks kicked in when there was still a hefty queue snaking around the building, and nobody could get in or out of the place until around daybreak. But whatever happened, people always came. And in their droves. So this was something of a mystery to them all.

David's phone rang in his pocket, and he was so quick in pulling it out that he lost his grip and started hamfistedly juggling it above his head. "Phone call! Phone call!" he shouted in a panic. "It's going to be good news, I know it!"

"Calm yourself man and get a grip on the damn thing!" Shani mocked.

"Got it! Got it!" he cried in triumphal delight as he finally brought the phone under control and thrust it to his ear.

"Yes? Yes? How splendid!" he said with some excitement. "Yes, we'll be waiting to receive you. See you in a bit!"

"Who was that?" Shani asked seriously.

"It's the Finns," David replied. "The reckon their party's ended a bit early, and they want to know if they can come over and play a little set? They've got the Aussies and the Norwegians with them, plus all their party goers, too. They're heading this way now."

"Oh great," Shani replied, sarcastically. "First we've got nobody, and then we've got nothing but Finnish troll boys, Aussie piss heads and Norwegian fascists coming our way. Plus that canine freak sat in the corner there. We're going to scare off the small few people that we've got here at that rate."

"Oh I don't know," said David, enthusiastically. "If we start the night with a bit of authentic rock music it'll give us a bit of cred, surely?

Then we can build up to all the tasty club bangers later!"

"This isn't bloody Download, you great nit!" Shani barked at her partner. "It's a bloody Eurovision party. We can't be having all that noisy nonsense going on?"

At that moment, Shani's phone gave an insistent ring. She went calmly to her pocket and picked it out, casting David a dark gaze that said "See, not everybody is a phone cretin like you," and then answered it.

"Hello, Shani speaking. Yes. What? Oh how terrible? But she's alright though? Oh that's a relief. I take it that she won't be playing tonight though? Yes. Yes. Probably for the best. How long do you reckon? About half an hour? Good, good, we'll be ready for you. Yes thanks. See you soon!"

David stared at her for a couple of seconds, before plucking up the courage to speak. "That all sounded a bit serious," he said, nervously. "What's happened there then?" Shani took a deep breath and started to explain.

"That was our singer Uriella. She was on the Ukrainian boat party. She reckons that the Czech artist fell overboard and they had to stop and rescue her. I'd have just left the drunken bitch to drown if it was me. Anyway, they're just pulling up to the jetty now. Once they've loaded everyone onto the buses they should be here in about thirty minutes. All being well. Why does this always happen, David?"

I don't know, Shani, but it is uncanny how the bad luck always seems to follow us. Shall I go in and alert the DJ?"

"Yes David, good plan," Shani replied, now a little calmer in her manner. "You go and tell him to line up the backing tracks for the noisier acts, and hopefully they'll be here and done by the time the party buses arrive. We can even let that dog bloke have a go if they've not arrived yet. At least it'll keep the Mossad boys amused."

"Right you are," David said, chirpily, "See you in a bit."

And with that he skipped off across the cavernous dancehall. To the left of him, the girls running the Dead Sea Mud beauty products stall were looking bored and picking at their nails, and to the right the massed tables of free falafel were slowly going stale. In front of the stage a solitary pensioner was dancing to seventies Israeli Eurovision entries while half a dozen blue and white balloons just tumbled lazily around on the floor behind him. "The buses will arrive soon, and it'll all kick off lovely," thought David hopefully as he made his way to the DJ booth.

19

The next morning in the press office, Terry and Dean greeted a bleary-eyed Jeff and he stumbled in through the door.

"You hung around at the Israeli party then I see?" Terry enquired. "I just didn't have the stomach for it after all that boat business. Did it go on long?"

"I think it's still going on now, to be honest with you," Jeff replied. "It all kicked off so late that they still had dozens of acts left to do their turns, and some of them steadfastly refused to leave before they'd performed. When we got there that Aussie band were playing, and they were going mental, throwing half-full cans of beer everywhere. I heard that one of them knocked the little Irish lad clean out!"

"Oh the poor little sod," said Dean. "He really didn't have the best night of it."

"He's alright though," Jeff continued. "He got up with a smile and just carried on dancing."

"I just don't know why these acts have their parties the night before their rehearsals," Terry said, shaking his head. "Surely it's going to be bad for their performers?"

"Oh the Israeli girl did a little intro piece as soon as she arrived," said Jeff. "Mimed along to a couple of her songs, and was out of there not much past midnight. I'm sure she'll be right as rain."

"Glad to hear it," said Terry. "They're not silly, that delegation." "Any word on the Czech lass?" asked Jeff.

"Yes, I gave her HoD a call this morning," Terry explained. "Apparently she was practically in a coma until they got her up to her room. The hotel staff thought Juri was dragging a dead body into the building, she was that sparko. Anyway, they plonked her onto her bed, and she woke up with a start, sober as a judge and wondering why her hair was all wet. She's a strange one, that Jolana. We're going to have to keep a serious eye on her. I'm terrified of what she's likely to pull at the opening party if she gets any booze in her!"

He stopped for a moment to ponder the horrors that may lay ahead, before he snapped out of it and asked: "Actually, anyone seen Jan and Sunny?"

"Yeah, they were still going strong at the Israeli party last I looked," said Jeff. "Can't see them getting in much before noon."

"Well, it's their first Eurovision after all," said Terry, remaining strangely cool about the whole thing, "and we've all done it. I'll give them a free pass – this time. But don't you go getting any funny ideas, Deano!"

"I'll be good as gold!" Dean laughed.

"Right then, we've got one heck of a day ahead," said Terry, suddenly turning to business. "The last seven songs are all credible contenders to win this thing, and most of them have got ridiculous staging. And on top of that, some fool decided to not only draw Armenia and Azerbaijan right next to each other, but bloody Russia and Ukraine too. It's going to be an absolute bloodbath out there. I think our Filip was only thinking about the songs rather than the potential politics when he made the draw, but it's really not ideal. So we're all on double shifts until the waifs and strays of the press office finally drag their sorry behinds out of their pits. You good with that, fellas?"

"Yeah, we're good," said Dean and Jeff, keenly.

"Right, let's get on with it!" Terry announced purposefully.

On the other side of the arena, Filip was deep in discussion with Hanna and Ice from the stage crew.

"Right ladies, we're in for a bit of a tough one today. Everybody except Macedonia and the Dutch lady have got tons of props, and we don't want to have too many long shots from the back of the hall or chats with the green room while we sort out the log jams getting them on and off stage. But knowing you two I assume you're well on top of it?" he asked.

"Definitely, Filip," Hanna replied. "Me and Ice went over the drills when we were doing the stand-in rehearsals last week, and I think we've identified where all the major pinch points are likely to be."

"And don't forget, pay special attention to the transitions between both Azerbaijan and Armenia AND Ukraine and Russia," Filip added. "We don't want either of those pairings kicking off. So keep them apart in the stage queue, and make sure that one act is totally off stage before you bring the other one on. We don't want any dirty tricks or foul play going on – you just know at least one of that bunch is going to try to pull something."

"We've got that all accounted for, too," Ice added. "The costume check squad are going to hold Armenia and Russia back just that little bit longer, and the mic monkeys are going to rush the Azeris and the Ukrainians through more quickly than they usually would. It'll still be tricky on Thursday night, but we'll drape a big curtain between them if we have to. They're all new to this, so they won't know any different."

"Good, good," said Filip. "That's all very encouraging. So run me through all today's transitions again one more time, just so that we're clear."

"Great, so," said Hanna, steeling herself for a long explanation.

"Macedonia are easy. Just two kids with guitars, a park bench and a couple of backing singers. Just what we need after that Kazakh horse monster thing."

"Another bloody park bench?" said Filip, shaking his head disappointedly. "How many more of those are we going to have at this thing?"

"Suits us, Filip," said Hanna, " as they're a really simple on and off. Next comes Israel. They've got a fuck tonne of candlesticks scattered all over the stage. Easy enough, but we've got to make sure that we don't forget any. The Dutch are simple. Just Lieke up the front and a rank of five support singers at the back. Meat and potatoes for us. But then the crazy times start."

"Oh dear, what do we have to look forward to then?" Filip asked with a furrowed brow.

"Well now," Hanna continued, "the Azeris have gone for a campfire theme. The video screens at the back do most of the heavy lifting, but he's got huge great boulders, a big tent and a whole lot of actual sand. It's on a mat, but it could still keep the broom boys busy getting any stray grains off stage afterward. The Armenians on the other hand have gone full disco, with massive great scaffolding towers at the back for the dancers to gyrate on."

"Why do we still let them do this?" Filip asked. "It gets more extreme every year!"

"I dunno, Filip," laughed Ice. "That's your department. Put something in place for next year!" "I think I'm going to have to, Ice," he replied. "These people are just taking the piss now."

"So!" said Hanna, getting the conversation back to the point. "Those pesky Swedes have chosen to have their speciality moving walkways and independent lighting rigs again, curse them. But at least they're on wheels and an easy mark. Getting them back down the off ramp safely is going to be the issue here – especially as Ukraine are bringing a full bloody stadium show set up on stage with them."

"How so?" Filip asked.

"Big tall drum risers, guitarists on plinths, fire boxes, massive spinning cogs and that bloody kitchen sink at the back!" she replied. "It looks a bit stupid sat there on stage for the whole song before she eventually uses it at the end."

"I think the cameras are going to take care of that, keeping it out of sight of the viewers at home," Filip reasoned. "But I'll go and have a check with them just in case."

"Now we're onto the home straight," Hanna continued. "Russia are bringing a full bloody mountain onto the stage. And there's even a waterfall for young Gennady to gyrate under at the end. It'll be a huge pain in the arse, but luckily it comes in six separate parts, so hopefully we'll be able to just wheel it on and click the bits into place. You know what their people are like with the props, though. They'll be stood behind us and barking instructions into our ears for the first couple of run throughs – and you know how much my crew enjoy that!"

"Yes Hanna, that's never ideal," said Filip, sympathetically. "So how about those Australians to finish with?"

"Well it's good and bad, Filip," Hanna noted. "They're bringing a big wooden beer bar and a stand up toilet onto the stage. But again, they're on wheels, so if we've got the Russians nicely off and away it shouldn't be too much of a problem. Bless them though. They gave me a call last week and said that they were happy to help us wheel the things on themselves. No one's ever asked us if they could do that before."

"Perhaps they're not as dangerous as they look after all," Filip laughed.

"Oh they're famous for being a great bunch of lads with the stage crews," said Hanna. "They can just get a bit rowdy afterwards!"

"Yeah, and you've got to hope that they're not bringing any tinnies onto the stage with them," Ice laughed. "They peppered the crowd with them last night at the Israeli do. Nearly hospitalised the Irish lad, they did."

"I heard!" laughed Filip.

"Ooh, have you seen inside the bar though, Ice?" Hanna asked nervously. "It's absolutely chock full of cans!"

"Oh my," said Filip. "I'm going to have to have a word with them. Health and safety are going to go rural if they find out about that!"

"Good luck with that, mate!" Hanna laughed. "Have you ever tried to get between an Australian and his beer?"

"Ha, yes, good point." said Filip. "I'll be my usual diplomatic self. Right then, it looks like we're well on top of things. Let's get this show on the road!"

"Aye aye captain!" said Hanna and Ice, saluting Filip as if he was a pirate king.

"Oh don't take the piss you two," he laughed as he walked out of the door towards the arena.

Sure enough, the morning session went swimmingly. The first three acts just flew by as if their shows were on rails, and somebody had the bright idea of moving the lunch break to between the Azeri and Armenian rehearsals, which kept the rival nations apart for at least another day. After lunch, the Armenians and the Swedes got through their stints with little incident, too, although the Swedish singer Ebba did manage to fall off her travelator a couple of times, banging her head quite firmly on the hard stage floor on the second occasion.

"We'll really have to put some soft mats around those moving walkways," Filip said to Terry from the balcony. "I don't want anybody cracking their skull open on live TV on my first watch."

"You'd better give Ice a shout, Filip," Said Terry. "She's got all sorts of stuff like that sitting under the stage just in case we need it. But from what I hear about the Swedish girl she's notoriously clumsy – perhaps we'd better give her a crash helmet instead!"

"What, with that frock?" mocked Filip. "It'll clash terribly, darling!"

But now it came to the complicated final threesome, made even more difficult by the close proximity of those sworn rivals Ukraine and Russia.

"Don't worry too much about getting these on, Filip," Terry said, reassuringly, "I was chatting to Bohdana last night on the boat, and her whole operation is like a slick machine. It's getting her back off again before the Russians start to set up that's my biggest worry. We don't want to encourage an international incident now, do we."

"That's my biggest concern," Filip said anxiously. "That's why I'm out of the office watching it all right now. There could be all kinds of trouble with that changeover."

True to Terry's word, the Ukrainian staging slid on stage an into place as quick as a flash, and Bohdana herself looked like a dream to work with.

"As long as you let her flirt with you she'll be putty in the crew's hands," Terry noted of the Ukrainian performer."

"Ha! Ice will be in her element, then," Filip smirked.

Bohdana had her first run through and she breezed through it like a dream. Even the much feared kitchen sink moment looked incredible on the big screens. Her next two goes were near to perfect as well. It wasn't until her fourth and final performance that things began to get a little complicated.

"Stop! Stop!" Bohdana cried with a pained expression on her face just as the song's introduction was about to finish. "I can hear some terrible noises in my ear piece. Can any of you hear that out there?"

The crew all looked around at each other and shrugged. Up in the sound gantry, Skunk was twiddling a few knobs and called down to Hanna at the side of the stage.

"Nothing untoward up here, mate. All the channels are clean. Must be some kind of local interference in her monitor. Check with the mic monkeys stage side."

"Nope, we're good too," the mic crew responded on the radio. "It must be her ear piece. We'll switch it out for another one."

They quickly dashed on stage to change Bohdana's in ear monitor, and dashed off again just as fast.

"All good Bohdana?" Hanna asked the Ukrainian singer.

"Yes, that's much much better," she replied. "I think I can start now."

"And three-two-one... music please..." Hanna ordered over the monitor as she slowly walked backwards off the stage.

"The song's introduction began again, and just at the moment where Bohdana was going to sing, a flash of pain darted across her eyes and she held her hand up, in some apparent discomfort.

"No! No! It's back again!" she snapped angrily. "I think somebody is trying to sabotage me!" Filip looked concerned and quickly got onto his radio.

"Yes, cut the feed to the press hall," he said into the microphone, "We can't have that baying mob speculating over what's going on."

"What do you think's happening?" Terry asked, puzzled.

"It could be one of two things, I reckon," Filip replied. "One: she genuinely is having problems with her monitor. And if she is, we've got to hope that it's not the Russians trying to put her off by jamming her signal or anything like that. I'll get Håkan to have a look and see if there's anyone with any suspicious looking kit."

"What's the second, Filip?" asked Terry.

"Well in a way that's almost worse," said Filip. "How do you mean?" Terry asked.
"Well I've got a horrible feeling that she's swinging the lead and causing a deliberate distraction to try to annoy the Russians," said Filip with a doleful look on his face. "Everyone tends to err on the side of the Ukrainians in these matters, so it's a win-win for them. They'll get sympathy for being the perceived put upon party, and they get to make the Russians look bad while they're at it. But of course, it won't end well. Because even if the Russians are the innocent ones in all this, you can be damn sure that they'll find a way to get back at the Ukrainians somewhere further down the line. And whatever they do it'll probably make our lives even more difficult."

"What's your hunch, Filip? Who do you think is to blame?" said Terry.

"I wouldn't like to hazard a guess," Filip answered. "With their recent track records they could both be up to something. It is a bit suspicious though that they had three completely clean run throughs before all this happened."

"Yes, but that could be double bluff on the part of the Russians, surely?" Terry posited.

"I wouldn't bloody put it past them," Filip sighed. "Right then, I'll get Håkan on the radio, and you see if any of your boys on the ground are picking up any sniffs of info about what's going on."

Filip put the radio to his ear and switched to Håkan's private frequency. "Hawkman, are you seeing this?" he asked.

"I'm ahead of you Filip," the gruff voice replied. "I'm just heading down there now to have a bit of a nose about. I'll let you know if it looks like anything dodgy is happening."

"Right you are, Håkan," said Filip as he called off.

"I'm getting no word of any news from the boys," said Terry, eagerly. "This really is all a bit of a puzzle?"

"And of course, we can't accuse either of them of anything," said Filip wearily. "We could kick off a full scale war – in every sense of the word. We've got to play this one very tactically."

On stage, the mic crew were trying one last earpiece from the emergency box, and set it to a new frequency, just to be extra sure.

"Right then Bohdana ma'am, you try that one," one of the crew asked her. "It should be as good as gold."

"To be honest young man," she said with a cautious look on her face,

"I'm a bit scared to. What if that horrible noise comes back?"

"Well if it does, just put your hand straight up and we'll cut it out immediately." "I'll try, young man," said Bohdana. "I'll try."

Meanwhile, Håkan was back from his quick recce around the performance area and got back to Filip.

"Nothing too much to report mate," he said. "There were a couple of shifty looking Russians sitting a few rows back in the stalls, but I fixed them with one of my hard stares and they got up and left. I hope that they weren't anyone important."

"Ha! Good work, Hawkman!" said Filip, "I guess we'll see if this last run through goes according to plan."

"Fingers crossed mate!" came the gravelly voice down the radio.

"Is everybody ready and standing at their correct mark?" Hanna said, perhaps a little impatiently. "Yes? Good. Music!"

The introduction music began, and everyone in the room held their breath. On stage, Bohdana was visibly bracing herself for some in-ear pain, but it never came. Looking surprised, she launched into her elaborate song and completed it note perfectly.

"Damn, that's a relief," said Terry. "I thought we were never going to get that one finished with and get the Russians on!"

"Yes, but I still don't like it," said Filip. "We're still none the wiser. Did Håkan actually scare off some Russian marauders from the seats down there? Or were they even Russians at all? They weren't noticeably carrying any kind of jamming device either. Then on the other hand, did Bohdana realise that she couldn't push her luck any more and just got on with it? Or was there actually a genuine issue with the kit? At least we can get the sound crew to run tests on everything tonight to check that it won't happen again. But I get the most horrible feeling that we're going to get complaints in from both side of this scrap here. And I'm really not sure which way we ought to play it."

True to his predictions, both delegations did put in formal complaints against each other. Ukraine claimed that Russia were somehow jamming Bohdana's monitoring signal, causing her great physical discomfort, while Russia suggested that she was just faking it to try and make them look bad to the international community. And from the CTF's point of view it was impossible to prove or disprove either way. Was it all just another game in Russia's hybrid war with anyone who cared to fall for it? Or were Ukraine just being crafty and trying to join in with the silly mind games? Either way, Filip didn't want any part of it, so demanded that each respective Head of Delegation was ushered to his office first thing the next morning.

The Russian HoD was Kazimir Starsev, a wily old fox who'd been in this role for nine years now, and was also rumoured to have connections with the Russian secret services. His Ukrainian counterpart was Sasha Yaremchuk, a brash young TV executive who was just making a name for himself in his nation's light entertainment scene. Filip could see that this was going to be a complicated game of blame chess, so thought it best to demand that both men came to his office at the same time so that he could give them each a stern warning at the same time and not show favour to one or the other – much to each delegation's disapproval.

"I will not be in the same room as this young upstart who is accusing the most innocent Russian delegation of such terrible things," Kazimir stated as his opening gambit as he walked into the room.

"I'm afraid that your complaint will be instantly nullified if you refuse to take part in this meeting, Kazimir," said Filip starting with a cool hand. "And you wouldn't want your grievances to go unheard now, would you?"

Kazimir realised that he was up against a worthy opponent, so conceded the first point with very little protest. There was a knock at the door and Sasha entered, instantly flying into a minor rage.

"I told you, Fillip," the Ukrainian barked sternly, "I refuse to be in the same room as this... this... thing."

"Hello Sasha," said the Russian. "Very good to see you, my friend. Sit down... we can talk this over."

Sasha flew into even more of a rage, and Filip, seeing that this meeting could quickly get out of hand, urged Sasha to sit.

"I'll tell you what I've just told Kazimir," he said, coldly. "No joint meeting, no complaint."

Sasha pulled a grudging face and threw himself into the chair on the opposite side of the table to Kazimir.

"So gentlemen," said Filip, "I've called you both here today to attempt to sort out this little disagreement between you."

"It is not a disagreement," shouted Sasha. "His delegation quite distinctly tried to sabotage our performance with some electronic trickery. I don't know HOW they did it, but I do know that they DID do it!"

"How?" said Kazimir, calmly. "Show me your proof. You've got nothing, because nothing happened. You're just trying to gain sympathy with the gullible Western Europeans. But we're not going to play any of your childish little games."

"Little games?" said Sasha, leaping from his chair and banging both fists on the table. "I'll show you little games!"

"As you wish, Sasha," the Russian mocked, sneering at his opponent from his chair. Filip knew that he had to step in immediately or the meeting would be beyond repair.

"Gentlemen! Gentlemen!" he assertively cut in. "We can look at this three ways. Either you did it…"

He pointed his pen towards Kazimir, who nodded back with a deadpan expression. "Or you did it…" gesturing towards Sasha.

"Wait! No!" the younger man cried, before Filip held up his hand to calm matters down again.

"Or the third, most likely explanation to my eye, is that it was a completely coincidental technical issue, and one that we can get ironed out before your next rehearsal, Sasha."

"But no! Wait! It was them," Sasha said in a fluster.

"So. Here's what we do," Filip continued. "I can't prove it was you, and I can't prove it was you, either. So for the sanctity of this contest, let's just say that I'm right on this occasion and we shall go on as we were."

"That sounds like a very agreeable solution," Kazimir conceded. "Awww! Damn! Yes, I suppose so," stuttered Sasha. "I suppose so." "And," continued Filip, "if anything of the kind happens again, or there are any more of these 'coincidences', I shall take steps to sanction you both in not only this contest, but for the next three years as well. Now how does that sound to you, gentlemen."

Kazimir knew that he's been beaten by a better man – on this occasion at least – and gave a grudging approval of the scheme.

"Yes, I think that this is a very reasonable solution," he said. "I think my delegation can work with that."

"And you, Sasha," Filip asked.

Sasha was very well aware that he'd been painted into a corner, and partially of his own doing, too. But despite what he considered to be his better judgement, he also agreed with the plan.

"Hmm, well, yes, I suppose," he said. "But if anything like this happens again. Anything. Then I'm making sure I put in another formal complaint, and be damned with the consequences."

"Well let's just make sure that nothing of the kind happens again then gentlemen. Both of you." said Filip, calmly.

"Yes OK, I'm good with that," said Sasha standing and walking to the door. "I'm going to have to be. Now, if you'll excuse me, I have people to call."

"I shouldn't wonder," said Kazimir with an impish smirk.

Sasha stormed out of the room without another word, being sure to slam the door angrily behind him.

"You play a very good game of chess, Mr Ivanović," Kazimir said to Filip once he could be sure that his Ukrainian adversary was well out of earshot. "You should maybe consider joining your fine Serbian nation's diplomatic department. You'd have a great future ahead of you."

Filip smiled one of those smiles that you make when you know you're being professionally flattered.

"Oh you're too kind, Mr Starsev," he replied. "But I'm quite happy where I am, thank you very much.

Even on days like these."

Kazimir gave him a knowing nod, stood up and offered his hand to Filip. "Thank you for a most interesting meeting, Mr Ivanović. I hope that the next time we meet it will be in more, how should we say, relaxed circumstances."

"Oh I'm quite sure that it will be, Mr Starsev," replied Filip. "I'm quite sure that it will."

And with that, Kazimir shook Filip firmly by the hand, gave another knowing nod, and left the room. Filip slumped into his chair and let our a massive, relieved sigh.

"How in the name of hell did I just get away with that?!" he said to himself, shaking his head as he poured another cup of extra strong coffee.

20

With the first round of semi-final rehearsals out of the way, things began to get a little easier. The tech crew knew which songs were going to be simple and which were going to be complicated, so could plan accordingly, while Filip and the people from the CTF were now aware of who was going to be easy to work with and who they had to treat with kid gloves in order to keep the show flowing nicely. And with only the big six pre-qualifiers yet to arrive, 86% percent of the acts already had at least one solid performance under their belts and in the can. So if the worst came to the worst they could piece together a couple of semi-finals out of rehearsal clips. But everybody was pretty confident by now that it was never going to come to that.

As is traditional, the second round of rehearsals flew by with scarcely an issue. The Austrian lad had a bit of a hissy fit on the Thursday when his firework curtain refused to work at the end of his song, and the Lithuanian kids seemed even at odds with each other than they were before. With the rehearsals now condensed to run more songs in a day, the Saudi Prince finally turned up, but stood in the wings chattering about the lights for most of their rehearsal slot, then walked on stage to give a single word perfect performance of the song, before dashing off the moment the song had finished in one of a fleet of Range Rovers that he had parked by the loading bay of the arena.

Filip had rather smartly rearranged the commercial break slot to go in between Norway and Denmark, just to save the former from harassing the latter any more than is necessary. The Norwegian death metallers Stormgiver also deigned to give a press conference, but just sat there on their big thrones refusing to answer any questions that weren't about ancient Norse mythology or the true power of heavy metal. Unsurprisingly it didn't last long. They did however cause a bit of a stir when their head of press walked to the side of the stage carrying a large wooden box. Many of the crowd, thinking that the big container was harbouring a selection of valuable promotional CDs, stampeded over to where he was standing, only to discover that it was a box of dead nightingales, their feet and beaks bound by elaborately tied knots of willow bark. The same crowd who dashed to the front, quickly recoiled in horror as the stench of death flew out of the box and up into their nostrils. The press agent then began flinging them into the press conference crowd, causing anguished screams whenever one fell into somebody's unsuspecting lap. Hermóðr Heimdall just sat on his throne surveying the madness before him and laughing a deep, throaty, imperious laugh. But despite the somewhat ghoulish situation, there were still three of the poor dead birds up for sale on eBay for extortionate prices before the hour was out.

After that, the only remarkable things that happened were that the handsome young Estonian singer changed his suit – from a dark glittery black to an insipid shade of powder blue; Malta got through her slot without being accosted by the Czech singer; and Finland, as promised, declined to hang their dwarf. But they did have him acting as a butler throughout their performance, serving them drinks on a little tray crafted from the end of a log.

"They've got that idea from bloody Euroclub, haven't they Terry!" said Filip to his colleague up on the balcony.

"For the first day this week things have gone as easily as we'd hoped," Terry replied, "well apart from the Norwegian nightingale incident, obviously, but I'm sure you're going to have a word with them about that, aren't you?"

"I almost don't like to," said Filip. "We seem to have found them in a good place today – I even thought I saw the drummer smiling once. I guess we kind of have to say something, but more just to ask them politely not to do it again."

"Yeah, good luck with that mate," Terry scoffed.

"I know, right!" Filip replied, in mock horror, before changing the subject and clicking into business mode. "Right, that's another day over and done with. But tomorrow's the big one. The big five have finally arrived, and we've got Maxim giving us his first run through too – as well as all the rest of the pure insanity at the tag end of semi 2. We're going to start early and stay late tomorrow, so make sure that all of your team are primed and fresh and ready to go. We've got to be on top of this from the word go. Thank heavens we've got that dreary tune from Croatia on first to kick the day off. One singer, a backdrop, and absolutely no controversy. It's going to be like a dream considering the absolute mayhem we've got to follow. You ready for it, Terry?"

"I'm ready boss!"

"Right then, I'm off down to have a word with the Norwegians about nightingale-gate. Have we got the stench of death out of the press conference hall yet?

"Not yet, Filip. The essence of dead bird is proving tricky to shift," Terry laughed.

"Wish me luck, Terry mate," said Filip. "And if I'm gone too long, send out a search party!"

Filip puffed his cheeks and headed down to Stormgiver's dressing room. He'd had a chat in advance with Egil their HoD, and despite having finished their rehearsal stint some hours ago, the band were still camped out backstage. He nervously tapped on the door, and Hermóðr Heimdall's big booming voice once again bellowed "ENTER!". As Filip opened the door, he could scarcely believe his eyes. The Czech singer Jolana Nováková was tied to a table, stark naked, while the Saudi Sammarinese backing singers were circling around her, tipping red liquid out of goblets onto her exposed flesh.

"More wine! More wine!" she yelled lustily as the Saudi men, still in their clean white stage outfits, circled ever quicker to the sound of some old Norwegian folk music.

Filip blinked hard, twice, just to be sure that he was really seeing what he thought he was seeing.

"Welcome to our little rehearsal after party, Filip!" Hermóðr declared from his throne. "Would you like some bull's blood wine? It's got real bull's blood in it!"

"Er, no... thanks. I'm still working, Mr Heimdall sir," Filip stuttered anxiously. "I've just come to ask about those nightingales. You're not going to pul that kind of stunt in the live shows are you?"

"Unfamiliar with the stench of death are you, Filip?" Hermóðr said, finishing his words with a big cackling laugh.

"Well there is that, Mr Heimdall," but we've also got a very serious rule that there must be no livestock on stage – alive or dead – and contravention of this rule would lead to an instant disqualification if it were to happen."

"Fear not, Mr Ivanović," the Norwegian singer boomed. "This was naught but a mere gesture for the hounds of the press. A gesture to symbolise how you... the CTF... threatened to stop the nightingale... us... from singing our beautiful song. The nightingale has been silenced, but she will still be very much noticed on Tuesday evening. Do you understand, Mr Ivanović?"

"Erm, yes, I think I do," Filip, looking a little confused. "Possibly. So I have your absolute assurance that nothing that has formerly lived will be flung into the audience on Tuesday night on live international television?"

"You have my absolute assurance," Hermóðr replied. "Here, let us strike a blood oath!"

He again whipped a long, broad knife decorated in ancient runes out from his calf-length boot and prepared to draw the blade across his upturned palm."

"No, no," said Filip with a start, "that still won't be necessary. Your solemn word is more than good enough for me."

"So be it," said Hermóðr, sliding the knife carefully back into his footwear. "Until the next time we meet, then. May your journey be a restful one."

"Erm, yes, Hermóðr," said Filip, edging his way towards the door. "And yours too. I really must be going."

Just as he was about to leave this most unexpected of tableaus, a woman's voice burst out from the centre of the room.

"Filly baby," Jolana Nováková said seductively, "Come and lick some hot blood wine off my hot blooded body!"

"Erm, it's very kind of you to offer, Miss Nováková," said Filip, grabbing for the door handle. "Really it is. But I've got to go and sort out an issue with the staff catering. Another time maybe..."

He burst out into the light of the corridor and took a deep breath. He really didn't want to go back into that dressing room ever again if he could absolutely help it.

That evening, at his ranch on the edge of the city, Maxim Munteanu was making his final preparations for tomorrow's rehearsals.

"How many bits and bobs do you think I'll need to take, Michi lad," the old man asked. "What are they going to need from me?"

"Ooh, I don't know, Michi replied, "not too much I wouldn't have thought. I'd say the outfit that you're going to wear on stage, another change of smart clothes in case you have to do any kind of press calls afterwards, your medication, obviously, and anything you want to take along to make your dressing room look a little more homely."

"What about snacks and things like that?" Maxim pondered.

"Don't worry, they've got it all covered there Maxim," said Evgeny, his personal security man and driver. "Like they always do at the big shows."

"Yes yes, of course," said Maxim. "Oh, one more thing... I'm going to need my stage clothes, aren't I?"

Michi threw Evgeny a worried glance before the bigger man replied: "It's all been taken care of, Maxim. You have nothing left to worry about."

"Oh good, good," said Maxim. "Well I'll just make a last little trip down the corridor, as it were, and I'll think about heading off early to bed to get myself a good night's sleep. I'll need all my energy for tomorrow!"

Once he'd heard the bathroom door firmly slam shut, Michi walked towards Evgeny and quietly asked: "Is he quite alright? It's just... he seems a little muddled."

"Well, yes. And it is a bit of a worry, I must confess," said Evgeny.

"He usually gets a little bit stressed before a big show, but never quite this confused. I'm really concerned that the pressure of this whole thing had been getting to him. He's barely touched much more than a morsel of food all week, and his sleep cycle is all over the place. I really think that we need to get his regular doctor on standby at the venue, just in case anything happens. He can be a stubborn old goat, as you're beginning to learn, and he'll probably refuse to see anyone but his own physician. I'll give him a discrete call now and get him on standby for the next couple of days."

"I think that's wise," said Michi. "And do you think he'll be up for all that hectic press stuff afterwards tomorrow?"

"I reckon we'd best play that one by ear, Michi," said Evgeny. "Just monitor him all day and see if he'll be strong enough for it. But you know how he can be. He'll just flat out refuse to admit that he's not up to it and then wipe himself out answering questions and giving selfies to anyone who asks him. He's just physically unable to let down his fans. We've really got to try to steer him away from all of that – quite subtly, of course – or the old man might not make it until next weekend."

"Oh yes, we really don't want that to happen," said the younger man, anxiously, remembering Maxim's pledge that Michi would have to take his place on the show if anything happened that would keep him from performing.

The two men could hear the sound of flowing water from down the corridor, and Michi and Evgeny curtailed their little chat and readied themselves for Maxim's return.

"What were you chaps furiously whispering about just there?" Maxim asked. "I might be old, but my hearing's still in good working order."

"Oh we were just talking about the football," said Evgeny, quick as a flash. "Michi here is a Zimbru fan, but I'm strictly Politehnica! Come on you Machines!"

"Oh, the beautiful game, is it," Maxim replied, gleefully. "Well you know that I'm a Tiraspol boy at heart. But since my beloved Tiligul were disbanded I've found it hard to keep an interest in the sport, except for the national side, of course. I never did much care for that Sheriff lot, though. Too much money, if you ask me. But I do keep an eye out for Dinamo-Auto now and again. Their owner is a terrific chap, and a very old friend of mine."

"Ooh yes, that reminds me," the old man said, switching the subject in a flash. "I'd better take a spare change of clothes for that Russian do tomorrow night after the rehearsals, shouldn't I?"

Maxim's two attendants flashed their eyes across the room at each other in surprise. "Erm, what Russian do is that, Maxim?" Evgeny asked, cautiously.

"Oh I had a little invite for it last week. Did I not tell you? It's at their consulate in town. Just a quiet affair, I believe. Timur Turgenev's going to be there too. Terrible fellow, but one has to show their face at these things. I won't be there too long – just enough to get my face seen and shake a few hands."

Michi knew that this probably wasn't the best of ideas. They managed to steer him clear of the Romanian party without too much trouble, but this was going to be a much harder proposition to get out of. Still, he thought he'd better inject an element of doubt into Maxim's chain of thoughts, just to plant the seed.

"You see how tired you're feeling before you go making any party plans," Michi said with a smile. "You really don't want me taking your place on that big stage on Saturday week, do you now! The pride of the nation is on your shoulders!"

"Ha! Very good point, and very funny, young Michi. But you know me, I'm as strong as a lion! I'll be just fine. But if it does concern you tomorrow evening, check in on me and I'll see how I feel. And on that note I should be getting these old bones to bed. Sleep well, you two, and see you bright and early in the morning!"

Michi wished his old companion a hearty good night, but there was something deep within his soul that told him the next few days were going to get more and more complicated.

21

Friday morning had arrived, and the crew had all arrived early for a special backstage briefing by Filip from the CTF and Stefan from Moldova Smash.

"Right everybody," Filip began. "Thank you all for arriving extra early today, and for all of your hard work over the last week. You've been brilliant, every one of you. Things are really going to step up from today. But before I go too closely into the finer details, Stefan Smolenko from Moldova Smash would like a quick word with you all. Stefan..."

The Moldovan TV executive stepped forward and began to speak.

"So. Hello! Firstly, to our international colleagues, how are you all enjoying beautiful Moldova so far?" he asked as an icebreaker.

"Hardly seen any of it yet, apart from the hall and the hotel to be honest," Skunk grumped with a signature sneer. "Same as every year, really."

"Oh yes, busy busy!" said Stefan, laughing off Skunk's remark. "But how are you finding it working here, all you people from outside of Moldova?"

There was an awkward shuffling within the ranks, and a few grudging grunts and agreements from some of the bolder members of the crew.

"Oh you won't get much out of this lot," Håkan cut in. "They're professionally unimpressed. You could have them working out in Dubai sitting on gold chairs and they'd grumble that their arse was too hot! As far as I can see it, they're doing just fine – and the rehearsals are going like a dream, shy of the usual one or two complications. But you've got to expect that on a production of this complexity."

"Good, good!" Stefan continued. "And how are you Moldovans getting on with your international counterparts?" he asked.

"It's difficult," came a voice from the back of the room. "Some of them march around like they own

the place, and a few of them talk to us like we're just children fresh off the farm. It doesn't create the best atmosphere."

"I see, I see," said Stefan, worrying that he might have bitten off more than he can chew with this line of questioning. "So how can we rectify this, going forward? I'd like to hope that now we are getting close to our first broadcast day we can all start working together as equals. Can we do that?"

"Yeah, I'm as equal as everybody else here," said Skunk. "Anyone can come up to me and ask me anything. Just don't be surprised if I snap back at you every now and again. I don't mean anything by it – it's just my nature."

"See, this is our problem," said Artiom Balan, the head of the local crew. "Our two sides don't share the same sense of humour. And what might seem like fun to all the non-Moldovans can seem like the height of rudeness to our people. I think we've both got to get an understanding of how each other work if we are to move on and get this show done efficiently. Otherwise we may have problems further down the line. Already many of my staff have put in complaints about Mr Skunk, and Ari on the lights. But at the same time they all seem to work well with Hanna and Ice on the stage, so it shows how well things can be done if the right measures are taken."

"I'll have a quick word with the lads after we've finished this little chat," Håkan offered. "That alright with you, Skunk and Ari?"

Both men nodded, impassionately.

"Good, we've sorted that out calmly and efficiently," Stefan said, slightly relieved that the meeting hadn't turned into a petty grievance free-for-all. "And I have one more announcement. When our very own Maxim Munteanu makes his rehearsal today, we are expecting a visit from our chief financier Timur Turgenev. He is a very important man in this city, so expect to see security ramped a fair bit. And if he decides to talk to any of you, local or otherwise, please just agree with everything that he says, and answer any questions in as plain a manner as you possibly can. It's not unfair to say that he can be a little volatile in conversation, so if we keep everything civil and non-committal we should just about be OK. So, everybody, good luck with today, and if any of you have any questions – from either side of the crew – then please do come and knock on my office door."

"Great!" said Filip. "Thank you for your notices, Stefan. And let me reiterate the importance of keeping Mr Turgenev sweet. Just treat him with the same reverence as you would a member of your local royal family – or an equivalent high ranking political entity – and we should be just fine."

"Do we have to doff and genuflect?" said Skunk, sardonically.

"No more than you normally would!" Håkan laughed, and the meeting descended into mild chattering chaos for a few moments. Once the laughs had finally subsided, Filip continued with his speech.

"So, there's a lot of potential issues that we must address today. The first few acts up this morning are as good as gold, although we're still expecting the Latvian singer to act up at some point over the next few days, so tread very carefully around her. I also understand that there will be some changes to the song from Kazakhstan, but I believe you stageside have been fully briefed by their HoD. And remember, when the last six finally start to arrive, we're back to the first rehearsal timings. So take your time, and be patient with them. They're all new here, and might be a little overawed by the surroundings. On top of that, be very gentle around the Moldovan singer. I'm hearing that he's not in the best of health. But he's got no props to speak of, and he's just singing with a small choir of backing singers, so it should be a nice easy way to end the day.

While I have you all here, a quick word about tomorrow. I've managed to cram a break in between Ukraine and Russia, so that should lighten the mood a little in the middle of the day. But that means that Azerbaijan and Armenia are following each other directly again, so do your very best to keep them as far apart as possible. The back end of Semi 2 is as prop heavy as before, but I think we're just about on top of that now. Then there's just the last six with their second rehearsals on Sunday and its on to the interval acts, which shouldn't take too much time, as most of it is pre-recorded video work.

Again, thank you all for your tireless work since we've been down here on the ground. I understand that sometimes tempers can get frayed – it's the nature of a big busy production, after all. But if you could all do your best to work out your differences and get along, then this thing is going to go like a dream. I have every faith in you, ladies and gentlemen. It's all action from this point on, so let's do this! Are you with me?"

The crowd in front of him let out a half-hearted murmur of agreement. "That's no good," Filip chirped, "I want to hear you roar! Are you with me!"

"YES!" the crew all yelled, much louder than before, some sarcastically, some half-grudgingly, but every one of them utterly behind their boss. For now at least.

"Right then, let's all go and do this thing!" Filip shouted. "Good luck, and thank you!"

A mild round of applause rippled through the crowd of crew as they all made their way to their stations.

"Good job!" said Stefan. "Sounds like you're really on top of this lot."

"Well, you would hope," said Filip, "But there's still a long way to go between now and Saturday night. A lot of things could still happen before then, so we've got to remain cautious."

*

"Erm, Filip," said Terry urgently over the phone. "I think that you'll be wanting a look at EuroStorm's front page before the rest of the world tries to get hold of you."

"Oh no, what's that idiot done now," said Filip as he opened his laptop and navigated towards his least favourite site. "OH SHIT! He can't say that. He really, really can't say that. I don't care how good his numbers are, the man's out of here the minute I catch up with him!"

The story in front of him told an utterly made up and unsourced tale about the North Macedonian entrants.

"He/She?" read the headline, "More like She/He!"

The piece then went on to suggest, most salaciously, that the brother and sister act were actually sister and brother, and that both of them had recently transitioned at the same time.

"Where's he got this from?" asked Filip angrily. "There's no truth to it, right?"

"NO!" said Terry. "Not at all. Nothing. Not one single iota. He's made it up completely out of his hat based on a supposition relating to the name. And now the poor kids are absolutely terrified about what they're going to do next."

"How do you mean, Terry?" asked Filip.

"Well, they've not transitioned," said Terry. "They've explained that to me themselves. But they're worried about how they're going to broach the subject without coming across as transphobic."

"Oh, they're good sweet kids," said Filip. "I'm sure they'll manage to do that delicately."

"Oh I'm sure that they will," Terry replied. "But then there's the problem of what happens when they get home. North Macedonia isn't exactly the most LGBTQ+ friendly country on our list of competitors, and when their local papers see a foreign news source making a statement like that they're bound to start asking some awkward questions. This is all going to make their lives ridiculously complicated, and they've got to prepare themselves for their second rehearsal in a couple of hours. I really wouldn't want to be in their shoes right now. And the worst thing is that they've done absolutely nothing wrong. It's just that bloody Kiwi half-wit running off at the mouth on a wonky hunch."

"Oh yes, I can see how difficult it must be for them, the poor little souls," said Filip, sympathetically. "I've got a plan. I'll go and find that horrible monster Storm and get him dragged off the site by his delicate parts, and you go down to Dusana and Jovan and make a formal apology from the CTF, assure them that they are in no way at fault for this, and let them know that from today, EuroStorm is finished at this contest."

"Good idea, Filip," Terry replied. "Shall I carefully draft them a statement explaining their situation so that they don't have to worry about that part of the equation?"

"Yes!" said Filip. "Bang on! Now first things first, let's get that nasty little bastard kicked out of this compound for good!"

Filip got The Ox on the phone and asked the security man to meet him at the front desk of the press centre. This was in part to protect Filip in case Michael Storm decided to get violent, but also to help evict him from the Eurovision complex with perhaps just a little bit more force than was altogether necessary.

"Do I need to hit him first?" asked The Ox. "I'd be happy to."

"No no, I'll just talk to him first," said Filip, "To make sure that he fully understands what he's done wrong, and to let all of the people around him in the press centre know quite how badly he's behaved. Then you can try to usher him out politely if he doesn't make a scene."

"And THEN I hit him?" said The Ox.

"Try not to resort to any kind of physical violence in the view of any other people – especially when there are press cameras and live-streamers about."

"Fully understood, Filip sir," said The Ox with a professional nod. "We have our own private places where we can take him."

"Well as long as I don't know anything about where they are or what you do to him, I'll be happy with whatever you decide is the right course of action," said Filip, coldly. "Right, are you ready? Let's go in!"

As Filip and The Ox marched over towards the EuroStorm table, heads were bobbing up like meerkats right across the press hall as people cottoned on to what was about to happen.

"Oh here we go!" said Radouane Thill from EuroStorm's biggest rival, ESC Cargo. "I think they've finally got that odious little man!"

A buzz picked up around the room, and upon seeing their manager marching purposefully towards the middle of the building, the other security guards primed themselves for a rumble and edged closer into the room from their stations. Michael Storm had his back to the fast aproaching trouble, and was oblivious to what was about to happen, instead loudly bragging about his latest antics on a live stream. He only realised that Filip was marching up behind him when he caught a glimpse of him looking angry in the corner of his screen.

"Michael Storm?" said Filip quite sternly. "I'm afraid I'm going to have to rescind your press badge immediately!"

Instantly there was a loud peel of applause from around the room. Storm looked away from his screen ready to start an argument with Filip when he saw The Ox towering above him.

"What on Earth made you think that it was a good idea to publish that story, Michael?" said Filip. "It's going to cost you and your operation dear."

"Erm, what story was that, Filip?" Storm replied nonchalantly, clearly playing for time.

"You know full well it was the story about the North Macedonian kids," Filip continued. "You've caused them great distress, and because of it I'm afraid that we're going to have to evacuate you from the premises."

"Oh that?" Storm replied evasively, with the air of a man who still thought that he could talk his way out of this situation. "No biggie. I'll just take it down and all will be lovely."

"No, Michael, I'm afraid not," said Filip. "The damage is done. The story has already been reported in their press back home, and they're getting deluged with interview requests asking them if it's true or not. The poor kids just wanted to come here and sing their pretty little song with no fuss, and you have to go and ruin it for them with that big mouth of yours!"

"How terribly rude!" said Storm. "I've half a mind to put in a complaint about you!"

"To who, exactly?" said Filip. "The buck stops with me at this competition, and I want you out of here. Whatever possessed you to write such a story anyway?"

"Well, we were back at the hotel, and we were talking about how Dusana looked a little bit boyish, and how Jovan appeared a little bit girlish, and it all slotted into place. I mean it's obvious! Just look at them. The name He/She is like a cry for help to let everybody know what has happened. It's as plain as the nose on your face!"

"Did you not for one minute think to ask someone on the North Macedonian delegation about it? Or to look into their biogs? The pair of them have been playing brother and sister on a Macedonian soap since they were both seven. Do you not think somebody might have noticed by now?"

"Oh facts are for losers!" said Storm, smugly. "And why should I ever believe anyone on that delegation. They're bound to be covering up for them. And the most important thing is that I got the story first. That's it. I win."

Filip could feel the anger welling up inside him, but he centred himself for a moment, turned to The Ox and said dispassionately: "Take him away!"

"It'll be my pleasure, sir," The Ox replied, as he grabbed him by the scruff of the neck and lifted him clean off the ground.

"Ooh, but wait just one moment, Ox," said Filip, stopping the big man in his tracks. "Put him down

for a moment. There's just one more thing that will make this moment complete. Michael Storm – hand over your accreditation badge – right now!"

"Not a chance, Filip!" Storm shouted, defiantly, "You're not taking it. It's my right to keep hold of this badge for as long as I want to!"

"I control this building, I decide your rights," said Filip sternly. "Mr Ox, take that badge off him!" "With pleasure Mr Ivanović!" The Ox replied. The big man bent down towards Michael Storm, thrusting his massive face within inches of the New Zealander.

"Badge!" he said curtly.

"No way man, this badge means everything to me," Storm began to whine.

"Badge!!!" said The Ox again, this time with a little more malice and with his head tilted menacingly.

"Fine!" said Storm as he threw his accreditation angrily to the floor, " You take it. But keep it safe, as I'll be talking to my lawyers as soon as I leave this building. And then who'll be sorry?!"

"Erm you, quite possibly," said Filip. "The Macedonians have already begun defamation proceedings, and the CTF is going to make very sure that we support them all the way. And we're already formulating a case against you for bringing this competition into disrepute, too. We gave you every chance to play nice, but you just had to be an arse again, didn't you! Now, get on your way!"

The Ox picked Michael Storm up by the scruff of the neck once more, wrenched his right arm behind his back and began to frogmarch him out of the room to massive cheers from the rest of the press corps.

"You can't do this to me!" Storm complained. "Don't you know who I am?"

"It's happening exactly because of who you are, you horrible prick!" shouted Radouane Thill in a rare display of emotion.

As The Ox got nearer and nearer to the exit, all the other journalists began a rousing recitation of the old football song "Cheerio Cheerio Cheerio" as they stood on the tables and waved him goodbye.

But Filip wasn't finished with the rest of the EuroStorm crew.

"Right then you lot," he said, "your passes will be cancelled tonight at the stroke of midnight. So don't even think about coming back tomorrow, because security won't let you in. I want you to pack up all of Michael's stuff and get it safely back to him – I wouldn't want him trying to sue us for loss of property or anything petty like that. Then I want you, fella there, sorry I don't know your name, to take down that North Macedonian story right away. And that lady sitting next to you can write a formal and heartfelt apology that will go onto the front page of your site inside the next hour. And if anyone takes it down before the end of play today you'll all receive the same treatment as your boss and get marched out of here. And you wouldn't want that to happen, would you now?"

"No, Mister Ivanović," they all said meekly.

"Right then, I've got to go and sort out some weeping North Macedonians," said Filip. "So if it's all the same to you, I'll take my leave. Thank you for your understanding."

As Filip walked purposely towards the door, every single person in the press room, bar the EuroStorm crew of course, rose to their feet and gave him a massive round of applause.

"See," he said to himself with a smile at the corner of his lips, "it IS worth all the endless hassle and aggravation after all!"

*

"Right, so here's what we've got," said Terry, walking into Filip's office with a sheet of paper. "Tell me what you think..."

Filip took the paper and began to read.

"This morning we had to remove Michael Storm from the Eurovision compound and rescind his accreditation for his website's continual flouting of both copyright laws and editorial standards. EuroStorm will also cease operating from within the Eurovision press room as of midnight tonight.

Already on a final warning, Mr Storm continued to publish stories that not only had no grounding in the truth, but also flirted seriously with international libel laws, and this final incident has caused the North Macedonian delegation deep distress, but has also caused grave upset to our friends and allies within the transexual community.

We would like to wholeheartedly apologise to both parties on behalf of the Eurovision family, and seek to reassure that any similar behaviour in the future will be stamped out immediately.

We stand by our ethos that The Eurovision Contest is a fun and inclusive event, and that everybody in attendance, be they artists, workers or fans, should feel as safe and welcome as possible. With that in mind, we will be helping the North Macedonian delegation with their legal case against Mr Storm, and will be donating a percentage of the proceeds of all merchandise at this year's events to charities supporting transexual issues.

We will answer no further questions on this matter at this time pending the ongoing legal case against Mr Storm.

Thank you, Filip Ivanović"

"That's perfect," said Filip. "You got the tone just right, you've made it very clear that it was Michael Storm who was at fault, and you've underlined our commitment to aftercare with the artists – not to mention your delicate handling of the trans issue. You've also done well not to accuse the Macedonian people back home of anything, which to be honest I'd have struggled with. Strong work, sir. Strong work."

"It had to be done, Filip. Those poor Macedonian kids are utterly overwhelmed by the whole sorry affair, and it's not as if the trans community need any more hassle right now, either. I just thought we'd better do what we could to help, and make a stand against any further shitheadery."

"Yeah, but you know my new concern? Just what's that Storm arsehole going to start writing about now?" said Filip, looking worried. "At least we had something of a control over him when he was in our premises. Now the little bastard can write pretty much whatever he wants, and we can't grab him by the collar quite so easily."

"Ooh yes," said Terry, "I'd not really looked at it that way. That could be a problem. I suppose the good thing now though – if you can call it a good thing – is that we don't have to worry about being seen to do the right thing any more."

"How do you mean, Terry?" asked Filip, looking a little puzzled.

"Well, when he was here we couldn't be seen to get security to drag him round the back of the bins and give him a good pasting," said Terry with a devious expression on his face. "But now he's out in the wild... well, who knows what might happen to him if he ran his mouth off in the wrong place at the wrong time. Especially if it was in the vicinity of some of The Ox's off duty colleagues..."

"Oh Terry," said Filip, alarmed. "I'm seeing a whole different side to you this week... good work!"

"Well, we've got to be able to use the unique circumstances of our current location for some good, haven't we, Filip?" Terry said with a wink.

"Yes, yes, but just as long as I never get to hear about it, OK," Filip replied with mock horror. "At least not on the books, that is..."

"Right then, that's got that dirty little matter out of the way. Shall we get on with the songs?" said Terry.

"I think we most probably ought," said Filip with a smile. "Who have we had so far?"

"Well Croatia floated by unnoticed like a magnolia cloud, Iceland did his doggy thing with no real issues, and the Swiss were all very cold and efficient, as you'd expect. Latvia's due on next, but she's been behaving herself against all predictions, and then we take a break after the Serbian gentleman does his business. But he's so bloody slick he'll be on and off in no time. But then it all begins to get a little lumpy."

"Oh yes, that enormous prop storm followed by the big six," said Filip. "Thank heavens we've had such a relatively quiet morning, song wise at least."

"And that's the bit that's most important, at the end of the day," said Terry. "None of this backstage messing about amounts to a hill of beans when it comes to the three big live shows."

"Very true," Filip nodded. "Right then, I've got a couple of hours of office work to do. You get that release circulated, and then we can meet on the balcony just after the first break. Despite all the odds, I think we're finally getting ourselves on top of this one!"

"Oooh Filip, shhhhhhhhhh!" said Terry, "You don't want to tempt fate. With all the songs and egos that are coming up this afternoon, anything could happen. Absolutely bloody anything!"

22

"Right, prepare yourself for this one, Terry," said Filip with a wince. "It's even more horrifying in real life than it is on video. That voice of hers just resonates through the hall and rattles all the seats."

"I can't wait, Filip," Terry replied with some excitement, "It's moments like these that make Eurovision for me!"

"You say that now, mind," Filip smirked.

The singer from Kazakhstan, Rayana Bayzhanova, walked purposefully into the stage, looking every bit as devastating as before. The animated horse puppet took its place behind her and the song's introduction began to play.

"Brace! Brace!" said Filip, barely controlling a laugh.

And then it happened. Quite unexpectedly, Ms Bayzhanova opened her mouth and the most beautiful sound wafted around the arena.

"Eh?" said Filip, looking more than a little surprised.

"Eh???" chanted pretty much everybody in the hall who'd witnessed her previous rehearsal.

"Now wait a minute!" said Terry, looking like he'd been robbed of a rare treat. "I think we're being had on here!"

"In what way?" asked Filip.

"Well you're not telling me that just a handful of days ago she sang like a bruised foghorn, but now suddenly she's got the voice of an angel. No vocal coach or healing tincture in the world is that good!" Terry replied. "Hold on, something's missing. Where's that dancer I saw on the video?"

"Well Hanna did suggest that the staging was going to be a little different today, perhaps that's it?" Filip suggested.

"Yeah, but you know what that means, don't you. There's only five on stage. They've got to be hiding another singer somewhere!"

Filip and Terry strained their eyes through the gloom, scanning the outer fringes of the stage to see if there was anybody with a mic hidden in the shadows.

"There!" cried Terry. "Just there, right at the very edge of the big screen, all dressed in black with a black hood on. Look! See! She's singing all the words while Rayana lip synchs along. The crafty bloody devils!"

"Ooh, how terribly cunning," said Filip, rather impressed at the nerve of the Kazakhs. "You're the rulebook expert though Terry. Is that altogether allowed?"

"Well as long as the hidden singer is standing on the actual stage, which she is, and is in full view of at least one audience member, which again she is because we can see her, then they're entirely within their rights to do this. It's going entirely against the spirit of the competition, obviously, but there's not a darned thing about it that is illegal going by the letter of the law. I reckon they've pulled an absolute blinder here. Right back in the game, the cheeky shits!"

Meanwhile, over in the press hall, the professional gamblers were rapidly backing Kazakhstan again at their recently more agreeable odds.

"I wish they'd hurry up and decide whether they're rubbish or not," said one of their number. "All of this going backwards and forwards is giving me an RSI!"

Back on the balcony, Filip and Terry were deep in conversation.

"You really think that this is a contender now Terry?" Filip asked nervously.

"Damn straight!" he replied. "I mean, just look at it. It's got the lot. The only thing that could damage her chances would be if it got out that she can't actually sing a note herself, but even then I reckon that could play in her favour if they play it right. Prepare yourself Filip, we could all be off to Nur-Sultan this time next year."

"Oh god, I'd never even entertained that as an option before," said a worried Filip. "We've practically destroyed the secret emergency contingency fund on this one. Lord knows what weirdness that's likely to throw up! Curse that bloody Cory Kjellberg and his legacy project!"

"Ha, yes!" laughed Terry. "It's at times like these that EuroStorm would actually come in useful for a change though. Y'know, feeding them a story about the hidden singer and letting them spread some vile gossip."

"Oh don't start," said Filip with a smile. "We've only just got rid of them!" Filip suddenly sat bolt upright in his seat.
"Shit!" he proclaimed loudly.

"What is it?" said Terry. "What's up?"

"I just remembered that Timur Turgenev is due in the building in a couple of hours, and I'm quite sure that he's going to want a private guided tour by yours truly. Damn, I'm going to have to get Dumi and Stefan on board for this one. They'll know more about how to play him than I ever could. I'd better be off."

"Give it another few minutes though," Terry suggested. "The North Macedonians are about to come on, and I think it would be good politics to be seen giving them our support."

"Very good point," said Filip. "I'll text Dumi to warn him I'm coming over, and I'll head off once we've got through the first run through."

Just then they noticed some commotion going on at the entrance to the auditorium below them. Accredited fans and members of the press were allowed into the hall for the second round of rehearsals, but up to now only the same small handful of keen photographers had bothered making the winding trek from the press centre and around the back of the bins to the arena. But now floods of people were bursting into the hall through every available door.

"What's going on, Terry?" asked Filip. "This all looks a little bit weird."

"If I'm not mistaken, I think they're all coming in to offer their support to the little Macedonian kids after all that EuroStorm business this morning."

"Really?" said Filip. "They've not come to give them any hassle, have they?"

"Oh no, I can't see any pitchforks or flaming torches or anything like that," Terry laughed. "And look, rather a lot of them are carrying Macedonian flags. I get the feeling that we're in for a bit of a special moment here, you know."

And it was. Dusana and Jovan both looked terrified as they walked up the ramp onto the stage, but as soon as the crowds noticed them they burst into a warm and welcoming ovation. The two young Macedonians visibly swelled with relief as the crowd began to chant "He/She, He/She, He/She" over and over again. Unsure whether to take their mark to prepare for their rehearsal, Hanna ushered them to the front of the stage to bathe in their most welcome reception for a moment.

"Thank you, thank you," Dusana said down the microphone, her voice cracking with emotion. "We didn't know if we were even going to come out here today, but you've made us feel so very welcome."

"And solidarity to our trans brothers and sisters," Jovan cried, as a massive wave of cheers flooded through the hall.

"Y'see Terry," said Filip, leaning towards his colleague in order to be heard over the noise. "Our fandom can be a strange and curious beast. But at the best of times, when they all get together to do something good, there's absolutely no better set of people on the planet. And to be honest with you mate, I'm welling up here. Right now, I feel like a proud father."

He looked over, and Terry was just nodding in agreement, totally unable to speak.

*

The rest of the afternoon passed by with little incident. Israel managed to keep all their candles upright and avoided setting light to the stage, the crew were successful in their attempts to keep the Azerbaijani and the Armenian delegations far enough apart to avoid any possible confrontations, and the Swedish singer only fell off her travelator the one time. Even Ukraine and Russia were on their best behaviour, and it transpired that the cans in Australia's bar prop were actually made of a spongey material, so they wouldn't hurt if they came into contact with any of the crowd's faces. Somehow all of the expected pitfalls of a potentially troublesome day were avoided, and the crew could happily recalibrate their systems for the day's bigger challenge – the arrival of the Big Five and the hosts Moldova.

Italy were up first. Their performer Explodo casually ambled onto the stage like he owned the place, surveyed the expansive hall for a couple of minutes, before nodding regally and declaring "This will do" in Italian. His song had put a few noses out of joint by being overtly political. He'd got around the issue of explicitly mentioning Italian MPs by replacing their names with those of farmyard animals, which enraged supporters of the respective political parties back home even more, but utterly delighted everybody else who thought it was a most apt solution.

He was also notoriously difficult to work with, generally doing things in his own time and demanding the Earth from everybody around him. But for this rehearsal he was on his best behaviour, only calling out the crew on the one occasion when a firework didn't go off at precisely the correct moment in the chorus of his sleazy salsa grime tune.

"No bomb on 'Grande'," he snapped angrily at the nearest crew member. "One bomb on 'Boom', one bomb on 'Bang'. It's simple you dumb motherfucker!"

Hanna had been tipped off by the Italian delegation that their artist could be a little volatile, so made sure to warn her crew what he was going to be like. So taking his antics with a pinch of salt the rest of the rehearsal passed by without too much more of his pop starry nonsense.

France were next, and Zuzi's perky little jazz number went by in a flash. Not only was she a dream to work with, but all her props, from a fake bedroom wall to a chintzy sofa, standard lamp and about a dozen suitcases were light and easy to manage. However, one of the crew missed a suitcase that was hiding in shadow at the edge of the stage, and by the time the United Kingdom's Jason Brown came on for his first run through it was still sat there rather awkwardly.

"The case! The case!" one of the UK delegation shouted from the front of the stage as Jason began his first attempt at his song, and it put him right off his game, nervously staring at it as he sang, and missing his cue for his one brief walk across the stage. This was quickly rectified for his second performance, which he absolutely sailed through, but by then the Eurovision press corps watching on the big screens, all entirely unaware of the case issue, had posted their first judgements. And they were a punishing read.

"Brown looked completely out of sorts," read one, "ambling across the stage awkwardly like a pine wardrobe, and looking utterly distracted throughout his performance".

"The poor lad looked thoroughly overwhelmed by the situation," said another, "I'm not sure what they can do to improve this mess in such a short time."

"Another last place for the UK?" a third suggested.

It wasn't the start to their Eurovision adventure that the Brits would have wanted, but surely things could only get better from there on in. They hoped.

Thankfully the UK was followed immediately by the Germans. The third song in the competition with the title Strong, Filip was concerned that there could be another ugly incident in the hall, so put out an all points bulletin to security before this rehearsal slot began.

"Whatever you do, try your best to keep both the Czech and the Maltese performers away from the arena while Germany are rehearsing. Especially the Czech girl. We are not expecting either of them to be in today, but just be on your best vigilance!" the executive director had breifed them.

Thankfully there was none of the feared trouble, and the German rehearsal passed quickly and simply. Sissi And Sal, the two singers, clearly had major issues with each other though, and chose to remain on their respective sides of the stage, never once looking the other's way until they had to face each other at the very end of the song.

Spain, however, caused no such problems. Their performer, Emiliano Ganador, bounded onto the stage with the enthusiasm of a puppy who'd just learned how to walk, then jumped and gyrated along with his dancers with a joyful aplomb throughout each scheduled three minutes – and even beyond. Although the song was never expected to cause too much damage to the scoreboard, his endless positivity made it like working with a happy fluffy cloud after some of the heavier, more complicated performances that had gone before him.

All that remained was the very last rehearsal of the day, the home entry from Moldova. But Maxim Munteanu was nowhere to be seen. Filip got on the radio to Hanna to find out what was going on.

"Erm, do we have a Moldovan folk legend anywhere down there, Hanna?" he asked.

"Not yet," she replied. I'll send a runner down to the dressing room to find out what's happening. They've given him a room just around the back of the stage, so it shouldn't take too long."

In the dressing room, Maxim was going through his final preparations, but he wasn't looking too steady on his feet.

"Are you absolutely sure that you're OK to go on, Maxim?" said Michi, looking at his elderly friend with some concern.

"Don't you worry about me, young man," Maxim replied. "I'll be just fine. I just need to snap myself into show mode and I'll be ready to go!"

"Well if you're certain, I'll help you get your stage shoes on and we'll get you out there," said Michi, still unclear as to whether Maxim was entirely up to the job right now.

There was a tap on the door, and the runner stepped into the room.

"We are ready for you now, Mr Munteanu," said the young Moldovan timidly, clearly in awe of the man standing unsteadily before him.

"Fine! Fine!" said Maxim, puffing his chest out proudly. "Tell them I'm on my way!"

And with that, he grabbed Michi by the arm and slowly shuffled towards the dressing room door. But the moment they crossed the threshold into the backstage area, Maxim underwent the most miraculous transformation. Suddenly he was walking more steadily, and standing a good two inches taller. The years seemed to fall off him before Michi's eyes, and he was now looking a good twenty years younger than his actual age and started to speak in a more bold and purposeful manner.

"That's his stage persona," Evgeny whispered into Michi's ear. "He does this every time. You can think that he's out for the count, but the second the man feels the warmth of the stage lights on his skin he's like a different creature. It really is remarkable. But it seems to take more and more out of him every time. We've really got to treat him gently when he comes off stage."

Michi nodded with agreement as the old man let go of his arm and walked up the ramp and onto the stage.

At that same moment there was a knock on the door of the CTF viewing balcony. Terry got up to answer it, and a rank of dead-faced men in sunglasses stood before him.

"Filip Ivanović?" the middlemost man asked in a disaffected manner.

"No, but he's just over here, would you like to come in?" Terry replied. "Yes," said the man, curtly. "We are Timur Turgenev."

And with that Timur's party walked in. First the security guards, then Mr Turgenev, who was much smaller than Terry had imagined and glowing a curious shade of orange, followed by Dumi and Stefan from Moldova Smash, and then another rank of security guards.

"Hello Mr Ivanović," the tiny oligarch said, offering his hand for Filip to shake.

"You can call me Filip," he replied, nervously taking Timur's hand, only for it to be crushed in a vice- like grip.

"Am I in time for my good friend Maxim, Mr Ivanović?" said Timur. "I hope I haven't missed him." "No no, you're good, Mr Turgenev," said Filip. "He's just coming onto the stage now."

"Ahh, great, just in time!" Timur laughed. And as he laughed, all of his security detail let out an obliged and emotionless laugh too. Dumi stared at Filip and gestured with his head that it would perhaps be best if Filip laughed too, and he duly obliged.

"Then after we have watched Maxim, you must take me on a tour of all the buildings, Mr Ivanović, so I can see how well my money is being used." Again Timur let out a brief cold laugh, and his minions followed, every bit as coldly.

"Oh, it'll be my pleasure," said Filip, lying through his teeth. "I think you're going to be very impressed with what we've done with the place."

"I hope so, Mr Ivanović. I sincerely hope so."

The air turned cold and awkward for a moment, but Filip was saved by the husky voice of Hanna counting Maxim in.

"And three-two-one... music..." she said, as the most beautiful symphonic introduction wafted out of the speakers.

"We have improved the song a little since O Melodie Pentru Moldova, Mr Turgenev," Stefan explained. "It's now sounding much fuller and more in tune with the old times."

Timur held his hand up as if to silence Stefan, and leaned forward, resting his chin on his cane.

"Maxim is a very special performer for me. I have seen him sing many, many times, but it fills me with great pride to see him on this stage – a stage that I built – representing Transnistria to the world."

Terry briefly breathed in to mention that it was actually Moldova that Maxim was representing, but looked at the bulky security men who were crowding the balcony and thought better of it.

"Wait," said Timur, "he's about to sing. He really does have the most beautiful, evocative voice."

And sure enough he did. When Maxim began to sing, everybody's worries started to wash away. His warm, honest intonations were at once nostalgic yet still speaking to both young and old, and not a single person in that whole enormous room could take their eyes off the old man, even for a second. By the time the song had come to an end there wasn't a dry face in the house, and Filip could see some moisture forming in the corner of Timur's eyes.

"He reminds me so much of my own father," said Timur, wiping the tear away with the back of his brown suede glove. "He is all of our fathers. Maxim is the very embodiment of the father of our nation, and he must be cherished and loved as such. Is he going to sing again?"

"Possibly another four times," said Terry.

"Oh my heart can hardly bear it," said Timur, poetically. "This is one of the proudest moments of my entire life."

After Maxim finished his first run through, Michi edged onto the stage to check that everything was alright with his elderly friend. But as he walked towards his elderly friend he became a little overwhelmed with the sheer scale of what spread out before him.

"Drink it in, Michi lad," said Maxim, warmly. "One day all of this will be yours. I guarantee it!" "Hopefully not for a while yet," Michi laughed, nervously.

"Oh there's no danger of that, my young man," Maxim replied. "When I walk onto this stage I become a lion. An eagle swooping over the heads of the crowd. A mighty whale gracefully lending its song to the ocean. I am the moon and the stars and I give every part of me to the audience.

Just try it for a moment Michi. Here, step up to the microphone and sing."

"Oh. Oh no, I couldn't," said Michi in a panic. "There's a schedule and everything, and the crew have had a long day."

"Oh dash the schedule, Michi," said Maxim with a smile. "You forget, I am the star here. They work around me, even if it is Eurovision. Go on, just say a few words and get to feel the power of your voice in a big room like this."

"If you insist, Maxim," said Michi, stalling for time.

"I do, I do," Maxim replied, before turning around to Hanna and asking, "While we prepare for the next performance, do you mind if my young friend says a few words into the microphone? I am trying to prepare him for stardom."

Michi visibly recoiled with embarrassment, but when Hanna said, "Of course, by all means, he can have about ten seconds if he likes," the room magnified by about a hundred times in front of him, and he felt as though he was suddenly the only person on the planet.

"Go on, boy," said Maxim. "Now's your chance!"

Michi stepped up to the microphone and could hear his anxious breathing coming out of the massive speakers suspended from the ceiling above him. Nervously he said a quick mumbled "Hello" into the mic, and as his anxious voice echoed around the giant hall, he suddenly understood what Maxim had been telling him, and attempted a line from the song Moldova's Landscape in his fragile, willowy voice. It wasn't perfect, by any means, but the power of the microphone flushed through him, and he quickly wanted another go.

But Hanna's voice suddenly wrenched him out of his dreamlike state.

"Thank you, we must move on now," she said, and Michi turned towards Maxim and mouthed the words "Thank you!".

"See, what did I tell you young man! Wasn't it good!" Michi nodded, now totally unable to speak.

"It's like taking a drug for the first time. It fills your veins and makes you feel 1000 times better about yourself. But this drug will only make you stronger, not weak and ill. And I can sense that you've definitely got a taste for it now! Right, I'd better get on. That delightful Hanna there is giving me a very serious look!"

Michi walked off stage, stopping once to look over his shoulder at the auditorium for a few more seconds. Before today, the biggest place that he had ever performed was at the Moldova Smash studio, and even that was relatively tiny. Other than that it has been nothing but cramped basement bars and community music rooms. But Maxim had helped prise the door open into another magical world, and Michi knew that his life had been changed forever. Again.

Up on the balcony, Timur Turgenev turned to Filip and asked angrily: "Who was that shrieking idiot trying to sing the great Maxim's song just then? He was absolutely dreadful! Be sure that this never, ever happens again, you hear!"

*

Maxim finished his rehearsal triumphantly. In fact he was so good that even the crew stood in ranks and clapped him off the stage. But the nearer he got to the dressing room, the more he shrank with tiredness, and the moment he got through the door he slumped into his chair and visibly aged about thirty years. At that same moment, Dumi from Moldova Smash stuck his head around the door.

"Mr Munteanu sir," he asked.

"Call me Maxim," the old man mumbled with a warm but exhausted voice.

"Thank you," Dumi replied. "Maxim, are you ready to come and view your performance to see if the sound and visuals are to you approval?"

"Oh I don't much care for those kind of things, Dumi my lad," Maxim said. "You understand television. You can do it for me!"

"Are you sure, Maxim sir? It's only down the corridor," said Dumi.

"Yes, yes, you do it," said Maxim. "I have no idea what I'm looking for, to be honest, and I never much enjoy seeing myself on a screen. Take one of my delegation laddies along with you and you can work it out between yourselves."

"As you wish, Maxim sir?" said Dumi. "And will you be engaging in a meet and greet with the press in around an hour?"

"Oh, I'm not sure that I've got the energy, to be honest with you,

Dumi. I'll tell you what. I'll give you one on Monday when I've got nothing else on. How does that sound to you?"

"That sounds perfect to me, Maxim sir," said Dumi. "I'll notify the press guys and let them know. Right then, I'm off to check out your video. But I'm sure it will be fine."

"I'm quite sure that it will be," said Maxim. "Thanks terribly for sorting all that out for me." "It's my pleasure, sir," said Dumi as he was closing the door. "My absolute pleasure."

"That's unlike you to turn anything down, Maxim," said Evgeny. "Are you sure that you're feeling OK?"

"To be honest with you, old friend, that took more out of me than I'd expected," Maxim weakly mumbled. "It must have been those hot stage lights or something. I'm sure I'll be back at the top of my game by tomorrow. Now, is there any water anywhere for me to drink? I'm absolutely parched."

And with that, the old man fell into a deep sleep.

"Is he OK, Evgeny," asked Michi with a worried look on his face. "Does he do this kind of thing often."

"Not very much," Maxim's close personal aide replied. "But it is happening more often in recent years. I think the pressure of representing his country on an international stage is getting to him. We've got to make sure we keep him fully hydrated at all times."

Evgeny paused for a moment, apparently deep in thought, before uttering the words that Michi was dreading.

"And if I were you I'd be sure to memorise the words to his song as if they were second nature, just in case the worst happens and Maxim is unable to go on."

This small statement whisked Michi into a panic.

"What? Really? Me?" he said in a fluster. "Do you really think that is going to happen?"

"Well I wouldn't usually. But I've never seen him this tired after such a short performance before. We've really got to prepare for every possibility."

Michi's head began to spin. All he could see were spiralling stars and pulsating orange clouds, and his heart felt as though it was pushing up into his mouth and trying to escape his body. Certainly he'd enjoyed his few seconds behind the mic on that giant stage just now. But had it really given him the confidence to be able to represent his country in front of millions of television viewers around the world? He felt sick at the very thought of it. It's one thing having dreams of being a rock star in the bedroom of your tower block flat, but it was quite another being called in to substitute for most popular human being in the country and keep their honour intact – let alone remembering all the words.

"Michi? Michi!" Evgeny's deep, harsh voice snapped him out his visions. "I think Maxim is waking up. Quick, get him a drink."

"Erm, yes. Yes! Right away Evgeny!" he said as he dashed towards the fridge.

"Oh, did I nod off?" said the old man rubbing his eyes. "How very rude of me. I must have been terribly tired. Right then, let me get this make up off and then we can pop back to the ranch to spruce myself up for this evening's do at the Russian Consulate."

"Are you sure that's awfully wise, Maxim sir?" Evgeny asked. "You do seem terribly tired, after all." "Nonsense lad, I've never been fitter! Let's get this show on the road!"

23

"So where is this Russian Consulate, Elvis?" Terry asked his regular cabbie. "It seems like we're taking an awful lot of of back lanes."

"At end of 25th October Street, Terry my friend, by Monument To First Moldavian Power Plant," Elvis replied. "Euro Village made main road closed, so we must find a new way."

"Monument to what?" Sunny laughed from the middle of the back seat.

"First Moldavian Power Plant, Sunny sir," Elvis replied. "Very proud history, very beautiful monument."

"Oh I'm quite sure that it is!" said Sunny, "and it sounds 100% Tiraspol!"

"Ahh, we are here," said Elvis after turning right out of a broken back alley. "The beautiful Russian Consulate building! I park up."

"Oh, that wasn't quite what I was expecting," said Dean. "I thought it would be something far grander."

Across the road stood a pair of squat white single story buildings with a big sliding gate filling the space between them. Somewhere in the distance the boys could hear some traditional Russian music being played and a lot of loud chattering.

"Yep, this is definitely the place," said Jeff. "Look, there's the monument to the power thingy. How terribly, erm, knobbly."

"Right then chaps," said Terry, stirringly. "Invites out, we're going in! We've got to make the most of this as it's the only Consulate party this year."

"It's the only Consulate in the city," laughed Jeff. "Unless you count Abkhazia and South Ossetia, of course, but I don't think we'll be having them in the contest just yet."

"Psst, Terry," whispered Sunny. "I've got a spare invite because one of the lads from the front desk didn't want to come. Should we give it to Elvis?"

"Oh I don't see why not," said Terry. "We've had some pretty good service out of him over the last week. He can think of it as a tip."

"Erm, I was wondering," asked Jan with a furrowed brow, "why don't we get Vasile or one of the other official drivers to cart us about around the city for free?"

"Well for one," Terry answered, "Vasile is detailed to Filip, so we could only guarantee his service if our leader has done with him for the night. And for another, none of the rest of the lads ever want to drive out to the places that we want to go in their big posh mercs. So Elvis is the King. And what are we paying him? Three Euro a night or something silly like that? Plus, we get the full off-piste tour guide business out of him as well. What's not to love? Here, give him your spare."

"Elvis mate," Sunny called after the cabbie, who was still sitting in his Lada by the monument. "How do you fancy coming into the party with us?"

"Oh thank you Sunny, sir, you are very kind," Elvis humbly answered. "But I already have invite. My nephew works on gate. But thank you for the special thought."

"Strewth," said Dean under his breath, "He's better connected in this city than the mayor himself!" "We'll see you in there then, Elvis," Terry shouted across the road.

"Just doing my hair," Elvis smiled, as the lads walked towards the gate.

"Invitations?" the inscrutable security guard barked coldly. "Accreditations?" he continued. "Guns, knives, fireworks?" he asked.

"What, we need weapons to get in?" joked Sunny.

"Shhh, mate," said Dean. "I'm not sure this is the time for jokes!"

"No, no we're clean," said Terry, more of an old hand at these things than the other four.

"Stand here," the guard said sternly, as he passed a handheld metal detector across their bodies. "Oh shit!" said Sunny, with some concern.

"What's up mate?" Dean asked. "You'll see," he replied with a wink. As it got to Sunny's turn to be scanned, the detector let off a loud beep as the guard passed it around the top of his trousers.

"Empty pockets," the guard said.

"They're empty," Sunny replied matter-of-factly. "It's my Prince Albert."

The other four lads did their best to stifle their laughs as this scene progressed. "What is Prince Albert?" the guard asked, puzzled. "Show me."

"Ahh!" Sunny continued with a knowing smile. "You might not want me to do that."

He quickly started scrolling through the pictures on his phone until he found the one that best described his predicament.

"Here, see," said Sunny as he thrust his phone towards the guard's face.

"Oh!" exclaimed the guard with a start. "I see. Very good, sir. You go in. You all go in!"

The guard quietly chuckled to himself, by now quite sure that this wouldn't be the strangest thing he saw all night.

"Sunny, I never knew!" said Dean with some surprise. "But how come that never sets off the security beeper when we go into the press centre?"

"Oh I've got a little arrangement with the guy who runs the machine down there," Sunny replied with a knowing smirk. "Let's just say that he discovered it for himself the first night that we were in town..."

"You're a right dark horse you are, Sunny!" Dean laughed. "I dread to ask if there's anything else you haven't told us yet!"

The boys walked down the passageway between the two white buildings towards the scrubby-looking garden around the back. The Russians had done a pretty good job at trying to make the place look classy. Big banners in the colours of their flag were draped across the trees, tables covered in gold lamé were scattered around the groundspace, and tall burning torches stood at each corner, marking out the mingling area. Along one side of the gardens stood a line of tables, each laden with Russian delicacies – everything from pelmeni to pirozhki via golubtsy to little piles of the finest caviar perched upon gold-flecked blini. Along the other side stood a long bar, constantly doling out a steady flood of flavoured vodkas, rich Georgian wines, and champagne.

Between them, at the far end of the garden, stood a big stage, covered again in gold fabric, with the word Gennady written in bold on a big screen at the back.

"Oh man," said Dean, stuffing a handful of cabbage rolls into his face, "all this great grub and we're going to get a Gennady gig too. Ambassador, you really are spoiling us!"

Suddenly there was a commotion back towards the gate.

"Who's that old guy coming in?" asked Jeff. "Everybody seems to know him." "Oh, I think that's Maxim Munteanu, the Moldovan singer," Terry offered.

"Really?" Jeff replied with some surprise. "That guy I saw on stage this afternoon looked a good twenty years younger. If not more!"

"The stage and the cameras can take years off a boy," Sunny laughed. "Well I'd better get up there myself if that's the case!" joked Dean.

Maxim made his way through the crowd, being sure to spend a little time shaking the hand of everyone he passed and giving them a kindly word.

"Man, he looks like royalty," said Jeff.

"He very much is around these parts," Terry replied. "He's just about the biggest hero this nation's got. No wonder they chose him to do their song this year."

"Yeah, but he doesn't look like he's going to make it to the end of the night, let alone get up on stage and represent Moldova to the whole world next week," said Dean. "I reckon we've got to keep a close eye on that old goat. Are there any contingency plans just in case any of the acts can't make it on the big night?"

"Well, not as such," said Terry, knowledgeably. "But we have discussed this back in Lucerne. The consensus is that should a main singer be unable to perform for whatever reason, they, or their delegation, would suggest a replacement, who would then take their place by proxy. It's not something that we've ever had to worry about before, but I can really see what you're getting at. I think I'd better have a chat with Filip about it in the morning and find out if anything is in the books to facilitate such a matter."

"Well you'd better do it quick," said Dean. "That old fella looks like he's on his last legs!"

There was another stir among the crowd as Timur Turgenev stepped out of one of the Consulate buildings to take a seat on a verandah overlooking the party area. Maxim Munteanu slowly and unsteadily made his way up there to join him and the lights began to fade.

A man in a drab business suit climbed up onto the stage, looking slightly awkward to be amongst the showbiz glitz and glamour around him.

"Hello partygoers!" he said with little conviction. "My name is Zakhar Entin, and I'd like to welcome you to my beautiful garden. Made all the more beautiful by having all you beautiful people in it."

"Stop saying beautiful!" Sunny said under his breath, before Terry quietly kicked him in the foot. "It is with great pleasure that I invite you to sample a taste of Russian hospitality, and to enjoy some Russian entertainment on the stage here in front of you. Eat, drink and dance in the Russian style, and I thank you all for coming!"

There was a polite ripple of applause as Mr Entin left the stage, before a troupe of dancers in furry hats came on stage and began hopping about in a very traditional way.

"Right, bar then," Sunny proclaimed, as he headed to the left of the stage to fill himself with as much complimentary booze as he could manage. But as he turned to to his friends he noticed Elvis on the verandah behind them.

"Hey, there's our cabbie up there, talking to the Moldovan singer and that local King guy," he shouted, pointing up to the verandah.

"Bloody hell, yes it is," said Jeff. "How the hell did he get up there? Do you think he's some kind of agent sent here to keep an eye on us?"

"In this city," said Terry, "it's probably best not to ask. And most definitely best not to find out. Anyway, the dancers are coming off. I think we're about to get a bit of Gennady."

Sure enough, a gaggle of musicians appeared on stage and began to play a long, Vegas-style intro to Gennady's song. Suddenly a voice came out of nowhere.

"Hello Tiraspol!" it chirped energetically. "Are you ready to make party?"

And with that a slight but impossibly handsome young man flew out of a trap door in the stage floor and began to gyrate around as he hummed the melody to his Eurovision song.

"Has he forgotten the words?" Dean laughed.

"Nah mate," replied Jeff. "It's art, innit. Jazz art. At least we know now that he's not a hologram now."

"Still don't believe it!" said Dean, mockingly. "Look, the light passes right through his body and I can see the drummer flailing about behind him."

After a long preamble, Gennady launched into his Eurovision song with a performance so energetic and enjoyable that even a few of the stone faced dignitaries at the back began to jig about in their sensible suits.

"Oh man, I think we've got another potential winner here," said Jeff. "How many's that now?" "Oh, at least ten, I reckon!" said Jan. "It's anybody's game."

"Yeah, but you bet when something does eventually win it'll be so darned obvious that we'll all be cross at not having realised it," said Jeff.

"Same as every year then," Terry laughed. "Yep, same as every year," Jeff replied.

Gennady came to the end of his song, and just as everyone was about to head to the bar again, he stopped them in their tracks with an announcement.

"And now I would like to invite a huge hero of mine to the stage so that I can sing his own very special Eurovision song along with him. Ladies and gentlemen... may I introduce to you... Maxim Munteanu!"

"Ooh, this could be interesting," said Jeff. "Is he even going to make it up those stairs?"

The old man slowly clambered onto the stage, and with each step he appeared to get five years younger. By the time he got to the microphone he appeared full of his usual vigour and ready to perform.

He opened his arms, as if to figuratively hug the whole crowd, and started to speak.

"My friends," he said warmly. "It is with great pleasure that I come to sing for you today with my young friend Gennady here. He is a great talent. It is so very special for me to welcome you all to my wonderful country. Are you all having a good time?"

Even the cynical Jeff found himself hollering "Yeah!", quite against his better nature.

"Heck, this guy's like some kind of emotional hypnotist!" said Jeff. "I'm not entirely sure why, but I love him already!"

"So now for my song, Moldova's Landscape," said Maxim. "It's about the ground that you are standing on and the air that you are breathing."

And with that he launched into the most beautiful warm and heartfelt rendition of his song. Gennady joined in with him on the first chorus, but quickly realised that he was offering nothing to the performance and very graciously stepped back to let the old man continue alone. By the time he'd finished there wasn't a dry eye to be seen, and a massive cheer came forth from behind the Consulate's gates from locals who'd recognised their national hero's voice and came to listen for themselves.

"Thank you," he said. "Thank you all. Enjoy yourselves for the rest of the evening!"

He turned to walk off stage, but as he planted one foot on the first step his knee gave way and he took a tumble down the short flight of stairs. Fortunately Evgeny was there to catch him and break his fall, but there was still a loud collective gasp from the audience.

"Don't worry," Maxim shouted out, apparently unconcerned. "That birch bark vodka is mighty strong stuff!"

But the crowd were concerned. They could suddenly see the old man's frailties displayed starkly in front of them, and a loud anxious muttering rippled around the garden as Maxim disappeared off into the Consulate buildings.

"I tell you what," said Jeff. "That song was utterly beautiful, and his charisma is well beyond anything I've ever seen with my own eyes. But I'm really concerned that he's not going to make it to next Saturday. He's either going to win this thing by a mile or die trying. And I've got serious fears that it's going to be the latter."

WEEK TWO

24

The second set of rehearsals for the Big Five and the hosts Moldova all went relatively smoothly. Explodo didn't explode, Jolana Nováková didn't invade the stage for the German performance, and despite his stumble the previous night, Maxim Munteanu eased through his rehearsal with the look of a man at the top of his game. Even Jason Brown from the UK looked more confident with each passing performance. And with just the six songs to rehearse on the Sunday, it gave all the artists plenty of time to prepare themselves for the grand opening party in the grand hall of the Government Offices in the centre of the city that night.

As many of the stalls from the Euro Village ran along the other side of the road from the stark Stalinist building, local residents and any Eurovision fans who'd arrived in town early were able to cheer all the artists as they walked from their buses up the red carpet and in through the building's austere main entrance. The carpet was red this year rather than the traditional pink in part because the local government were keen not to overplay the gay aspect too much in case it caused tensions locally – but also out of deference to Lenin, whose statue lay on the route into the party venue, and who many Transnistrians still held in some regard. The delegation buses were queued up around the block, ready to spill each new contestant out onto the pavement in alphabetical order. Although they decided to leave the hosts until last so that Maxim could have a bit of a nap back at his ranch.

Xhyljeta, the Albanian singer, was the first to arrive, looking stunning in a brocaded deep blue velvet dress while tottering skilfully in four inch high-heeled boots. She was followed by Armenia's Takouhi

Vardanyan in a flimsy peach gossamer affair, with tattered frills billowing in the gentle Spring breeze. Australian band The Space Truckers caused the first real stir as they clumped off their bus in their signature vest and shorts combo, although they had made just a little bit of an effort as each member of the band was wearing a dicky bow around their weather beaten necks. Then the Austrian lad Danny B skipped out of his delegation transport and proceeded to moonwalk down the red carpet, scuffing it up just enough so that the diminutive Azerbaijani singer Murad Orujov stumbled over the first fold in his built up shoes.

Filip and Terry stood at the top of the steps to the grand building, surveying all that went before them, just to check that everything was going to plan. The moment he saw Murad's near pratfall he got on the radio to one of the production crew nearer the red carpet.

"Can someone carpet side whip down and straighten out the mat?" he said efficiently. "We don't want any more of these goons tripping up on live Moldovan tea time telly. Oh, and while you're there, can you tell Danny B to stop arseing about.

"Will do sir!" replied the voice on the radio, and about a hundred yards away two figures in black scurried out from the wings to smooth the carpet back down again.

"Ahh, the power!" said Filip, affecting an imperial stance.

"Don't let it go to your head, Filip old boy," Terry laughed. "We've got the Czech girl coming up in a few buses, and you know what that could mean."

"Oh gawd," said Filip, deflating a little. "It's going to be a horror story with her all night, isn't it! I've had a word with Juri from her delegation, and he said he's going to try to keep her on a leash, but the poor lad's got his hands full there!"

"Fingers crossed for a good outcome," said Terry. "And at least it'll get us on the international news if she acts up!"

"Yeah, but not in a good way," Filip scowled.

With each passing bus the pair began to get more and more anxious, and as the Cypriot singer began her walk up the red carpet, the Czech bus was still nowhere to be seen.

"Oh my good heavens, she's milking it!" said Terry.

"Either that or she's made her bus crash and they're all lying bleeding in a ditch somewhere," Filip quipped.

"Oh, don't," Terry laughed. "The way this year has been going I wouldn't be at all surprised if that had actually happened.

After what seemed like an endless minute-and-a-half, the Czech bus came into view, flashing its lights and sounding its horn. Filip feared for the worst.

"Brace yourself Terry," he said with a wince. "I'm getting a bad feeling about this."

The bus pulled up and its doors opened, but nobody came came out for several seconds.

"Oh no, they're just prolonging the agony!" said Filip. "Hang about, can you hear barking? Iceland aren't due for another eight buses, surely?"

Finally Jolana Nováková stepped off the bus, and the big crowd of photographers who were fenced off in a corral at one end of the red carpet let out a collective gasp. She was wearing a tight black bodystocking, with whiskers painted on her face, and a pair of big dog's ears on a headband poking through her scraped back hair. Then Juri, her head of delegation, stepped out from the bus behind her holding a long leather lead, and began to parade her down the aisle as if he was taking a family pet for a walk down the local park.

"Juri wasn't wrong when he said he was going to keep her on a leash," said Filip, aghast, "but I never imagined it was going to be an actual, proper dog leash. Boy, this is either brilliant or tragic, and I'm not sure which!"

"I think it's a little of each," said Terry. "But Vikingur from Iceland is going to be bloody livid. He's going to think she's taking the piss!"

"Ooh, we'll cross that bridge when we come to it," said Filip. "We've got to get her up the red carpet without leaving any little messes or humping another contestant's leg first."

After a few doggy-shaped antics, Jolana reached the interview area where this year's hosts – Elina Gospodinova from O Melodie Pentru Moldova and the talk show host Ruslan Rusu – were waiting to give her a brief interview. But instead of speaking she just started to bark again.

"Oh, you're looking forward to a little meeting with the Icelandic puppydog are you?" said Elina, quick as a flash.

Jolana then started to growl, before saying "I'm a good girl," over and over again as Juri led her off to meet the ranks of press lined up alongside route to the party.

"At least that's got her out of the view of the TV cameras and halfway to the hall," said Filip, relieved. "It could have been a whole lot worse. As long as Juri keeps her away from the booze then we should be alright. Now we've just got to hope that the rest of this year's problem children behave themselves!"

And for the most part they did. The Finnish trolls larked about in their costumes, but didn't cause any great offence to anybody, Sissi and Sal walked very obviously up different sides of the red carpet to each other in a display of mild mutual loathing, and the Greek singer Adonis jumped out of the bus wearing boxing gloves and a big blue and white robe, jabbing and moving his way up the carpet like a prize fighter on the way into the ring for a title eliminator. Even Iceland's Vikingur seemed relatively normal as he disembarked, wearing a sharp black tuxedo to compliment the head, hands and feet of his plushy dog costume.

"You know who we've got to worry about next, though," said Terry with dread in his voice. "Who's that then?" Filip asked.

Terry effected a death metal growl and pulled the devil horns gesture with his two outstretched fists.

"Oh shit, Norway," he panicked. "What in the name of heaven – or more worryingly, hell – are they going to pull."

True to form, the Norwegian bus pulled up with loud Wagnerian music pounding out of a large pile of speakers on its roof and smoke billowing out through its windows.

"Here we go!" Filip said, nervously. "Anything could happen in the next sixty seconds."

The doors of the bus opened and smoke cascaded down the steps. Through the haze, the first few figures could be seen disembarking. As the mist cleared, Filip could see each member of Stormgiver standing buck naked in full corpse paint, shy of a small leather pouch that was just about protecting their decency. And over the right shoulder of each of them was the corpse of a young pig, just hanging there and bleeding slightly.

"Oh. My. Days." said Terry. "This is going to put the good people of Moldova off their Sunday tea!"

The Norwegians marched in single file at a funereal pace, stopping only to say a stark "NO!" at the interview post, before eventually reaching the statue of Lenin. The band stopped walking, and each man in turn laid their pig at the base of the statue, kissing it tenderly on the head before they continued on into the building.

"I have absolutely no idea what that's supposed to mean," said Filip, by now in something of a fluster, "But it's really going to annoy someone somewhere, and I'm expecting to get a flood of calls about it any second now."

Sure enough his phone rang. It was Stefan Smolenko from Moldova Smash who was standing on the other side of the the steps.

"Did you see that, Filip?" he spat, in a panic.

"I certainly did, Stefan," Filip replied. "Was that in any way symbolic?"

"Well not to my knowledge," Stefan continued, "But the old guard around here really aren't going to like it. I think we'll have to put extra security on that lot for the rest of the week, because I can think of a few local agitators who might want to take them to task for it. And probably not in the most polite manner!"

"I'll be sure to get an extra detail on them as soon as we're done here, Stefan. Thanks for filling me in!"

The rest of the red carpet parade ran relatively to plan, once the stage crew had managed to get the dead pigs out of sight and scrub off any remaining residue from the plinth. But there were a few more highlights still to come. Gennady from Russia rode along in front of his bus on a big white horse, and managed to get as far as the steps up to the building before he had to dismount. The Saudi team from San Marino had employed a little Arabian folk band to follow them wherever they went, and Ukraine's Bohdana was carried the whole way from her bus to the party venue while kneeling on a golden platform, waving serenely as she went, and held aloft at each corner by four oiled up and muscular men.

Now they just had to wait for Maxim Munteanu to arrive and this complicated part of the event would be complete. They waited, and they waited, until finally a bus festooned in the colours of both Transnistria and the wider Moldova came into view. As it pulled up, Maxim climbed casually down the steps without a care in the world. Filip and Terry looked at each other puzzled as to what might have caused the delay.

"I had a horrible feeling that he may have died on the way to the party, for a moment there," said Filip, and Terry just cast him one of his "I know!" looks.

As Maxim approached the interview area, both CTF men strained their ears to hear what the problem may have been.

"We thought you'd deserted us for one horrible moment there, Maxim," said Ruslan with a warm grin. "What kept you, old friend?"

Maxim stood and smiled for a moment, before he replied. "Well the strangest thing happened, Ruslan. Just as I was about to leave the ranch, my favourite horse started to give birth in the field right in front of me. So I had to stay to see if she managed to finish the job successfully."

"And did she?" asked Ruslan.

"Oh yes, very well," the old man replied. "And I've named the little foal Michi, after my loyal young friend here."

Michi turned to Maxim on the verge of tears. Already his new friend had given him so much more than he could ever have wished for, but this latest honour was just a little bit more than he'd ever expected.

"You must be a hell of a guy then Michi," said Ruslan, whacking the confused looking goth on the back with a hefty slap.

"Oh I'm nobody. Nobody at all," said Michi. "Maxim is the hero here. He helped birth the horse with his own hands."

A spontaneous round of applause burst out across the watching crowd, as Maxim turned to make his way up the red carpet, stopping and shaking the hand of practically everybody he passed.

"Right, that's the easy bit over and done with, Terry," said Filip, turning to enter the building. "Now for the ordeal. With that lot all in the same room at the same time for the first time, absolutely anything could happen. And I suspect that it quite probably might."

*

As the two men passed through the doors they were almost surprised to see the polite-yet-busy event buzzing away before them. The artists and their delegations were standing in little groups, getting photo ops with each other, while waiting staff dressed in national costume were quickly whipping any finished glasses out of the attendees' hands and replacing them with a full one of the same colour. Every now and again there'd be a little hubbub as the photographers and TV cameras noticed a couple of performers starting to have a chat, and were instantly surrounded by the world's press all trying to get a decent snap for their papers. So they would suddenly have to pretend that they were talking about each others' outfits rather than if they knew anyone who could supply some decent cocaine around these parts.

At one end of the big room a squat balding man in a grey suit nervously tapped the microphone on a small stage and began to make a speech. It was Miroslav Grankin, the mayor of Tiraspol, and he looked incredibly uncomfortable.

"Hello? Hello! Yes, hello," he muttered anxiously. "As mayor of this great city of ours, I would like to welcome all you talented people from all over Europe and beyond to taste some true Transnistrian hospitality."

Mayor Grankin delivered his lines with all the excitement of a company accounts clerk reading out that year's stationery spending figures, and the excitable crowd quickly went back to their conversations. This hubbub was starting to drown the poor old fella out, and Lucian Dobre, the brash owner of Moldova Smash, was pacing in the wings, frustrated at the city grandee's lack of dynamism.

"Let me up there with him!" he said to Dumi. "I can quickly get this party going again!"

"Ooh, I wouldn't just yet," Dumi replied, "If for nothing else than in deference to our local hosts. The last thing we need right now is for the locals to take offence at us loud Moldovans butting into their party. Just give the old goat a minute and I'm sure he'll be finished soon."

"I guess you're right this time, Dumi," Lucien agreed. "But we can't leave him up there much longer, mate. He's totally killing the vibe."

Unfortunately Mayor Grankin was nowhere near finished, and as he was thanking what felt like the fiftieth local dignitary, the crowd were getting restless.

"Put a sock in it, fella," shouted one of the Space Truckers. "we're here to get wasted and have a great night. We don't need you waffling along!"

"Yeah man!" Austria's Danny B added, "I'm just here to Dance Dance. Less talk more party!"

But still Mayor Grankin ploughed on, even though the agitated rumble from the hall began to get louder and louder.

"That's it, I've had enough of this shit! I'm going in to save this show!" barked Lucien, as his huge frame ambled up the steps at the side of the stage."

"Oh God no!" Dumi fretted to himself, before shouting up at Lucien: "At least be diplomatic!"

Lucien gave Dumi a shrug of assurance as he slowly walked up to the the dreary man at the mic. The locals who recognised who he was began to let out little chirrups of delight, and a small peel of applause rippled around the hall. Mayor Grankin, who hadn't yet noticed the stage invader, thought the applause was for him and looked visibly buoyed at this response, before sinking on his heels as soon as he felt Lucien's massive presence shuffle up beside him. He looked up at the former basketball player towering above him, raised his eyes and let out a big sigh. You got the feeling that this kind of thing happened to him a lot.

"Mayor Grankin!" Lucien effused. "Thank you for such a warm and kind welcome to your amazing city!" As he spoke he encouraged the crowd to applaud with a little hand gesture to the Mayor's blindside. "Is there anything more you'd like to tell us?"

There was a momentary pause before a single voice in the centre of the room cried out a panicked "For the love of God no!"

The Mayor knew when he was beaten, shrugged his shoulders, and coldly announced "I now declare this year's Eurovision Song Contest officially open!"

Once again Lucien surreptitiously led the cheering, before subtly nudging the Mayor away from the mic and announcing: "The the food hall is now ready!" His sturdy long arms made a sweeping gesture before him as a set of massive doors at the back of the room swung open to reveal a cornucopia of local culinary delights. Everybody's heads swivelled around, and there was a polite stampede in high heels and posh suits as the delegates clamoured for their free food.

"AND!" Lucien continued, "To entertain you all I'd like to welcome the musical pride of our nation, the Bessarabian Turbo Squad! Make some motherfucking noise, brothers and sisters!"

And with that, a big curtain was swept aside behind him and last year's Eurovision winners launched into a full set of their most popular songs. As the pair walked off the stage, Lucien put a big caring arm around Mayor Grankin's shoulder and said "Good job, old fella! I think you really won them over there!"

"Oh, do you think?" the meek city official questioned.

"Oh most definitely!" said Lucien with a massive grin. "Just look at them all going batshit bananas out there. You helped do that!"

"Yes, maybe I did!" said Mayor Grankin as he straightened his faded red tie and walked to the backstage area with a spring in his step.

"I have no idea how you just managed that," said Dumi, once the Mayor was out of ear shot, "but I'm incredibly glad that you did! Good job sir!"

"What do you mean?" said Lucien, pretending to be affronted. "With this charm I can make the flowers grow and coax the bees out of their hives!"

"Yes, and I full well know about your sting, too!" Dumi laughed. "But thanks for helping out there sir. I thought people were going to start throwing stuff for a minute, and that really wouldn't do!"

Meanwhile, in the food hall, Filip and Terry were anxiously surveying the scene for any kind of trouble. The caterers for the city hall had placed a fifty foot long table with free shots of the local firewater along the back wall of the room, but some of the more bold members of the delegations were working their way down the line to try to have a go on each of the garishly coloured liquids.

"Oh my days," said Terry, "If Jolana sees this lot here we're done for!"

"Oh good heavens yes," said Filip. "We've got to keep an eye out for her and try to steer her away from danger."

"Easier said than done, I fear," Terry replied, before he fell silent and his jaw dropped a little. "What is it, Terry?" Filip asked, a little concerned. "What have you seen?"

"Fair play to Juri!" Terry responded, "he's only gone and done it! Look there, and see for yourself!"

Filip turned to see that Jolana now had a muzzle fitted to the front of her face, and no matter how hard she tried to drink from a glass she just couldn't get a significant amount to pass her lips before Juri tugged her away on her lead.

"God damn it, the man's a genius!" Filip conceded with an amazed look. "He's keeping in the house style for the night while he's keeping her – and indeed everybody else – away from booze flavoured danger. Class move, Juri!"

"I know!" laughed Terry in response. "We've just got to make sure that we hide all the bastard straws in the building!"

The rest of the evening passed by perfectly. A few artists may have got a little more sozzled than they ought – especially considering that they had an early call for the first full dress rehearsal in the morning – and a few dancers disappeared off into the night with a few backing singers, but nothing majorly untoward. Juri even managed to keep Jolana away from the Icelandic dog boy for the whole event, despite the constant efforts of the press corps to try to bring them together. Having no difficulty in keeping themselves apart, however, were the two German singers, who made great pains to stand on opposite sides of the room all evening. Also rather noticeable was the fact that both the Armenian and Azerbaijani singers melted away into the night quite early on. The rumour mill was suggesting that they'd been having a little fling on the quiet, but their respective heads of delegations were quietly denying it, stating that it would be worth the journalists' while in the long run if they kept this story to themselves. Of course, now this tasty bit of tittle tattle had started to do the rounds, more and more people were approaching the two respective HoDs just in case it earned them some kind of reward further down the line. Such is the way of the Eurovision press corps.

Oh, and the Norwegians? They just stood there quietly in their own corner all night, glowering at anyone who came near them. But one had the suspicion that they still had something terrible up hidden away up their studded black leather sleeves.

25

Monday morning finally arrived, and it was time to glue all the rehearsed bits and pieces together into something vaguely resembling a Eurovision show. This afternoon's first full dress rehearsal for semi-final one was going to be a complete run-through of Tuesday's night's broadcast show, complete with hosts, postcards, interval acts, green room larks and some dummy qualifier announcements at the end. After all the individual rehearsals this was the first opportunity to run it all in order and see if it not only actually worked in a big straight line, but fitted in with the planned broadcast timings too.

The first full dress rehearsal of the week always ran a little wonky. It was the one big chance to check on all the potential logjams and iron everything out, but that didn't stop the fan press from getting themselves into a major panic about everything that appeared to be going wrong, and then pontificate about how it was such a stupid idea to let Country X host the thing in the first place.

Every. Single. Year. But with twenty minutes until show time, things were running smoothly. Almost too smoothly for Filip's liking.

"Something's not right," he said, as he anxiously paced about on the CTF viewing balcony. "It's all going too damn... well!"

"I know, right," his sidekick responded. "Something doesn't quite sit right. With all the freakazoids that we've got on the bill today something's sure to blow up somewhere – and hopefully not literally!"

"Oh don't, Terry! The last thing we need is another terror panic incident just because a bit of pyro went pop at the wrong time!"

"True. True. But someone, somewhere is going to upset the applecart,

I'm sure of it. And I'll bet they're wearing corpse paint!"

"And anyway Terry, where have all these people come from?" said Filip, pointing to the large crowds that were filing into the arena. "It's usually only the press, families and hangers on that come into this one, isn't it?"

"Usually," Terry replied. "But the demand for tickets over the whole week was so massive locally that Moldova Smash thought it would be a nice idea to give all the schools and people from the neighbourhoods some extra cheap tickets for this show so that they could get a feel of what it's all about. And actually, I think that's rather a sweet idea on their part."

"A very sweet idea," said Filip. "Usually. But with the gaggle of easily aggravated egos that are about to perform for us I get a terrible feeling it's a PR move that could very easily backfire on us."

Five minutes to go and the backstage area is crowded and anxious. The first half-dozen acts were waiting in line, getting their in-ear monitors fitted and having the last touches to their hair and make up sorted out. In every other available space, more than a hundred dancers and musicians in local costume were bouncing about nervously, ready to burst out on to the stage and the aisles and perform their opening song and dance routine once the introductory video had finished playing.

Hanna was already doing her best to calm down the most terrified among them and keeping everyone on their mark, while Linnea the crew ganger had her mob poised like greyhounds in their traps, ready to spring onto stage the second the hosts walked off to sweep up any stray feathers and boot prints and get the first act set up before their performance. And for those Montenegrin steam punks it was going to be quite a task to do all that in 45 seconds or less.

A minute before the planned kick off time, Hanna walked up onto the stage, and alongside her an interpreter gave the crowd a quick explanation of when to cheer and how to behave when the acts were on stage. The crowd were clapping her every word, which she found a little disconcerting, but she figured that they're just excited to be there. Ten seconds to go and the arena goes dark. Hanna gives them all one final up stir with her clipboard, and the famous Eurovision theme tune kicks in.

The crowd go absolutely wild.

"I'll tell you what, mate" said Terry with a slightly moist eye, "I don't know how many times I might hear that piece of music in a year, but it still gives me the goosebumps every single time."

"I know what you mean," Filip replied. "And these crowds! If this is what it's like when it's three- quarters full on a Monday afternoon, how amazing is it going to be for the big show on Saturday?!"

Up on the big screens a film showed The Bessarabian Turbo Squad winning last year's competition and arriving back home in Moldova as heroes. The crowd went even more berserk than before, as a brief travelogue shows the countryside and cities of the nation, being sure to get as much of Transnistria in as possible – although to be honest there really wasn't all that much to show. A drone shot from above a cornfield quickly zooms in to a small child playing on a panpipe, before a single spotlight in the hall bursts onto a satellite stage in the middle of the audience where the same small child is nervously awaiting her cue. The film cuts out and she begins to mime her piece – before the deepest, most bowel-cleansing burst of feedback you could ever imagine started to throb dirtily out of the PA. The crowd grabbed their ears in horror, the sound crew urgently levelled out every fader, and the little girl with the panpipe quietly wept on her plinth.

At that moment Hanna shouted "Stop! Stop! What is that terrible noise!" Some wag in the audience chirped up "It's only a little kid playing a tooty whistle – don't be so cruel!" This lightened the mood a little, but it still worried the two CTF executives on the balcony.

"Tell me that's normal, Terry, and that they're going to sort it out quickly," said Filip with a furrowed brow.

"Yeah, this thing seems to happen every now and again with a big PA," Terry replied. "It's no real biggy. They'll have it all cleared up in a minute."

"I do hope so," said Filip. "I'd just settled myself in for a nice show, and then that happened. I'd better give Skunk the sound guy a shout, just to be sure."

He picked up his radio ready to give Skunk a call when there was another short burst of the same punishingly loud feedback that rattled every fixture in the hall.

"Skunk mate, it's Filip. What's going on up there at the desk?"

"Ahh Filip, I've been expecting your call," Skunk laughed. "Seems like we've got ourselves a bit of brown noise in the system. Probably a rogue twiddly knob somewhere. We're trying them all out one-by-one as we speak..."

There was third loud throb that led the audience to grab their ears in distress once more.

"We'll probably be another five minutes, boss," Skunk continued. "The local boys seem to have it in hand. I'll put out a shout when we're sorted. Better now than Saturday night, eh!"

"Well that's one way of looking at it, Skunk," said Filip only half satisfied with the answer. "Keep me posted."

"Will do boss!" Skunk sang, as he rang off.

"Well they're on top of it at least," Filip said to Terry, before another micro boom of pure noise pummelled out of the speakers. "Almost..."

"Oh they'll sort it soon enough," said Terry, before changing his expression and saying, "but I think you'll want to take a look at this... " while pointing to his iPad.

"Eurovision Latest: PA blows up, show in fear of cancellation!" said the headline.

"Who the hell did this?" barked Filip, before Terry pointed at the site's URL. "Oh EuroStorm! I might have flipping known! Hang about, didn't we kick them off the premises last week?"

"We did, Filip," Terry replied "but they've been operating out of Michael Storm's hotel room, ripping off everybody else's reports and photos wholesale. But it feels awfully like they've got someone in the hall right now. Look, there's even a video clip of the feedback!"

"Shit, we've got to get this sorted out quick smart," said Filip in a minor panic. "There's people who still believe his nonsense, and if that filters back to the proper press then we're going to be answering questions about it for the rest of the week. Can't we work out where the film was taken from by the angle of the shot?"

"Ooh, good point!" said Terry, scanning the crowd. "By my reckoning it should be just... about... there! Got him! Third row behind the moshpit, left of stage."

"Oh yeah, there's some bloke down there with a hat on who looks like he's streaming it on his phone," Filip replied. "Hang about! It's only bloody Michael Storm in a fake beard and local headgear. How the heck did he manage to sneak in?"

"No idea. But we'd better get security to drag him out by his ear before he causes any more damage. I'll get on the blower to Ox right away."

"Nice one," said Filip, and the pair watched fascinated as a handful of burly figures ghosted their way towards the disguised character, surrounding him before he even knew they were there.

"Excuse me sir," said Ox politely to Michael Storm. "Do you mind coming with me?"

Storm looked shocked to have been discovered so soon, but immediately got on his feet to try and argue with the burly men.

"I got my ticket for this show fair and square – after a fashion," he complained, "I have every right to be here!"

"And you will understand, Mr Storm sir," said Ox, "that I have every right to remove you from this venue for contravening international copyright laws. Now, would you like to do this the hard way, or the easy way? And I'll warn you, the easy way still isn't very nice."

Michael Storm found himself breathing in to utter the words "You just try it, buster!" before he looked around at the seven massive mountains of muscle surrounding him and decided that it was probably the right choice to go quietly – just this once. He could always send someone else in to get the shots. Just then there was a massive clumsy nudge to his right hand, and his phone and microphone fell to the floor.

"Oops!" said Ox. "I appear to have accidentally stepped on your filming equipment. Six times. How very unfortunate. I can only apologise. Ooh, look, I did it two times more. Sorry again!"

The indignation was boiling up within Michael Storm and he found himself yelling "You just wait until I get my lawyers on this!" before one of Ox's men picked him up by the scruff of the neck – with just the pinch of two fingers, mind – and he felt Ox leaning in towards him to whisper the words that few people ever want to hear: "Oh goody, you want to do this the hard way. Come!" He beckoned to the seven heavies, and they frogmarched Storm out to a darkened back room.

"You know what, Terry?" said Filip, observing the security operation from the balcony like a benign Nero figure. "There can be a benefit to bringing this show to these more old fashioned countries. Although I could never possibly say that out loud, could I now?"

"Oh no, Filip," Terry replied. "Perish the thought!"

In the distance the two men could hear Hanna addressing the audience over the front of house mic.

"OK, that's the sound sorted out. This time we go for the whole show in one go! Are we ready? In three... two... one..."

26

It's now a little after 2am on Monday night – or rather Tuesday morning – and the competition's chief organisers, Filip, Hanna and Terry from the CTF, Stefan and Dumi from Moldova Smash, plus Håkan from the Sparkle Crew and Artiom Balan from the local staff were all crammed into Filip's office to have a debrief about the day's events.

"So after that tiny issue with the sound at the start of the day everything ran refreshingly well for the rest of the day," said Filip, almost surprised at this success. "I'm not sure that we've had a first dress rehearsal Monday run that well in a long time. So thank you to everybody and all your teams for helping to make it work so painlessly."

The rest of the meeting's attendees all nodded in agreement.

"The acts all behaved themselves too," Håkan added. "I really thought we were going to get some misbehaviour from the Norwegians at the very least. And that Czech girl was on her best behaviour, too. Well, apart from the corpse paint, that is."

"Yes," Filip replied, "it might have been funny for us, but I really don't think that was her best move being at the jury final and all. I reckon she's done us all a favour there, though, and effectively knocked herself out of the final."

"Which would be a relief to us all," laughed Hanna with a knowing wink.

For those of you not up to date with Eurovision lore and lingo, the jury shows take place the night before each televised show. These full evening dress rehearsals are the ones that each nation's jury watches in order to put together their scores, which are then collated and announced on the following night's live televised show. If an act has a shocker of a performance that night, or doesn't take it seriously enough, it can have a major effect on their total score. Originally the term Jury Final was simply a method used to try to sell more tickets for these rehearsals, as they are filmed and put on standby just in case anything happens to stop the live shows from being broadcast. So the organisers wanted to ensure that they had a full and lively crowd inside the arena, just in case. But they soon developed a culture of their own, and have since become every bit as important as the main shows.

It also means that, having seen how the juries have voted for each of the songs, the organisers are best able to build the tension with the announcement of the votes and the reveals of the qualifiers on the three broadcast TV shows. On top of that it also gives them time to analyse any irregularities in the voting. In the past it's not been unknown for the five jurors from a specific jury to all post identical scores for the songs, while an occasional juror has posted their scores on their social media, too – both of which are in direct contravention of the rules, and can lead to the scores for that country being ruled out of the competition. So it's always an exciting moment when the first set of scores come into the office for the analysis of the organising committee. However this year there were going to be a few uncomfortable surprises.

The inbox alarm on Terry's laptop made its customary bing, and he quickly alerted the committee to the arrival of that evening's jury results.

"And the scores for semi-final one are in!" he chirped with excitement. "Let's have a little look at this lot!"

Each of the seven people in the room quickly fired up their laptops and tablets, clicked onto the email and stared deeply into their screens.

"Ooh!" said Terry with a worried look etched into his brow. "That looks, erm, complicated."

"What am I looking for, Terry?" asked Dumi. "Remember, me, Stefan and Artiom are new to this, so talk us through the numbers."

"Well," Terry began to explain, "You're familiar with the traditional 12-10-8 scoring system of course?"

"Yes, of course," the Moldovans replied – although Artiom wasn't looking quite so sure.

"So, the top ten on each jury's list get the points, with the most popular one getting the 12, and the bottom eight getting nothing," Terry continued.

"Ah yes," said Artiom, as if a lightbulb had just gone on in his head," I understand now!"

"Well now, take a look at the results for San Marino," said Terry. "They've got eleven sets of twelve points…"

"Yes…?" Filip queried.

"And absolutely nothing else from anyone!" Terry announced with dismay. "Nothing. No eights, no fours, no ones. Just twelves and zeroes. That never, ever happens, and it looks just the tiniest bit fishy!"

"How so?" asked Dumi.

"Well," said Terry, "every now and again a song will get a single rogue twelve-pointer and nothing else. Sometimes a song will appeal to one particular jury in a way that it fails to with all the others. It's worthy of note, but not really worth getting concerned about. But on every other occasion in voting history, if a song has got more than a couple of twelves they always, on every occasion, pick up a handful of other assorted scores along the way, too. But this kind of scoring pattern just doesn't happen, and is an indicator that something fishy might be going on."

"Out of interest," asked Filip, "who are the countries that gave them the maximums? I'm too tired to pick my way through the score sheet at the moment."

"Well without pointing any fingers, Filip, it's mainly the ones that we've filed discretely in the Usual Suspects folder."

"Say no more," Filip replied. "I know pretty much exactly who you mean."

"Sounds a bit like the old brown envelope gambit to me, people," Håkan laughed. "And that Saudi prince they've got singing for them does have awfully big pockets!"

"That's the fear, Hawkman," said Filip. "But of course, we can't say any of this out loud in public until we get to the bottom of it."

"Understood, Filly!" Håkan replied, earnestly.

"So where does this leave us going forward?" asked Dumi. "Do we have to do disqualify anyone or anything? That won't look terribly good for the show."

"Not at this stage," Filip replied. "They've probably done just enough to qualify for the final already, which will be a popular move amongst fankind. But I can't see them having a broad enough appeal to dredge in too many points from the public voters, so I'm pretty sure that we'll be safe come

Saturday night."

"And on top of that," Terry added, "we can put round a non-specific briefing to the jury supervisors stating we've identified some potentially questionable voting in the first semi-final, and impress upon them that we hope we don't see any repeat of the unusual scoring patterns in the rest of the shows. That way, the guilty parties will know we're onto them and hopefully think better of it for the rest of the week, while nobody has lost face by being formally accused of anything – which probably works best for everybody. Probably."

"Any other anomalies or surprises, Terry?" Filip asked.

"Well it all looks quite usual and above board for the most part," Terry answered, "although I must say that it's a bit of a surprise that Portugal finished up on the top of the table!"

"Eh what?" said Filip, puzzled. "Portugal? Are they even in this semi?"

"Yeah, you know," said Terry, "that handsome long-haired lad with the beard who's sitting on a little stool with a guitar. The juries went absolutely bonkers for him!"

"Well that really is a surprise," Filip answered. "We're here every day, hearing all the songs, but that one's completely washed over me. Oh, good for him! We could do with something nice and unassuming doing well. Who else is up there?"

"Well, as expected Poland and Romania are up near the top, the Belgian girl is doing surprisingly well, and Austria and Belarus are struggling a bit. Everyone else is bunched up in the middle order, so almost anything could happen tomorrow night".

"Ooh, that should be exciting for the viewers!" Filip replied, "but how about those potential complications from Norway and Czechia? Are they likely to qualify?"

"Touch and go, Filip," said Terry. "They're both pretty much bang centre midfield. It could go either way for both of them."

"Oh damn. I know I'm not supposed to have my favourites, but for the ease of our job we could do with losing at least one of that pair," said Filip.

"Surely they both can't make it?" said Hanna. "Surely? It'll make my life a whole lot easier if we shed them both."

"It's all down to the glorious international public lottery that is Eurovision, I'm afraid," said Filip. "We'll just have to cross our fingers and hope that they don't let us down tomorrow night. Right, I think that's just about it for today, unless anyone's got any other business? No? Let's call it a night then. I think we're in a reasonably good place."

"Reasonably's the key word there," said Terry, only half joking.

27

It's Tuesday morning, and the crew in the CTF press office were making their final preparations for the day when the phone rang. Jeff raced to answer it, and his face immediately set to an expression of deep concern.

"Yes? Oh yes? Oh!" he said with a start. "Oh dear. Ooh. A monk you say? When was that? 1974? I see. Yes, yes, that could be a problem. Could you hold the phone for just a moment? Thanks..."

Jeff muted the phone, turned to his colleagues, and let out an almighty roar. "Shiiiiiiiiiiiiiit!" he exclaimed.

"Quite clearly something appears to be wrong, Jeff mate," said Sunny. "Anything we can do to help?"

"Get Terry in here now," said Jeff, the colour draining out of his face. "This could actually be quite serious."

Sunny skipped over to the office across the corridor, poked his head round Filip's door and asked "You got a moment, Terry? Jeff seems to think it's a bit important."

"Yep, I'll be there now," said Terry, grabbing his coffee. "I'll give you a shout if it actually is important, Filip."

"What is it? What's up?" Terry asked as they made the short walk to the press office.

"I don't know. But Jeff went a funny beige colour about ten seconds into a phone call, so I fear it might be a bit serious."

"Sounds ominous," said Terry, as he walked through the office door.

"Jeff sir, what's up?"

"This could be a bit awkward," said Jeff looking concerned. "We've got a monk on the phone here..."

"A monk?" Terry asked, puzzled.

"Yeah, a bona fide monk. Anyway, he reckons that he was listening to his radio in the cloisters this morning and heard a song that he thought recognised. Turns out that he wrote and recorded it himself back in 1974 and put it out on a limited vinyl release. He's ringing in to ask if he gets any royalties from it being on the show tonight, because he wants to donate it all to his church."

"Oh shit! You're right," said Terry. This could get serious. "Nip over and get Filip would you, Sunny." "On it now, boss," said Sunny as he dashed back out of the door.

"Ooh, I forgot to ask, which song was it again?" asked Terry. "The Portuguese one."

"Phew, at least it's not one of the serious contenders," Dean said relieved, just as Filip burst through the door.

"The Portuguese song?" said Filip, who had clearly heard the conversation as he was coming in through the door. "Oh bollocks!"

"Why's that, Filip?" asked Jeff. "Surely it's a no hoper?"

"Well, you'd have thought," said Filip, anxiously, "And you've not heard this, right – none of you have, understand – but that song absolutely walked the jury vote last night, and this could put us quite deeply in the mire if it's true."

"Eh?" said Sunny. "I couldn't hum that song back to you if it was playing in the office right now!" "Well, you know what the juries are like," said Terry. "Worthiness over funtimes, every time!"

"Right, let's not get ahead of ourselves here," said Filip, settling himself a little. "This could just be another of those plagiarism crackpots who thinks a song's a copy just because it's got the same three words in a row as something that finished seventeenth in a Belgian final in the sixties. Let's have a little chat with him, why don't we. Jeff, can you pass him over?"

"No worries!" Jeff took the phone off hold and spoke to the monk once more. "Hello, Mr Monk..." "Hello! Call me Brother Jose," said the cheery voice on the phone.

"Yes, yes, hello Brother Jose," said Jeff. "My boss would like a word with you. Can you tell him exactly what you've just told me."

"Why certainly young man, put him on," said the monk.

"Hello Brother Jose!" said Filip brightly. "Filip Ivanović from the CTF here. Nice to speak to you. What seems to be the issue here?"

"Well Filip, as I was just saying to your colleague Jeff there, I was listening to the radio at the monastery here in Braga this morning and I heard a song that I wrote back in 1974. I'm so pleased and excited that it's finally being recognised and is going to represent my beautiful country of Portugal at the Eurovision tonight. One of the younger monks told me that it will be liable for some royalties if it gets played on TV, so I was just wondering if they could be diverted to the charity wing of my church, because I have no real need for money myself, living here in the monastery as I do."

"I see," said Filip. "But before we get too involved with all that, we just have to confirm that your song is indeed the same one that Rodrigo is going to sing tonight. It's not that I doubt your word as a man of the cloth, of course, but we have processes and protocols in place for this kind of thing. I'm sure you understand."

"Oh completely," said Brother Jose. "How shall we do this then?"

"Well, is there a copy of your song on YouTube or Spotify or anything like that?" Filip asked hopefully.

"I'm not sure that I even know what any of that means, to be honest with you," said Brother Jose with a warm laugh. "But I do have the record in my room. I can go and play it to you on the monastery's stereogram if you like?"

"If that works for you, Brother Jose, let's go with it," said Filip.

"Excellent!" the monk replied. "Now it'll probably take me a few minutes to find the record and set it all up. Shall I call you back?"

"Yes, yes, that'll be fine," said Filip. "It'll save you spending all your royalties on an international call. Here's my number – give me a quick shout when you're ready and I'll ring you right back!"

"OK, that's very kind. Thanks then. Talk in a little while," said Brother Jose as he rang off.

"Oh bless him," said Filip. "He's going to play it on his stereogram! I'm sure we've got absolutely nothing to worry about here, but it's a lovely little unexpected interlude to our day!"

"I still can't believe that anonymous little song won with the juries last night," said Sunny. "I mean, it's sweet and lovely and everything, but a winner?"

"Yes, but like I said, you keep that to yourself," said Filip with an assertive snap, "and don't you go putting a bet on or anything, either! That kind of information would be like gold dust to the lads at the betting table, and they'll hammer the exchanges if they get wind of it. If the odds begin to drop the punters will get wind that something is afoot. And if this song is what dear old Brother Jose claims it is, then we could get into serious problems."

"Fully understood!" said Sunny, earnestly.

There then followed an anxious ten minutes as everyone in the room sat silently staring at the phone, willing Brother Jose to hurry up and call back.

"Come on old fella, I've got an international song contest to organise, mate!" said Filip, only half jokingly. "I can't settle and do anything else until we get this sorted!"

Finally, after what seemed like an age, the phone rang. "I'll bet it's not him after all this," Sunny joked.

"If it's your Nan after tickets again, Jeff, I'll throttle you," laughed Terry.

"Heh, yeah," said Jeff, "she's convinced that Moldova is just the other side of Wolverhampton!" "Right, I'm going in," said Filip. "Wish me luck!"

He answered the phone.

"Hello, Filip Ivanović here. How may I help you? Ahh, Brother Jose!" The rest of the room gave out a visible sigh.

"You've got it all set up have you? Good, good! Just give me a second and I'll click onto speaker phone. My colleagues are bigger musical experts than me."

Terry gave Filip a big thumbs up of thanks.

"Hello, hello, can you all hear me?" said Brother Jose. "Yes we can!" said Sunny. "Hello Brother Jose!"

"Excellent," the monk replied. "I'll put the needle on the record, as I believe the youth all say these days."

Through the phone's tinny speakers the occupants of the press room could hear the pop of the stylus as Brother Jose carefully placed it onto the record, followed by the reassuring rumble of needle on vinyl as it rolled fatefully toward the song. Finally the music began, and a familiar gentle guitar intro wafted out of the phone.

"Well the intro's certainly very reminiscent of Rodrigo's song," said Terry with a worried look on his face. That must be the only similarity though."

"You hope!" laughed Sunny, whose face dropped the moment the vocal began. "Oh damn, it's the same song, isn't it?"

"Every last bit of it so far," said Terry, shaking his head in disbelief. "Let's just hope it changes when it gets to the chorus."

It got to the chorus and it didn't change. Not one bit. Note for note and word for word, it was clearly and undeniably the same song as Rodrigo Braga's Portuguese Eurovision entry. The record came to an end, and Brother Jose came back onto the phone.

"A lovely little tune, isn't it, even if I say so myself," he said sweetly. "I must say that I was amazed to hear it on the radio this morning. We only pressed a couple of hundred copies for sales among my church community. I've got no idea how it got to be sung on the Eurovision so many years later."

"No, me either," said Filip. "And Brother Jose, can I just check one more thing?" "Certainly," the monk replied.

"What is the title of this song of yours?"

"Oh, it's O Que Era Uma Vez, just like the song on the radio," said Brother Jose.

Terry mouthed a bad word towards Filip, as his boss put his head in his hands in disbelief, mouthing "I know!" back at him.

After settling himself for a moment, Filip spoke again.

"Yes, Brother Jose, I can confirm that it is indeed the same song," said Filip. "And I must say that I think your version is even nicer than Rodrigo's."

"Well thank you for saying so, Filip," said the monk.

"And thank you for bringing it to our attention," Filip continued. "Now, with the amount that your beautiful little song has been played on the radio, and with all the broadcast and recording rights and whatnot, I'd like to offer you an upfront payment of five thousand Euro, and we'll follow that up with a percentage of any further sales and royalties from here on in. I think your church is going to be very happy at the outcome here. Now, who should I make the cheque out to?"

"Oh that's terribly kind of you, Filip," said Brother Jose with the delight of a man who'd just received an unexpected windfall. "That really is way more than I was expecting. I thought it was going to be no more that about eighty Euro or so."

"Well there's a lot of money in songwriting if you get it right, Brother Jose," said Filip. "And on this occasion you've got it very right. But I must ask you just the one big favour in return."

"Oh I'd be delighted to do whatever I can to help," said the monk.

"Lovely," Filip replied. "So because we've already printed all the programmes and album sleeves and all that kind of thing, it'll prove quite expensive to change them all at such short notice if we reveal you as a songwriter for your brilliant tune. So if you could just keep it all under your hat for a while, we'll work out what we can do about it after the contest has finished. Would that all be fine with you?"

"That would be no problem at all, Filip," the monk replied. "I'll be happy to be of assistance in any way that I can. And to be honest, just hearing a song that I wrote all those years ago on the television will be reward enough for me, so I don't need to worry about any kind of formal recognition for it or anything like that."

"Well that's very generous of you, sir," said Filip. "We'll get that money transferred to you first thing in the morning."

"Splendid," said Brother Jose, "You've all been very kind."

"Well, it's only right and proper that you are fully rewarded for your efforts, especially as it's going to such a good cause."

"Thank you again," said the monk. "I shall look forward to seeing my song on your programme tonight."

"Oh, you're going to enjoy it, for sure," said Filip. "Right you are, Brother Jose, it's been lovely speaking to you, but I'd better get on. I have a show to put on this afternoon."

"OK, talk again soon," said Brother Jose as he rang off. "Goodbye and God bless!" "Erm Filip," said Terry with a disturbed look on his face, "did you just bribe a monk?"

"I don't like to think of it as a bribe," Filip laughed. "More a well-deserved payment for writing a quite lovely song, and bringing a possible pitfall to our attention. Now, let's get the Portuguese HoD on the blower and we can try to engineer a situation that's best for everyone without it being too obvious to the folks watching on the TV back home. We've got to ensure that Portugal just miss out on qualification in a way that doesn't look too fishy. I'm quite sure that their HoD would prefer that to being disqualified from the show at this late stage. That wouldn't be good for anyone, let alone lovely Brother Jose."

Filip called his old friend and Portuguese Head of Delegation Gustavo Ambrósio immediately. He wanted to get this issue solved as quickly as possible, but it wasn't going to be a lot of fun telling one of his closest associates at the competition that his nation's song was a ringer, and that whatever happened in the scoring, it couldn't be allowed to qualify for the big final on Saturday, lest it be outed as a cover version.

"Yeah, Gustavo," he said nervously down the phone, "Filip from the CTF here."

"Filip my old friend!" Gustavo roared with delight. "How's it going up there in the big office? It's a shame we haven't got to meet up yet this year. I guess you're a bit more busy than usual. Did you see our boy last night? God he was amazing, and the crowd absolutely lapped him up. But of course I know you can't tell me how he did with the juries though, can you?"

Now Filip was even more anxious about telling Gustavo the bad news. Portugal has had so little to get excited about over the years at Eurovision that it felt like he was about to hit an excitable little puppy with a rolled up newspaper until it looked sad. But he really had no choice. If anybody else found out that Rodrigo Braga had stolen his song from a lovely old monk – and more to the point, discover that Filip knew about it – it could cause all sorts of problems for the credibility of the organisation.

He shook his shoulders out, took a deep breath and began to speak.

"Yeah Gustavo, it's about that," he calmly began. "It turns out that we've got a little bit of a problem with your song."

"How so, Filip?" Gustavo asked, puzzled.

"Well it transpires that your lovely new original song is actually a cover version, and..." Gustavo cut Filip off mid stream.

"Nooooooo!" he cried. "Tell me this is not true? How did you find out?"

"Yep, sorry mate, but it's true solid fact," said Filip. "We had this monk from Braga ring us up this morning reckoning that he wrote and recorded it back in 1974. We thought it was just another crank call until he played us the record down the phone... and it's 110% the same song."

"Oh shit!" exclaimed Gustavo. "The little rat assured us that it was absolutely his creation. He claims that it's based on a little ditty his mother used to sing to him as a child. How can we be sure that this isn't just some prank by someone with a grudge against us? Spain, for instance."

"We've just got to put it to Rodrigo himself and see how he reacts, I guess," suggested Filip. "But sadly, Gustavo, if Brother Jose really did write the song all those years ago then I'm afraid it can't be allowed into the final on Saturday, however well it does tonight."

"Yes, yes, I can quite see your position on this," Gustavo conceded. "You're stuck between a rock and a hard place and you can't be seen to be doing anyone a favour – especially in your first year on the job, and even more so after the Kjellberg incident."

"Yeah man, it's a bitter blow to us all, but we'll have to find some way of ensuring that you don't make it through," Filip explained.

"Not that we ever do!" Gustavo laughed, injecting a little humour into this awkward situation.

"No, quite," said Filip with a wry smile, keeping his knowledge of the jury result close to his chest. "But first things first, let's check with Rodrigo, just to make sure that this isn't all just one giant misunderstanding."

"Great idea!" Gustavo answered. "Shall I bring him up to you now?"

"No, probably best I come down to you. Then it just looks like I'm on my regular pre-show rounds," said Filip. "If you lot all marched up here it would look like you'd been sent to see the headmaster, and that might arouse suspicions. Remember, we've got to keep every last bit of this under our hats. The only people who have any knowledge of it at the moment are the lads in the press office and old Brother Jose himself. Fortunately he has no idea how either this show or indeed copyright works. There doesn't seem to be any trace of the original recording anywhere on the internet, but we can't take any risks of the news sneaking out before the big night. If Brother Jose heard it on the radio and recognised it, I can't begin to believe that nobody else has. So can we just keep this between you and I for now?"

"No problem at all, boss," said Gustavo.

"Right, give me twenty minutes and I'll be down," said Filip. "And don't give him any clue that anything is wrong. We don't want him cooking up an escape plan between now and then, do we!"

"OK then old friend, I'll get him in the dressing room and we'll see you in a bit." Filip put down the phone and turned to his colleagues in the press room.

"This is getting more and more complicated, chaps," he said. "Gustavo was previously of the impression that it's all above board, but I'm popping down to give Rodrigo a gentle grilling in a minute. What can we do though? Would we be able to fiddle with the results in a way that wouldn't get noticed? The adjudicators already know last night's scores, and he's darned nearly got enough points to go through already. So we'll probably have to do something with tonight's votes. But it doesn't feel right to even talk about doing it."

"You say that," said Terry, "but it wouldn't look quite as fishy with the Portuguese as it would with some of the other acts."

"How do you mean?" Filip asked.

"Well thinking about it, the song's got jury bait written all over it. Bloke with a beard and a waistcoat with a guitar on his knee and looking all earnest – them muso bastards lap that kind of dreary stuff right up. But there's always a jury contender who absolutely bombs with the punters, so it's our job to try to engineer a situation where that's going to be Rodrigo this year."

"If, of course, he actually is pulling a fast one," said Filip. "For all we know it could be Brother Jose who's the conman and we've just agreed to send him five grand!"

"Oh damn, I'd never even considered that," Terry said with a shocked look on his face. "Jeff, you've got the name of his monastery haven't you?"

"Yes Tel, I have."

"Well, could you track down their main office number via the local directory enquiries, and ask the head monk if this fella actually exists or not?"

"On it now, Terry."

"Right then, I'm heading down to quietly confront the Portuguese laddie," said Filip, rising to his feet. "You keep me posted as to the voracity of Brother Jose's monkdom, and I'll let you know if there's anything we need to do at this end. If the worst comes to the worst we could just come clean and DQ him, but if we can do it by any other means, then we'll have to entertain that option too. Wish me luck, I'm going in!"

Seven minutes later and Filip is walking down the contestant corridor, glad handing any delegation members who passed his way, but running over what he was going to ask Rodrigo again and again in his head. Should he just come clean and ask him straight out if he'd ripped the song off an elderly ecclesiastical? Or should he be more subtle than that? As he stopped to knock on the Portuguese dressing room door, he elected to go for the slightly less nuclear option.

"Hello yes, come in!" Gustavo's friendly voice boomed out from inside the room.

"Hey yes, hello Gustavo. And hello Rodrigo! Nice to finally meet you! How's it all going?"

"Oh hi man!" the singer replied, looking ridiculously chilled out for a man on the cusp of playing his biggest gig ever. "Yeah, just hanging out, getting my zen on for tonight. I think it went really well yesterday, didn't you? I've got a feeling in my bones that something good is going to come of all this."

"Good, good," said Filip, desperately trying to swerve the niceties. "Now, I'm just on my rounds before it all gets too hectic and serious, and I'm doing the final checks to make sure that all the songs are exactly as they should be."

"Oh cool man," said Rodrigo, laying back on the white sofa and emitting an air of calm. "Yeah, it's just a little song that my mama used to sing to me when I was small. If anything I should have given the writing credit to her, but she didn't want to hear a word about it, and said that she wanted me to take all the glory."

"Oh how terribly sweet of her," said Filip, his eyes now flickering around the room grasping for any kind of clue that might help get him out of this increasingly complicated fix. "She sounds like a lovely mum!"

"Oh she is," said Rodrigo. "And when you consider the hardships that she had as a kid, it's amazing how sunny and sharing she's become as an adult."

"How do you mean," Filip enquired. "If you don't mind me asking?"

"Well," said the singer, "her parents – my grandparents – were killed in a terrible accident when she was just a little girl. She had to grow up in an orphanage attached to a monastery in Braga. But she pulled herself up by the bootstrings and really made something of herself, becoming the most wonderful and attentive mother a boy could ever wish for. I guess losing her own parents made her realise that she had to be the best mum that she could possibly be to us kids."

Filip's ears pricked up at the mention of Braga. "A monastery, you say?"

"Yeah man, she was brought up by monks, and they used to teach her all these beautiful songs and showed her how to play the guitar," said Rodrigo. "I think that's where I got my musical ear from."

Filip realised that he might be on to something and probed a little deeper.

"Now, I'm not accusing anybody of anything here," he said, "and music is of course always a matter of influences and borrowings. Just as it has been throughout time. But you don't think that the song your mother taught you was actually one that the monks taught her, do you?"

"Oh man, I'd never even thought of that," said the singer, now sitting up on the sofa and looking thoughtful. "Yeah, I guess it could have been, now you come to mention it. Oh, is that bad?"

"Not necessarily," Filip half-truthed to the singer. "I guess we'd better find out from your mother if the song is older than you thought it was, and then work out a strategy from there."

"Yeah man, that sounds like a plan," said Rodrigo. "I don't want to get you into any trouble or anything."

Filip was now certain that this young man was absolutely sincere about the origin of his song. Dumber than paint, quite possibly, but there was no way that he was trying to pull a fast one regarding the ownership of the composition. Just then his phone alerted him to a text. It was Jeff.

"The monk's story holds up. Good luck at your end!"

"That's one worry out of the way," Filip thought to himself, "now let's try to see how we can solve this one!"

He settled himself for a moment before asking Rodrigo for a little favour.

"You don't suppose you could give your mother a quick call, could you?" he asked. "Just to settle this once and for all?"

"Oh yeah man, I'd love to. I was just about to call her anyway. Now where's my phone?' He picked up his massive but well-battered smart phone and made the call.

"Hey Mama! Yeah, lovely to hear your voice too... Yes, not long now... Yes, I'm looking after my voice, and I'm wearing those socks you gave me... Yes... Yes... So, I've got a little question to ask you about the song... Yes, it is beautiful... Did you actually make it up yourself?... Oh?... You didn't?... It was on a little record that Brother Jose gave you?... I see... Oh no reason – I was just wondering... Anyway, I'd better go now – not long until my make-up call... Yes, yes, I'll behave myself in the green room... Gotta go... Love you mum... Love you..."

Filip looked at Gustavo, who'd sunk on his haunches as if somebody had released his stopper and let out all his air.

"Well," said Rodrigo, "it turns out that she heard it on a record that a monk gave her when she was a kid. That isn't going to be a problem is it?"

"Ooh no," lied Filip, "I shouldn't think so. Just as long as we know this and can be prepared in case this monk comes looking for royalties. Everybody wants a buck out of you when you're famous!"

"Ha yes, I quite understand. Yeah, we wouldn't want to rip off the church or anything," Rodrigo said sweetly. "I'm not sure that God would be terribly happy if we did!"

"Oh I'm sure he'd let you off, Rodrigo," said Filip with a smile. "How could anyone ever be cross with a sweet lad like you? Right, I've got to get on with my day. Thanks for your help, Rodrigo. And thanks to you too, Gustavo. I'll get in touch about that other issue we were talking about."

Gustavo nodded with resignation and Filip left the dressing room. As he closed the door behind him he let out a massive sigh and propped himself up against the wall to gather his thoughts.

"What more?" he thought to himself. "What more can possibly happen before those bloody credits come rolling up the screen on Saturday night? I'm cursed, I tell you. Cursed!"

28

Considering everything that had gone on behind the scenes in the over the last week-and-a-half, the live running of the first televised semi-final show went by with scarcely a hitch. Montenegro's elaborate opening was now so well rehearsed that the crew got them on and off the stage with time to spare, the Saudi Sammarinese act got to where they were supposed to be, on time, and with very little fuss, and even the Czech singer Jolana Nováková behaved herself, forgoing the corpse paint this time for a fairly standard performance of her emotive-yet-generic song. The only act that made things complicated in any way were the Norwegians, which by now wasn't a surprise to any one connected to the show. As they walked onto the stage, each member stuck a short length of gaffa tape across their mouths, and they proceeded to perform their song with no vocals at all, and with the words "No voice" written in many languages on the backs of their hands, which they waved at the cameras at every opportunity. They still did the church burning though, which was met by a mix of horror and delight by the audience. Only at the very end of the song did singer Hermóðr Heimdall rip off the tape and utter the word "Silenced" in a deep, guttural voice, before kicking the mic stand off the stage and marching away with his arm raised in the devil horns salute, wincing just a little at the delayed pain of his tape removal.

"Well at least he didn't say anything too contentious at the end there," Terry said to Filip on the CTF balcony. "And I reckon their silent job as put paid to their chances of qualifying."

"At this stage, Terry," Filip replied, "I wouldn't be sure of anything. But let's hope that's the last we've seen of them. And at any rate, as they've deviated from the published lyric we're well within our rights to disqualify them for it – but obviously I'm pretty sure that it's not going to come to that."

"Hopefully!" Terry asserted.

"Yeah, hope's all we've got!" Filip replied with a smile. "Right then, let's wait and see who's going to qualify and cross our fingers that they're all relatively easy to work with and scandal free."

After an interval act packed with local dancing and folk music that seemed to go on for an age, the hosts Elina and Ruslan climbed onto the announcement podium and proclaimed that the qualification reveal was about to begin. The tension music cranked up, and the two of them began to string things out a bit.

"So... here we are... and the first country to qualify for next Saturday's final is..." said Elina, as she stared into the mid distance, waiting for her next line. The wait went on and on until she got the signal to make the reveal.

"...POLAND!"

The handful of Polish fans sitting deep in the bowels of the hall went berserk, as the cameras dashed to the corner of the green room where their act Hold Tight were celebrating like crazy.

"The Poles look happy," winged Ruslan, somewhat flatly. "And now on to the second qualifier... who are..."

The wait strung out even longer, before he revealed... "...BELGIUM!"

There was a gasp around the audience. Although everybody held the Belgian song in warm regard, nobody gave it much of a chance of qualifying, deeming it to be perhaps just a little too arty for the voting public. Sunny and Jeff turned to each other in the press room and did a little cheer.

"Oh, I couldn't be happier!" said Sunny. "Bloody love Gladys, I do!"

"Yeah," said Jeff, "but it's already looking like it's going to be one of those nights. Absolutely anything could happen here!"

Back on the CTF balcony, Filip ran his eye down the list of qualified countries as he assessed the order that he was going to feed them into the hosts' ear-pieces.

"Oh thank heavens for that!" he cried, relieved. "That's going to save us a bit of a headache! But oh. Oh bloody hell..."

"What? What?" said Terry, trying to squeeze an eye onto Filip's list.

"You just sit back and enjoy the reveal with the punters," Filip laughed. "There's good, there's strange, there's very useful, and there's potentially very awkward. It'll be more fun if you learn with the room. Well, I say fun..."

"You terrible tease, Filip," said Terry in a huff. "I'm sure I'll thank you at the end of it all, but don't blame me if I try to catch a peep of your laptop screen!"

"I'll hunch over it then," said Filip, as he affected the stance of a schoolchild hiding their work from the cheat on the desk behind. "Look, I'm hunching!"

"Oh my days," said Terry, "that list has addled your brain. I dread to think what's on it!"

Filip raised an eyebrow like a cheap horror movie actor and turned to complete his evening's work.

Five more countries had been revealed as qualifiers: Malta, Greece, Romania, Denmark, and to massive surprised shrieks from the audience, Estonia, which nobody could entirely remember. Now there were only three songs left to reveal from the eighteen nervous acts who were still perched anxiously on the edges of their comfy sofas in the green room. All except Norway, of course, who were calmly reading massive hardback books with Latin and Old Norse titles.

"Still no Portugal, no Norway, No Austria then?" said Terry, hoping to extract a grain of info from Filip. "You're ordering this reveal specifically just to annoy me, aren't you!"

"Ha!" laughed Filip, "Good theory, but no. Well, not entirely. If the way we're announcing this lot is making you fidget, imagine what it's doing to the folks back home. They're our first consideration."

"Good point," Terry replied, "but you're still milking it for larks, I suspect!" "Maybe..." said Filip with a smirk.

"There's just three songs left to announce," shrieked Elina, almost beside herself with excitement. "Who's it going to be?"

Immediately the audience shouted out their favourites in a mass cacophony.

"Who is that? I can't hear you," yelled Elina as she teased the crowd a little more. The masses gradually fell near silent, but not before one wag near the front screamed "Burkina Faso!" at the top of their lungs. This caused the hosts to immediately get the giggles and lose their composure. The reveal sequence had been dragging on for long enough anyway, so Filip quickly had to calm the pair down and get on with the show.

"Elina! Ruslan! Please quit with the corpsing and get on with the announcements." Elina put her finger to her ear, took a deep breath and tried to settle herself.

"The eighth song... hehe... to qualify... heh... for Saturday's final... is..."

Filip quietly fed the name of the next country down her earpiece, and she only just managed to spit it out incredulously before bursting into even more fits of laughter.

"SAN MARINO??? WHAT?!!"

The audience let out their biggest gasp of the night and looked around at each other utterly bewildered.

"You what?!!" said Jeff in the press room, spitting out his tea. "They've done what?!! I mean, it's San Marino – everybody's happy. Kinda. But with THAT?"

"Yeah, but you've heard the rumours, right?" said Sunny. "Actually no," said Jeff. "What's the scoop?"

"Well the sniff goes that our moneybags prince here has bought up every hooky call centre in Europe to spam the phones and get him qualified," Sunny replied. "I don't know how much truth there is in that tale, but somebody was going to do it sooner or later. I'm just surprised that it was this lot!"

"Might have been this lot, you mean," Jeff asserted. "And remember, we can't say a word about these suspicions online or to the general public. This one's for these four walls and no further unless anything comes out in the proper press."

"Fully understood," Sunny replied with an unusual seriousness. Terry turned to Filip with a grudging shrug.

"Well we kinda knew that one was coming. But if you've given that one out in eighth, what more horrors are yet to come?"

"Oh you just wait, Terry," he said mercurially. "You just wait!"

It was Ruslan's turn to announce the next qualifier. He popped his cuffs, jutted out his chin and proclaimed...

"OK! So now for the ninth qualifier," he announced in his rich, deep voice. "And it's going to be..." He hung the gap for an absolute age, and long after Filip fed him his line.

"The honourable Republic of..."

"Don't milk it, Ruslan," Filip spat into his earpiece. "We're close to running over as it is!"

Ruslan smiled, gave a cheeky nod to the balcony and proclaimed...
"...BELARUS!"

Now the audience really were confused. The announcement of Kirill Kisly as a qualifier led to more of a collective gulp of astonishment than any kind of congratulatory applause, and there was still a loud, mystified muttering around the audience as Elina started to announce the last qualifier.

"How the heck did that just happen?" Terry said astonished. "That must have been in a distant tenth place, surely? So I'm guessing that it can only be Portugal left to announce now?"

"Nothing is certain in this life," said Filip, by now looking a bit manically at his laptop. "I think you're going to be, how shall we say, entertained by this last one."

"Wait? No?" said Terry in shock. "Not the Czech woman?" "You just wait and see, Terry..."

"So. Here it is," said Elina. "The tenth and last qualifier. Good luck to the nine acts that are left to await their fate. Only one of you will remain happy after I've made this announcement."

In the green room, camera crews began to huddle around a few of the acts who hadn't qualified yet. Suddenly the Czech singer Jolana Nováková realised that she wasn't among them. And she wasn't best pleased.

She stood up shakily on top of the coffee table in front of her white sofa and yelled: "Hey! Where's my bloody camera? Over here, boys! This is where your last qualifier is sitting."

But nobody noticed her in the clamour to film the reactions of the lucky tenth delegation. So she raised her voice a little louder.

"Hey! You lot with the cameras! Over here! This is where the real star of this show is sitting. If that Maltese bitch got through with that shitball rip-off of a song, the last qualifier can only be me! Oi! Look at me!"

And with that she picked up the empty Eurovision-liveried carafe of water in front of her and flung it vaguely in the direction of one of the camera crews. But her anger was such that it sailed straight over their heads and whacked the green room host Bobby Odobescu plumb on the back of his head, showering broken granules of glass all over the Irish delegation. But while little Billy McNamara the Irish singer looked terrified and tried to hide underneath the low table in front of them, his burly brothers who'd come along to support him for the night were less impressed and made a march in the direction of the carafe's flight. At the same time, Jolana was staggering angrily towards the crowds of cameramen, with Juri her HoD trying in vain to wrestle her back to her seat. Even though the green room was situated at the back of the hall, the commotion was so loud that you could hear it over the presenters' mics.

Filip had noticed that things were starting to get a bit lively amongst the artists in the green room and hurried Elina along.

"For God's sake, just spit it out and let's get out of here!" he cried down his mic. Elina, ever the professional, nodded her confirmation and quickly continued. "The tenth and last qualifier... is... NORWAY!" Deep shock instantly ran around the hall like a tidal wave of confusion. Terry turned to Filip and mouthed the words "What the actual?!" Sunny, Jeff and all the lads in the press room could only pull confused faces at each other, and the Norwegians in the green room quietly stood up and graciously applauded all the other acts in a surprise gesture of magnanimity.

Elina attempted to make one last announcement.

"Now, if the ten acts who have qualified could make their way to the stage, we'd like to celebrate their good fortune. And let's have a big round of applause for the unlucky eight who didn't make it, but who helped make this such a magnificently exciting show!"

Just as Elina finished her speech, Jolana let out an almighty roar that could clearly be heard throughout the arena.

"BITCH!!!" she yelled, as she made a beeline for the Maltese singer, who was happily on her way to the stage.

At the same time, the Irish marauders were heading over to where they thought the carafe had flown over from, and seeing the Danes on their feet, all happy and laughing, assumed that they were the miscreants and so piled in with fists flying. While this was happening, Jolana had shoved her way through the camera crews and spotted Lia Maria, the Maltese singer. Shaking off Juri, she launched herself towards Lia and grabbed her by the back of her jet black hair, forcing her to the ground, and raining brutal punches onto the frightened young woman. It took four security guards to wrestle her away, but not before Lia had suffered a bloodied nose and a severely torn glittery gown.

Meanwhile, the misplaced disagreement between the Irish and the Danes was escalating into a full-blown brawl. While the Happy Band themselves weren't terribly keen on all the fighting, the rest of their delegation most certainly where, and punches began to swing in left and right. Soon, many of the other delegations were joining in, with tables being thrown and sofas being turned over. Filip had to act quickly before the whole thing got completely out of hand.

"Right, gallery, run credits, and only use the cameras that are pointing at the stage. And for heaven's sake turn the ambient mics down. We don't want the sounds of showbiz rioting filling the living rooms of the continent now. We're bang on time as it is, so let's wrap this thing up while we can! And cancel the qualifiers' press conference before this thing turns into a full-blown war!"

"That didn't go quite as expected there, did it now?" said Terry calmly to Filip as the broadcast came to a close.

"No Terry, it most certainly didn't. Now let's hope that we kept the bulk of that off the TV and we can tootle along as if nothing had happened. Right then, you get the boys in the office crafting a couple of press releases. The first congratulating the ten qualifiers on their success – the usual template

will do and I'm sure the boys are onto it already. But then a second apologising for the behaviour of Ms Nováková there. We'll hold that one on standby just in case anybody asks us about it."

He took a deep breath as the chaos played out in the hall beneath him, shrugged his shoulders and calmly declared: "Right. I'm off to prepare the post show debrief with the broadcasters. I think we can take a lot of positives from this show – if we leave out that minor bit of public insurrection at the end there, that is..."

*

It's now half-past-two in the morning, and Filip and Terry from the CTF are having a quick debrief about the events of that evening's

319

show with Dumi and Stefan from Moldova Smash, plus Håkan and Artiom from the crew. On any normal evening it would be a simple case of reporting any production issues, scouring the scores for irregularities, and making an early assessment on which of the ten lucky qualifiers are likely to go where in the eventual running order for the final on Saturday night. But there was a whole lot more than usual to unpack tonight, starting with that little green room squabble at the end.

"See, I told you, Filip!" said Dumi. "You have to expect a little hurly burly – it's the Moldovan way!"

"Ha! Yes, Dumi, very good. The only problem with that theory being that none of the people involved in the scrap were actually Moldovan."

"Ooh yes, I see your point, sir," Dumi conceded. "It must be something in the water! So how can you see us making sure that this doesn't happen again?"

"Well, for one thing, our principal agent provocateur, the Czech lass, has been eliminated, so all being well we shouldn't have any trouble with her again. However, we do still have a couple of, how shall we say, complicated blips in the running order for the second semi. So as long as we can keep both Armenia and Azerbaijan plus Russia and Ukraine well away from each other in the green room we should be just about OK. Hopefully..."

"Yes!" barked Håkan in his deep, rasping, cigarette-stained voice. "What fool decided to stick that lot together in the running order?"

Filip looked sheepish and stuck his finger up to indicate his guilt.

"Look, it's my first go, right," he laughed, "I was thinking of the songs rather than each nation's international relations. I think I've learned my lesson!"

Artiom Balan, the head of the local crew, piped up with a practical idea.

"How about if we station a couple of members of our security detail in civilian gear in with the delegations in the green room. If anyone thinks that they are being watched or spied upon, we can tell them that it's for their own protection. The viewers at home will just think that they're some minor local TV executive or something if they catch a glance of them. From my memories of the show there's always someone who looks like they're not supposed to be there sitting in amongst them all."

"Brilliant idea, Artiom," said Filip. "Israel have been doing it with their own people for years now, so it kind of makes sense. Can you action it to The Ox, and we can dry run it in tomorrow night's jury final."

"Positivity in action!" Håkan laughed, and the whole room nodded and shrugged approvingly at each other.

All of a sudden there was a knock at the door. It was Jeff from the press office with the full breakdown of the results, delivered to him by the show's voting auditors in a fiendishly sealed envelope.

"Scores breakdown, gentlemen!" Jeff shouted as he burst into the room. "I've not had a crafty look, either – these new envelopes are impossible to sneak into."

"Very good Jeff," Filip smiled. "Top work, as always."

Jeff stood about for a bit, hoping that he might be privy to which songs got what scores from who.

"That'll be all, Jeff," laughed Filip. "I know you're a safe pair of hands with information, but we can't risk anything getting out this year. Sorry mate!"

"Ha! It was worth a try!" said Jeff as he was leaving the room. "I'll find out soon enough!"

Jeff left the room, and Filip waited for a moment until he heard his footsteps moving down the hall before he picked open the seal of the security envelope.

"Right then, let's have a look at this little lot then," said Filip as he pulled the papers out and tapped them into a neat order.

"Oh!" he said, as his face turned a dull shade of beige. "Oh shit."

"What is it, Filip? What's up?" asked Terry, concerned at his friend's sudden shocked demeanour. "Take a look for yourself, fella," said Filip as a passed over the print out.

"Oh!" said Terry, a similar look of dismay flashing across his features. "Oh bloody fuck! What the hell are we going to do about that?"

"Come on Filip, mate" said Dumi, "Share the bad news."

"Well, it appears that San Marino have won tonight's show by a massive margin," he replied, ashen.

"Ooh!" said Dumi, "Fair enough, that is a bit weird. But why so shocking?"

"It's the scores, Dumi. The scores," Filip replied. "They've only gone and got top marks in the phone vote from every last country."

"Is that bad?" Stefan asked. "Surely the most popular song gets the most votes?"

"Yes, they do," Filip explained. "But even the biggest of all landslide winners have rarely got more than a dozen sets of twelves. This lot have got all forty-one. And that never, ever happens. Not even close.

It's practically impossible. Surely something fishy is going on here?"

"The boys in the press office were muttering something about this earlier, but I didn't give it much mind," said Terry.

"What's that?" Filip asked, anxiously.

"Well the rumour has it that our Saudi Prince there has employed a call centre in every country in Europe to flood the phone lines and vote himself into qualification," Terry explained.

"Oh damn," said Filip with his head in his hands. "You'd have thought they would have at least have attempted to be a bit more subtle about it. Every bloody country though? The fools. The darned fools."

"So what's our answer to this then?" Stefan asked. "Do we disqualify them?"

"Only if we absolutely have to," he replied. "And then in a roundabout kind of way." "How do you mean," asked Dumi.

"Well it's not really the done thing to start messing around with the points, for one thing," said Filip. "We can only really dock points from a nation if there's clear and obvious evidence of a misdeed. Usually that only amounts to one or two countries coming to an arrangement between themselves, or everybody in the jury from a particular country declaring identical scores to each other. But if we announce that something on this scale has taken place we're effectively admitting to a fundamental flaw in the voting system. And if some of the more unscrupulous nations get wind of it they're all going to be trying it next year."

"Yes, but just think of the extra revenue on the phone lines!" Håkan guffawed.

"That is a somewhat positive by-product of all this horror, yes," said Filip, shaking his head, "But it doesn't really help us sort this problem out!"

"True, true," said Håkan. "I'll keep quiet."

"I didn't catch the full results, because I was too distracted by the top of the table," said Filip. "So out of interest, Terry, who came eleventh tonight, just in case we do have to DQ San Marino?"

"Let's have a look now," said Terry, running his finger down the list, before stopping with a start. "Ooh, you're not going to like it."

"Oh no! Who is it?" said a worried Filip. "Portugal!"

Fillip let out a low, slow groan of displeasure.

"What's the problem there, Filip?" said Dumi. "Surely that's a good thing? It's a great little song, and everybody loves a Portuguese success, don't they?"

"Ordinarily," said Filip. "But in this case there's the little matter of the song being an accidental cover version. We'd have had to disqualify it if he'd qualified."

"Oh yes, I can see the problem here," Dumi replied. "So if we DQ San Marino we'll have to then DQ Portugal as well?"

"Exactly that," said Filip. "I was kinda hoping that the Portuguese problem had solved itself, but this is going to prove doubly hard to countenance. I dread to ask, Terry. Who was in twelfth?"

Terry sucked air harshly through his teeth and affected a pained expression. "Oh God, who is it?" Filip asked. "Oh no, don't tell me..."

"Yup, Czechia!" said Terry.

"Kill me. Just kill me now!" said Filip, looking like he was at the very end of his patience.

"Is there nothing else that we could do to make the best possible outcome for everybody?" asked Stefan. "You know, by a little bit of creative accounting?"

"We can't, Stefan," Filip replied with an exasperated voice. "For a start, we're not really allowed to. People have paid money to vote in good faith, and we have to provide officially audited vote tallies to the people upstairs at the CTF in our report next week. And for another thing, there's too many variables. Even if at the most simple level we dock San Marino just enough points that it stops looking quite so dodgy, then we'll probably bring Portugal back into the top ten at somebody else's expense. Who would that be, Terry?"

"Erm, it's looking like it would probably be Denmark at first glance."

"And we definitely don't want to be upsetting them any more after tonight's green room debacle," said Filip, the complications mounting up on his tired shoulders by the second. "And if that happens we'll probably have to kick Portugal out anyway, as we can't have some fan of obscure Portuguese religious music suddenly piping up and telling his local paper that he already had the song in his record collection. But if we do kick them out, we're almost certainly going to have to kick out San Marino for their, how shall we say, unconventional points collection schemes. And if we do that, we're going to have to readmit the most disruptive single human being we've ever had on these shows to the final! We're deep in the shit whichever way we stir the pot!"

"I reckon we've got a good case for binning the Czechs off too, though," Terry suggested. "That violent incident she started in the green room contravenes all our good behaviour policies, so they wouldn't have a leg to stand on if we had to kick them out as well."

"Ooh yes, that's a very good point," said Filip, looking just a tad less worried. "Well done!"

"But would it be terribly becoming to disqualify three songs from the same semi-final in your first year on the job?" said Håkan. "You might end up looking either slightly careless or excessively authoritarian."

"Actually I think you're onto something there, Hawkman," Filip said with a little more positivity in his voice. "I could definitely play the whole new broom sweeping out old rubbish card. It'll let those pesky delegations know that the CTF isn't going to take any of their nonsense any more, and if they try to pull any strokes they're going to be severely dealt with. If we kick out all three of them for their varying misdemeanours it'll send a strong message to everyone in the future – and that way we won't get accused of any kind of corruption that we might have done if we tried to cook the books to keep everyone sweet. Thank heavens this was only the first semi-final – it means that we have a bit of time to get approval from our overlords in Lucerne, tell the effected delegations of their respective good and bad fortune, and sort out how we're going to explain this to the masses in the morning. And if we do have to go down to thirteenth on the list to pick our last qualifier, then so be it. Who was that, Terry? Just out of interest?"

Terry let out a hearty roar. "Montenegro!" he laughed.

"Oh my days," said Håkan. "I can tell you now that they're going on after the first advert break!"

29

It's around 9:30 on Wednesday morning, and Filip has just got off the phone after a two-hour call to Lucerne.

"You're looking tired but slightly relieved," said Terry. "Good news? Or merely news?"

"Goodish," Filip replied. "When I first suggested the potential triple disqualification gambit they hit the roof – and quite understandably. But then when I carefully explained all of the available options they started to come round the the idea. The only thing I'm slightly in the mire for is not booting out the Portuguese song as soon as I heard the news, although they did understand my reasoning there in the end. But we do have the go ahead to action all three expulsions, though, and as soon as possible. The legal team's just got to check with San Marino's people that they're not going to sue us through the pipe if we boot them out. But there's really nothing else we can do about it. It's a clear violation of both the rules and the spirit of the competition, and we've got to be seen to be nipping this kind of thing in the bud, no matter how rich the perpetrators are."

"I hear you," said Terry. "But how are we going to get around it when we release the results of the semis on Saturday night? The press are going to take one look at those numbers and start screaming. The maths will be obvious."

"Actually, the overlords had a pretty good workaround for that," said Filip. "We don't publicise the scores that any of the expelled countries got – just put them at the bottom of the table with a big DQ alongside their name."

"But won't it be slightly noticeable that there aren't any twelve pointers on the whole list of scores?"

"Again, they were on to that one," Filip explained. "As soon as I brought up the idea of disqualification, they got one of their stats lads to work out what all the scores would have been had none of the miscreants been in the show, and fortunately for us, Austria were so far behind in fourteenth that it wouldn't have made a blind bit of difference. It does, however, mean that Belgium ended up topping the semi, which I suspect will be a popular result amongst the fan press, and keep them off our backs for a little while."

"Oh you know what they're like," said Terry. "One whiff of scandal and they'll be making up their own narratives like nobody's business."

"Ain't that the truth," Filip said with a smile. "But as long as we put a contact for more information on the press release, the grown up papers are sure to ask us for the real story and hopefully bypass the tittle tattle of the fan lot. Jeff's good at that kind of thing – put his number down."

"Oh he's going to just love that, the grumpy old sod," Terry laughed.

"Right then," said Filip, rising from his chair, "You start carefully crafting that press release, and I'll go and see the respective delegations. It's Gustavo that I feel the most sorry for in all this. I tried my best to keep them out of this, but we've got no other realistic option than to let them go, I'm afraid. Make sure that your explanation of their demise is as kind and gentle as possible. You can let rip with the other two as much as you like – just don't give too many fine details about San Marino, though, or else they'll all be giving it ago. And when you're done, drop it my way for a quick eye over and we'll get it out there as quickly as possible."

"Right you are," said Terry, immediately setting to work. "And good luck with the delegations!" "I'm reckon going to need it!" he sighed. Filip immediately made his way to the hotel where both the Czech and Portuguese delegations were staying, and thought it most polite to go and talk to his old friend first. He knocked on the door, and Gustavo promptly answered.

"Filip!" he said in a warm, happy tone, "So good to see you! What a stroke of luck that everything worked itself out in the end last night without us having to come to any kind of mathematical arrangement. Best result for everyone! But what brings you here so early?"

"Well, it's about that, Gustavo," Filip said with his most serious face on.

"Uh-oh, this sounds ominous," Gustavo procaimed with mock horror on his face.

"Well it kind of is," said Filip as he began to explain this deeply complicated situation. "We had to kick San Marino out for voting irregularities you see..."

"I knew it!" Gustavo blurted loudly. "I knew there was something dodgy about that lot this year. The people at the station back home gave me a thinly veiled warning about brown envelopes and glossy baubles – but none of the tight bastards came to me with any furtive offers! This is all very interesting, but how does it effect us?"

"Ordinarily it wouldn't have done, Gussy mate," said Filip, "But were eleventh on the scoreboard and would have qualified by rights... had your song not been a second-hand church singalong."

"Ooh yes, get you now," said Gustavo, "and I quite understand. Do what you've got to do, fella. We'll quite happily fall on our sword if it helps you out. I've got the hump with Rodrigo for being quite so dumb and trusting anyway. Just be gentle with us, OK?"

"Oh I've got Terry on it right now, and he's going to cast you lot as the most innocent party of the three disqualifications."

"Three, you say?!" said Gustavo with a start. "Who's the other one?"

"Have a guess, Gus," said Filip with a smile.

"Oh it's got to be that Czech lady, surely?" he replied. "Great for an unhinged night out, not so great if you're trying to arrange a televised song contest, I'd wager. What have you got her on?"

"Well, inciting that riot in the green room will do for starters," said Filip. "Although I'm sure we could pick out a good half-dozen other contraventions of the rules if we put our minds to it."

"I guess if you're disqualifying us and that other mob, your hands are tied when it comes to her?"

"Oh totally," said Filip. "And it turns out that I get to play the Hardman of Eurovision role and assert myself on my first year in the job. I reckon I could grow into that!"

"Oh I'm quite sure that you will," laughed Gustavo. "Thanks for being so honest with us, though mate. We all really appreciate it."

"No problem at all, Gus. At least you weren't either trying to pull a fast one on us – or hospitalise another contestant. I'll make sure that you get an extra good spot in the running order next year for your troubles – just as long as you can guarantee that nobody's ever released your song before, that is."

Gustavo let out a hearty laugh and said "We'll do our very best, Filip! We'll do our very best."

"Right, thanks for being so understanding, Gussy," said Filip. "I've got the Czechs to sort out next, and I'm really not looking forward to that. Wish me luck!"

"Oh, you're going to need it son!" Gustavo laughed. "I'll book you an ambulance, just in case."

And with that Filip walked out of Gustavo's room, and headed down a floor to where the Czech delegation were staying. He could tell he was in the right part of the hotel by the sight of all the red wine stains, shards of broken glass and big boot prints on the wall. Indeed, when he got to Juri's suite there were massive dents in the wood of the door, and what looked like threatening messages written in lipstick, judging by the amount of exclamation marks angrily dotted behind each string of words. He thought it best to gently but assertively knock first, just so that Juri knew that it was safe. Juri opened the door tentatively and let out a sigh of relief.

"Oh, thank God it's you!" said Juri. "I thought it might have been, y'know, her, for one horrible moment. And to be perfectly honest, I've been expecting you. Is it going to be bad?"

"Badish!" said Filip with a smile, trying to keep things light.

"Well that's a start, I suppose," Juri chuckled back. "Come in, sir."

Filip sat down behind a broken coffee table and started to explain the situation.

"So Juri," he began, "you know that we're going to have to censure the Czech delegation after her majesty's behaviour in the green room last night..."

"Yeah," Juri said wearily, "I could see this coming. You'd better give it to me with both barrels!"

"No, don't worry, it's not going to be THAT bad," the CTF man assured the Czech HoD. "We fully realise that the situation spiralled out of anybody's control last night, so we're just going to keep it simple..."

"Yeah, sorry about that," said Juri, shaking his head and staring at the carpet. "We told the green room crew to keep our area completely dry of alcohol, but Ms Nováková smuggled in a hip flask in her boot.

Plus some little turds on the Belarussian delegation thought it would be funny to keep pimping her their booze over the backs of the sofas. I'm amazed we kept her in reasonably good behaviour for most of the evening, to be honest with you. I hope nobody was seriously hurt? Or are going to sue?"

"No no, we're all good on that front, Juri," Filip assured his old associate. "Everyone's been calmed and placated. But I'm afraid that we're going to have to DQ you from the show and have all of your votes expunged."

"Really?" said Juri, surprised, "That's it? No fines? No long-term bans, or anything like that?"

"No, we're good," said Filip. "We realise that these were extraordinary circumstances, and we don't want to penalise your whole nation for the behaviour of your singer."

Juri nodded in thanks. "I reckon this is the most sensible solution all round," he said. "I mean, it's hardly like we were going to win or anything, were we. Actually, out of interest, where did we come in the table last night?"

"Now Juri, you know I can't tell you that until Saturday night," said Filip over his glasses with a school masterly lilt to his voice.

"Oh go on, mate," Juri pressed. "Just between you and me."

"Right, this goes no further," Filip conceded. "Let's be clear, you have to keep tight-lipped on this!" "You have my word," said Juri, solemnly.

"OK, so, I can't tell you everything about it," Filip began to explain, "but you're not the only country from last night to get the chop…"

"Oh really?" said Juri, his interest now peaked. "This could get interesting… tell me more."

"Well, we've had to let San Marino go after we discovered some, how shall we say, irregularities in their voting…"

"Of course!" barked Juri. "I bloody knew it! Early last week I had some heavy looking characters come knocking on my door there, waving some massive wads of cash and hinting at a potential little arrangement."

"So what did you do?" asked Filip, now hanging on Juri's every word.

"I politely closed the door on them," said Juri. "I enjoy working on this show too much to let it all go by back-pocketing any bribes. And anyway, what can I do on my own to engineer a vote for them? Our station is a big bureaucratic beast of an organisation, and everyone's going to want their piece of the pie – so I'd hardly have been left with my bus fare home! But I'm guessing that there were a few countries who took the bait?"

"It wouldn't be right for me to point fingers," said Filip, coyly. "But I'm sure you'd have an idea of where they'd be pointing if I did…"

"Enough said, Filip. "I'll definitely keep my own counsel on this."

"Thanks Juri. But there's another thing. It turns out that another song last night was lifted in its entirety from an old religious tune from the seventies. And we've had to let it go too."

"What, there's going to be three DQs?" asked a shocked Juri. "On your first ever show? Way to go, Filip old chap! You're certainly showing them who's boss!"

"It was a bit of a chain reaction, if I have to be perfectly honest," explained Filip. "If one went, you all had to go. We were going to try to sweep Jolana's behaviour under the carpet, but because of the two songs above her on the table getting the old heave-ho, we had to let her go too."

"Wait? So we came twelfth?" said Juri, now looking even more surprised, "After everything that's gone on this week? Result!"

"Yes," Filip replied. "But only unofficially. And you can never tell anybody about any of this. I know you're solid, so I'm sure that I can trust you."

"Totally," Juri assured his friend. "That's just for me."

"Good to know," said Filip. "But officially, you came equal last with zero points, as because of the Sammarinese incident we've had to expunge their voting from the record, and to make things fair and simple we thought it best to do the same with you and Portugal as well."

"Portugal was it?" said Juri. "What a darned shame. I loved that song!"

"Yeah, well, it was either that cooking the books," said Filip, "and you're always going to get found out if you try to pull that stunt. So I thought it was best if we came clean and played the authoritarian card. The punters aren't going to like it, but it's the best of a whole load of very bad options."

"I totally get you Filip. Thanks for doing me the courtesy of letting me know before you released the news officially. I really appreciate it, bud."

"No problem at all, Juri," Filip replied. "You're one of the good guys at this show, and we want to keep you coming back for more. Oh, and thanks for the information about the attempted bribery. That gives me fuel for my next visit – the San Marino delegation don't know they've been kicked out of the show yet!"

"Ooh, that's going to be a lot of fun for you," laughed Juri. "Good luck with that!"

"Oh yes, and before I go... how's Jolana doing this morning?" asked Filip, hopefully. "I'd imagine that she's woken up with her tail between her legs this morning."

"No bloody idea!" said Juri, with an exasperated look on his face. "Not seen hide nor hair of her since she stormed out of the arena last night. I lost sight of her, but one of her backing singers reckon that she walked down into the audience, got pally with some of the punters, then hopped into a maxi cab with a bunch of them to who knows where! And I can't call her, because she left her bag with her phone and all her other important stuff on the green room table. So we've been checking social media to see if anyone's showing off that they've got her back in their hotel rooms. And good luck to them if they have, I say! It's a damn shame too, because on a human – sober – level I get on really well with her, and she's an absolute dream to work with on stage. It's just that when she starts to party she really doesn't know when to stop, and turns into a whirlwind of chaos at the mere sniff of a barman's apron. Having said all that, I'm definitely going out on the lash with her when we get back. She knows places in Prague that I've never even heard of, and I've lived there all my life – and once I don't have the job of minding her on a professional basis I reckon she'd be a right good laugh! Anyway, Filip, I'll let you get on. Good luck with that other matter mate!"

"And good luck with finding Jolana," Filip laughed. "I reckon she's gone feral. You should have clipped a radar tag to her ear like they do on the wildlife shows."

"Yeah, I reckon next time I will!" Juri chuckled. "No, wait a minute.

Next time we're going to send a bunch of nuns or a school choir or something. Anything for a quieter life!"

*

After a short journey, Filip's driver Vasile dropped him off at the Sammarinese delegation's hotel out on the very edges of the city… although he gave him a gentle warning as he climbed out of the car.

"Before you go in, Filip sir," he said, "I'd better give you some information about this place. It's long rumoured to have been the front for all manner of criminal activity, and I've always suspected that people who've found their fortune in some of the – how best to put this delicately – less traditional industries spend a big part of their lives in here. You'll rarely ever see the police anywhere near this place, either… unless they've got a meeting with the owners of course… so I'll keep my engine running, just to be on the safe side."

"Oh!" said Filip with some concern. "Why didn't you warn me about all this before we started the journey?"

"Well, you seemed in such a hurry," said Vasile, "and I was trying to think of the best way to raise the subject. Still, we're here now, and I'm sure that everything will be OK."

"You're not just winding me up, are you?" asked Filip suspiciously. "Because after the twenty-four hours I've just had it wouldn't be advisable."

"Oh no, Filip sir," Vasile answered earnestly. "It's all true. I went in there once many years ago for a wedding, and it's not like any other hotel I've ever been to. So just be wary and keep your wits about you."

"OK Vasile," said Filip, still unsure as to the voracity of his driver's claims. "But if I find out you've been messing me about I'll be terribly cross."

"You'll see for yourself as soon as you get through the doors, I assure you sir," said the driver. "Now, good luck!"

"Oh you've stressed me out before I've even started," said Filip as he got out of the car. I'm sure it won't be as bad as you're suggesting."

As he straightened himself and took a look at his surroundings he began to get the idea that maybe Vasile wasn't joking with him after all. Every window on the six storey building had bronzed mirrored glass, and the establishment's name 'Hotel Majestic' was written in big golden letters surrounded by tiny twinkling lights. In the window of the lobby a red neon light flashed the words 'Casino Tonight!', and as he walked into the building, the only other that he could see were tall women in outfits as sharp as their cheekbones looking distinctly bored as they sat draped across the low red velvet sofas littered around the foyer. Indeed, there was an awful lot of red velvet and gold lamé around the place, and Filip began to wonder if he'd stepped into some kind of alternative universe. It was very unlike the more bland and serious hotels he was used to visiting as a part of his job with the CTF.

Filip nervously made his way to the counter to look for the concierge. He rang the ruby-encrusted bell and a tired looking man with a lilac-coloured Russian cigarette wedged into the corner of his mouth stepped out of a back room.

"Yes?" the man said grumpily. "What do you want? A room or a service?"

"A bit confused by what this could possibly mean, he sputtered "Erm, well actually I'm looking for the Eurovision delegation from San Marino. Is Elio Gasperoni available pl..."

"No!" the concierge snapped curtly. "No one is available."

"Well it is rather important," Filip continued. "And I need to speak to him quite urgently." "I make no calls," the concierge snapped again.

"You call him!"

And with that he stamped back into the room behind the counter and slammed the door just hard enough so that Filip could tell it was deliberate.

"I guess I've got his number," Filip thought to himself. "Now that I'm here perhaps I'd better give him a call."

As he got out his phone he heard a loud "Pssssssssst!" behind him. A scruffy looking bellboy in a red velvet suit adorned with golden brocade appeared out of nowhere.

"I wouldn't use your cellphone in here, sir," said the bellboy in perfect English, "You never know quite who is listening in!"

"Oh. OK," said Filip, now even more disoriented, "but it really is important that I see Mr Gasperoni this morning. Do you happen to know where he is?"

"Yes!" said the bellboy, who then stood staring into the middle distance with a steely glare. "Oh good. Well can you take me to him?" Filip asked.

"Yes!" said the bellboy, now with the first germs of annoyance in his voice.

Filip stopped and thought for a moment, and then realised that the bellboy must have been angling for a tip before he took him any further. He peeled a 20 Euro out of his pocket, and was just about to pass it to the bellboy when the young man let out an agitated cough. Filip took this to mean that he'd not offered him enough, and was just taking out another tenner from his wad when the lad whispered out of the corner of his mouth.

"US Dollars only, sir," he said. "Thirty will do for now."

Fortunately Filip had been advised by his colleagues at Moldova Smash to always keep a small handful of US currency with him, and slipped the bills to the bellboy.

"Right sir," he suddenly perked up. "I'd be happy to take you there. Follow me to the elevator on your right..."

Filip did exactly as he was instructed. As the elevator doors opened, another tall, well-dressed woman stepped out, accompanied by a squat looking middle-aged man in expensive sunglasses and a leather coat.

"Never ask," the bellboy whispered to Filip. "That way you'll never know. And to never know is the safest possible option in this place."

Filip confirmed his understanding, but still wasn't entirely sure what the bellboy meant.

As the lift began to rise to the fifth floor, sleazy brass-heavy music began to ooze out of its speakers, as this was some prohibition era Chicago clip joint. As it neared its destination, Filip could hear the ever-loudening sound of Middle Eastern music, and when the doors eventually opened there was clear evidence of an almighty shindig strewn all along the corridor.

"Room 513, directly in front of you sir," said the bellboy. "I'm sure you can find it."

And with that he disappeared almost as instantly as he'd arrived. Filip knocked on the door with a cautious rap.

"Che cosa? Cos'è ora?" came a gruff Italian voice from the bowels of the room. "It's me, Elio, Filip Ivanović from the CTF. I've come with important news."

"Oh Filip, thank goodness it's you," said Elio through the door, his voice now brighter than before. "I've had those Saudi dancers knocking at my door all night, trying to get me to party with them. I've had next to no sleep at all!"

As Elio opened the door, Filip could see the dark rings around his eyes, so immediately knew that he would have to go easy on the beleaguered Sammarinese TV exec.

"So, Filip, what can I do for you?" said Elio warmly as he ushered Filip in. He looked around and was astonished by the plush surroundings in Elio's suite.

"Oh this!" Elio smiled. "Yeah, it wouldn't have been my first choice, but it's kinda cool for the Instagram shots! Prince bin Faisal insisted on the place, though. He said it was for security reasons, but I very quickly got the impression that he'd stayed here before. Everyone on the staff seemed to know who he was. But it seems like the kind of place where you don't ask too many questions, so I haven't!"

"Yes, the bellboy was suggesting that, too," said Filip.

"Wise, very wise," Elio replied, "and for heaven's sake don't even think about using your phone in here. I'm pretty sure that the place is heavily bugged, so I've had to get a burner phone just for Eurovision business."

"And that's kind of why I'm here," said Filip, attempting to swiftly gear change the conversation. "How did the Prince take his qualification last night?"

"Actually, he responded like it was the least surprising thing in the world," said Elio. "Just like it was another day at work to him – whatever work these princely types actually do. His entourage, however, have gone absolutely berserk and haven't stopped partying since."

"And how are the good people of San Marino taking it?" Filip enquired further. "Are they pleased about all these goings on?"

"Well they're glad we've actually qualified for once," Elio joked, "but there is rather a lot of disquiet about the way that we've done it. There's a general feeling around The Most Serene Principality that something doesn't quite sit right."

"Ah yes," said Filip, preparing to broach the difficult news, "which is why I've come here, actually?' "Oh damn, has he been buying votes?" said Elio with a world-weary tone. "He has, hasn't he!" Filip did an awkward shrug that told Elio everything he needed to know.

"I knew it!" said Elio. "I knew that sly old fox was up to something! And did we just scrape by with the votes he bought?"

"I wouldn't say 'scrape by' so much as 'finished top of the table by an all-time record amount'," said Filip.

"Oh the idiot," Elio replied. "The absolute idiot. Never ones for ever doing anything subtly, those Princes. And where would we have come without that little extra help?"

"It's difficult to say definitively, but we roughly estimated it as last but one, I'm afraid," said Filip, "but you would have beaten Ireland!"

"Well that's hardly a consolation, is it now," Elio laughed. "I guess we're going to have to fall on our rather finely decorated swords and withdraw now then, aren't we?"

"That's alright," said Filip, "we've kind of done it for you. But don't worry, there's been two other DQs as well, so at least it'll take a little bit of the heat off."

"Oh yes," said Elio, "you have to take your positives where you can find them. So how much can I say about all of this?"

"We'd prefer it if you directed all inquiries to us," Filip explained. "For the moment we're just going with the 'voting irregularities' line. That way people will hopefully only suspect that he's attempted to feather the nests of a few of the usual suspects, rather than the wholesale televote fraud he's just pulled off."

"Oh he didn't, did he?" said Elio, exasperated but unshocked. "All the HoDs have all been saying that someone's going to attempt a call centre sting one of these years, and to be honest I'm not terribly surprised that it was him that did it. The fella's got bottomless pockets. How many countries did he work that one on, if I might be so bold to ask?"

"All of them!" said Filip. "Every last one!"

"Oh the great big tit!" Elio guffawed. "You'd have thought he'd have at least tried to be a little bit cute about it. But no, you're right, after that news we're quite happy to stand down from this one."

"I thank you for your graciousness on this matter," said Filip. "It's reassuring to know that there are still some good guys left at this competition. But can you do me just the one big favour next year?"

"What's that Filip?" Elio asked.

"Can you hold a national final entirely made up of local artists – just this one time?" said Filip. "We'll help you with the costs and the running of it. After all the trials and tribulations that we've had this year I just want the next contest to go as smoothly as possible."

Elio let out a hearty roar! "Right you are, Filip! We'll be combing the bus shelters of Serravalle and Acquaviva for talent!"

Filip joined in with Elio's laughter, realising the difficulty of the task that he'd just set him.

"But seriously, we'd be happy to if it makes your life easier for a year, Filip," said Elio. "And we must have at least one multi-millionaire who wants to buy their son, nephew or secret fancy piece a place in the competition. Leave it with me, sir, and I'll see what I can do."

"Thank you so much, Elio. I knew you'd take it well."

"To be honest with you it's something of a relief," said Elio. "This delegation are the biggest handful I've ever had to look after, and I could do with the sleep. And on top of that, I can't say that I'll be unhappy to see the back of this place. I've never felt so emotionally sticky!"

"Cheers, Elio," said Filip. "I'd like to stay and chat, but I've got another show to put on this afternoon, and we've got to release this news now that we know you're good with it. Good luck with telling the Prince."

"Yeah, that's going to be a whole lot of fun, I can tell you," said Elio, ironically. "Oh, and before you leave, I have two bits of advice for your journey out of the building. Don't touch anything, as you'll feel like you have to keep washing your hands for the rest of the day – and for heaven's sake don't take the left-hand lift back to the lobby!"

"Why's that, mate?" Filip inquired, curiously.

"Just don't!" said Elio. "I'll tell you all about it when we're well away from here, OK." "Nice one Elio," said Filip. "Talk soon!"

And with that, Filip made his way down to the lobby, being very sure to use the right-hand lift, and swiftly skipped out of the building and into Vasile's limo, the car pulling away the very moment he closed the passenger door.

"You got out safely I see," said Vasile. "I was beginning to worry.

343

You'd been gone for an awfully long time."

"Oh I don't know," said Filip. "That must have only been about ten minutes, surely?"

"That's still long enough," Vasile smiled. "And here, use this hand sanitiser. Just to be on the safe side!"

After throughly cleansing his hands, Filip gave Terry a call back at the arena.

"We're on, Terry," he said. "All three delegations are good with it. Are we all ready to send out the release if it's serviceable?"

"Yes boss," Terry replied. "We've got it all into pretty good shape with the least information required. Shall I press send, or do you want to run your eyes over it first?"

"No no, I trust you on this one, Terry. And we need to get semi-two on the go to distract the masses from all this controversy. You get going on that and I'll be there in about 25 minutes."

"Right you are, Filip," said Terry. "Preparing for fan press meltdown in three... two... one... sent!"

30

Later that morning, Michi Rotari was helping Maxim Munteanu prepare himself for his appearance at the second Eurovision semi-final dress rehearsal that afternoon. Each year, the six automatic qualifiers were divided into two sets of three and performed their songs after one or the other of the semi-final run throughs. In part this was to give their performance a run out in front of an audience, but also so that an excerpt could be recorded and shown on the live broadcast semi-final shows the following evening. A long time ago somebody decided that this would be the best way to help everyone at home familiarise themselves with the big six – although by that point in the show most of the viewers were either making a quick cuppa or had dashed to the bathroom for a comfort break. But it made the people upstairs at the CTF happy in the knowledge that they were doing something to at least try to even the playing field for every song in the contest, no matter how much of a perfunctory gesture it really was.

However, Maxim hadn't really been his ebullient self since the opening party, and Michi was starting to worry whether he'd be up to the job. The veteran singer had a long history of ploughing on with a show when he wasn't in the best of health, and this last few weeks had already taken its toll on him – and he hadn't even got to sing a note in anger yet.

"I don't want to sound like a broken record here, but are you quite sure that everything is alright, Maxim," Michi asked caringly. "You really don't seem yourself this morning."

"Nonsense!" snapped the old man, quite uncharacteristically. "I just take a bit longer to get going some mornings than others, and this is one of those days. I'll be right as rain as soon as I've had a couple of cupfuls of Evgeny's chewy coffee."

"Alright, if you say so," Michi continued. "But if at any point you think it's all too much for you, just say the word and we can take today off. The guys at Moldova Smash said that they recorded your last rehearsal performance the other day, and they can show that tonight night if needs be. It's not like there's going to be lots of shots of a dancing crowd throughout your performance or anything."

"I know your game," Maxim said sarcastically. "You just want to get me out of the way so that you can take my place and take all the glory, don't you! I should have known you were a gold digger right from the start!"

"No no no!" said Michi, looking hurt and horrified at the old man's suggestion. "Nothing could be further from my thoughts. The good people of Moldova don't want to see me on their TVs. It's all about you, Maxim sir. I just want to make sure that you make it to Saturday night all in one piece."

"Yes, you're right," said the old man, "I'm sorry for even suggesting such a thing. It's these new pills my doctor has me on. They're making me a bit snappy and short tempered. I really ought to stop taking them."

"Yes, but suddenly stopping them could be as harmful as taking them in the first place," warned Michi. "Who knows what damage such an abrupt change of dose could do to your insides. I always remember my dear grandmother. She smoked sixty cigarettes a day from the age of seven. By the time she got to eighty-nine the doctor said that she really ought to give them up. So she did, and the shock of going cold turkey killed her in three days! I know it's not the same as what you're taking, but we've really got to consider these things."

"Oh I know that you've got my best interests at heart," said Maxim. "But I trust what my body tells me. Maybe I'll give that doctor a call later and see what he suggests."

"You just mind that you do," said Michi, affecting a comedy turn of voice. "If nothing else, the last thing I want to be doing on Saturday night is making a fool of myself in front of half the planet!"

"Ha yes, I didn't think of it that way, Michi young fella," Maxim laughed.

Evgeny, Maxim's driver and right-hand man entered the old man's bedroom, looking like he meant business.

"Right Maxim, you've got about half-an-hour to collect yourself and your belongings before we have to start making a move towards the arena," he said coldly. "Now, is there anything you really need or need to do before we go?"

"Oh, the usual. I'll just pop into the bathroom for a moment, and then I'll start getting dressed," the old man said compliantly. "Have you got any of your special coffee on the go?"

"It's almost stewed and ready, sir," Evgeny said with the traces of a smile at the corner of his mouth.

"Good, good," said Maxim. "Give me a minute and I'll be with you."

As their charge tottered off to the bathroom on unsteady feet, Evgeny leaned towards Michi and whispered conspiratorially.

"When he's like this you really have to make him think that everything is his idea," he said. "He used to have a day like this once in a blue moon, but now they're getting too close together for my liking. And I don't know what kind of rubbish that doctor has got him on, but it's affecting his mood. It's supposed to be for his blood pressure and bone strength, but it's making him anxious. I'm really not sure what we can do about it. Probably nothing in the short term, because our priority is getting him through the next four days. We can worry about everything else afterwards."

Michi wasn't too sure about that plan, but went along with it, because, after all, Evgeny had known Maxim a lot longer than he had, and surely had a more intimate knowledge or all his quirks and foibles – not to mention his various health problems.

A few short minutes later Maxim stepped out of the bathroom, scuttled towards the coffee pot that was bubbling away in the corner, and poured himself a small cup.

"Ahhh, nectar of the Gods!" he sang as he took his first sip of the dark liquid. "I've never had anything else that's ever got me going in the morning as well as Evgeny's coffee. Try a bit, Michi lad, why don't you!"

"Oh I wouldn't want to deprive you of your special tonic," Michi smiled.

"Oh there's enough in that pot to wake a cemetery," Maxim laughed. "Go on, try a bit." "Oh, OK then," Michi conceded.

He poured a small dash of the rich brew into a glass cup, swilled it around for a moment and took a sip. Instantly his head was swirling and he began to cough.

"That's certainly a bit... cough... strong... cough... isn't it Maxim!" he sputtered. "The perfect way to start the day," Maxim replied.

Michi now was convinced of the liquid's ability to awaken even the most slumbering of beasts, but he wasn't entirely sure that it was the best thing to be giving to an old man who appeared as increasingly frail as his old friend.

"Come on gentlemen, time to go!" Evgeny politely called into the bedroom, and with that the three men made their way to the limo and headed for the arena.

"How's the reaction looking amongst the press corps?" said Filip as he burst through the door of the press office, still a little flustered by his trip to the Sammarinese hotel.

"Surprisingly good, actually," said Jeff. "Most of them are fully in agreement with the decision, and are talking you up as the hand of authority that the competition has been crying out for."

"Well that is surprising," said Filip. "But you said 'most of them'. Do we have any dissenters?" "Well there's the usual freaks and conspiracy theorists paddling around at the bottom of the gene pool, but none that have terribly large circulations. The only two biggies that are looking at things in any depth are ESC Cargo, who are just asking their usual over-serious editorial questions, and EuroStorm, who appear to just be making stuff up out of their hat – as usual. But no one has cottoned on to what really happened with San Marino yet. They just think it was the odd dodgy juror here and there."

"Good, good" said Filip. "Let's make it stay that way – at least until the contest is done and dusted and we're last week's news."

He stopped and pondered for a moment, before he asked Jeff a question that he knew he really didn't want to hear the answer to.

"So what are Storm saying? I thought we'd got them as far away from the contest as possible."

"Oh they're still operating out of their hotel," Jeff informed him, "and we've got no jurisdiction over them there…"

"Well, not entirely legal ones…" Filip cut in with a smirk.

"Quite," said Jeff. "Although last I saw of him, Michael Storm was looking a little worse for wear, so hopefully he's beginning to learn the lessons of shooting his gob off in unfamiliar countries."

"Oh I doubt that very much with the ego that boy's got on him," said Filip. "Anyway, what have they been saying?

"Well somewhat unexpectedly," Jeff began, "they're all on board with the Czech disqualification." "Really?" said Filip, a little bit startled.

"Yeah, they reckon that however much of a character she was, she damaged the reputation of the contest with her green room antics."

"Well fair play to them on that count, at least," said Filip. "I'm suspecting that the next couple of things that you tell me aren't going to be quite so agreeable."

"Bang on Filip!" Jeff laughed. "For Portugal, they're saying that they knew it was a plagiarism all along. But they've made a couple of comparison videos that are so wide of the mark that they're just laughable."

"Yeah, that lot have always had difficulty understanding any kind of music from outside of the Eurovision realm," said Filip. "So far, so usual. What about the last one?"

"Oh, this is the doosie," said Jeff, with an enthusiastic smile on his face. "Sit down, because it gets complicated."

"Ooh, I'm not sure that I like the sound of this Jeff!"

"Oh but you will, you will. So, they've taken the bait and have suggested that San Marino tried to bribe a couple of juries at least..."

"Yes, yes," said Filip, "but this is sounding ominous now!"

"Oh yes!" said Jeff, now rubbing his hands together. "But they reckon the only reason that you kicked them out is because the Russians have invested an enormous amount of money in the Montenegrin entry this year, and slipped you a back-hander to ensure they qualified – wherever they finished in the table!"

"Wait! What? How have they even...?" Filip spat with a confused look splashed across his face. "I know," said Jeff. "Delicious, isn't it!"
"Well yes and no, Jeff." Filip replied. "Yes, because it's so gloriously swivel-eyed that it can only be a pack of lies. But no because it's accusing me of bribery straight out, without the slightest hint of suggestion or possibility. And you just know that some of that shit's going to stick amongst the rank and file – not to mention the people upstairs after the Kjellberg incident. We've really got to nip this one in the bud before it gets out of hand. Where's Terry? Is he about?"

"He's just off briefing that lot from Montenegro about what they can and cannot say regarding their unexpected slot in the final on Saturday," said Jeff. "I really can't tell you how excited they were when he told them they'd qualified earlier on this morning. I could hear them yelping down Terry's phone from this side of the room!"

"Great, at least they're on side then!" said Filip assertively. "They're a good lot, anyway, and I'm sure they wouldn't want any accusations of Russian money flying their way. Get Terry to give me a shout when he's done with them, you keep monitoring the nonsense that EuroStorm are pumping out. Jan and Dean, can you get on social media to try and track down where Michael Storm is operating from, and I'll get onto our legal department in Lucerne to see if we can throw a cease and desist at him at the very least, and establish whether we can sue the arse out of him for even suggesting that I'd taken a bung. And once that's done we've got another bloody show to run in about three hours. Surely that can't go as eventfully as the last one? Surely...?"

31

After the manic events of the last day or so, Filip just couldn't wait to get the first full dress rehearsal of the second semi-final up and running so that he could have a nice sit down and watch some songs. He still feared that he'd be spending much of the time trying to anticipate what problems were likely to befall him from amongst this disparate bunch of quarrelling nations. He knew that the back end of the show held a couple of potential flash points with the Azerbaijan/ Armenia and Ukraine/Russia interfaces, but the bonus pay-off to all that was that it was going to make for one heck of a show for the viewers back home. So unless those bitter rivalries spilled out onto the stage in front of the cameras or accidentally kickstarted any bitter localised wars then everything should be fine, he thought.

So as he settled into his comfortable chair on the viewing balcony, his thoughts were on nothing more than the two-and-a-bit hours of light entertainment that were about to flow gracefully before him. As he let his eyes adjust to the darkness of the hall he felt a sudden tap on the shoulder. It was Sunny from the press office.

"Sir! Sir!" he whispered urgently. "You'd better come quickly."
"What is it, Sunny?" Filip grumped. "Can't you see I'm busy?"

"Yes, but this is kind of important," Sunny explained. "Prince bin Faisal is in your office and he's not very happy. And what's more, he's got a sword!"

"Oh shit, I'd better go and deal with it then," said Filip wearily. "Sunny, you get hold of Ox and tell him to meet me outside my office. I've just got a couple of bits and bobs to sort out first and I'll be right there."

"You'd better hurry," said Sunny. "He's already been waving it about in a very unseemly fashion."

"I'll be there in three," Filip asserted, and sat back in his chair to centre himself before he entered into yet another fray.

"It's the semi-final that refuses to die!" he chuckled to himself as he stared out into the calming blue light that cast across the rapidly filling auditorium for just a moment longer.

"Right, I'd better go and sort this all out," he said with a start as he jumped out of his chair and dashed into the corridor. "If I get this solved quickly I might just make it back for the first song."

Filip took the short walk to his office, where Ox and a handful of his men were waiting outside, each of them pulling on some tight black leather gloves.

"Hey Ox Man!" he said to the event's head of security. "Hopefully it won't come to fisticuffs!" Ox laughed, leaned in towards Filip and said "Yes, but we don't want him to know that!"

Filip gave a knowing smile and opened the door. Inside his office stood an angry Saudi prince, surrounded by half-a-dozen of his aides. The moment he saw Ox and his men burst into the room he drew his sword and set himself into a defensive position, while his men stood in a broad arc around him, each with a dagger drawn. Somewhere in the background someone was holding a kestrel.

"Stop! Stop!" Filip yelled. "We're not going to have any violence here now. From either party!"

"OK!" said one of the Prince's henchmen. "But when you're a Prince you are liable to all kinds of attacks and kidnap attempts, so we can never be too careful!"

He said a few words in Arabic and the men put down their weapons – all bar the Prince who was still standing firm.

"Prince bin Faisal, sir!" said Filip, calmly. "How may I help you, sir? And it would make this conversation so much easier if you just put down your sword and sat down nicely in that chair just there."

"I prefer to stand," said the Prince. "And I want to know why you've disqualified our song? What is wrong with it?"

"Well there's nothing wrong with the song in itself," Filip explained. "The song we very much liked. In fact, we think that it added something very valuable to last night's show. But when we were auditing all the votes we noticed some clear and obvious irregularities in the points that you accrued. We've talked with some of the other delegations involved, and with your head of delegation, and decided that it is only fair to the other contestants to withdraw you from the contest at this time."

"What is fair about that?" the Prince huffed. "I have spent good money to ensure that my song passed this early stage of the contest, and you're telling me that it is all wasted and for nothing?"

Filip sensed that the Prince was about to paint himself into a guilty corner, and subtly quizzed him on what he'd just let slip.

"Erm Prince bin Faisal sir. Do you mind if I ask quite how you spent that money?"

"On hiring call centres to arrange a favourable vote for me across the nations," he admitted in a matter-of-fact tone as if it was the most normal thing in the world. "Plus a few little incentives for some of the jury members. Nothing illegal, I checked the rules."

Filip was taken aback at this stark and somewhat honest confession by the Prince. It made his life a whole lot easier, but he needed to put him right on one or two little matters.

"Actually, sir, it really IS just a little bit illegal," he explained, "you know, in international law and everything. And while the call centre seeding isn't strictly mentioned in the official Eurovision rule book, it goes against the spirit of everything that Eurovision itself stands for. If news of this got out into the public sphere it could lead to the worst kind of bad press and bad feeling across the continent, not only for you personally, but for your nation, and indeed poor San Marino who have been an innocent party in all this."

The Prince stopped and pondered Filip's words for a moment. "Hmm, such things are common practice in my world. I guess I hadn't stopped to consider the cultural differences between what we do and what you do. As disappointing as this is for me personally I think that I understand the reasons for your actions now, and I'm so sorry to have put the fine reputation of the contest under such risk. Here, let me make some financial recompense to you for this most unfortunate misunderstanding."

The Prince pulled out a chequebook and a dazzling gold pen from a small leather satchel that was slung over his shoulder and began to write out a cheque.

"Who should I make it out to?" he asked.

"Stop! Stop again!" said Filip in a bit of a panic. "We can't accept any money from you regarding this matter. We are an international organisation with checks and balances and everything, and professional behaviour must be adhered to at all times."

The Prince looked puzzled.

Filip thought for a moment, before offering a solution. "I tell you what, sir. If you would like to make a donation to anyone, maybe you should ask your HoD whether there's any charities back in San Marino that need a helping hand," he suggested. "That would probably be the best way to make some lasting good out of this whole affair."

"Very well," said the Prince. "Then so be it. That sounds like a very agreeable compromise." Filip let out a barely disguised sigh of relief. "Right then," said the Prince. "We must go now. I have an important business meeting back at the Hotel Majestic in an hour and I need to prepare myself for it."

Filip thought it best not to ask any more questions on the matter, thanked the Prince for his honesty, and indeed generosity, made his excuses and dashed back to the arena, leaving Sunny to finish up in the office.

"Well that was a whole lot easier than I first anticipated," he muttered internally as he plonked himself down in his chair and swivelled it slightly for the best view of the big stage.

Moments later Terry came and sat down beside him. "Have I missed anything?" he asked.
"Oh not much, Terry old friend," Filip smiled, "shy of a Saudi Prince wanting to run his sword through me. Just a normal day in the office."

32

Maxim Munteanu was waiting in the wings, all set to go on stage to perform his song for the recording after the hosts had finished practising their lines. The rest of the show that afternoon had gone completely to plan, which was a surprise to everyone considering some of the complicated transitions involved, and so the Moldovan delegation had been called to get in place about fifteen minutes earlier than expected. But Michi was still concerned that his elderly friend was looking a bit frail.

"Now are you sure that you've got everything you need, Maxim?" he asked gently. "All I need is my voice," Maxim replied. "everything else follows that."

"Good, good," said Michi. "But just don't be afraid to ask if you do need anything. This show isn't going out on live TV, so we're able to stop and start again if you need to."

"Yes, but what about all the beautiful people in the audience?" the singer began to explain. "These people can't afford tickets to see the real show, so this might be their only chance to see me in person. I have to give it my everything just for them. After all, they mean the world to me."

"That's a beautiful point," Michi conceded as Hanna the stage manager walked down the ramp to give them their cue.

"Right Maxim sir, when the stage goes dark it's time to go," she said, "I'll show you where you need to go, and when the postcard music stops you're on."

"Why thank you Madam Hanna," Maxim said graciously. "I very much appreciate your help."

"OK, in three-two-one... lights out... let's go!" said Hanna as she began to lead the old man and his backing singers onto the stage. At first his steps were unsure and faltering, but as he got his first sight of the audience he appeared to visibly grow again, and by the time he got to the microphone it was as if he'd shed twenty years in age once more."

"I just don't know how he does that," said Michi to Evgeny.

"He's a simple man," Maxim's right-hand man replied. "The audience is his medicine. It's what keeps him going, and they very much fill him with the power to perform."

"It's a very beautiful thing," said Michi.

"It is," Evgeny replied. "But I fear that it's the thing that's going to ultimately see his demise."

At that same moment the crowd caught the first sight of Maxim and went wild. The noise grew in waves as he first gestured to one side of the arena and then to the other, drawing the love from the audience like a skilled craftsman before he'd even sung a note.

"Right, let's hold this for a moment," said the show's director in the gallery. "This is just too special to cut off.

So Maxim stood at the microphone for another thirty seconds, his arms opened broadly as if to physically embrace all the applause from the crowd.

"Sorry cameras, I don't think this is going to end unless we start to play his music," the director instructed down the crew's earpieces. "Now... cue music..."

The intro to Maxim's song began, but the crowd didn't let up with their adoration. If anything it only made them louder. Maxim held his hands out in front of him and made a calming gesture, and they began to quieten a little just before it was his time to sing. And boy did he sing. His warm yet fragile baritone oozed out of him with such ease it was as if the song was a part of his very soul. The crowd, who up to now had been mouthing every word, began to sing more heartily in the chorus, and before long the whole performance had become a massive communal choir, with Maxim conducting affairs at the centre of it all.

By the time it came to the last chorus, Maxim stepped back from the mic, held his arms aloft like the conductor of an orchestra, and let the audience sing the words for him. There wasn't a dry eye in the house, as every single person in that big hall – crowd, security, cameramen, TV executives, the lot of them – had been utterly demolished by the old man's charm.

Terry turned to Filip on the viewing balcony, and struggled to mutter a few words to his colleague.

"I... I think we're in trouble here boss," he said. "If this old gimmer has this effect on Saturday night and sings it directly down the camera to all the people at home we could very easily be coming back this way again this time next year."

"Oh don't, Terry," Filip said with a weepy sniff. "Although to be honest I was just thinking – no, fearing – pretty much the same thing myself. This is one of the most incredible live performances I've ever seen – and it's only just under three minutes long!"

"I know!" said Terry in wonderment. "What are we going to do if it wins?"

"Let us cross that bridge when we come to it," said Filip. "And there's a lot of water to flow under it between now and Saturday night."

As Filip finished his sentence, the song ended. If the crowd were loud before the song was performed, then they escalated to a whole new strata of volume and excitement now. Maxim just stood there on stage, soaking up the applause, which grew and grew and grew. Somewhere in the wings the UK's Jason Brown was waiting and quietly shaking, terrified at the thought of having to follow that. As Maxim finally turned to walk off stage, the crowd only got louder. When he was finally out of sight they began to boo loudly, and as the British singer was ushered on stage they started to throw programmes and half-finished plastic cups of beer at him.

"Note for the future, Terry," said Filip. "Always put the home artist on last for their first dress rehearsal appearance."

"Most duly noted," said Terry, while in the background poor Jason struggled to perform his song over the hubbub as the crowd were still chanting Maxim's name.

But backstage it was a different story. As Maxim started to move out of the gaze of his adoring audience he began to visibly shrink, and by the time he got to the bottom of the ramp where Michi and Evgeny were waiting he'd become a shadow of the man they'd just seen perform on stage.

"Get me a chair, Michi lad," he weakly asked. "That ramp was a bit steep and it's fair worn me out."

Michi and Evgeny cast each other a knowing look as both men knew full well that the ramp had very little to do with Maxim's fatigue, and once they'd got him sitting down they started to fan him with towels like a boxer before the last round of a title fight.

"Do you know what, lads?" Maxim continued with a frail voice. "I think I'll just rest up here for a moment. You sort out everything else that you need to do, and come and get me when you're ready. Thank you. Thank you so much."

And with that he fell into a deep sleep that neither man could wake him from.

"Erm, Evegeny," said Michi with a worried tone in his voice. "I'm no expert, but that looks more like a coma than a quick nap. I think you'd better call the medics..."

"Man down backstage!" came the anxious sounding voice over the production radio channel. "Call medics to exit ramp position three quick!"

"Oh no!" said Filip, in worried tones. "Has the old boy taken a tumble? I knew we should have lit that corner of the off ramp better for his exit."

"Do you want me to scoot down there to have a check see?" asked Terry.

"No no, it's fine," Filip replied. "I'd better go down myself, just in case there are any potential legal issues."

"No worries," said Terry. "I'll hold the fort here and take notes if anything untoward happens." As Filip made his way to the rear of the stage he could sense the commotion increasing.

Concerned looking Moldovans were dashing about with fearful looks on their faces, and when he got to the backstage area he could see a big group of people standing in an arc around a little recess in the curtained area, with the people at the back craning their necks for a look at what was going on.

"Stand back!" Filip said assertively. "CTF official coming through!"

The crowd parted, and he could see Maxim sitting slumped on a chair, apparently fully asleep, but with an unnervingly serene look on his face. Dumi from Moldova Smash was by his side, along with Michi and Evgeny.

"What appears to be the problem, gentlemen?" he asked tentatively.

"It's... it's... Maxim," Michi stuttered. "He came off stage after that amazing performance, said he needed a sit down. Then he sank into this deep sleep and we just can't rouse him."

"Has be ever done this before?" Filip enquired?

"No," said Evgeny, curtly. "Never before. And I have worked for him for 25 years. This is new." Just then the medics arrived.

"You took your time," said Filip with a stern tone. "I came from way up in the gods there and still beat you to it. You're supposed to be stationed back here, anyway!"

"Yes, sorry about that, sir," one of the medics replied. "We had an unprecedented rush on fainting grandmothers when Maxim performed just then. There have been quite a few nasty bumps to the head out there, so all the medical crews were rushed into the arena. So, what do we have here then?"

"Maxim Munteanu, unspecified age, gently passed out when he came off stage, and now we can't wake him up," Filip calmly explained.

"Let's have a look at him then," said the medic, as he took Maxim's pulse and checked his eyes.

"Ooh!" he said curtly, which made the surrounding gaggle instantly take a collective step back in fear.

"He's got a very weak pulse, and his pupils aren't reacting to the torch in the way we'd usually expect," said the medic. "I think we'd better get him to the hospital, just as a precaution. Get a few vital fluids into him and boost his strength a bit."

By now there was quite a crowd surrounding the old man, and their fearful mutterings could be heard on stage, just as the UK's Jason Brown was coming to the quiet and emotional sequence of his song. Unaware of the events taking place backstage, his eyes kept flickering to the side of the performance area in an attempt to see what was going on, and he became so distracted that he missed his cue for the chorus and continued his song about half a beat out of time.

News of Maxim's unwelcome turn hadn't filtered out beyond the backstage area yet, so as far as the press room could work out, here was a nervous young British singer totally out of his depth and absolutely blowing his chances of a decent result on the Saturday night.

"He's bloody rubbish!" shouted a Portuguese voice from the centre of the room.

"Who is this idiot?" yelled another more Germanic sounding critic. "He doesn't deserve a place on the Eurovision stage. Look at him, he's a rank amateur!"

"Hey, cut him some slack!" a Scottish voice cut through, "You don't know what it's like to be up there on that massive stage."

"If he's not up to it he should be there, you fool," carped someone with a mocking tone and a Serbian accent.

"Who are you calling a fool?" snapped the Scot, angrily.

"You, ya big prick!" mocked a man with a deep Dublin accent, which caused the Scot to charge across the press hall with his fists flying. Out of nowhere a massive brawl kicked off. Tables were turned over, chairs were thrown, and people were slapping completely random strangers at their tables just for the fun of it. While all this was going on, Radouane Thill from ESC Cargo stood on his chair in the furthest corner of the room live streaming the whole thing to the media player on the front page of his site.

"Something like this was always going to happen," he remarked stoically into his phone. "There are so many petty rivalries and jealousies in this hall that the whole place was like a tinderbox just waiting for the first spark. But at the same time, it is all rather amusing..." he added, before quickly ducking as one of those giant water cooler bottles flew perilously close to his head.

Jeff, who was sheltering in a little side office and watching these events unfold through a crack in the door, had alerted Terry to this almighty punch up, who arrived at the top of the steps down to the press tables just as the hostilities reached their peak. He took a deep breath and yelled at the top of his voice...

"STOP! STOP THE VIOLENCE EVERYBODY! MAXIM MUNTEANU HAS JUST BEEN RUSHED TO HOSPITAL!"

The fighting stopped immediately as everyone turned to each other with shocked looks on their faces.

"Thank you ladies and gentlemen," said Terry more calmly. "We have no further news, but we're assured that it's not serious. We'll be issuing a press release as soon as we get any further news. Now, in the meantime, could you all start tidying this mess up?"

"Sorry Terry!" came the collective shame-filled mumble from the centre of the hall as the rioters began to pick up their chairs and set the tables right.

Meanwhile, over on the betting tables in the bowels of the hall, the professional gamblers were heavily laying the United Kingdom, but absolutely throwing the money onto Moldova, oblivious to the carnage around them.

"Sympathy vote," one of them could be heard to say. "It's got to be. Classic tactics, innit."

33

"Any word on Maxim?" Dumi asked as he popped his head around Filip's office door about half an hour before the start of that evening's jury final.

"I'd have thought that would have been more your territory," Filip replied. "I don't tend to get news about any Moldovan matters unless it comes from one of the cleaners or the security mob."

"Oh, I just wondered if anything official had worked its way back from the hospital via the news channels, that's all," Dumi answered.

"How did he look to you, though?" said Filip. "You were one of the last people to see him before they loaded him into the wagon."

"It was weird. His body was all weak and limp, but his face had the strangest expression. It was like he was still listening to everything that was going on around him, and he was in utter peace with the world. They say he's in a coma, but it didn't look like any kind of coma I've ever seen."

A terrible thought flashed through Filip's mind.

"Oh God!" he said to Dumi. "We've not killed off the most popular living Moldovan by pushing him a bit to hard on our silly little singing show, have we? We'll never get out of here alive if we have!"

"I don't think so, Filip. I mean, he didn't look great, but he has been in generally good health for a man of his age."

"But that's just it," said Filip. "What actually is his age?"

"Nobody knows for certain," Dumi replied. "Some rumours suggest that he could be as old as ninety, although I don't believe that for a minute. But however old he is, we've got to ensure that he gets the best care possible if we're going to get him up on that stage on Saturday."

"No way, Dumi man," said Filip. "There's no way I'm going to risk the very strong likelihood of a live death in front of a transglobal audience of four hundred million people. Nobody wants to see that on a human level, and it would damage the brand beyond belief. You must have considered some kind of contingency plan in case the lovely old fella took ill?"

"Well kinda," said Dumi, awkwardly. "Maxim made us sign a legal caveat before he finally agreed to take part this year. If anything were to happen to him that meant he was unable to perform on Saturday, he left strict instructions that a replacement singer, as nominated by him, would sing in his place."

"And do we know who that singer is?" Filip asked. "That's just the problem – we do. It's Michi Rotari." Filip could scarcely believe his ears.

"What, that freaky Goth laddie who nearly caused a riot at your national final?" he yelled. "He can hardly sing a bloody note!"

"Yes, we know," said Dumi, looking a little embarrassed. "But Maxim has taken something of a shine to him. He's always been such a strong old goat that we didn't think it would ever be an issue, so we just signed the caveat to humour him. We never imagined that we'd actually be stuck with Michi."

"Oh my days," said Filip, pacing up and down in his office. "This is the last thing that I needed to hear. There's surely something that we can do about it? What's that Michi lad actually like? Will we be able to work with him if the worst comes to the worst?"

"Actually he's a much nicer chap than his image would suggest –

although he's very raw. I'm not entirely sure that he'd be able to handle the pressure though, between you and me. And the song is totally unsuited for his reedy little voice. I'll get my head down with Stefan from the station to see what plans we can come up with tonight. It 100% has to be the same song though, right?"

"I'm afraid it does," said Filip. "We can make exceptions to some of the rules in extreme circumstances, but it definitely has to be the same song. It's on all the livery, the programmes, the CD album, everything. We'll make it possible for there to be another singer for it, but we'd rather have someone who can, y'know, actually sing to perform it, if there's a legal way of getting around the issue, of course Br?"

"Well that's one of my ideas gone right down the drain already!" Dumi laughed. "But seriously though, we'll test this Michi out tomorrow and keep monitoring how Maxim is doing in hospital, then hopefully I can give you a definitive answer this time tomorrow, if not earlier."

"That would really help," said Filip, "so we can sort all this out in good time before we have to work through the aftermath of tomorrow night's semi."

"We'll try our very best!" said Dumi, only half confidently. "Ooh, and are we still on for the jury final debrief after the show tonight?"

"Yep, same time, same place," said Filip. "Acts of God and freaks of nature allowing. And I hope to God that it doesn't get as complicated as the last one, or you can book me the hospital bed next to Maxim right now!"

*

Thankfully the Jury Final for the second semi-final passed with remarkably little incident. Slovenia had a little difficulty getting out of their crate again, and once more had to pick it up from inside, scuttling along with it to get off the stage, which was a little embarrassing for them. But at least nobody could see their faces. And after a stunned silence at the beginning of his performance, Iceland had the crowd laughing so loudly that poor Vikingur stormed off down the ramp the before his backing music had even finished playing. Azerbaijan and Armenia played nicely though, with no significant incidents during their changeover. But Ukraine seemed to take an absolute age to get off the stage when their song was done, and one of the crew forgot to remove the kitchen sink from behind their other props, which led to a delay in getting Russia's even bigger props in place. The Russians had already put in an official complaint, but from its wording it looked as though it had been written well in advance of that evening's events. The surprise package of the night, though, were Australia, who despite all predictions of a semi-final failure struck a chord with all the punters in the hall and ended the show in a rousing, if not slightly unruly fashion.

Back in Filip's office, an hour-and-a-half after the show had finished, the representatives from the CTF, the crew and the local organisers were having a quick debrief.

"I shan't keep you long tonight, people, as we had a pretty smooth running, for once," said Filip. "I get the feeling that Ukraine were taking the Mickey a little bit on the changeover there. But Artiom, can you make sure that Ice sharpens up the stagehands so that they don't miss any vital bits of equipment during that changeover in particular? I appreciate that they were being bamboozled by all those giant props going off and on, but we've really got to be on top of that by tomorrow night otherwise both of those sainted nations are liable to start claiming we're favouring one or the other of them."

"Noted, Filip," said Artiom.

"And all that laughing at the end of the poor Icelandic fella," Filip continued. "Look, I know he's a bit of a strange one, but we still want to present him in the best light possible. Håkan, can you have a word with Skunk on the sound desk to see if he can cut the ambient hall mics if it happens again? Maybe drop in some recorded crowd noise if it's possible. We want to give the poor sod at least a bit of a fighting chance with the people watching on the TV."

"I can ask him, at the very least," said Håkan.

"And that seems to be about it until we get the jury results in," said Filip. "Jeff's just running up with them now," said Terry.

There was a knock on the door. "Postie's here!" Jeff shouted camply.

"Yes, come in Jeff," Filip laughed. "Now let's have a look at what we're dealing with. I hope the juries have done us a couple of favours tonight."

Filip prised open the sealed envelope from the auditors and took a quick scan.

"Ooh, that's awkward," he said. "The juries didn't seem to care terribly much for either Russia OR Ukraine, and have them both sitting just outside the top ten. We kind of want either both or neither of them in the final otherwise we're going to be up till late tomorrow night listening to their official complaints!"

"Surely they'll both make it through on the televote though?" asked Dumi.

"Oh that's almost certainly a given," Filip replied. "But it does leave a little scope for complications, so we'd better prepare ourselves for every possibility."

"Who did they actually like, though?" asked Terry, trying to catch a glimpse at the results sheet.

"It's pretty seriously backloaded, to be honest with you," said Filip.

"Australia, Armenia, Azerbaijan, The Netherlands surprisingly, North Macedonia, Serbia, Kazakhstan – all there or there abouts. They're probably the shoe-ins unless the nice people at home take an inexplicable dislike to anything. Then it's three spots from eight!"

"No Sweden?" Terry asked, a little confused.

"They finished tenth," said Filip. "But they were a long way adrift from Cyprus in ninth." "Ooh, they're not going to be very happy about that!" Håkan rasped from the corner.

"Well they shouldn't keep sending the same flipping song every year then, should they now," joked Terry.

"Who came last though?" asked Dumi.

"Erm, Slovenia, it says here. I did tell them that the crate wasn't perhaps the best of ideas." "What, not Iceland?" said Dumi in amazement.

"Nope," Filip replied. "Those judges can clearly see some art in the thing that none of the rest of us could and put it up in thirteenth, would you believe."

"Either that or we've go a whole load of 'That's soooooo Eurovision!' jokers on the panels this year?" Terry teased.

"Oh heaven forbid!" Filip laughed in mock horror.

"Still, however wonky they may seem in places, the results all appear above board, with no blatantly obvious San Marino incidents going on. So I think we can leave it there for the night, people, and head off to our beds. Thank you for all your constantly brilliant efforts, folks. See you all in the office first thing – oh and Dumi, let me know if you've come to any decision about that other matter we were talking about earlier. I think we need to clear that up sooner rather than later."

34

"Any news from the hospital yet?" Dumi asked down the telephone.

"Not yet, Mr Enache sir," said a tired sounding Evgeny. "There's been no change. They still have him on fluids, but he's stable. He might not be getting any worse, but he's not getting any better either. At least he's in a private room, and only one doctor and one nurse have been told who he is."

"Hopefully that should keep the news quiet locally until we have the chance to announce it after tonight's show," said Dumi. "Thanks Evgeny, we appreciate what you're doing for us down there."

"It is no problem," Evgeny replied. "I will call if anything changes." "Thank you so much, sir. Bye."

Dumi was sitting in an emergency morning meeting with his close associate from Moldova Smash Stefan Smolenko, the station's owner Lucian Dobre, and its head of programming Iurie Mirea.

"What did they say?" asked Iurie.

"No change either way," Dumi reported. "So we're going to have to make a decision in the next few hours regarding what we're going to do about all of this."

"There is no decision," said Lucian loudly, " we wake the old man and prop him up there with a stick if we have to!"

"Unfortunately the CTF are very much against that scenario," warned Dumi. "I can't see them allowing us to bust him out of hospital to do the show."

"It is our country and our show!" said Lucian angrily, banging both fists onto the table in a mild rage.

"Yes, but there's the small matter of being physically able to wake Maxim up," said Stefan. "We can't just roll him up there in his hospital bed wearing his jim jams and let the music play out behind him?"

"Why not?" said Lucian. "That would make amazing television! And I reckon we'd still come in top five with all the sympathy we'd get!"

"Don't you think that would be just a little tasteless though, Lucian?" asked Iurie. "Of course!" Lucian roared. "That's why it would be so brilliant!"

"Unfortunately, even if we do sweep all notions of taste under the carpet and go with that option," said Dumi, "I'm afraid that the CTF just won't allow it."

"We'll find a way!" said Lucian, now bristling with excitable nervous energy. "You've all seen Weekend At Bernie's haven't you? We can tie strings to him and make it look like he's moving, then play a tape of him singing over the top of it. Nobody at home will know..."

Lucian suddenly became very aware that the rest of the people in the meeting were all giving him a very hard stare.

"What?" he said indignantly. "I think it's a brilliant idea!"

"No!" said Iurie. "Just no, Lucian. We're not going to harm the dignity of our most important musical hero on an international broadcast just for a few cheap laughs. I know that you own the station, but I really won't allow it."

"Yeah, OK," said Lucian sheepishly. "I guess I was just getting carried away and riffing on an idea."

"So, do we have any more... sensible suggestions?" said Dumi to the room, cutting Lucian a sarcastic glance over his glasses as he spoke.

"Well how I see it there's only three things that we can do," suggested Stefan. "One: go with Maxim's wishes and let Michi Rotari sing the song..."

"What, that freak?" barked Lucian. "Never!"

"Two: go against Maxim's wishes and find another singer..."

"But who would ever be bold enough to step into the old man's shoes?" asked Dumi. "And that's before we even start on the legal caveat we'll have broken if Maxim ever wakes up!"

"And three: pull out of the competition altogether!"

"No!" shouted the other three people in the room, instantly.

"No way, man!" said Lucian. "This is probably our biggest moment on an international stage. We can't just step away with our tail between our legs. If it absolutely has to be Michi or nothing, then it has to be Michi. Do you think the kid has got it in him though?"

There was an awkward silence around the room as the other three TV executives looked at each other nervously.

"In a word, probably not," said Iurie. "But he's been working closely with Maxim since he won O Melodie Pentru Moldova, and he definitely knows all the words. If we get him rehearsing vigorously for the rest of the the night, then we can slot him into Friday's first full dress rehearsal, tell the audience that Maxim is resting his voice, and then just see how it flies from there."

"I'm not digging it," said Lucian with a worried look on his face, "but it's the best option we've got. Although... Weekend At Bernie's? No? Dammit, let's go with the kid. Get him on the phone right away and tell him the news. I'm sure he'll be over the moon when he hears."

Dumi called Evgeny's number again and waited for an answer.

"Hello!" Evgeny curtly answered. "No more news since five minutes ago." "Actually it's about something else," Dumi said gently. "Erm, is Michi there?"

"Yes," came the sharp reply. Dumi could hear Evgeny talking to Michi in the background. "For you. It's Dumi."

"For me, you say?" said Michi nervously. "Whatever could he want?" He took the phone and gave an enquiring "Hello?"

"Ah Michi, good to speak to you sir," said Dumi. "We've had a meeting of the local organising committee and we've decided that should he not recover in time – and we most sincerely hope that he does – that we must adhere to Maxim's wishes and allow you to take his place on the Eurovision stage."

Michi's brain suddenly exploded in his head. All he could see were clouds of stars and blue smoke, and it felt as though he had been fired off into the cosmos without a spacesuit and was struggling to breath amongst the cold beauty of the cosmos. But through the rush of blood pounding around his ears he could hear an insistent voice.

"Michi? Michi? Are you still there?"

Michi's attention snapped back into the room. He shook the fog of confusion out of his head, took a deep breath and answered.

"Yes, sorry Dumi, I was a bit taken aback for a moment there. It's quite an important thing that you're asking me to do, and I'm not really sure

375

that I'm up to the job just yet if I have to be absolutely honest with you."

"I admire your candour, Michi lad," said Dumi. "But we have every faith in you at Moldova Smash, and we'll give you every bit of help that you could possibly ask for. And who knows, the old man might wake up perfectly refreshed after his long, well-deserved rest and you won't need to do it. But if you at least take his place during the dress rehearsals we can work out everything else when it comes to it."

Michi's head was a whirl of fears and bad thoughts. This was a moment that he'd dreamed of for most of his life, but it would come at such a cost to both him and his nation. Surely he could never fill the massive shoes of his elderly friend and mentor? Surely nobody would accept him taking the place of such a revered national figure at such an important moment in Moldovan history? Surely he wasn't up to the job, either artistically and emotionally? What could he possibly do in such an impossible situation?

"So what do you think, Michi?" asked Dumi.

"Erm... well... I suppose I can give it a try. And if it doesn't work out we can get some proper singer to do it. I'm sure Maxim wouldn't mind."

"Oh he was very insistent that you were the only alternative option," said Dumi, trying to bolster the clearly terrified young man's confidence. "But we're going to need you to start rehearsals right away. Are you still at the hospital?"

"Erm... yes... but..." Michi stuttered.

"Great!" said Dumi, steamrollering the frightened singer into making a decision. "We'll send a car round right away, then bring you back to one of the practise studios at the arena and get you all rehearsed and polished up until nobody would ever believe that it wasn't your song! Are we good Michi?"

"Erm... yes? I guess?"

"Great! See you in about forty minutes then! And if there's anything you need just let us know!"

As Dumi rang off, Lucian, Stefan and Iurie all leant forward across the table, wide-eyed with anticipation.

"Yep, he's in!" Dumi gladly announced. "He doesn't sound terribly keen on the idea right now, but we'll drill it into him."

The three other men sat back in their chairs, with a strange blend of relief and abject horror written across their faces.

"Right, now to give the CTF the, erm, good news," said Dumi. "I'm sure they'll be beside themselves..."

*

"I've just had the weirdest phone call from Dumi," Filip said to Terry on the balcony just as the second-semi final was about to start.

"What's up then?" Terry asked.

"Well he started muttering something about Weekend At Bernie's, but then swiftly changed the subject and was nervously telling me about how well Michi Rotari was coping with his rehearsals. So it sounds like they actually are going to go with that Gothic horror of a singer. I'm not altogether sure what I think of that?"

"Well I suppose it's better than nothing?" said Terry, quizzically. "But even nothing's better than having a real life death on stage, I guess?"

"Yes, you're right... really," said Filip, rubbing his eyes with dismay. "And in the wider scheme of things, when you consider Moldova's history at this contest it won't be the worst thing they've ever sent. It's just that everybody has such high hopes for them now they've actually gone and won the thing once."

"At least they'll have someone out there attempting the song," said Terry, "although I'm not sure how the local punters will take it when their one true hero fails to turn up and some haunted-looking pipe-cleaner in leather trousers tries to warble out the song instead. We've already learned that their audiences can be a bit volatile, to say the least. And there'll be people who've splashed out a lot of money on tickets simply because they want to see Maxim sing one song on that big stage there. It could go very bad, very quickly."

"Hmm yes, I can very much see your point," said Filip."I guess we'd better draft in some extra security for the big show, just in case. I'll gauge the response in the crowd during the rehearsals tomorrow and try to devise a plan accordingly.

Suddenly the hall went dark in front of them, and Te Deum boomed out through the massive speakers suspended from the ceiling.

"Right then Terry, eyes down for a full house! Let's hope this semi is a bit more incident free than the last one!"

And it very much was. Cyprus opened the show with a welcome dancey bounce, setting the tone perfectly for the rest of the evening. Slovenia managed to keep their great big crate under control, as ludicrous as it looked, the Finnish Troll metallers had a whale of a time, and the audience even behaved themselves for Iceland this time. Azerbaijan and Armenia were still getting on remarkably well, which, if rumours about the two singers having secret late night assignations were to be believed, could explain a lot – but it could also cause a whole heap of ructions back home if the news ever got out. And even Ukraine and Russia were on their best behaviour, which suggests that they may have got wind of a few of the jury scores and decided to concentrate more on themselves than each other.

And once again Australia closed the show with a flourish. The crowd in the hall had, against all normal logic, warmed to their coarse rock'n'roll ways, and it took a fair while for the noise to die down after they'd finished their song and the hosts could be heard. Mind you, they had been ferrying Space Truckers branded beer cans to the audience for most of the show, so that may have helped to get themselves in the good books of the punters.

But the songs had now finished, the interval acts had done their bit, and the stage was clear for the big reveal. Elina and Ruslan were standing behind their plinths, nervously filling before they revealed which lucky ten songs were going to progress to the final.

"So!" said Ruslan. "It is time... finally... to discover which songs will complete the line up for Saturday's Eurovision Song Contest Grand Final. Do you have a favourite?"

"Australia!" came an almost universal roar from the crowd, still clearly fuelled up on the free Aussie beer.

"Damn, I didn't see that one coming thirty six hours ago," Terry whispered to Filip. "I thought that was a borderline qualifier at best. But the punters were just lapping it up."

"Well, if it keeps the Aussies with us for another year then it's done its job," said Filip. "I just hope the bastards don't go and win the thing, because that could open up a whole new world of pain for the lot of us!"

"Oh wouldn't it just!" Terry smiled.

On stage, Ruslan put on his most serious voice.

"OK. So who is it to be? The first country to qualify from this second semi-final... is..." There was a long painful wait before Ruslan ripped open the envelope and shouted... "ICELAND!"

"What?!!!" yelled Terry as he spat his drink over the edge of the balcony. "The bloody dog man? How in the name of hell did that happen?"

Filip laughed. "Ha! I thought I'd keep that one from you especially. Seems like the folks at home loved him just enough to sneak him across the qualification line. He might have been a nightmare to work with, but his qualification guarantees that we're going to get the final on every version of Gogglebox across the planet in the next fortnight!"

"Well that's one way of looking at it," Terry shrugged. "But, I mean... come on!"

It was Elina's turn to reveal the next qualifier, but the crowd were still in shock over the first announcement and she had to calm down the chatter before she continued.

"Everybody, peace..." she called assertively, and the room fell quiet – apart from one voice at the back who kept making very loud dog noises.

"Have him put down would you, he sounds in terrible pain..." Elina ad libbed, and the whole place erupted once more, only this time with laughter.

Beside her, Ruslan had got a serious case of the giggles, but ever the professional she flicked some imaginary dust from her shoulder, let out a big sniff, and continued with the announcement.

"Anyway..." she sang loudly, "the second of tonight's ten qualifiers is..."

Again, there was a long pause while the jeopardy music rumbled menacingly along in the background, before she dramatically ripped open the envelope and declared...

"CYPRUS!"

Again, this brought on some shocked muttering from the audience. Everybody enjoyed it, of course, but nobody ever imagined that it was going to be one of the qualifiers.

Terry leaned over to Filip and whispered...

"That's two from the first half already!" he said in some shock. "Does this mean that we're going to lose somebody pretty serious from the back end of the draw tonight?"

"You know that I'm not going to spoil the fun and tell you that!" said Filip with a knowing smile. "You always tell me that you want to find out at the same time as the folks back home, don't you!"

"Yeah, but we're only two in and the tension is killing me already!" said Terry.

"And I won't be giving anything away if I tell you it's only going to get worse," Filip teased. "Oh you!" said Terry, in mock frustration. "And the third qualifier," said Ruslan, his voice booming above the noise. "Is..." The arena was suddenly hushed in anticipation. "Our new friends... KAZAKHSTAN!"

There was a massive cheer of approval, as everybody seemed to enjoy that one. "Right," said Elina. "Time for the fourth qualifier. Who is..." This time the wait seemed unbearably long, but the host was milking every single moment of it. "CROATIA!'

"Wait! What?" said Terry. "That dull old thing?"

"Remember Terry, it was prime jury bait," said Filip. "and it got just enough punter love to haul it through."

"Yeah, but," said Terry in utter bewilderment. "That's all four from the first half now. The next six announcements are going to be an absolute blood bath!"

"Just you wait!" said Filip with a wry grin.

The next three reveals were all as to be expected, with Azerbaijan, Armenia and Ukraine all making it through. So there were three countries yet to be called, and a whole load of heavy hitters still in the hat.

"This is making my head go all fuzzy," said Terry. "I'm not sure that I can take the tension." "It's only just got started, my friend," laughed Filip.

"Oh don't say that? You're just winding me up now," Terry snapped crossly. "Maybe I am, maybe I'm not..."

Back on stage, Elina quietened the audience once more and announced the next qualifier. "And in eighth... comes..."

Everybody in the room held their breath for her next utterance. "Well done cobbers... AUSTRALIA!"

"Phew, at least another normal one," said Terry. "Well, relatively normal. I reckon there would have been a riot in here if they didn't make it through."

It was Ruslan's last turn to call the next qualifier. "So, two to go. Anyone have any favourites?"

The crowd all shouted a jumble of different names before the host quickly shouted... "SERBIA!"

"Eh?" said seemingly everyone in the hall at the same time.

"I'd clean forgotten you lot were still in it!" Terry said to Filip, jokingly. "To be perfectly honest, Terry mate, so had I!"

"But wait," said Terry with a serious look on his face. "One announcement yet to be made and Russia are still there, Sweden are still there, The Netherlands are still there. We're going to lose someone pretty major in the next three minutes. Oh my days is this going to cause some trouble!"

Elina took her last turn at the mic, and she was looking anxious.

"This is it. The final qualifier. The last country to go forward to Saturday's big Eurovision final. And it is..."

The massive hall went so silent that you could have heard a pin drop – from outside. Everybody was glued to the big screens, trying to work out what mouth shapes Elina was fixing up before her big announcement.

"NORTH MACEDONIA!"

The audience stayed silent, shocked into a stupor by the two words Elina had just uttered, although somewhere in the distance you could hear a small handful of North Macedonian fans going thoroughly berserk.

Terry sat there blinking with disbelief, almost shellshocked at what he'd just seen.

"No Russia? No bloody Sweden? Oh my days this is going to get weird," he drawled. "Wait, stop, where did Russia actually come?"

Filip opened his results papers and subtly showed them to Terry.

"Eleventh?" he said in some shock. "Wait... level on points with Iceland? My life, this is almost priceless."

"Yep," said Filip, "Russia may have had the most big scores out of the pair, but Vikingur got lots and lots of little amounts of points from almost every jury, and that got him the win on countback. It tastes pretty darned sweet, doesn't it!"

"Yes, yes, it does," Terry replied. "And they're going to be absolutely livid!"

"My phone's gone insane with messages in cyrillic already, Terry old chap. One suspects that this is going to be a long night!"

"And Sweden fourteenth? Oh dear! But where are all the points that would head to Russia and Sweden going to go on Saturday night?"

"Your guess is as good as mine, old chap. But one thing's for certain, this has suddenly become the most open contest that I can remember in a long time. Anything could happen in the next forty eight hours. Absolutely anything. Now let's go and start working out this running order…"

35

Filip, Dumi, Hanna and Håkan were locked away in one of the big conference rooms at The Teapot with a big wad of Post-It notes, each with a qualified country's name written on it, trying to work out what the best running order for the Eurovision final should be. Filip had been in half a mind of which songs were likely to go where for a while now, but Tuesday's disqualifications and a couple of surprise qualifiers from tonight had put his plans into something of a skew.

Aside from the usual musical and aesthetic reasons for ordering the performance line up, there were some practical considerations to take into account too, which is why Håkan and Hanna were there to make an input. The songs with massive props and production elements like Montenegro, Ukraine and Norway clearly had to be kept apart – for the health and well-being of Ice's stage crew at the very least. But at the same time they couldn't put too many of the quieter, more understated songs in a row or the folks at home might start to get bored and switch channels, which really wouldn't help with the televoting income.

At least they didn't have Russia to contend with when considering the running order. Although their show was the kind of prop-heavy spectacular that the viewers at home tended to love and enjoy, the crew no longer had to worry about getting its many enormous elements of staging on and off the performance area in the alloted 45 seconds, while Filip would have less of a logistical headache now that he didn't have to worry about which countries to avoid politically when matching them together on the bill. Now he only had the two battling Caucasian states to worry about. He'd learned his lesson with the running order of that night's semi, and so now he could very deliberately stick them at opposite ends of the show to keep them well out of each other's way.

This was a job that really shouldn't be rushed, but at the same time kind of had to be, as the first few artists had to prepare themselves for an early make up and costume call for tomorrow afternoon's first full dress rehearsal, and they'd need to know when they had to be up before they went to bed. And on top of all that, there were the notorious cursed positions to contend with.

Throughout the competition's history there had been some slots in the running order that had never provided a winner. The positions 21, 25 and 26 had not had the honour of a victory before, but mainly by dint of having been in the show less frequently since it first began in 1956. Slot 16 was also bereft of success, but its notoriety as an unlucky draw was far overshadowed by the one remaining spot of doom – number 2. Long considered an instant kiss of death, it was always seen as a bit of bad luck for any song that found itself dumped there back when the draw was conducted totally randomly. But since the running order became entirely producer led in a move to make the shows as exciting as possible, any song finding itself in that position could only consider itself to be held in low regard by the organisation. Which to be fair, they frequently were.

"Norway!" said Filip. "It's got to be Norway. That way we get them out of the way early, but they're not the first thing the punters see. And they can also see it as something of a retribution for the way they've behaved this past fortnight. They're into all that symbolism and numerology nonsense, they'll quite understand."

"Yeah man," rasped Håkan, "I agree with that in principle. But if they're going second, who the hell do we start with? It's going to have be something pretty show-stopping, but also something that isn't too heavy on the props. And we don't want to blow all our rock'n'roll goods right at the start! So definitely not Australia or Montenegro."

"Hmm, yes, I get your point, Hawkman," said Filip. "But who could that be?"

"I've got it!" said Hanna. "You might think this is a stupid idea, but it's a massive song with absolutely no props at all, shy of the pyro..."

"Go on, Hanna?" said Filip, tentatively. "Italy!"
"Brilliant!" barked Håkan.

"That's a great idea!" enthused Dumi.

"Oooh now, I'm not so sure..." said Filip with some concern. "A big fiver opening the show. They're going to moan like all hell."

"Yeah, but think of the showbiz," said Hanna. "Enormous hip hop banger on first, ludicrous black metal on second, and I reckon something dumb and dancy in third, like Greece. What an opening gambit that trio would be! Then we can put in something nicey nicey and mid tempo for the Nans, ease that into a ballad, and then dog tooth the rest of the show between the quick ones and the slow ones until ending on something immense like Australia, Ukraine or Kazakhstan."

"Bloody hell, Hanna," said Filip, "I think you're onto something here. Let's start off with that as a framework, and hang the other songs around it and see how it flies."

"I reckon Australia last again, though," Håkan suggested. "That way there'll be less panic about that bloody great shed of theirs, and we already know that they're a great act to finish on. But whatever else we do, we have to make sure that Montenegro come after an ad break. That way we can get that bloke on the wires nicely hitched up in good time to lower him onto the stage."

"Nice one," said Dumi. "But we've got one other slightly pressing issue – where the heck do we put Iceland?"

"Ooh yes," said Filip, "that is a bit of a problem, I must confess."

"Chuck him in sixteenth – the secret slot of death – then surround him with big hitters," said Hanna. "He'll be far enough into the show that people will enjoy him, but at the same time they'll hardly remember him after the big finish."

"That's just perfect!" said Filip. "Can we have you in here helping every year, please Hanna? You've made all of our lives a whole lot easier in just ten minutes."

"Well, you get to notice a thing or two when you're dragging them all on stage and getting them ready to go," said Hanna, proudly. "The whole ebb and flow becomes almost organic, so you just know when it all feels right."

"Perfect!" said Filip. "Right now, let's get on with filling all the other slots..."

Just as he turned to the wall and began to shuffle all his Post-It notes about there was an angry pounding on the door.

"Where is he?" bellowed and angry Slavic-sounding voice. "I'm going to mash him!"

It was Kazimir Starsev, the Russian Head of Delegation, and he didn't sound best pleased.

"Oh dear," said Filip anxiously. "I guess we knew that this was likely to happen, but I was rather hoping he'd at least wait until the morning."

"You know the Russian psyche as well as I do," said Dumi. "That was never going to happen."

"Yeah, I should have known better, really," said Filip, "and posted some guards on the door. I have a deep fear now that Kazimir's going to burst his way in here and upset the applecart!"

Filip called Ox to redirect some of his security heavies to the area, just in case, then moved toward the door to try and reason with the angry Russian.

"Is that Mr Starsev there?" he asked nervously.

"Of course it fucking is!" came the angry voice from outside in the corridor. "Who else did you think it would be?"

"Well there's a lot of disappointed delegations out there tonight, and they're all dealing with it in a much more adult way than you are right now."

On reflection Filip realised that this perhaps wasn't the best way to have begun this discussion, as it only enraged the Russian in the corridor further.

"Who? Who?!!" he yelled, sounding like he was going to explode with anger. "Good old 'we never qualify but we have a jolly nice time' Slovenia? The 'we won once and that'll do for us' Latvians? Fucking Switzerland?!"

"Well the Swedes must be every bit as disappointed as you, but they're not making quite so much of a scene."

"Oh they made a scene alright!" Kasimir sarcastically spat. "They raised an eyebrow and offered a disapproving look. That's the best you'll ever get from those reasonable bastards. But we're Russian, and we take things to heart. Let me in so that I can fight someone. Anyone will do, I'm not fussy!"

"Now you know that I can't do that, Kasimir," said Filip. "Not only do I have a duty of care to my employees and colleagues, but we're doing some very important and incredibly confidential work in here right now and I couldn't let you in even if I wanted to."

"Then come out here and I'll fight you in the corridor!"

"I'm afraid that's not going to happen either, Kasimir. Now, I quite understand that you're disappointed, sir, but what is really at the heart of your grievance?" Filip asked calmly.

"Isn't it damn obvious?" came the voice from outside the room. "We didn't qualify! How could we not get through when that shit from Macedonia and Australia and Cyprus and Iceland did? I mean, Iceland for Christ sake!"

"Well the simple answer is, Mr Starsev, that people enjoyed those other songs just that little bit more than yours," said Filip, now fully into his diplomatic stride. "How can you be so confident that yours should have done better than them?"

"Well I know for a fact that we got at least seven lots of twelve points from the juries. That must have got us over the qualification line on its own!" Kasimir ranted.

"Ooh now Mr Starsev," said Filip, fuelled up with some new ammunition for the fight. "When you say 'Know for a fact', how can this be? We're not planning to release the scores from the semi- finals until after the big show on Saturday night, and yet here you are claiming that you know some of the scores. If this is true then we'd like to know who it was that told you about them so we can discount their scores from tonight as it's completely and utterly against the rules. If you don't mind."

Kasimir was clearly flustered at this proposition and took some time to answer.

"Well... erm... I don't know for an actual fact, you must understand," he stuttered, "but those seven countries have always and consistently given us big points in the past, so, erm, it's fairly reasonable to assume that they'd have done the same thing tonight."

"How can you be so confident, Mr Starsev?" Filip continued. "It could make a person wonder if you maybe had some kind of arrangement with these countries – if that person were of a cynical mindset, of course. Not that we are here at the CTF, oh no. But we're just looking at it from every possible view. You know how people like to gossip."

Once again, Kasimir began to sputter behind the door. Filip clearly had him on the ropes.

"No... no... nothing of the sort!" he said sheepishly. "You just instinctively know over the years which countries are likely to enjoy the songs that you produce. Yes, that's it!"

"Well I'll take your word for it, Mr Starsev," said Filip, sticking the metaphorical knife in just that little bit deeper. "But I have seen the scores, remember. And while I can't tell you exactly what points you received and from whom, I can say that, as a whole, the juries weren't terribly impressed with your song. Many of the spokespeople told me that it was perhaps a little too poshlost for them?"

"But how can this be?" said Kasimir, astonished. "Surely we provided them with the best possible show that money can buy? We spent nearly eleven million Euro on that performance, and not a penny of it was wasted!"

"That's just it," said Filip with a sympathetic voice. "Perhaps the rest of Europe just don't connect with that kind of post-Soviet excess any more. Maybe to all the Russians living around our constituent countries such extravagance might be seen as a surefire winning move. But to the average Ma and Pa and their little ones sitting at home in front of the telly on a Saturday night in May, maybe having burning tightrope walkers, men dressed as apes on stilts and an enormous great tower block for the performer to climb awkwardly while struggling to sing the song is perhaps just a little too... well... flashy?"

There was a long, uncomfortable silence from outside in the corridor, before Kasimir answered.

"Do you think?" he said meekly. "Do you think that might have been what's cost us our chances this year?"

"I think there's a very distinct possibility that it was," Filip offered.

"But... but... it's the Russian way," said Kasimir, sounding a little hurt. "What can we do now if we can't do that?"

"Oh by all means keep on doing it," said Filip encouragingly. "It all helps to make ours shows exciting and dynamic. But just take your chances with everybody else, and don't expect that you're more entitled to qualify than the others."

At that moment Filip sensed a commotion outside. The security had arrived, and he could hear Ox's big booming voice speaking loudly and assertively in Russian.

"Aurochs? Aurochs mate?" Filip shouted though the door. "Don't worry fella, we're all sorted here now, and Mr Starsev was just leaving."

"If you're sure, sir?" The Ox replied.

"Yes, yes thanks," said Filip. "But if you could just leave one of the lads outside in case anyone else wants to come up here and have a pop, that would be lovely sir!"

"It would be my pleasure, Mr Ivanović," said The Ox. "Oh and

Kasimir," Filip added. "Are we good now?"

"Yeah, I suppose we are," said the Russian HoD, sounding slightly crestfallen. "Sorry for being so angry at you, my friend. Pride can be such a terrible mistress."

"Well you mind how you go, mate," said Filip jauntily. "And I'll see you tomorrow at some point for a coffee and a chat?"

"If they don't send us home immediately," said Kasimir dolefully as he ambled disconsolately down the corridor.

"Whoa Filip, fella!" said Håkan, fully impressed at what he'd just seen. "You ought to have a career in diplomacy or hostage negotiation or something. How did you talk him down so easily?"

"I have absolutely no idea, Hawkman," Filip laughed. "But it seemed to do the trick!"

"I have one question though," asked Hanna. "You used a word that I've never heard before, and that seemed to change the whole tone of the conversation. What was that?"

"Oh poshlost?" Filip replied. "It's a distinctly Russian concept that suggests that the greatest joys can only be bought, and that by making such a purchase it somehow ennobles the buyer.

You've seen how they splash their cash around at these things, and some of the hugely expensive outfits and rings and watches that the richer amongst them seem to wear. It's all part of the idea of poshlost. It's not about how useful or appropriate a particular item is, but how much it cost them.

And in this particular instance it appears to have cost them a place in the final on Saturday!" He quietly smiled to himself, reset his shoulders and nodded to his three companions. "Right, back to the Post-Its then..."

36

It was Friday morning, and finally, after a full year of negotiations, planning, drama and dozens and dozens of national selection shows, the full line up of this year's Eurovision Song Contest final was preparing for its first complete rehearsal. But despite many weeks of long range weather forecasts that insisted the weather was going to be blue skies and sunshine all weekend, the day had started with the most torrential rain.

"It's the Russians!" said Dumi at the morning management briefing. "They're seeding the clouds somehow out of pure spite for being knocked out last night!"

"Do you really think they could create this kind of heavy weather at such incredibly short notice though?" questioned Filip. "Are they really that capable of such feats?"

"I wouldn't put anything past them!" said Dumi with a smile.

"They've also been seeding the news agenda," said Terry with a scowl. "Kasimir Starsev has given an exclusive interview to EuroStorm saying how it's all been one big conspiracy this year to keep Russia out of the final!"

"Oh gawd, that's all we need," said Filip, wearily. "Here, let's have a look at that..." Filip navigated his browser to the offending article and gave it some close inspection.

"Actually," said Filip, "he said nothing of the kind. Look, there's hardly any quotes at all, and what he does say might sound disgruntled and disappointed, but it doesn't point the finger at anyone at all. It's that bloody Michael Storm who's filled in the gaps and written all the propaganda for them. I wonder what treats they've offered him to be such a useful idiot?"

"Is that lowlife STILL hammering out his made up stories?" said Dumi. "I thought we'd laid a massive legal threat on his shoulders."

"We have," said Filip. "But the man just doesn't know when to shut up!"

"Ox, my friend," said Dumi conspiratorially. "I know I can't officially ask you to do anything of this nature, so please disregard this suggestion. But hypothetically, do we know anybody with a secure pig shed in the countryside that we could lock him up in for the next 48 hours? I'm only enquiring out of interest, you must understand, not as a practical solution."

"Oh!" said The Ox. "Perish the very thought of it! But apropos of nothing, it does so happen that one of my cousins runs such a farm just outside of Hrustoveni, right in the very North of Transnistria. I haven't spoken to him for a long time – I really must pay him a visit one of these days."

"Erm, gentlemen?" said Filip with a little concern etched on his face. "What have I just witnessed here?"

"Oh nothing!" laughed Dumi. "Just a little Moldovan family chit chat. Nothing for you to be concerned about!"

"Good! Good!" Filip replied, unconvinced. "Well don't let me be hearing any more of this kind of talk. At least not in my earshot, do you understand!"

Filip quickly changed the subject to more musical matters. "So Dumi, do we have any more word on Maxim's health?" "He's stable, but there's apparently been no change."

"So we're stuck with the Prince Of Darkness then?" Filip mocked. "I'm very afraid we are," said Dumi. "For today at least."

"How are his rehearsals coming along?" Filip asked nervously.

"Well, there's two ways of looking at it," Dumi answered cryptically. "On the one hand, they're going a whole lot better than we'd expected."

"That sounds as though we're going to get a massive caveat on the other hand though, Dumi," said Filip.

"Well, I'm not one to judge, Filip. But his voice is bloody awful, and he looks more awkward than if we'd just shoved a nine-year-old boy up there and told him to dance," Dumi confessed. "I'm really not sure how we're going to get through this one without losing any credibility."

"That is a worry," said Filip. "Do you think there's any room to do some kind of a work around?"

"Well, we're trying to get the backing singers to do most of the hard yards, but we still need him up front to do the actual show business, and he has all the charisma of a damp blanket. Ah yes, but there was one thing that I was meaning to ask you. Is it too late to change the video content that we'll have running on the back screen."

"Ooh, good point!" said Filip. "Not that I'm aware of. I think we always keep it open just in case something on the backdrop is deemed inappropriate by sudden changes in the world news. What were you thinking of?"

"Well you know how it was going to be lots of lovely long shots of the Moldovan landscape swirling around behind the performers?"

"I remember. It looked smashing!"

"Well, we recorded the official video with Maxim standing in front of most of those big sweeping scenes," Dumi explained. "If we could run that one instead, at least in the rehearsals, we could say that it was a tribute to the old man. Then the people in the audience – and at home if it comes to it – will get to see Maxim in some capacity at least."

"Do you think Michi would be good with it though?" Filip asked. "I know that he's got a bit of a fragile ego."

"I reckon he'd jump at the chance," said Dumi. "He and Maxim have become such firm friends that he'd do whatever we asked him if it showed the old fella off to a world audience."

"Brilliant!" said Filip enthusiastically. "Håkan, do you reckon such a late switch is doable?"

"I don't see why not?" he replied. "From what I remember, the official clip was shot in a pretty wide screen ratio, so that should fit just lovely across the screens at the back. I'll get on to the gallery right away and tell them what's going on. We've got a couple of hours to run it around a few times, and then I'll let you know how it's going."

"Perfect, just perfect," said Filip, the stress appearing to roll right off him. "Now let's go and do a show and see how well this whole thing fits together!"

*

Much to everybody's delight it all fitted together rather well. After the dynamic opening threesome practically blew the heads off the audience, the show soon set into a more natural ebb and flow, with the big bangers being followed by more understated numbers. There was a moderate dip in the high energy action in the last quarter, with Germany, Belarus, Belgium and Serbia all offering a different flavour of down tempo, before another dynamic threesome powered in to finish it all off: Armenia's enormous dance number, followed by the mammoth home crowd pleaser from Moldova, and finishing on Australia's three minutes of noisy knockabout fun.

The Moldovan performance did start a little shakily though. When a clearly terrified Michi Rotari walked out onto the stage there was a sense of disquiet from some sections of the audience, with a low level of booing and cat-calling directed towards the stage. This put Michi off his stride and he missed his opening cue. But thankfully he had the presence of mind to raise his hand and ask for the music to be stopped so that he could start again. In the awkward few seconds of silence that it took the sound technicians to cue up and restart the song, a number of unkind comments could be heard from the audience.

"Where's Maxim?" came one.

"We don't want this freak singing for us! It's Maxim or nothing!" came another.

"You're rubbish! Go back to Sectorul Ciocana and stop submitting us to such pain!" came the most hurtful.

Michi felt that he couldn't let the show progress without making a comment. So he summoned up all his emotional strength and raised the microphone to his lips.

"Look, ladies and gentlemen," he said with a wavering voice. "I don't like this any more than you do. I would much prefer my good friend Maxim to be standing here in my place to sing for you. But you know as well as I do that he's not able to come and perform today. Hopefully he'll be well enough to be here by tomorrow night. But for now, it was his choice that I take his place until he's ready, so why don't we all just celebrate our most cherished performer and make a wish together for his quick recovery. And if you'd all like to sing along with me, then that would be lovely too!"

"Bloody hell!" said Terry on the balcony. "Where did that come from? He seems so meek in real life!"

398

"I don't know, Mate," said Filip. "But I think he's pulled it out of the bag there... somehow."

But there was still some muttering of unrest amongst the locals in the crowd, until a tall, ruddy- faced man in his sixties yelled out...

"Stop! All of you! Give the boy a chance! Let's help him, not harm him – he's got a damned difficult job to do here! Let him sing!"

And with that a small ripple of applause began to build in the centre of the crowd, which soon swelled to a whirlwind of noise that span around the Teapot and almost lifted Michi off his feet.

"I am ready!" he said. The music started, and then the most beautiful thing happened.

As he opened his mouth to sing, every Moldovan in the audience began to sing along with him. Quietly at first, but when it got to the choruses they were hurling out the words wholeheartedly and with deep emotion. But it got better. The moment Maxim's face finally appeared on the big screen at the back of the stage the whole arena erupted with joy and delight, and by the end, Michi was just holding the microphone to the crowd, conducting the singalong. When the song eventually finished it got one of the biggest ovations that anyone could ever remember at a Eurovision show – and remember, this was just the first dress rehearsal. Whatever was it going to be like on the big night?

"Erm, can you see that?" said Terry pointing to his arm. "Every single hair on my body is standing on end!"

"Me too, Terry," Filip replied. "How in the name of heaven did he just pull that off?"

"I don't know, but I hope he can keep the magic going until tomorrow night, because we might have a completely different contest on our hands again!"

"Oh mate, we're not coming back here again next year are we?" Filip joked. "After what we've just seen there, my friend, I certainly wouldn't bet against it!"

Down on the stage Michi finally found the strength to uproot himself from his mark and stumble down the off ramp. Behind him the Australian punk and rollers walked nervously up the ramp on the other side of the hall, wondering how they could even come close to following that. But follow it they did – just about – and the competitive portion of the show came to a close with an excitable buzz zapping around the crowd.

As the interval act piled into their excitable song and dance routine and the hosts prepared themselves for the mock voting, Filip turned to Terry with a big beaming smile.

"Do you know what, Terry," he said as the weight of pressure of the last few months just flew off his shoulders. "I think that somehow, despite everything that's gone on, we've managed to put together one of the finest Eurovision shows that I've certainly ever seen. How the hell did we manage that?!"

"I don't know Filip," Terry replied. "But let's not tempt fate, eh. We've still got the best part of a day- and-a-half to get through before we can truly count this thing as a success."

"True," said Filip. "So very true. I'd better keep my enthusiasm dampened down until we're well into the big show tomorrow night, hadn't I!"

As he uttered those words, a great big drop of water fell from the ceiling and splashed down on the tip of his nose.

"Ha, talk about dampened!" he laughed. "Must be condensation from all the hot breath and excitement in the room!"

"Actually Filip," said Terry with a more serious look on his face, "it sounds like it's still raining pretty heavily out there. "You don't think that the roof's starting to leak under the weight of all the water, do you?"

"Oh bloody hell, you might be right!" said Filip, now looking a little panicked. "Look, there's massive big drips sploshing down all over the place. That's not a special effect or anything is it?"

"Certainly not," said Terry. "And with the electrical equipment that we've got hanging from the roof I've got grave concerns that perhaps we'd better start getting people out of here in case there's a safety incident."

"Oh damn yes," said Filip, "I reckon you're right. I'll get onto the crew." He picked up his radio and spoke in his most clear and serious voice.
"Code Cyclamen. I repeat, Code Cyclamen. On stage shutdown procedure to commence immediately. Skunk, stop the music. Hanna, clear everybody off the stage and get Ice to usher them to the safe muster point, then make an announcement to the crowd to calmly leave by the nearest available exit. Front of House, help the audience out of the building as quickly and safely as you can, please. And tech, the moment the last punter is out of the arena, slam the power down immediately and prepare for emergency setting. We've got an awful lot of kit to protect in a very short space of time, so all hands on deck, please."

Filip put the radio down on the desk in front of him, turned to Terry and said... "Me and my big mouth, eh!

*

Half-an-hour later, with everyone safely out of the building and a darkened Teapot lit only by emergency lamps, Filip, Håkan, Artiom and Dumi were having an emergency meeting in a gantry high above the stage in the arena's roof. Around them, the technical crew were battling tooth and nail to get all the vital electrical works covered up with tarpaulins that Ice had magically produced from beneath the stage.

"The problem here Filip," asserted Artiom, "is that the works that your crew did in the roof to put the lights up has damaged the outer shell and it's let the water flood in. I knew it would be a problem if it rained."

"Nonsense!" barked Håkan, looking like he wanted to punch Artiom right in the mouth. "We went nowhere near the outer shell when we put the props up. If we hadn't done that the building could have come down like a house of cards. This whole place was chucked up in a couple of months without testing or consultation with our building inspectors, so there was bound to be the occasional leak."

"Are you disrespecting our fine Moldovan architects and builders, Håkan?" Artiom replied crossly, "Because it sounds an awful lot like you are!"

Filip quickly flashed Håkan a gaze that suggested he ought to take a more diplomatic tone, and the Hawkman got the hint.

"Not at all, Artiom," he said more calmly. "These things happen. I'm just suggesting that there were some areas of the roof where water appears to be accumulating, and the pressure of all that water has led to some of said H_2O working its way into the auditorium. Nobody could have predicted that it was going to rain this hard and for this long. So what we've got to do now is work out a way that we can make the roof safe before tomorrow."

Artiom sucked his teeth, as he knew that he'd seem unreasonable if he continued his line of attack.

"Come on Artiom," Håkan added, "let's all work together to fix this problem. With our background and your local knowledge we can get it done by the morning.

"Wait!" said Filip. "Morning you said? What about tonight's Jury Final?"

"There's no way we can even consider letting the punters into this building until we've made that roof watertight – let alone allow the performers to go on stage beneath all that tonnage and wattage of lights," Håkan explained.

"It is true," Artiom agreed. "I don't want to put the Moldovan public at risk in a building that's been made unsafe by foreigners. We just can't risk it."

"Artiom!" Dumi scowled at his head of local crew. "We're past that bit now, remember!"

"I'm sorry Dumi," he replied. "I still feel like we're being blamed for something we didn't do."

"There's no blame here, Artiom," Håkan replied. "The only thing at fault is the weather, and we've got to make sure that doesn't play any further part in scuppering our plans to put on the best Eurovision show ever. Come on Artiom, are you with me?"

Artiom scowled grudgingly before replying "I suppose so. Come on, let's get to it!"

"But what are we going to do about tonight's show?" said Filip. "We've got half the overall points to sort out for starters, and several thousand punters expecting to come in, too. If we can't run tonight's show that gives us a massive set of complications to deal with."

"This is true," said Håkan. "But our biggest responsibility is for public safety, and that must always come first. Our crews are going to have to work until the small hours to sort this out. So make sure that there's enough coffee and hot towels to keep us going while we find a solution. That's for Artiom and me to sort out. The politics of the actual competition is your forte, Filip and Dumi, so we'll leave that to you. Right then, where's the emergency gaffa tape vault…?"

And with that Håkan and Artiom climbed up into the roof space and disappeared out of sight. "So what ARE we going to do?" said Dumi, looking increasingly concerned.

"First things first, we alert the HoDs," Filip replied. "We tell them what the situation is and put a few options to them."

"But what options do we have?"

"Not too many, to be brutally honest," said Filip. "And I can only think of three at the moment." "Which are…?" asked Dumi, puzzled. "One: Tell the delegations that the juries are going to vote tonight based solely on their preview videos."

"Wait a minute!" said Dumi. "Some of them have spent thousands of Euros on a big budget movie, while others have just got a few casual clips of their singers having fun in the studio. They're never going to go for that as a collective, surely?"

"Exactly!" said Filip, "You've always got to have one option that almost nobody is going to agree on. That way they're more likely to opt for one of the other more sensible proposals!"

"I can see where you're coming from, Filip," said Dumi, impressed at his opposite number's guile. "What are the other two?"

"Well Option Two is a little like Option One, only we send the juries clips of the semi-final performances and the Big Six rehearsals."

"Ooh," said Dumi, "I can foresee problems there too."

"How so, Dumi?" Filip asked.

"Well, all the semi-final qualifiers made their performances in a fully competitive frame of mind, while the pre-qualified mob may just have ghosted through their performances in rehearsal mode. Plus we've got the whole Maxim/Michi issue. There could be problems here."

"Hmmm yes, I think you're probably right. But it might be the best option that we have."

"Why, what's the third one?" Dumi asked, puzzled.

"To totally disregard the juries and make tomorrow's final 100% televote," said Filip with dread in his voice.

"Ooh yes," said Dumi, "That could be a little awkward. Although to be perfectly honest I'm not completely against that thought. I've always been in favour of leaving it to the people, rather than giving equal weighting to a handful of self-appointed experts."

"In any other year I'd have almost agreed with you Dumi," said Filip. "But we can't be so naive as to imagine that nobody else has got wind of San Marino's call centre schemes. Surely someone else is going to try to give that a slightly more subtle stab eventually, so if we leave it entirely to the phones something weird or terrible might happen."

"Ooh yes, I'd forgotten about all that nasty business," said Dumi.

"So it's kind of got to be option two then, really, hasn't it?"

"I think it probably has," Filip replied. "It's the nearest that we can get to the original agreed rules given the short time that we have to sort this out, and we'll still be able to use our planned voting dynamic at the end of tomorrow night's final show. I'll put all three options to the delegations and go with the consensus, but I'll heavily hint at the middle way as being the best for everyone. That's the easy bit though. But what do we do with the ticket-holding crowd members who are all dressed up and ready to party?"

"Actually I think I've got the germ of a plan there," said Dumi. "What's your thinking, sir?"

"Well, all we had planned for Euro Village tonight was a big watch of the Jury Final. So how about if we get the artists down to perform their songs in simple form, and give tonight's ticketed crowd exclusive access to the compound, with free food and drink all night? It might cost us a little bit more than we'd have hoped, but it'll be so much cheaper than giving full refunds to everyone, and that way everybody who's paid will get to see all the artists perform live in at least some manner. We'll sell it as a unique event – they're bound to lap it up. Well, most of them should."

"Genius idea!" said Filip, impressed at his Moldovan friend's suggestion. "We could even have some manner of rudimentary voting system for the night, just for fun like. I'm not sure that all the artists will want to sing outdoors on a damp old night, but we can at least ask them!"

"Great!" said Dumi, "I'll get onto the ground crew at the Village and alert them. Then we'll get the news sent round to all the local TV and radio stations. Will you get a press release put out to all your internet channels?"

"Sure thing Dumi!" said Filip enthusiastically. "You know what, I reckon we can rescue this while offering maximum fun for the punters, too. It won't be 100% the same, but as long as we get a show out at 9pm Central European Time tomorrow night, that's all we've got to worry about. Now let's just hope that the boys in the roof can get it all sorted out by morning.

37

Artiom was beginning to wonder if clambering up onto the Teapot's roof in a full-on howling storm was really such a good idea after all, but Håkan and his crew were skipping up the access ladders like mountain goats. Still clinging on for dear life, he stopped to look up after he heard his name being called.

"Look!" shouted Håkan. "There are big dips that are collecting water into small pools all over this roof. That's what's causing the leaks. Although I concede that perhaps some of the connections for the supporting structure that we put in might have compromised the integrity of the seal. But this was a problem just waiting to happen and it would have happened sooner rather than later, so it's a good job that we found it now, as I dread to think what might have befallen us had we not caught it!"

Artiom nodded in agreement, wishing that he was back on solid ground.

"Here!" yelled Håkan through the wind and water as he threw Artiom a bucket. "You start bailing these pools out while we erect a big tarp over them to keep the worst of the elements out. Then when it's all dried out we'll get to sealing it off."

Artiom was puzzled. "How... how are you going to do that? I don't see any kind of welding equipment up here?"

"Techie magic!" Håkan smiled, waving an arm covered in rolls of extra wide gaffa tape. "This is the hardcore stuff. Sets like concrete and is impervious to water for about three months – which should just about carry us over until tomorrow night. After that we can arrange for some engineers to get up here and reimagine to roof design. But for now we've just got to make the old girl watertight so we can get our show on tomorrow. We might be up here all night, but we're going to get it done!"

Artiom, while pleased at his Scandinavian colleague's confidence, wasn't entirely convinced that this plan was going to work, but he still wanted to give it a go. So he planted his feet firmly on each side of the first recess and began to bail with a little yellow plastic bucket that Håkan threw him.

The hollow seemed to refill every bit as quickly as he was emptying it out, but when the team finally got the tarpaulins up and sealed them to the structure's surface the flow began to subside a little and he eventually got to the bottom of the pool. But still he wasn't entirely sure how they were going to get the surface dry in such terrible conditions before they sealed the leaks with tape.

"Mind out Artiom!" yelled Håkan, before unzipping his leather jacket and whipping out a spongey mop head to get the last few drops of water away from the surface. It was all the local man could do to stand upright in these conditions, but Håkan and his crew were hopping around the roof and clinging on to the most perilous of perches like pirates climbing up the mast of their ship in a big storm to get the sails down. He'd never seen anything like it, and was amazed at the speed and efficiency with which the Sparkle Crew were working.

"I'm done here, Hawk man!" he yelled.

"Good work!" Håkan affirmed. "Now scramble over to the next one, if you would. The lads are setting the tarps up and it's almost ready for bailing!"

"Will do!" Artiom shouted, now beginning to find his feet on the slippy roof.

"But for heaven's sake don't take any risks!" Håkan warned as an afterthought. "We do this kind of thing all the time, but it's easy to get a bit too confident and slide off the edge. And in all this wind and rain we wouldn't hear you go, so extra careful OK!"

Those words immediately stopped Artiom in his tracks, and he became almost afraid to move any further. But watching the other crew members darting about with such ease he felt that he should give it another go – albeit a little more carefully than the others. He slowly mounted the ridged section of the roof that divided off the next little recess and began to bail.

Three-and-a-half hours later and he was bailing out the last pond. After the first two or three he got into his stride, and was soon leaping about all over the roof at almost the same speed as Håkan's men.

"Is this the last one?" he yelled randomly into the air, hoping that someone could confirm his task was over.

"Yep mate!" Håkan confirmed. "You've done a great job. Now carefully stow your bucket so that it doesn't fly off in the wind and wallop someone on the ground, then get the floor dried off with this spongey broom and start to apply some tape to the floor. You've seen how we do it – all one way first, then the other next, followed by a zig-zag criss-cross all up the side of the recess and over the top. Give it six layers and we should be done!"

Håkan threw Artiom the mop with one hand and a half dozen rolls of gaffa tape from a big canvas sack on his back with the other and went back to wrapping tape around the joint where the flagpole met the roof in the very centre of the building.

"Can't be too safe, after all old fella!" he laughed. "We'll get this thing shining like new lead by the time the morning sun glints on it!"

After what seemed like hours, but was probably only more like 45 minutes, Artiom gingerly scaled the service ladders back to the door into the roof space and finally got inside and out of the gale. Håkan gave him a hearty slap on the back, before putting one of his big, bearlike arms around his shoulder.

"Great work out there, man!" he said approvingly. "When I saw the look on your face when you first got up on top I didn't think you'd be able to hack it. But fifteen minutes in and you were scuttling around that roof like the best of us. What are you doing when this is all done? I reckon I could easily find a spot for you on our crew if you wanted it. And don't worry – most of what we do is considerably drier than this!"

Artiom was visibly taken aback. For the whole of the production of this enormous show he'd felt as though the Sparkle Crew were treating him and his staff like second class citizens. But now he could see that although they could be curt and cutting at times, they just wanted to get the job done in the quickest and most efficient way possible, and that they were actually a pretty decent mob of people.

"I'll have to think about it, Hawkman!" he smiled. "Although I'm not too busy in the immediate future..."

"You're in mate!" Håkan bellowed. "We'll talk more about it at the wrap party. But for now we've got to get those big lights into the rice."

Artiom stopped and looked puzzled. "Rice?" he asked, quizzically.

"Yeah, rice," Håkan smiled. "You know how when you drop your phone down the toilet you have to put it into a bag of rice to get all the moisture out? Well we do that on a much larger scale with the lights. Fortunately only a couple of strips suffered from any kind of damage – and thank the good Lord that the big vid screen only got hit by a couple of little splashes. But we've got a deal with the caterers to order in an excess of rice for the duration of the production – and that way if we have any watery misfortunes we can whip the sacks out from the kitchen and bury the electricals in them for a few hours. You really wouldn't think it, but it works remarkably well!"

"So that's why there's been nothing but curry and paella in the works canteen then?" Artiom laughed.

"That's exactly why, old friend!" Håkan bellowed. "The sneaky tricks of event production! And tonight, good sir, you have joined the army – whether you like it or not!"

*

2.37am, and Filip Ivanović was half slumbering in his hotel room when the loud trilling ringtone of his phone wrenched him out of his torpor.

"Hello?" he mumbled, his brain slow to thaw out. "It is done!" came a loud rasping reply.

"Håkan?" Filip, enquired.

"The same!" the voice laughed. "We got that roof sealed up and tasty in double quick time. She should hold until the middle of next month – but we'll be long gone from here by then, so we can leave that to the locals. We've got the wet electricals in the rice, and the rest of the crew are swabbing the floors as we speak. We're back on for tomorrow, Filipé, old son! Both shows!"

In his drowsy state, maybe only half of those words made complete sense to him. But he did fully understand the last bit.

"Great news, Hawkman!" he said with a chirp in his voice. "I can't thank you enough for all your hard work tonight."

"It's what we're here for, sir!" Håkan laughed, saluting the phone.

"Great stuff!" Filip answered "I'll get onto... well, I'll get onto everyone and tell them the good news. You go and get some rest."

"Oh, I'll be up all night now," Håkan replied. "We're off out drinking with the locals. I'll catch some zeds when it gets light, and you can send someone to drag me out of the pit when the first show's starting to prep in the morning."

"I'll be sure to do that," Filip laughed. "Thanks again!"

Filip knew that he had a lot of work to do over the next hour or so, and quickly dropped a note of confirmation to the HoD WhatsApp group, preparing himself for an influx of enquiries. He'd already had a busy night lobbying them about the preferred options for the replacement vote in lieu of that night's jury final, and was still waiting for a definitive response – which is when he'd briefly nodded off in his room, leaving him even more tired and groggy than he was before.

He thought he'd better give Terry a quick call before the HoD's started getting back to him, to fill him in on the latest developments. As Terry answered the phone, Filip could hear music and frivolity going on in the background.

"Erm, sorry Filip, I'm in the bar and it's a bit noisy. I'll move out into the corridor," Terry said, apologetically.

Filip could hear the background gradually noise getting quieter before Terry spoke again. "Yeah, sorry about that. Me and the lads from the office were having an uncertainty party in the hotel bar, just in case the whole thing got called off, and a few of the delegations popped down to join in for a bit. Any news from the crew?"

"Yeah, the roof's safe again and the show is back on, as scheduled."
"Oh that's great news – the best! You can always rely on Håkan!"

"Well, usually always," Filip replied, wryly. "I think he's going native again tonight though, so who knows what state he'll be in the morning."

"Still, the job's done now, eh!" said Terry. "I'll tell the lads."

"And you'll have to put a stop to the revelry, I'm afraid, as we've got a lot of work to do between now and morning," said Filip in his serious work voice. "We'll need a press release sorting out to let the world know we're back on – and that the venue's safe! Then I still need to get a hold of a few of the HoDs..."

Terry cut in. "I think a lot of them are still down at the Eurovillage. That all turned into one massive great party – I wished we'd beamed it out live to the world, 'cos it was a brilliant night. The Polish lot were still DJing when we left at about half-one, and we keep seeing the delegations dragging themselves into the hotel even now."

"Oh my days!" said Filip in full concern mode. "They do know that they've still got two full shows to do tomorrow, don't they?"

"Well they didn't – but they will now!" Terry smirked. "I'll go and round up the troops, and then warn any delegations that are still hanging about that tomorrow's back on. We got a ruling on the jury situation yet?"

"Unfortunately not," Filip replied. "Sounds like the HoDs have all been having too fine a time to get back to me about anything unimportant like how we're going to score a show that's going out in less than 24 hours. But you know us – we'll just wing it as usual!"

"We had any responses at all yet?" asked Terry.

"Probably about half of them have troubled themselves to reply," Filip sarcastically answered. "And we're still split around 50/50 between judging on the performance videos and having no jury element at all. Only the Kazakhs have wanted to take the promotional video route so far, but then that thing did look like it cost them about fifty million Euro to produce."

"Probably a bit late to suggest this," said Terry, "but can't we just get the juries to watch the last dress rehearsal live tomorrow and judge on that?"

"That's almost a great idea, Terry mate. And we did look into it. But half the jurors either have daytime radio shows or they've got other work on and they can't do it. So we've either got to rush them into looking at all the clips in the morning tomorrow, or we've got to get rid of the juries altogether – which isn't entirely ideal. But at this late stage it might be the only option we've got. I mean, you would have thought the HoDs would have all been quick to give us their opinion on how they wanted to be scored."

"Yeah, but the last few hours have been a bit weird and hectic, haven't they." Terry reasoned. "And do you know what? Would it be the worst thing in the world if we went 100% punter, just this time? Label it the people's Eurovision and sell it as a positive. I've never entirely warmed to the jury vote, I have to confess. It's like telling the viewers that although we're glad of their televote money, we don't entirely trust them to do the right thing. This way they'll only have themselves to blame!"

"I'm kind of coming around to that way of thinking myself," Filip conceded. "Although after the San Marino incident I've got massive fears about what could end up happening. It's clear that we've got to change the way we decide on a winner sooner rather than later, what with all these call centres and VPNs and brown envelopes that have been creeping into the game. So why don't we just have one last historic blow out with the viewers and see what happens?! Do you know what, Terry? If I don't hear from the rest of the HoDs in the next half hour we're going to do just that! To hell with the juries – let's go fully democratic!"

Filip could hear a little squeal of delight at the other end of the phone.

"Oh good! This is going to be great!" Terry sang. "I'll get drafting that release right now, and get it over for your approval within the half hour. Then we append any new ruling regarding the jury decision onto the end of it and we'll be all ready to go! You know what, I'm actually getting pretty excited about it already!"

"Me too, Terry. Me too. Let's just hope that it all pays off in the end. Gotta go, mate. My phone's just started pinging like crazy. I think the news has started to filter round..."

*

7.37am, and Filip was fully and soundly asleep when his phone ripped him from his dreams once more. After only a couple of hours slumber he was fully disorientated, and so gave himself a couple of moments to gather himself as the phone screamed insistently for a couple of rotations. His eyes began to clear and he could see that it was a Serbian number that he didn't immediately recognise, so he thought he'd better answer it in case it was somebody from the family back home.

"Hello? Is this Filip Ivanović?" a deep, sonorous voice enquired. "Yes, that's me," Filip mumbled sketchily. "Who is this, please?"

"It is I, Zivko Bodrožić, the famous Serbian singer," the voice proudly announced. "What is this that I hear about the juries being cancelled and the whole competition relying on the telephone votes? Can this be true?"

"Erm, yes, yes it is," said Filip, scrambling to full cognisance. "Why do you ask?" "And did you make the decision?" the dark voice continued.

"Well not entirely Mr Bodrožić sir. Your HoD may have told you that in light of last night's events, the matter of having a safe and trustworthy jury vote this year became incredibly complicated, and so we put it to the vote amongst the heads of delegations. And by a clear majority the preferred option was to do away with the juries for just this year alone and put the result in the hands of the viewers."

"I see," said the singer, in a long, drawn out tone. "So you couldn't have changed this?"

"Well I could have done," said Filip. "But we're a fully democratic organisation, and prefer to listen to the opinions of our members and go with the consensus wherever practically possible."

"I see," said the singer again. "So you know what you have done, don't you?" "I don't quite follow, Mr Bodrožić?" Filip replied, by now rather puzzled.

"You have put an end to your own nation's chances of winning this competition," said the singer. "We designed this song purely for the juries, as we know that they always love this kind of thing. Then we were confident that we'd pick up just enough of the phone votes to take home the prize. But now the opportunity has died – and for this you must be considered a traitor to our beautiful country's cultural well-being."

This riled Filip up just a touch, and it was as much as he could do not to call the Serbian singer a succession of very bad names. But he took a deep breath and clicked into assertive mode.

"Now hold on a minute, Zivko," said Filip. "I may be a Serb by birth, yes. And very proudly so. But when I am at work on this competition I become and impartial European, and I will do nothing to damage the integrity of the show. What you told me about your plans is very unfortunate, and I can only apologise if you think that you have been wronged. But it is the same for everyone, and you'll have to hope that if your song is as good as you say, it will appeal to the hearts of the people all over Europe, and that your message will spread across borders to make them all pick up the phones to vote for it. Nobody ever wins by jury alone, so let's put it to the people to decide, eh?"

The phone went silent for a moment, with nothing but Zivko's deep, agitated breathing to be heard.

"OK," he eventually conceded. "I understand your point of view. I will sing directly to the camera with all my soul, and if the people will it, then it shall be done. But I fear that one of those insignificant modern boom boom songs is going to appeal to them more."

"Then that is the people's choice – and who are we to think that we know better than them?" Filip replied.

Again there was a moment's silence, before Zivko curtly answered. "OK, goodbye now," and rang off abruptly.

"Anyway," Filip said to himself, "Serbia has been trying that exact same formula for years now, and it rarely does us any good!"

He smiled as he rubbed the sleepy dust from the corner of his eyes, and then sat up with a start.

"Wait a moment," he thought. "I never did cast an eye over exactly who voted for what option. I was just pleased that we came to a decision and thought nothing more of it!"

He quickly grabbed his tally sheet and ran his fingers along it.

"Pop banger? No jury. Pop banger? No jury. Ballad? Jury. Mid tempo? Jury. Pop banger? No jury."

He stopped again, staring at the list in bewilderment. Every single nation with a poppy up tempo number had voted to do away with the jury, while each of the slower songs had elected to go to the jury option. The only exception to this rule were the Kazakhs and their expensive promo video who chose the number one option.

"Oh well," Filip said to himself. "Looks like we're getting another party anthem this year then!" His phone rang again. It was Terry.

417

"Err Filip," he said anxiously. "I just noticed something, erm, intriguing, about the HoD choices from last night."

"That all the bangers voted to have no jury?" Filip suggested. "Exactly that!" said Terry. "But you know what this could mean?" "What's that, Terry?"

"That they could all cancel each other out and something bold and impressive from the Slow Joe camp powers through the middle to win it!"

"At this stage Terry, as long as we get the show on without any further hitches tomorrow night I almost don't care what happens. To be honest, almost anybody could win it at this point and I kinda like it that way. We've got enough wild card songs in there for the people to really get behind and make it a really memorable show for the viewers – and that, after all, is what we're really here for. Not to select the location of our work-based jollies for the next twelve months."

"Oh, I'm fully behind that philosophy Filip," said Terry. "Let's just get out there and do this thing and worry about what happens next when it's all finished and done."

"Exactly Terry. Exactly."

THE FINAL
38

The morning of the Eurovision final in the host city always carries with it a curious febrile atmosphere. Where the months and weeks running up to the contest engender a mounting whirl of excitement and anticipation, the Saturday morning of final day sees much nervous pacing about and people with glassy faced expressions wandering around the town, with most conversations consisting of little more than "Who's going to win?" or "Where are you watching from tonight?" And as the day goes on and it gets nearer and nearer to showtime, the streets begin to fill with people in glittery outfits, feather boas and national dress shuffling about with little else to do but worry about how their favourites are going to get on, and making mental lists of hotels to book in their preferred host cities for the next contest.

Over the last few years a strange phenomenon amongst Eurovision fandom has begun to build. Tickets for the final are always limited, and seem to sell out in seconds after their release. But more and more people every year seem to find themselves drawn to the host city, whether they've managed to bag entry into any of the shows or not. This has led to them becoming massive melting pots of nations and denominations, all wandering around in increasingly elaborate party garb just looking for somewhere to have fun. This feels strange enough in a big European city that's well used to hosting tourism and international events, but in a place that's as small and little visited as Tiraspol it's caused an unprecedented clash of multi-cultures, with the locals either embracing the visitors like new family members, or running a mile from anything relating to the contest for fear of catching showbiz germs from the thousands of strange visitors to their otherwise sleepy backwater.

With little else do do in town, Eurovillage had been packed to creaking every night since it opened over a fortnight ago, and fearing an overcrowding incident the city's council had been urged to put up big screens in every significant square and public place within two miles of the town centre to cope with the overflow. Tiraspol hadn't seen so many people since the last couple of times invading forces had passed through on their way to somewhere more fruitful, and the local traders and businessmen were milking it for everything they could get – and quite rightly so.

The regional textiles trade had been whipping up a profitable line in knock-off merchandise. This had gained something of a cult status amongst the Eurovision faithful, who felt it was a more faithful representation of their time in the city than the considerably more expensive corporate official merch on offer from the tented booths that were scattered around the city. Pop-up bars had started to appear at every empty shop front and street corner and were constantly crammed with revellers day and night, and practically every business in the city had brought in a big screen and was advertising a Eurovision viewing party for that evening.

After that morning's final full dress rehearsal, Terry van Boom from the Eurovision press office had wandered into town with a couple of his colleagues to try and soak up some of the atmosphere.

"This is insane!" said Terry. "I've been to fourteen of these things over the years, as both a punter and a worker, and I've never witnessed an atmosphere like it. You could almost chew the anticipation!"

"It's utterly boiling with excitement, isn't it Tel!" said Jeff, with a considerably less cynical tone than usual.

"Oh man, this would be the place to watch it tonight if we weren't working!" Sunny added. "Especially if that roof is still on the fritz!"

"I hear you Sunny," Terry replied. "But something tells me that we're going to need all hands on deck at the arena tonight. The way things have been going over the last couple of weeks there's no way that it's going to run as smoothly as usual. So we've got to sit in that office drafting up pre-emptive strikes just in case anything unsavoury does happen."

"Yeah," said Jeff. "But I'll bet that if anything odd does happen, it won't be anything that any of us could ever have predicted. This year's just been too weird for there to be any kind of normal issues."

"Who do you think's going to win though?" asked Sunny. "JINX!" shouted Terry and Jeff as one.

"Come on Sunny, you know the rules." Terry laughed. "We're all barred from even suggesting that as a question! Chuck a fiver in the local currency into the pot for the hotel after-party after-party booze fund."

"We'll be able to buy a whole distillery for that around here, mind," said Sunny with a smile. "Well if we don't spend it all we can roll it over to next year," said Jeff. "Wherever that may be!"

"Ooh, you're skirting perilously close to the question that must not be asked there, Jeff mate," said Terry.

"Yeah, I guess so. But without getting into specifics, it's an idea that we've got to at least entertain in broader terms. What kind of place do we want to end up in next time around? Somewhere nice and boring and Western, or somewhere as equally batshit as here?"

"Is there anywhere more batshit than here?" Sunny asked.

"Oh you bet your life there could be," said Terry. "And the main one begins with the letter K."

"Yeah, but at least they're likely to throw a few more million at it than here – as much as I've grown to absolutely love the place," said Jeff.

"I think Jeff's gone down with a touch of the old Stockholm Syndrome!" Terry laughed. "Don't worry though, mate, we all get it. It's part of the whole Eurovision fever! By this time next week we'll be pining for the industrial strength home-brewed spirits and the terrible squat toilets."

"And do we actually know what will happen if Australia go and win the thing?" asked Sunny.

"Well the official story is that it'll go to somewhere like Berlin because of record company affiliations and the such like," said Terry.

"But unofficially," Jeff added, "we've heard stories that an Aussie billionaire wants to ship the whole thing down to the Gold Coast, and will even pay for a couple of hundred members of the press to get down there too. The only thing with that is that we'd have to hold the contest at something stupid like seven in the morning."

"Ooh, imagine the after party for that!" laughed Sunny. "It would be like a violent brunch!"

As the three of them continued their walk through the streets of Tiraspol they were overwhelmed by the absolute scenes before them.

"Y'see gents," said Terry, philosophically, "this is why we do it. Where else do you ever get to see an atmosphere like this? It's a travelling circus of songing and campery, or a World Cup with all the teams playing in the same town on the same day."

"Only with more glitter and comedy regional hats!" Jeff joked. "Exactly those things," Terry smiled.

"And can you even imagine what it's going to be like after the show.

It's a damn shame that we've got to deal with the winners press conference afterwards, as I'd love to be down here to soak it all up."

"A by-product of the job, I'm afraid," said Terry. "But for all the things that we miss, we certainly double up in incredible access to the all the other nonsense."

"Amen to that!" said Sunny, as they strolled off through the revelry in the late afternoon sunshine.

Meanwhile, across the city in a private room at the Republican Clinical Hospital, Michi and Dumi were sitting by Maxim's bedside, telling the sleeping singer how well Michi's performances had been going, and hoping that maybe a little spark of recognition would crack across the old man's face.

"Really, Maxim," said Michi, still caked in his stage make up from that afternoon's performance, "I hardly have to do a thing. I just start with the first few lines of the song and the audience does the rest for me. The rehearsal that we just came out of was one of the greatest, most humbling experiences of my life. But I still wish that it was you up there, and that I was watching you sing from the side of the stage."

Dumi checked his watch.

"Come on Michi," he said. "We've got to get back to the Teapot for the early call. I know we're on late and all, but we've still got to be there to wave at the cameras at the start – and you know how that Hanna lady likes to insist we're all in our dressing rooms well in advance of our stage time.

Say goodbye to Maxim and we'll be off."

"OK Dumi," Michi replied, looking doleful, before turning to the old man's bed. "Thank you Maxim. Thank you for giving me this opportunity and for all of your kind help. It's way more than I can ever have expected. You sleep well, and I'll come and see you in the morning, whatever happens."

He leaned over to kiss Maxim fondly on the forehead, but froze solid as the old man began to stir beneath him.

"Erm, is he waking up, Dumi?" Michi asked.

"I'm not entirely sure, Michi. He's probably just moving about in his dreams. Come on, we'd better go."

"No, wait, I think he's opening his eyes," Michi said.

And he was right. Slowly the old man began to crack open his eyelids and stared directly at Michi.

"Well that's weird," said Dumi. "His eyes are open, but he still appears to be totally out of it. I'll go get a doctor."

"Yes. Yes you must," said Michi as he clasped onto Maxim's hand. "Just in case anything is wrong."

Suddenly he felt resistance in the old man's fingers. It was as if Michi was being pulled towards him. And then, quite magically, Maxim's eyes turned from a glassy otherworld stare into the twinkling pools of fun and warmth that Michi was more accustomed to. He opened his lips and gently began to speak in a dry rasping voice.

"Well done... young man, I knew you... could do it!" he said in faltering pulses. "Now... you go out there... and win the thing. For me..."

Michi stepped back in shock, but Maxim's hand gripped tighter and pulled him back towards the hospital bed.

"The people... will help you..." Maxim stuttered. "Good luck... Michi boy!"

And with that he closed his eyes, loosened his grip, and fell back into a deep, deep sleep.

At the exact same moment Dumi rushed in with a doctor, who immediately began to study the machines that were attached to Maxim and note down the readings. Michi thought it best not to mention Maxim's message in case Dumi and the doctor thought he was making it up. Instead he just gave them some vague detail of what had happened.

"He opened his eyes for just a moment, but then he was gone again," he told them. "Encouraging signs! Encouraging signs indeed!" said the doctor as he went about his tests.

"Come on Michi, leave him to sleep. We've really got to race now, and the old fella wouldn't want you to miss your big moment, would he."

"No, no he wouldn't," said Michi, smiling inside at the message that Maxim had just given him. "Let's go and do this show... for him."

*

It's now just two hours before the show was due to begin, and the crowds were already starting to mill outside the teapot. Those holding tickets for the standing area in front of the stage were already jostling for position by the entry gates, and first in the queue was a serious looking gentleman carrying an inflatable hammer festooned in the Israeli flag.

"He's here every year," said a Dutch fan to one of his less experienced countrymen. "Always first in line, too. But he never appears to be having any kind of fun."

"Oh leave him alone," said the first timer, "He's as much a fixture of this show as anybody else. I guess we all experience this thing in our own way, and I for one can't wait to get in there and soak it all up for myself."

I guess you're right," said the old hand, "but let's make sure that we're not standing anywhere near him, OK. He always makes me nervous."

Inside the Teapot, Filip was pacing nervously around his office, waiting for the OK from The Ox, the venue's head of security, to open the gates to the audience. As it was a live television broadcast featuring crowds and performers from so many different countries and cultures, the CTF had to be extra vigilant with the safety and security of the event. For two hours before the doors opened the entire compound was cleared of non-essential staff, and closely inspected for any unusual lumps and bumps and suspect devices. The security staff had systematically checked underneath every seat in the auditorium, in every locker back stage, and inside every prop that was due to be used during the show, and were now starting to carefully scan every single person who was scheduled to perform that evening, just to be extra double sure that there were going to be no nasty surprises as they beamed the show live to hundreds of millions of people across the globe.

Finally The Ox gave Filip the nod of approval, who in turn sent a signal to the front of house staff to open the doors to the venue. This heralded the most anxiety-inducing couple of minutes of the whole event, as the first few members of the audience dashed into the hall to bag their favourite viewing position and the crew made their final preparations for the big show. As Filip watched the auditorium slowly fill from his position on the viewing balcony his emotions were welling up within him. Part of him was starting to relax, knowing that this whole marathon was finally rounding the back straight on the last lap to being over and done with. But another part was starting to tighten with anxiety, in fear of all the possible pitfalls and pratfalls that could happen over the next few hours. His entire career rested on how well the show was executed tonight, and so he knew that he wouldn't be able to settle in his own skin until the show was well under way.

If you're new to the world of Eurovision, nothing can prepare you for the mounting excitement in the arena in the last hour before the show begins. On the concourse outside the concert hall, friends are meeting up for possibly the last time that year before they all go off and find their seats and standing positions and wait for the show to begin. The flags of a multitude of nations all start to mix as fans from different creeds and cultures get their pictures taken with newfound soul mates, while the more hardened regulars are attempting to ferry as much beer as they can into the arena so they don't have to miss a single moment of the show, with their comfort breaks carefully factored in during the songs they favour the least. And everyone, everywhere, is asking even the most vague of acquaintances that one fatal question – who do you think is going to win? And this year, of all years, very few people could give a confident answer.

Minute by minute the arena filled with a slow flood of multicoloured revellers, and with about ten minutes to go before showtime, Hanna made her first steps onto the stage to give the crowd their instructions.

"Right then you horrible lot," she shouted with a big grin on her face. "Are we going to make this the best Eurovision there's ever been?"

The crowd, as you would expect, went berserk.

"Great news!" Hanna replied. "But in order to make that happen, there's a few rules that we've all got to follow." She paused a moment for dramatic effect. "I tell you what, let's not call them rules. Let's call them ingredients."

The crowd quietened slightly and collectively leaned forward to listen to what she had to say.

"First of all, when you hear the Eurovision theme tune at the very top of the show, make sure that you go absolutely crazy with noise

– but I'm sure that you won't have any trouble with that!"

The crowd laughed.

"Then, when each of the postcards is about to finish, give every act your utmost love and respect. It doesn't matter if you don't especially like it, just make the act feel loved – and be sure to cheer it

even more loudly at the end, too. If we hear anybody booing any of the artists we'll be in there with a big shepherd's crook to fish them out, and they'll be firmly kicked out of the arena, never to return. And you wouldn't want that now, would you?!"

The crowd all looked at the floor, shuffled uncomfortably and replied "Yes miss," as if they were still in junior school.

"And if you're lucky enough to have the camera pointing at you, make sure that you look like you're having fun. We don't want to beam pictures of you picking your nose into the living rooms of half the planet, do we now. So, onto the fun stuff. We're going to need some extra help for a few of the songs, so when the big screens tell you to get your phones out and turn on your torches it would be lovely if you could quickly get that done before the start of the song. And remember, while we love having all your flags and banners down there, could you do your best to keep them low when the songs are on. The people at home want to see the singers, not all your funny little bits and bobs. And that includes you, Mr Inflatable Hammer Man. If that thing gets in the way tonight we'll be sending security in with a pin!"

The crowd let out their biggest cheer yet and began to cackle with laughter and point at the poor fella, who looked crestfallen as he was attempting to inflate up his bouncy blue and white weapon of irritation.

"Ooh, and don't forget to watch out for the boom cameras," Hanna added. "They'll be swinging about mere inches from the tops of your heads, so if anyone gets up on their friends' shoulders they might very quickly get a bash on the nut! But most of all, we want you to have fun, and we want the good people at home to see that you're having fun. Are you all with me?"

The crowd let out a hearty "Yes!"

"Really? I said, are you all with me?" Hanna yelled, milking them for every bit of excitement that she could.

"YES!!!" the crowd yelled at the top of their lungs.

"Great! That's it! We've got five minutes until showtime. Let's make it the best Eurovision Song Contest that there's ever been, eh!"

And with that she was off down the ramp to brief the opening act on where they needed to be. "She's damned good at this," said Terry to Filip as they settled into their seats.

"The best!" said Filip gleefully. "I mean, this crowd is a gift without any prompting, but somehow she manages to bring an extra fifty percent out of them, and that really comes across on the TV".

They both went quiet for a moment and surveyed the colourful mass of seething humanity before them.

"This is what we do it for, isn't it," said Filip. "This is what makes it all worthwhile."

"Damn straight!" his colleague replied. "There's not a single face down there that isn't having the absolute time of their lives. Seriously, I don't think there's a darned thing that can match this show for atmosphere in all sport or showbiz."

"It's a thing of beauty, isn't it Terry. It kind of makes all the hassle we've been through over the last few weeks so totally worthwhile."

"Doesn't it just, Filip. Doesn't it just."

With that, the lights began to lower, Te Deum began to crack out across the hall's big speakers and the crowd went absolutely insane.

"Here we go then," said Filip. "It begins."

*

The lights lowered some more and the audience hushed a little. A charming travelogue film saw birds from each of the competing nations winging their way towards Moldova from their home countries. Over fields and cities they flew, before symbolically settling on the roof of the Teapot.

"They'd better not put too much weight on that roof or they'll bring the whole bloody lot down!" joked Terry.

"Shhh, we can't be seen to be larking about for a bit," whispered Filip, "we're going to be on international TV any second now!"

Back on the big screens, the Moldovan bird was shown to be looking through a tiny window in the roof, and by the magic of television we were transported silently down into the arena towards the stage. Suddenly there was a loud crash as the Bessarabian Turbo Squad kicked into their winning song from last year and the whole place erupted with delight and excitement.

"You certainly can't knock that as an opening to the show," said Filip, brimming with pride. "These Moldovans do know how to make an entrance!"

"Don't they ever!" said Terry, now standing up at his seat and clapping along.

After a short but stunning performance, BTS strode triumphantly off the stage to be replaced by the evening's hosts, Elina Gospodinova and Ruslan Rusu. They breezed through the usual introductory niceties in English, French, and perhaps rather less expectedly, Russian, before stepping back, raising their arms and proudly announcing "May the show begin!"

Terry looked at his watch.

"Eleven minutes and thirty seconds!" he exclaimed. "That's the shortest opening in years!"

"Yeah, things flow along quite nicely now we've done away with the flag march," Filip replied. "I don't know why my predecessors insisted so strongly on that. Just having all the contestants waving from the green room works a treat."

"I know right," said Terry, before stopping in his tracks. "Ooh, ooh, Italian postcard. Here we go, Song One. Come on Explodo, give us a start to remember!"

Little did they know that he was about to do exactly that – only not in any way that they might have hoped for. The postcard came to an end, the hall went dark, the gentle pulsing music that proceeded the start of each of the songs came and went, and the camera zoomed gently from the back of the hall. Then nothing.

"Where the hell is he?" Filip barked into his radio. "Get him on stage now!"

"He's being difficult," Hanna replied, with the edge of frustration in her voice. "He claims his fizzy water isn't fizzy enough."

"Well tell him he can have all the fizzy water he wants when he's finished, and if he's not on stage in five seconds we'll personally invoice him for the whole of Italy's competition fees!"

"Hold on, he's heading up the ramp now," said Hanna, "but he doesn't look happy!"

"Well just as long as he sings the bloody song and gets off, I don't care what mood he's in," said Filip.

He quickly began to rue those words, as the backing track had only been on for a mere six or seven seconds before a clearly irritated Explodo held up his hand shouting "Fermare! Stop! Stop! I can't hear the fucking music!"

"Oh no! F-bomb!" said Terry, concerned that the show had got off to a sweary start.

"Don't worry Terry mate, we've got a seven second delay, so hopefully the sound boys dinked that out before the nice people at home got to hear it," Filip reassured his colleague. "Mind you, it appears that all the commentators are doing some hasty apologies by the looks on all their faces up in the boxes there. I'd better give Hanna a shout again. What seems to be the problem down there, Hanna?"

"It's a problem entirely of his own making," she replied. "He refused to wear his in-ear and said the on-stage monitors would be enough. Which they clearly aren't."

"I'll get onto the desk to boost the stage sound to just above comfortable levels," said Filip, "then we can watch the little shit squirm in a problem of his own making!"

"Good job!" said Hanna. "Right, we're ready to roll again."

All this time, Explodo was pacing the front of the stage like a caged tiger in an East European zoo, arguing with audience members near the front and casting distinctly Italian hand gestures towards the wider crowd. Gradually they lost patience with the Italian rapper and began to give him the slow handclap.

"Get the track on now or we'll loose the audience!" Filip snapped into the radio.

The music started instantly, and Explodo grudgingly began to perform, albeit with the minimum effort. But as the song progressed and the pyro started to go off around him he got more and more involved, and by the song's end he was strutting around the stage like a peacock in expensive sportswear. As the music finished, he stuck his middle finger up to the steadicam that had been following his aimless skulk around the stage and grumbled "Fuck you, Europe! Fuck you!"

The audience, who by that time had almost come around to his song, started to boo heartily, while boiled sweets and half-empty plastic glasses of beer began to rain onto the stage. At this, Explodo flung his expensively bejewelled microphone into the crowd and ran off stage. The audience member who caught it had just enough time to shout "Wanker!" before the mic was quickly turned off.

"Oh my days," said Filip. "This is already a bloody disaster. The press will be all over this! At least he's gone now and all that's over with…" But then he froze open mouthed, the colour draining from his already sallow features. "Oh shit," he said with a tremble in his voice. "It's bloody Norway next, isn't it!"

Filip and Terry both leaned forward in their seats, elbows on their desks and their heads in their hands, absolutely dreading what the next three minutes might bring. Stormgiver sprinted onto the stage like a crack sports team, and set up in seconds, appearing to help the crew as much as they possibly could along the way. In the seconds before the song was due to start, the band's singer, Hermóðr Heimdall, looked up to Filip on the balcony and gave him an enthusiastic thumbs up, before cracking a big, beaming smile.

Both Filip and Terry sat bolt upright. "Did you just see that, Terry?"
"Yes. Yes I did. What do you think it meant?"

"Well hopefully they've decided to be reasonable and polite after that Explodo incident and get through their song with the minimum of unscheduled incident."

"Well, that's what we hope is about to happen, Filip. But there's something in me that just doesn't trust them."

"I know what you mean, Terry. They're being just that bit too polite and accommodating."

The pair leaned forward again and hung on every move that the band were making. But despite being aggressively harsh and loud, with guttural, unintelligible vocals and a terrifying stage presence, the band did seem to be behaving themselves – albeit with a massive burning church on the stage behind them. As the last few chords of the song began to die down, and the band all stood with their fists in the air making devil horns and pulling grim faces, Filip's shoulders began to loosen a little and he settled down into his seat with a relieved look on his face. But he relaxed too soon. For on the stage in the middle of the burning church came an almighty explosion, and sparks rained down across the first thirty rows of the audience.

"What the hell was that?" said Terry, the air almost sucked out of his lungs by the massive sonic blast. "Was that supposed to happen?"

"I don't know, Terry. But they certainly left a lasting impression. That's one of the few times you could ever say that about the second song in the running order."

Stormgiver finally turned to leave the stage as the crew dismantled their gear around them, and Hermóðr Heimdall turned to the production balcony one last time and gave Filip a big knowing wink.

"They did it on purpose, the little shitbags!" Filip cried.

Yeah, but at least they didn't say anything dodgy this time, or chuck any raw meat into the crowd," Terry replied. "I suppose we've got to be grateful for small mercies."

"That we have, old friend. That we have. And thank the heavens we've got a nice little run of usualists coming up over the next few songs that shouldn't give us too much to worry about."

Filip was right. Despite the crowd muttering loudly about the Italian and Norwegian performances throughout the entire Greek song, everything ran totally to plan throughout Denmark, Azerbaijan, and Croatia, and by the time Cyprus left the stage the whole place was buzzing like a proper Eurovision party again.

Next it was the UK's turn. But as Jason Brown began to anxiously totter onto the stage, huge swathes of the crowd began file out of the exits. The poor lad looked visibly shaken by this.

"What's happening?" said Terry. "Is this some kind of boycott against the Brits?"

"Scheduled piss break more like," Filip answered with a smile. "It's been quite an intense opening, after all. And even the Croatian girl kept them engaged with all her emotive warbling. But our poor little Scottish lad here is just a tad too beige for his own good, so I reckon they've all taken the opportunity to dash out for a quick tinkle before the tempo picks up again over the next few songs."

"But there's a mini ad break in two songs time?" Terry wondered.

"Couldn't they have hung on for that?"

"Apparently not, it seems. Look, there's a good third of the crowd already gone. I feel for the poor boy. But as long as he remembers to sing for the people at home and not the crowd he'll be just fine."

He didn't though. As the crowd clamoured around the exits on their way out, his eyes flickered about the big hall anxiously, which looked especially unnerving on the big screens above the stage. By about the minute mark, with big empty swathes of seats in the arena, the sound started to echo around as if he was singing in a giant cave. But it got worse, for as the early urinators began to dash back to their seats, the loud buzz of the crowd chattering bled noticeably through his mic, and for the entire final minute of his song Jason appeared increasingly deflated. So when he finally finished his song he just shuffled off defeated to nothing more than a ripple of polite applause.

"Ooh, that was a bit difficult to watch," said Terry with a wince.

"Yeah, your heart goes out to the lad," Filip replied. "You can't fault him, though. He did his absolute best in difficult circumstances. But if his broadcaster keeps sending in these bland anonymous songs then what do they expect. Their run of bad results has got nothing to do with politics in the way they're are always moaning about — it's just a criminal lack of imagination from the people who sign off their songs. The poor lad's been hung out to dry there. I hope he gets over it quickly and it doesn't damage his career too much."

Suddenly in the background the crowd began to bristle. "Uh-oh, here comes Ukraine!" said Terry smiling.

"Yeah, that'll put a spring back into the audience's step," Filip laughed!

"Helllllllllooooooooo Tiraspol!" came a loud shrill cry from off stage. "Are you ready to rock?!" "Hell yeah!" the crowd exploded, is if someone had sprinkled instant party dust all over them. "Well let's go!" Bohdana cried. "Holy Cow!"

There then followed the most ludicrously enjoyable three minutes of unabashed high energy fun that anyone could remember seeing on a Eurovision stage, as the larger-than-life singer prowled around the stage, squeezing every inch of showbiz out of the opportunity. And by the time she whipped the glitter cloth off the kitchen sink and began to bash it rhythmically to the music, the entire crowd were in the palm of her hand.

"I think we've got our first contender here, you know," said Terry enthusiastically.

"Yeah, it's got winning germs all over it," Filip replied. "And of course, you know that she'll want to host the show if she does win, don't you?"

"Really?" said Terry, a little bit frightened. "That'll be, erm, challenging at best."

"Don't I know it!" said Filip. "Let's hope that somebody else pulls a win out of the bag, because the folks at home are going to go absolutely bonkers over that one."

"Ooh yes, Filip. Very good point. Still, we've got some pretty strong songs coming up in the next segment. I reckon at least one of them will be good enough to nick it off her."

"Yeah. As much as I like her song, and indeed Bohdana herself, after the year we've just had I could really do without the aggravation."

39

After Bohdana milked her riotous post-performance applause for all it was worth, the houselights darkened and the audience were treated to a comedy film clip about the history of Moldova at Eurovision. This was shown to fill up the space used for the ad breaks in countries where the contest isn't shown on commercial television, and it was utterly delightful. Meanwhile down around the stage area, Linnea and her crew were struggling to get the Montenegrin act set up and ready for when the cameras returned from the adverts.

From his position on the balcony, Filip could see that the crew were having trouble getting everything ready in time, so he radioed down to Linnea for an update.

"What seems to be the problem, Ice? You look like you're struggling."

"It's not us," she replied testily, "It's the equipment. Our Montenegrin boy here is currently suspended two feet below the rafters, and if we can't get the electric hoist running properly we're going to have to winch him down by hand. We may have to stand by for a minute or so after the ad break, so get the hosts briefed."

"Thanks for warning us, mate," said Filip. "I'll get onto the gantry."

He quickly switched channels and barked "We've got issues on stage, so get Bobby to stand by in the green room for some ad hoc interviews. But for heaven's sake make sure that he doesn't go anywhere near Italy or Norway or this could go very wrong."

"Sorry Filip, the line's a bit crackly," came the voice of the director, "but I think we got that. Green room cameras in position... now!"

"Right, that's bought us about another 90 seconds," said Filip, relieved.

"Just in the nick of time too," said Terry, "the interval clip's just about to finish."

As the heartwarming little film came to an end, the crowd let out a communal cry of "Awww!" and the cameras cut to the green room. Bobby Odobescu was standing there looking a bit shocked, like he'd just been woken up and shoved in front of a camera.

"Yes, so here we are in the green room, and I'm going to have some talks with the cool Italian rapper Explodo!"

"Noooooooooo!" cried pretty much everybody on the production balcony at the same time.

Back in the green room, things were starting to get edgy. Explodo was walled in behind a massive set of shades, his arms crossed in front of him in full on hip hop stylee, craftily pulling the middle finger salute with both hands.

"So Explodo, how do you think your performance went?" mumbled Bobby.

"Shit." said the rapper, curtly. "Real shit. I'm only still here for the free booze. Do you have any coke?"

"Yes, I think one of the waiters will have some Pepsi or something," Bobby innocently continued.

"Get that muppet away from the Italian," Filip roared into his radio.

Two seconds later, Bobby looked alarmed as instructions were barked into his ear and quickly rasped "Bye Explodo!", and shuffled awkwardly to the next table. The Norwegian table.

"Oh my days," said Filip. "This is going from bad to worse. Please be kind to us, Mr Heimdall. You owe us a massive favour."

"And now I'm with the delegation from Norway!" yelled Bobby, gleefully. "Stormgiver! Are you having a good time?"

Hermóðr Heimdall slowly looked up from a flesh-bound copy of the Necronomicon, stared deep into the camera and chirpily replied "Yes Bobby, sir, I'm having an absolutely swell time. Thank you for asking!"

Filip and Terry cast each other a confused side eye and waited pregnantly for something to go wrong. Suddenly the tension was broken by Ice on the radio.

"We've got the bastard free, and now we're slowly lowering him into position!" "Thank Christ for that!" said Filip. "Do the gallery know?" "We're all over it boss!" came the director's voice.

The shot of the green room suddenly cut to the hosts, who welcomed the audience back, made a couple of awkward jokes, and introduced the Montenegrin song.

"I reckon we dodged a couple of bullets there," said Terry. "We've sent out a message to the commentators to apologise for Explodo's language, but thank goodness he never said anything really bad."

"Yeah, and Hermóðr was weirdly agreeable too," said Filip, looking a little shell shocked. "I was expecting him to suddenly shout out 'Bring on the virgins!' or something equally Norse. Right, let's get on with the next few then and hope nothing else bad happens!"

Once again, Filip spoke too soon. As the singer from Steam Engine was being jerkily lowered from the rafters by a creaky hand crank, it became impossible to time his movements to the music, and when the hoist mechanism decided to lock solid, he was still dangling twenty feet above the stage.

"We can't move him!" said Linnea in a panic. "We'll just have to leave him there and pretend that it's part of the show. I'm sure the cameras will adjust accordingly."

And indeed they did. Despite the worried and confused looks on the band's faces, the people viewing at home would have had no idea that none of this was meant to happen, and the song got a rousing reception when it eventually finished. The problem now turned into a matter of how they were going to winch him back up and out of the camera's eye before the Maltese song began.

"He still looks like he's in shot!" said a now panicking Filip down the radio. "Can we do anything about it. Gallery, can we get the cameras to tighten in a bit?"

"Yes, we can do that a bit," the director replied. "But this is one of those songs that relies on the crowd putting their phone lights on, so there's a lot of long shots from the hall, and we won't be able to avoid seeing him dangling about in the background. All the cameramen have got their shot sheets ready, but I'll warn them to try and keep the poor fella out of sight wherever possible."

"We'd appreciate it if you could, sir," said Filip, exasperated.

But it didn't initially go as any of them had hoped. Many of the planned camera shots were designed to make the singer Lia took all small and alone at the bottom of the screen. But the first couple of times that they tried this the Montenegrin singer's big gothicky boots were clearly in shot, swaying about at the top of the screen.

"Abort the long shots!" the director instructed his cameramen, "we're going freestyle and I'm calling the shots! We're going to save this puppy if it kills us."

And to be fair, he did a pretty good job of it. There were a few moments where a quick sight of the dangling Balkan just couldn't be avoided, but on the whole they managed to cut him out of view wherever possible.

"Terry mate," Filip asked quietly. "Get the Maltese HoD on the phone and ask him if they want to go again at the end. It's only fair that we offer them the chance, as this balls up was entirely out of their control and they deserve a clean run at this. Just imagine the poor girl showing her grandchildren a video of this and there's this great big pair of steampunk boots swinging around above her like a hanged man. They love this contest like almost no other nation, the Maltese, so it wouldn't be right to just lumber them with this."

"That seems like a very fair and honest suggestion," said Terry. "I'll get onto him immediately."

Thankfully the dangling man was winched out of view in time for the Spanish performance, and Estonia, North Macedonia and Romania all passed by pretty trouble free, too. But next it was time for Iceland, and with the audience already in such a lively mood absolutely anything could happen.

"Oh gawd," said Filip. "I'd forgotten about this one. It was all moving along so swimmingly, too."

"Don't panic," said Terry. "As weird as he might be, he's a true pro. So he'll just do his business and get off."

"Perhaps that wasn't entirely the best turn of phrase to use in this instance," laughed Filip, "but I see what you mean. Fingers crossed that he behaves himself, and then we've got a free run of relatively normal songs until the end. Although having said that, the way things have been going tonight I won't be happy until I'm sat in the hotel room afterwards with a nice glass of single malt in my hand!"

"Right, here he comes," said Terry with a nervous wobble in his voice. "Let's hold our breath until this is all over and done with!"

Vikingur The Dog Boy skipped confidently onto the stage and the crowd went wild at their first sight of him.

Filip and Terry looked at each other, quite quite puzzled. "Eh?!!" they both said at the same time.

"Has he become some kind of a cult figure that we didn't know about?" Filip asked bewildered.

"I fear that he might have," said Terry, who was equally shocked at the Icelander's unexpectedly positive reception.

As the lights dimmed and the backing track began to play, the crowd went eerily silent. And then the most beautiful thing started to happen. As Vikingur began to howl like a dog, a few scattered members of the audience began to howl along with him. As the song progressed, more and more people joined in, and by the end it seemed like practically everybody in the building, including three-quarters of the crew, had answered his plaintive cry.

"That... that's... quite incredible," said Terry, completely stunned by what he'd just seen. "Twitter's gone absolutely insane over it too. It's the best reaction we've had on social media all night by a street..." He stopped what he was saying and turned to Filip, who was still open mouthed with shock.

"Fuuuuuuck," he said croakily. "That's going to bloody win this thing, isn't it. I mean, don't get me wrong, everyone would love an Icelandic win. But with... this? Oh my lord, what more weirdness could possibly happen tonight?"

Thankfully Poland quickly cut into his thoughts of impending doom with their massive party anthem, which had the whole arena standing on their seats and jiggling glowsticks. This performance quickly segued into the second commercial break, and everyone sat back in their chairs and breathed a sigh of relief as a short film about the best hairdos in Eurovision history played amiably in the background. Filip felt a tap on the shoulder. It was Dumi from Moldova Smash.

"Dumi sir! Great to see you. We'd been wondering where you'd gone."

"I had to receive the President's party, and go and sit with him and Timur Turgenev for the first couple of sections to explain what was going on. They've all nipped to the bar for a bit now until Michi goes on, so I thought I'd come and see how things were over here."

I won't lie, Dumi mate, it's been challenging," said Filip. "But we're on the home straight now. What did the dignitaries think about those sticky moments at the start, and with the Montenegrin cock up?"

"They bloody loved it," Dumi smiled. "They reckon we've encompassed the very spirit of Moldovan TV, and were laughing and clapping and singing along. I've rarely seen Mr Turgenev so much as smile, but he's having the time of his life up there!"

"Oh you do surprise me," said Filip. "And pleasantly so. I thought we were going to have trouble getting out of the country after all those complications. But if they're happy, I'm happy!"

"They're loving it on the socials too," Terry cut in. "'Best. Eurovision. Ever.' is trending number one, and 'Dog Boy', 'Dangler' and 'Kitchen Sink' are all in the top five too. You know what, I reckon we might have just about gotten away with this!"

"Don't tempt fate, Terry," warned Filip seriously. "There's an awful lot that could go wrong between now and the credits."

*

There were no further on stage issues after the second commercial break. Ice and the crew got Poland off and Kazakhstan on to the stage swiftly and simply, and the moment that the little interval film finished, the camera cut to the hosts Ruslan and Elina, who did a quick little skit about the official DVD and album.

"Have you see this one live, Dumi?" Terry asked. "It's pretty darned impressive, I can tell you."

I haven't, but I've heard great things," the Moldovan replied. "But I've also heard something else from the Twittersphere – that songs involving horses are almost always doomed to failure at this competition. There's an awful lot of people expecting this one to crash and burn terribly, so I can't wait to see it, just in case something strange does happen along the way."

"Oh don't say that," said Filip. "We've been rolling along without incident for a nice run of songs and links now. I do hope you haven't cursed it."

"Well he's added a nice little spot of jeopardy to the next three minutes at the very least," Terry laughed.

The hosts finished their piece to camera and the hall went dark. In the brief seconds of silence before the Kazakhstani postcard a handful of wags began to sing the My Lovely Horse song from Father Ted to mock the forthcoming song's title – My Beautiful Stallion. At first it was just a little ripple of noise, but as the postcard continued more and more people started to join in. So by the time the postcard was over and the performers were ready to start their show, a hearty chorus of 'My Lovely Horse Running Through The... FIEEEEEEEEELD' was echoing around the arena. The song's singer Rayana Bayzhanova just stood there looking a bit puzzled for a second or two until the first crashing chords of the song came in and obliterated the jocular noise coming from the hall.

"Bloody hell, that's a relief!" said Terry. "I really thought she was going to blow it there!"

"And thank the good Lord and little baby Jesus that she didn't," said Filip, relieved. "We've had enough incident already tonight – if anything else untoward happens it could send me right over the edge!"

"I wouldn't bet against it," said Dumi with a smile. "There's some pretty, how shall we say, lively characters coming up over the last few songs. I mean, whose idea was it to have Australia closing the show after Moldova's performance? That could go all kinds of ways."

"Oh my days!" said Filip. "I'd put all of that out of my mind. You've given me the proper jitters now!" "Ha!" Dumi laughed. "Glad to have been of service sir!"

On stage, Rayana was powering through her incredible visual spectacle. There was of course that life-sized horse marionette clip-clopping around, flames shooting in every direction, and film of beautiful stallions charging around the Kazakh Steppe on the giant screens behind her. Wind machines were blowing her long, voluminous scarves in colourful swirls as she prowled around the performance area building up to the big, explosive crescendo.

"This is it," said Filip fearfully. "This is where it could all go terribly wrong!"

But it didn't. Holding her arms aloft as pyro exploded all around them, she let out the last few plaintive wails of the song – or at least, the woman who was actually singing the song at the side of the stage was doing it for her. For a moment after the performance had ended the crowd stood in stunned silence, before offering up one of the loudest, most frenzied receptions of the night.

"She's done it! She's only gone and done it!" said Filip, relieved. "I was half expecting her to trip over one of her scarves, fall onto the pyro and blow her head off live on international TV. But we're safe!"

In the seconds after her near show-stopping performance, Rayana was soaking in her plaudits.

"Thank you! Thank you all!" she gushed, before her face turned to thunder and she pointed to the area directly in front of the stage where the choruses of My Lovely Horse had begun. "Except you," she said with a sneer. "Fuck you! Fuck you and all your families!"

Filip sank back into his chair as the crowd began to boo.

"Ah well, I knew it was too good to be true," he said wearily. "Still, at least we don't have to worry about carting this whole thing to Nur-Sultan next year after that little outburst."

"Yep," said Terry checking his phone. "'Swearyvision' is trending pretty highly now. I think she's done her chances over in one slip of the tongue there."

"Oh that wasn't a slip," laughed Dumi. "That was a laser guided salvo that she must have been planning for that whole performance. Good on her, I say!"

"At least we've got a little run of nice, happy, safe songs from highly professional performers coming up now," said Filip, hopefully. "And

Michi, of course. Then all we have to worry about is the ending and the scoring. Oh please go normally, you lot. Pretty please."

Much to Filip's delight, the French singer Zuzi skipped through her turn with an easy, coquettish grace, and strolled off the stage like a true pro, and the German duo Sissi And Sal didn't look like they were going to be any trouble either, despite clearly hating the very sight of each other. That is until the quiet moment before their first chorus was about to roll in. As the verse began to settle to a lull, a loud yell could be heard from the audience.

"BITCHES!" came the rasping cry. "YOU STOLE MY SONG!"

Filip, Terry and Dumi all looked at each other in horror and spat out one word in unison. "JOLANA!"

Sporting a bright orange wig, the disqualified Czech singer must have bagged a ticket from a disappointed Dutch fan and snuck into the arena undetected, and she was kicking up all kinds of fuss from the moshpit as the poor German girls tried their hardest to complete their song. Filip immediately got onto the radio.

"Ox sir! Can you and the security squad get in there and pluck her out her causing the least visible impact possible. If you need to put a sack on her head, then so be it. And be sure that there's at least a couple of women staff in there with you. We don't want to be accused of anything untoward!"

Filip quickly switched channels.

"Gallery. Make sure that you don't run any shots of the audience during the rest of this song. There may be some security issues. And get sound to turn down the crowd mics."

But while he spoke, Jolana was creating her own one woman riot and pushing towards the front of the stage.

"IT SHOULD BE ME UP THERE, NOT YOU!" she bellowed, as Sissi And Sal desperately tried to ignore her. But their song was paper thin as it was, and these unwelcome yells from the audience were putting them off their stride.

"It was always going to be bottom three, whatever happened during the performance," Terry said with a shrug. "I guess Jolana's just helping them along their way.

From their raised position towards the side of the stage, Filip could see The Ox and his security operatives creeping towards Jolana like cats after their quarry.

"The song's almost done," Filip whispered into his radio, "Wait until it ends and the applause starts, then bag her and bin her while the crowd noise is drowning her out."

"Fully understood sir," The Ox whispered back.

"This is fascinating!" said Dumi, rubbing his hands together with glee. "This is like watching one of those Attenborough wildlife films."

He put on a husky Moldovan version of an English accent and continued on his theme.

"And the hyenas... are circling their prey. The gazelle can't see them... but she senses that something is wrong."

The song ended, and the security team dashed in.

"And they pounce," said Dumi, still in character. "A successful hunt."

Down on the arena floor the guards were carefully coaxing the still-protesting Czech singer out towards the side exit while the Belarussian postcard began to play.

"Good job, Ox," said Filip into his radio. "I reckon we got her out with minimal strife. Now go and lock her up in one of the service sheds until after the show."

Filip turned to his colleagues on the balcony.

"Right nobody, and I mean NOBODY, even think of saying anything like 'It's all going to be alright from now on'! I'm not going to believe that until I'm sat having dinner round my Mother's house next Sunday!"

"Well at least we got that little problem out of the way quickly and easily," said Terry. "We're starting to get good at this!"

"Shhhhhh!" rasped Filip tersely with his finger in front of his lips. "We're not going to tempt the fates any more tonight. Let's just enjoy the show and smooth any further problems out as they happen, eh!"

Things flowed along more easily for the next quarter of an hour or so. Belarus breezed through their performance, although their tiny young singer Kirill was visibly shaking with fear throughout his song, bless him. The Belgian singer Gladys proved to be the biggest surprise of the night so far, as her previously unfancied slice of minimal electronica got the crowd up on their feet and singing along, while Serbia's Zivko Bodrožić sent sections of the audience to sleep with his sparse ballad – quite literally in fact, as one rather awkward camera shot showed a young family snoring away at the back of the hall during his performance. Takouhi Vardanyan from Armenia woke them all up again though with her stunning stage show and her bouncy singalong dance number.

The moment Armenia's applause began to ebb away the audience started to bristle with anticipation. It was the home entry from Moldova next, and Michi Rotari was standing at the side of the stage in absolute terror, awaiting his cue to go on. Stefan Smolenko from the Moldova Smash TV station was standing with him, giving all the encouragement he could muster.

"Now remember Michi, you're not alone up there. The crowd are with you all the way. They know the words as well as you do, and we'll be running them on the big screens above you, too. So if at any time you feel overwhelmed, or that your voice can't hit the notes, just point the microphone towards them and they'll take over for you."

"I just don't want to let Maxim down," said Michi, nervously.

"Oh you won't," said Stefan warmly. "You won't. He'll be watching – or at least listening – from his hospital bed, I'm sure, and he told me that he trusts you to do the best job that you possibly can. Plus we'll be showing him on the big screen behind you from about the halfway point of the song,

so he'll be with you in spirit at the very least."

"That is some comfort," said Michi, now beginning to warm to the task ahead of him a little. "You know, Stefan... this is something that I've wanted desperately for my whole life. But now that I'm here it doesn't feel anything like I ever imagined it would."

"Don't worry about that, my friend," said Stefan. "Just go out there and enjoy yourself. It's just three minutes of your life, and every single person in that crowd understands exactly what you've been through to get here. All you've got to do is be you, and they'll love you for it!"

Just then Hanna approached the pair and urged Michi to go and get ready for his performance. As the singer walked up the ramp and onto the stage, Stefan muttered something under his breath.

"Now don't you fuck it up you weird little creep or all our heads are on the block!"

The audience spotted Michi as he began to emerge from the gloom of backstage and went fully crazy. This is something that most of them had been hoping to see for their entire lives – a Moldovan artist stepping onto a Moldovan stage and representing his nation at Eurovision, and being broadcast across the whole planet. It may not have necessarily been the singer that they'd hoped for, but he was still theirs, and they wanted to give him all the encouragement that they could muster.

Back on the balcony, Dumi's expression suddenly switched from deep pride to one of abject fear. "Oh no!" he cried plaintively. "Oh no no no!"

"What is it?" asked Filip with concern in his voice.

"Well, do you see that little clump of people to the right of the stage in white t-shirts who've just raised a sea of white flags?"

"Yes?" said Filip, a bit puzzled. "Who are they?"

"Well they're from the Transnistrian Maxim Munteanu Fan Club They're about as politically radical as a bunch of musical supporters could ever be. And they're not terribly happy that Michi there is performing instead of their hero tonight."

"Ooh, is that likely to be an issue," asked Terry with some concern.

"It is when you factor in that group of people to the left of the stage with yellow flags and yellow t- shirts," Dumi continued.

"Who's that then?" Terry asked.

"That's ASLOM – the Anarchist Song League Of Moldova," said Dumi. "They're a self-styled bunch of art terrorists who very much lobbied for Michi's original song to be our representative at Eurovision this year. And the thing that is most important to know is that ASLOM and the TMMFC absolutely hate each other. Remember all that nasty business at the end of O Melodie Pentru a couple of months back? Well that was them kicking off against each other."

"Oh. Shit." said Filip starkly. "Should I get security on standby?"

"It's probably for the best," said Dumi. "But don't let them agitate either group though, because if anything lights the blue touch paper between the pair of them it could get seriously nasty. Right, I've got to dash off to sit with the President, as I can see that he's just dragged himself out of the bar. Call me if you need anything translating or explaining."

"Don't leave us now, Dumi!" cried Filip. "Not in our three minutes of potential need!"

"I'm afraid I've got to schmooze the top brass for a bit, lads. Our licence renewal is coming up soon! Hopefully I'll be back in a bit, though, 'cos I can't see them wanting to sit through the voting."

On stage the music whispered into its gentle start, and Michi took his last big breath before his vocal began.

"Come on Michi," came a cry from the ranks of the ASLOM supporters. "You can do it! All of Moldova is behind you!"

Immediately upon hearing this, another call came out from the TMMFC members on the other side of the hall.

"And do it for Maxim! We support you too!"

Terry snapped a confused gaze at his colleague on the balcony.

"Well I certainly wasn't expecting THAT!" he chirped. "A potential bit of tension relieved there, I feel!"

"Yeah, at least one thing has gone in our favour tonight," said Filip, looking relieved all over again.

Back on stage, Michi appeared visibly buoyed by the support from the crowd. Images of Maxim sitting up watching the show in his hospital bed flashed through his mind, and as he raised his head and gazed out across the audience, he could see a sea of positive, expectant faces all willing him on to succeed. The long, sentimental introduction finished and be began to sing. But much to even his own surprise the song somehow seemed to take over, and a deep, soulful voice flowed out of his mouth as if from the very depths of his soul. As soon as he uttered these first few words the audience let out an almighty round of applause and raised their telephones, torches lit, to the sky. A shiver went down Filip's back.

"This... this is quite, quite beautiful," he whispered. "And unexpectedly so. I wish that Dumi was still here with us, because I'd have loved to have seen his little face."

"He's sat directly opposite us," Terry pointed out. "Look, he's already got a wobbly chin. And wait, is that Timur Turgenev dabbing his eyes too? If he's got the power to do that to such a hard-faced oligarch, what in the name of daisy is this lad doing to the folks back home."

Filip suddenly looked a little worried again.

"Oh dear, this means that we're coming back again next year, doesn't it? I know that I've enjoyed it all in a wonky kind of way, but I'm not terribly sure that I want to revisit this whole experience again just yet."

"It's certainly a concern," Terry replied. "Just look at the crowd. There's not a dry eye in the house!"

Back on stage, Michi was now so absorbed in the song that he barely noticed what was going on in front of him. This was until Maxim's face appeared on the big screen behind him and the emotion in the audience ramped up even more. Suddenly the entire crowd linked arms and began to sing loudly to every word. Even the rival crews from ASLOM and TMMFC were hugging each other and crying along. The song may have only been two minutes and fifty-eight seconds long, but it seemed like an eternity as Michi delicately wove a story around each syllable with his new-found voice. When the whole performance eventually rolled to a finish, Michi just stood there, staring out into the distance as the crowd clapped and chanted his name.

"That was quite, quite splendid," said Terry, "If that doesn't win this it's going to come so damn close."

"Well it certainly deserves to, I have to confess," Filip replied, "however complicated it ends up making our lives over the next twelve months."

All of a sudden there was a cry from the centre of the audience and the mood in the hall turned instantly.

"You shouldn't even be up there, Michi Rotari," came the voice. "My boy Mikael was robbed, and he deserved to be there way more than you. You are a disgrace to your nation!"

It was Mrs Doibani, the car park attendant's mother who kicked off all the unrest at the final of O Melodie Pentru back in March. And she'd seriously annoyed many of the proud Moldovans who were standing around her.

"What are you saying, you silly witch?" shouted one woman of a similar age to Mrs Doibani.

"That's crazy talk!" yelled another sporting a TMMFC t-shirt. "This is one of the proudest moments in our nation's history and you're having a moan about your son? Get out of here!"

A scuffle quickly began as a small gaggle of women in their fifties and sixties began to tug at Mrs Doibani's clothes and hair. As they pushed and pulled their way around at the front of the stage, more and more people started to get involved, and soon the standing area became a small cauldron of anger. Michi's mood quickly switched from a deep spiritual elation to one of fear and dismay and he quickly dashed from the stage, with Maxim's backing singers all patting him on the back for a job well done.

"Great work, Michi," roared Stefan Smolenko with his arms outstretched. "You did your nation, and more importantly, Maxim Munteanu, proud. I just received a message from the President, and he wants to meet you as soon as possible."

"I... I don't know," said Michi. "I think it's all spoiled now. Just look at the crowd out there. I just want to run away and hide."

"Don't be so silly, Michi," Stefan reassured him. "That's the just the Moldovan way. It'll all be forgotten in a few minutes."

Meanwhile, on the other side of the stage, Hanna was checking that the Australian band Space Truckers still wanted to go on while the minor riot was taking place in the hall.

"We can delay for a couple of minutes if you want, fellas," she suggested. "We'll throw a little film on until it's all died down if you like?"

"No worries love," said Tony 'Tins' Barclay, the band's burly frontman, "this is exactly like one of our normal gigs back in Sydney. It'll make us feel right at home! Just chuck the stuff on stage now and we'll go out and tear up the party. It's exactly what we do!"

Space Truckers bounded onto the big stage in a sprightly manner quite unexpected for men of their advanced years. And weight. "Are you ready for a punk rock 'n' roll party?" yelled Tins as he surveyed the scuffles going on in front of him. "Ahh, I can see that you were expecting us!"

The opening chords of their noisy three-minute stomp cracked in and every single person who was able to jumped to their feet – most of them to get up and dance, but the rest to have a look at what was going on down the front. As the song proceeded, the band's two on-stage sidemen burst out of their toilet shed prop, dived into the big wooden bar and began to throw the spongey beer cans into the audience. However, unlike all their previous performances, these cans were actually soaked in beer and made quite a sloppy thwack if they hit anyone in the crowd. Unfortunately the man with the inflatable hammer was keeping an eye on Mrs Doibani and her tussles and wasn't paying full attention to the song, so caught one at full pelt right in the face. And that's when things got really unhinged.

You see, unbeknownst to anybody in Eurovision circles, Inflatable Hammer Guy was actually a secret Mossad security agent, historically placed there incognito to protect the Israeli acts and any Israeli fans who may be in the audience. The hammer was there to act as a marker for his fellow agents who were sitting up in the highest seats so that they could guide him towards any incidents that may have broken out. Of course, this was happy happy Eurovision, so in all the years that he'd been attending he'd never had a terrible amount to do. Over time he'd also become an alternative cult antihero amongst the fandom, so it would now be weird if he didn't attend. But this sudden and most unexpected beery assault kicked his survival instincts into gear. If something was kicking off around him, he was going make sure that he would protect his charges at all costs. So he grabbed a plastic taser out of his big fluffy blue-and-white boot, crouched into a defensive position and shouted at everybody else to back off. Which they very quickly did.

"Awww look," said Tins from the stage during the song's middle eight, "that lad in the blue and white there has got a little plastic toy gun! Go and have a dance with him!"

What Tins couldn't have known was that at least a dozen other countries had their own, slightly less obtrusive security agents positioned in the moshpit down the front, who at the sound of the word gun all sought out the Inflatable Hammer Guy, guided in turn by their own operatives sitting up in the Gods. And as the sudden appearance of the taser had caused a little empty circle to build around the Mossad man he was pretty easy to point out. The Lithuanian agent got to him first, and tackled him from behind. The German, Serbian and, strangely, Chinese heavies got to him next, and they all started getting into a tussle with each other over who was going to cuff the errant agent. From the stage, all Tins could see was a bit of a melee between a handful of burly fellas, so employing tactics learned from years of playing gigs at roughhouse music pubs in the bush he yelled "Pile on!", and flung himself from the stage backwards onto the heap of brawling men, still playing his guitar as he went.

At this precise moment, in another previously unseen bit of staging, a small group of stage crew began to throw toilet rolls into the audience from behind the little wooden bar, and the entire place turned into something more reminiscent of comedy bar fight from a cheap Western. Or a 1970s football match. But strangely enough it helped calm down the tense situation in the audience. It's difficult to be angry when you've got bogrolls bouncing off your skull and you're swathed in reams of toilet paper, and pretty soon even the most tetchy soul was joining in the chaos and chucking them about.

Filip and Terry sat open-mouthed from their vantage point high up at the side of the arena.

"Erm, was any of this actually scheduled to happen?" asked Filip, dumbfounded at what was unfolding before him.

"Erm, I'm not entirely sure," said Terry cautiously. "If it was it certainly wasn't presented to us in written form. But you've got to admit that it's some absolutely splendid chaos to end the show with – and the socials are going absolutely berserk!"

"At this point I don't know if that's an entirely good or bad thing," said Filip. "Or if it's even a thing at all. All I do know is that I'm more than happy that this is the last performance. We're nearly there, Terry. It'll end soon, and then we can finally rest. I hope."

The last few cacophonous chords of the Australian song came to an end, and the Space Truckers tottered to the front of the stage to soak in the chaos.

"Thanks you lovely European beauts!" shouted Tins with a manly tear at the corner of his eye. "You've made us all feel really welcome! It's just like being at home!" And with that the crowd went even wilder than before. Nobody had expected these old Aussie punkers to even get out of their semi-final, but now they surely had to be considered as serious contenders for the title.

Somewhere in the bowels of the press hall, the lads at the betting table who hadn't shifted from their seats in a fortnight were frantically laying all their previous favourites and lumping heavily on the Australians while the odds were still attractive.

As the cameras cut to the hosts standing at the back of the hall, looking a bit shell-shocked after the emotional rollercoaster of the last ten minutes, The Ox sent his men in to quietly deal with the audience turmoil. Again.

"So that was it," said Elina, clearly trying to ignore what was going on behind her, "the twenty-six acts have all performed their songs and they can do no more. Now it's up to you to decide who the winner is going to be."

"Yes!" said Ruslan, "In a change to recent years, the winner of this year's Eurovision Song Contest is going to be chosen entirely by you, the viewers. We're about to show you a quick recap of all the songs featuring the numbers to call so you can vote for your favourites. But remember, you can't vote for your own country. But before that, we're going to open the voting. So count down with us. Five-four-three-two-one... Europe, start voting!"

"Right, it's entirely out of our hands now!" said Filip as the recap video began to roll. Absolutely anything could happen over the next hour or so of our lives."

This is the most exciting bit," said Terry, enthusiastically. "It's the not knowing!"

"Yeah, that's actually the least fun bit for me," Filip laughed. "I was hoping that this was going to be a nice easy contest where there was one clear favourite and we could all mentally prepare ourselves for next year. But it's not going to be like that all all, is it now. I have absolutely no idea who's going to win this bloody thing, and there's so many potential outcomes that could make our lives so incredibly complicated for the next year. I'm dreading it mate, I'm telling you. Absolutely reading it."d

40

As the recap worked its way though the songs, Terry made note of which were the most popular amongst the crowd.

"You do realise that an ovation from the fans is rarely an indicator of ultimate success," said Filip, wisely. "Otherwise Spain would win every year!"

"Oh totally," Terry replied. "But it's a handy yardstick that can suggest to us which of the singers to keep the cameras on when the votes come in."

"Oh yes, I'd not actually thought of that!" said Filip. "Tell what you come up with and I'll let the gallery know."

"Well so far, Italy got loads of boos, Denmark did surprisingly well, Ukraine were up there..." "Oh Gawd!" said Filip.

"Quite," Terry continued. "Then Spain went massive, obv, Iceland, Poland and Kazakhstan all picked up a lot of noise, and then Moldova, of course, but that always happens to the home team.

But the most surprising of all were Belgium and Australia. I really think we need to keep an eye out for that pair. And seeing as it's 100% punter decided, I reckon these might be pretty good indicators of what the public are into."

"Good points all, Terry, said Filip, as the recap package ended and Elina and Ruslan were suddenly back in shot and looking a bit nervous.

"It seems as though the interval entertainment is taking a little bit longer to set up than we'd imagined," said Elina, "so while we get this amazing show ready, here's another chance to choose your favourite song with another quick recap!"

"What's up, Hanna?" Filip immediately spat down his radio.

"The Aussie shed is proving difficult to shift out of the way, and we've got fifty dancers about twenty metres away from where they should be," she answered. "We'll be literally a minute before we're all set and everybody's on their right mark."

"Glad to hear it!" said Filip. "Carry on with the great work!"

"Thank heavens for that," said Terry, looking relieved. "I got the fear that there was going to be another incident like that time at Turkvision where we ended up watching the recaps for three hours because somebody forgot to flick a switch. Some of the performers were actually on their flights home before anyone noticed!"

"Ha! Yes, I remember that!" laughed Filip. "Thankfully we're a little bit more organised than them – most of the time. And hopefully it'll give the folks back home more incentive to vote in multiples and put a few more pennies in the communal pot for next year! I've got a feeling that we might need it."

The second running of the reprise video came to an end and the house lights dimmed. A small child began to sing a plaintive song in the beam of a single spotlight at the centre of the performance area, before a multitude of colourful singers and dancers came streaming into the arena from every available nook and cranny.

"Haven't we seen this one before?" said Terry, puzzled.

"More times than we've seen a song called Shine," Filip laughed. "Still, it gives the folks at home a little bit of local colour, and gives us chance to have a moderately stress-free breather and get our slap on for the start of the voting."

"Oh heck," said Terry, looking worried. "In all this chaos and excitement I'd clean forgotten that we were going to be on camera – if only for a minute."

"Oh yes sir," said Filip proudly. "Now here comes the make-up crew ready to powder our noses and make our mothers proud of us!"

Terry sat there terrified while they took the shine off his forehead, which was quite a task on a humid Spring night in Tiraspol. As the interval act eventually ground to a halt, the voting was closed, and the last little comedy film for the locals was shown during an ad break, he got more and more nervous at the thought of being seen by hundreds of millions of people around the world.

"Don't worry about it, mate," said Filip reassuringly. "When it comes down to it, nobody gives a damn about us. We've just got to get this bit over with quickly and cleanly before they start the voting sequence."

"That's easy for you to say, Filip," his anxious sidekick stuttered. "You've sat in the background of this thing before. I'm still a first timer. What if I do something dreadful that takes the onus off you?"

"Well you'd better make sure that you don't," said Filip with a smile. "Just sit there with a blank expression on your face – that shouldn't be too hard. It's my first time doing the speaking bit, remember. Everyone will be looking at me to see if I have a new catchphrase or anything like that. It's sad to say, but unless you stand up and drop your trousers right beside me, not many people outside of your direct family will even notice that you're there. And you're not going do that, are you? I hope!"

"Oh no, not at all," Terry laughed. "Or at least I'll try not to..."

Suddenly Elina and Ruslan were taking their positions on stage behind the voting plinth, and Filip started to warm up his voice in preparation for the three sentences he was about to proclaim to the world.

"…and I'd like to welcome the new executive supervisor of the Eurovision Song Contest, Mr Filip Ivanović," announced Ruslan. "Filip, do we have a result?"

After allowing the audience to give him a small ripple of polite applause, he began to speak. "Yes Ruslan," he said with a dry sputter in his voice. "I can confirm that the votes have been counted and verified by our independent adjudicator, and we're ready to hear the results of the first jury. So let's get to it!"

The cameras cut back to the hosts, and the moment that he knew he was safely away from the screens of Europe, Terry leaned in to Filip and whispered…

"So let's get to it?" he mocked.

"Yeah, I know right," Filip replied. "I have absolutely no idea where that came from. I was going to do something far grander, but somehow I found those words just falling out of my mouth. I'm stuck with the bloody thing now, aren't I!"

Terry quickly checked Twitter.

"Yep, it's trending already, so I think you most probably are!" "Bloody social media!" Filip muttered under his breath.

As this was an entirely televoted procedure, there were none of the usual indications of how well the songs were doing that you'd usually get from a jury vote, so after all the eliminated semi-final countries had given their scores in alphabetical order, it was decided to go to the voting announcers of the finalists in the order that they had performed. This was mainly done to keep things simple, but after the unexpected success of Moldova and Australia – the last two nations to perform in tonight's show – it now meant that we could be in for a very tense and exciting end to the show.

After the initial sixteen sets of semi-finalist votes had been announced, there was no clear leader, and the songs from Denmark, Ukraine, Romania, Poland, Kazakhstan, Belgium, Moldova and Australia were all only a handful of points away from each other at the top, with Azerbaijan, Greece, and somewhat unexpectedly Iceland sitting only a little way behind. But then it was the turn of the evening's competing nations to announce their scores, and things started to get even more exciting. As there was no Russia, Sweden or The Netherlands in the final, the points that they would traditionally attract were going anywhere and everywhere, and it was impossible to predict what the final outcome was likely to be.

Italy's points announcer got severely booed by the audience, who scarcely heard her twelve points go to Moldova. This was perhaps a little unfair on the eighty–four–year–old woman reading the votes, as she obviously had nothing to do with Explodo's bad behaviour. The Norwegian spokesman, however, got a hearty laugh when he appeared wearing the same kind of corpse paint as his nation's performers. He then got a loud happy cheer as he announced their top marks were going to Denmark – the poor souls who had perhaps suffered most from the Norwegian singer's wrath. The next few sets of votes hammered along, and as they approached the first commercial break there were five clear leaders – Ukraine, Kazakhstan, Belgium, Moldova and Australia, with only Iceland sitting anywhere near enough to potentially catch them. At the bottom of the table, only Germany, Spain, Estonia and the United Kingdom were yet to receive any points at all.

"So then Filip," said Terry with a smile, "where do you most want to go to next year out of this little quintet?"

"Oh Belgium!" he immediately replied. "All day long. I mean, it may not be the most exciting winner we could have, but how much easier would it be to hold this thing there than in any of the others. I mean, don't get me wrong, I love all my Eurovision family members equally and with no favour to any of them. But Belgium. Please let it be Belgium."

"Iceland aren't completely out of it yet, mind," Terry teased. "Oh do shut up!" Filip snapped back, only half joking.

After a handful of awkward green room interviews with a completely out of his depth Bobby Odobescu, it was time to start the voting again. As each new spokesperson came and went they would without fail give their top six votes to the top six on the scoring table, with Iceland and their singing dogman still within reach of leading five.

"He's going to nip through and win this bloody thing," said Filip with a tremble in his voice. "I just know it! And how are we going to reply to the papers when they ask us about the song making a mockery of the whole competition?"

"No, surely he's too far behind to catch up now?" said Terry reassuringly. "He'd have to win every jury left and hope that all the others dropped a few points here and there, surely?"

"Yeah, but four of that five haven't announced their votes yet," Filip replied.

"Hey, wait a minute!" said Terry with a quizzical look on his face. "Don't you already know who's going to win this? Surely the adjudicators have slipped the result into your ear?"

"I thought I'd take a leaf out of your book and let it be a surprise this time," Filip said with a clenched expression. "And that's the last bloody time I ever do that! It's too stressful by half!"

"Couldn't you just ask them now?"

"Oh no mate, I'm in too deep. I've come this far, so I've got to ride it out with the rest of you, haven't I! Curse you and your silly cute ideas!"

During the final commercial break, the cameras again cut to Bobby in the green room, but the popular YouTuber clearly wasn't cut out for this kind of work.

"So Cyprus, did you enjoy your time on stage?" he mumbled hamfistedly.

"Erm, yes, Bobby," said the Cypriot singer Thea, who despite her immense energy while she was performing was clearly pretty timid off stage. "It was nice."

In Bobby's earpiece the director was shouting at him to make things more interesting.

"For Christ's sake Bobby, this is supposed to be a party atmosphere," he barked. "Try to get something exciting happening before the viewers all go to sleep."

Bobby nodded towards the camera and said "OK, here I go! Here's Takouhi from Armenia. I hear that you and Murad from Azerbaijan are getting on particularly well. There's talk that you've been seen out partying together. That's a great thing for relations between your two countries surely?"

Takouhi looked instantly mortified and started to attract disapproving looks from some of the older members of her delegation. Over her shoulder towards the back of the room, Murad could be seen nervously sneaking out of a side entrance. Over the radio the director yelled in a panic.

"Cut! Cut! Get the camera away from this fuckwit before he starts a war! Bobby and Elina, you're on, and you've got ninety seconds to fill!"

And to their credit, like the true professionals that they were, they did. But soon it was time for the final nine countries to announce their scores, and a nervous hush broke out across the arena.

Kazakhstan gave their twelve points to Ukraine, and their next four places were all taken up by the other songs still in contention. France went for Belgium, but with Iceland in second place, while Germany gave Iceland their top marks, the German spokesman howling like a puppy while he delivered them. Belarus went for Kazakhstan, and Serbia had Moldova as their favourite song. So as they approached the final three sets of votes, the top of the table looked like this...

Kazakhstan were placed first with 212 points. Ukraine and Moldova were tied in second with 209. Belgium were in fourth with 208, while Australia and Iceland were now tied on 204. At the bottom, Germany, Spain and the United Kingdom still sat pointless. Things were perilously close, but with two of the last three countries near the top of the table still yet to announce their scores, absolutely anything could happen.

"This is the most exciting Eurovision in years!" Terry yelled enthusiastically.

"It might be for you," Filip muttered, "but it's really not doing my blood pressure any good."

Armenia were the next country to announce their votes. Their spokesman was a chirpy chap who decided that now was a good time to crack a lot of jokes and praise the host Elina for her beauty. But this wasn't a popular move with the audience.

"Get on with it!" yelled one audience member. "Shut up!" yelled another.

But still he wittered on.

"And thank you for such an amaaaaazing show. As I sit here in front of the..."

The crowd were now booing and were beginning to look quite unruly again. Elina spotted this obvious unrest, and to avoid any more shenanigans from the audience she quickly cut the Armenian spokesman off.

"Your votes." she said curtly. "Your votes. Now, please." Loud cheers rang out from the arena.

"Oh yes, of course," said the spokesman, oblivious to annoyance he was causing across the globe. "So here are the votes, finally, of the Armenian public vote!"

Even louder, slightly more ironic cheers could be heard from the hall over the TVs of Europe and beyond. The first four sets of marks went to some of the low hanging fruit in the middle of the table, although Germany managed to bag their first point, which led to their delegation doing a little happy dance in the green room, despite the two singers sitting very deliberately at different ends of the sofas to each other. Unfortunately, the Armenian spokesman had decided that it would be a great idea to sing a little bit of each of the songs that he was announcing, which did little to calm the crowd down.

"Please, sir," said Elina's co-host Ruslan sharply. "No more singing. We want to get home at some point tonight."

The Armenian spokesman looked crestfallen at this telling off and continued with his announcements.

"Our five points go to... Belgium!"

Everyone in the arena began to mentally calculate what this could mean to the overall table, and tried to catch a look at the tiny numbers on the giant overhead screens.

"Our six points... belong to... Ukraine! Our seven points... go to... this year's beautiful host country... our new friends in... Moldova!"

The home crowd were altogether split on this one. Half of them were just happy to still be getting points and cheered heartily. But a big proportion had worked out that they could still dredge an unlikely second win and began to boo and whistle at such an apparently low set of points."

The spokesman continued.

"Our eight points go to... My Lovely Horse... Kazakhstan!"

The audience gasped. This score had the potential of making things very interesting, depending on how the next couple of sets of votes went.

"Our ten points... go to our second favourite song of the night..."

The spokesman then jumped up onto the desk in front of him on all fours and started to howl. "Iceland!"

Massive gasps went out through the crowd, followed by an almost instant silence as they waited to see what was going to come next.

"And our twelve points... go to..."

The spokesman dived out of shot momentarily and could be heard rustling in a bag, before diving back in front of the camera wearing a wide-brimmed hat with corks dangling from it and clutching a toy kangaroo.

"...our friends from Down Under... Australia!"

The gasps got louder as everyone gawped at the scoreboard trying to work out what effect those scores had on the competition.

"Bloody hell that Armenian fella drew things out!" said Filip. "I thought he'd never end."

"Hopefully the last couple of jurors will be more professional," Terry added, before they were both interrupted by a representative from the auditors who had just counted and verified the scores.

"Sir, we've got an issue with the results that needs addressing really urgently," said a serious looking woman in a crisp grey suit. "I thought you'd already been alerted to it, but one of the lads in the office told me that you were flying blind as far as all the scores went and I had to rush straight over."

Before they moved onto the Moldovan jury, Elina and Ruslan gave a quick catch-up of where the contest stood.

"Wow!" said Ruslan. "You folks at home have certainly made things very interesting on the scoreboard tonight!"

"Much more interesting than your jokes!" said Elina cuttingly.

"Anyway, things are even closer than before," he continued. "Kazakhstan are still leading on 220 points. But closing in behind on 216 points are both Australia and Moldova. Next it's Ukraine on 215 points, followed by Iceland on 214 and Belgium on 213!"

"Yes, with only seven points separating the top six songs, and only two juries left to give their scores, it's impossible to predict a winner," added Elina. "Any of the top six could still be the victors, so let's move to our next jury – our very own Lucian Dobre from Moldova!"

The locals in the audience at first let out a hearty cheer when they saw that the man who was responsible for finally bringing Eurovision to Moldova was going to present their votes. But then they almost as quickly slumped back into their seats, realising that they weren't going to get any points this time, which would probably cost them the title. This didn't seem to phase Lucian, who was as ebullient as ever as he stood on a big plinth at the back of the Teapot's auditorium.

"Good eeeeeeeevening Europe!" he bellowed, his massive hands enveloping the microphone. "And good evening Moldova! We can't tell you how excited we are to bring you this year's Eurovision Song Contest live from the beautiful ancient city of Tiraspol tonight. But I know that you don't want to hear me chattering on... you want to hear the results of the Moldovan jury! Am I right?"

The audience gave out an anxious cheer, and the big man started to read out the scores. The first three sets of points went to Azerbaijan, Germany and Poland respectively. But then things got really interesting.

"Our four points go to... Kazakhstan!"

The gasp factor in the audience ramped up several notches. Such a low score for the current leaders surely left everything up for grabs. An anxious silence fell over the auditorium.

"Our five points go to... our neighbours in Ukraine!"

He paused a moment to increase the tension, although to be honest, things were already unbearably tense as they were.

"Six points belong to... Belgium. Our seven score goes to... our other good neighbours in Romania!"

"Hang about," Terry thought to himself. "Moldova nearly always give

Romania their top marks. So who are the next three sets of points going to go to? This is just so impossibly complicated!"

Back in the press hall, the boys at the betting table were fanning each other down with the promotional t-shirts the delegation from Kazakhstan had been giving out for free.

Lucian continued.

"Eight points... for... who's it going to be...? Who do you think...? Australia!"

There was another long pause, before Elina nervously tried to hurry her employer along. "Yes, yes, I will continue..." he said, happily. "Our ten points, go to... Belarus!" Puzzlement suddenly dashed across the faces of everybody in the arena.

"And our big twelve... goes to... the United Kingdom!"

The camera cut to the green room, where the UK delegation were just staring at each other in belwilderment, while Jason Brown was making little heart symbols with his fingers and mouthing "Thank you! Thank you so much!" directly into the lens."

Up on the balcony, Filip returned to his seat, looking weary but content. "What was it, Filip?" said Terry. "Why did you have to dash off?"

"You'll thank me if I don't tell you," said Filip with a wry smile at the corner of his mouth. "But you'll enjoy it, trust me!"

"That all seemed a bit fishy those last few scores from Moldova there," said Terry, "especially as it still keeps them in the game."

"That was one of the reasons that I had to dash out," Filip replied. "But I can assure you that as weird as they may seem, they all seem to check out just fine. The auditors reckoned they had to scan them with a forensic eye just to be certain, but it really is all totally above board."

"That's done some pretty strange things to the scoreboard though," Terry said with breathless enthusiasm. "Wait, the hosts are just about to talk us though it all."

"So!" said Ruslan. "With only one jury left to give their scores, the top of the table looks like this... Australia have joined Kazakhstan in first place on 224 points. In third sit Ukraine on 220. Next come Belgium on 219 and Moldova with 216. And in sixth is Iceland on 214."

"But remember, Australia can't vote for themselves," Elina added. "So their fate is entirely in their own hands. Come in Sydney, can you hear us?"

"Yes we can," said Sally Demitriu, a popular Australian breakfast TV host. "It's a beautiful sunny Sunday morning on the beach here, and we're about to help decide who is going to win the Eurovision this year. Are you guys ready?"

"We're ready!" said pretty much everybody in the arena, before a deathly hush filled the room. "Our first point goes to... Malta!" Shrugs and mild muttering rippled gently through the crowd. "Our two points... go to... North Macedonia!"

Again, nobody bar a few folks from Skopje were all that bothered by these scores, and the tension began to rise as the numbers got higher. "Three points... go to... Estonia!"

The crowd fell eerily silent. With seven sets of votes to go, the entire top six still had a chance of winning. Sally Demitriu sniffed and settled her shoulders as if she had something important to announce.

"Australia's four points go to... Ukraine!"

There was a massive collective intake of breath from the audience.

"Shit!" shouted a startled Terry. "That puts them level with the top two now. I'm having trouble breathing. "What's going to happen, Filip? What's going to happen?"

"Now you know that I'm not going to reveal anything until the scores are fully announced," said Filip with a knowing nod. "But it's a bit good!"

Our five points," said Sally, milking her brief time on camera for everything she had, "goes... to... Belgium!"

"Noooo!" said Terry, even more bewildered than before. "Now they're on 224 points as well! This is now down to Kazakhstan, Moldova... and dare I say it... Iceland. No, no, that couldn't possibly happen! Could it?"

Filip just raised his eyes and looked mercurial.

Down in the green room, camera crews began to circle around Rayana from Kazakhstan, Vikingur from Iceland and Michi from Moldova. Michi was nervously perched on the very edge of the sofa, anxiously gnawing his nails. Stefan Smolenko turned to him and put a reassuring arm around his shoulders.

"Whatever happens next, Michi, you can be sure that you've done your country proud. Even if you don't win, your people will never forget what you've done for them all over this last week. You should be so, so pleased, wherever you eventually finish."

"But I feel like such a fraud, Stefan," said a sad looking Michi. "If I did this well, just imagine how Maxim would have done. I shouldn't even be here. It should be him!"

"There's no way anyone could ever know what might have happened," said Stefan, "what-ifs are just dreams in the wind. What we need to be more concerned about is the here and the now. And here we are, only a few minutes from the end of the Eurovision Song Contest, and there's still an outside chance that you could win it. Imagine what that's doing for the spirit of the nation. You're a hero, and that's all there is to it."

"I... I guess," sad Michi. "But I don't altogether feel like one. Wait, here come the next scores." The crowd fell silent again.

"Six big fat Australian points," Sally teased, "go to... Greece!" "Oh dammit," said Terry, "They're just prolonging the agony now. "Our seven points go to... my old granddad's backyard... Cyprus!"

"Three sets of points to go, and three songs can still win!" gasped Terry. "I don't think my heart can take it! Has it ever been this exciting?"

Filip just smiled, and gave Terry a look that said "You just wait, mate!"

"Right then," said Sally," we're at the business end now. The next three sets of votes might just determine who's going to win this thing! Who's getting our eight, then?"

The crowd all yelled out their favourites, but Elina was getting impatient. "Come on Sally, I'm going to have to rush you!"

"OK, here it is. Our eight points... go to... thank you for being such amazing hosts... Moldova!"

A brief excited cheer from the audience quickly subsided into glum disappointment as they looked at the scoreboard and realised that this also set them on 224 points.

Michi slumped back onto the sofa and looked thoroughly devastated. Stefan clasped him firmly on the shoulder.

"Don't worry mate. You did brilliantly. You can't finish any lower than third now. You're on the top table, and we got ourselves a darned respectable result. To be absolutely honest with you, I'm not sure that even Timur Turgenev's pockets are deep enough for us to be able to hold this thing again next year. That's the perfect result for us, and I couldn't be more happy."

"Are you sure?" said Michi. "Are you sure that I didn't let you down?"
"Far from it young fella. Far from it!"

Back on the balcony, Terry had done some working out.

"Kazakhstan have got this now," he affirmed. "It doesn't matter if they get ten or twelve. We're all off to the Steppe! That's going to be interesting, if nothing else."

"Let's just wait and see, shall we?" said Filip, calmly.

"Oh you're such a tease!" Terry laughed. "It's got to be them. It can't be anyone else, surely?"

"Right then," said Sally, hitching up her skirt. "Our ten points go to... Who let the dogs out!... Iceland!"

Stunned shrieks and yells of dismay filled the air, and with just the final twelve points left to announce, nobody was entirely sure of what was going to happen next.

"May I just stop you there for a moment Sally so that we can explain what's going on?" said Elina purposefully.

"Sure," said Sally, "fire away."

"This has never happened before in the long history of Eurovision, but we have six songs tied at the top of the table with only one set of points left to be announced. Let's just soak this all in for a moment."

A whole continent was perched on the edge of their comfortable chairs, holding their collective breath and waiting for the final score to be given.

"Sally, you may continue," said Ruslan masterfully.

"Thanks Ruslan. Here we go then. Our twelve points... and the honour of being Australia's favourite song this Eurovision... go to..."

You have never in your life heard the arena at a Eurovision Song Contest go quite so silent as everyone awaited Sally's final proclamation.

"Norway!"

"What?!" cried Terry. "Bloody Norway! They're still mucking us about and they're not even in contention. But hang about, what does all this mean to the scores?"

"You'd better get your TV face on, Terry lad," warned Filip, "'Cos we're about to go live!" Down on stage, the two hosts looked equally confused.

"Erm, that appears to be a six way tie for first place," said Elina. "But that doesn't mean that we've got six winners, does it now Ruslan."

"No," said her co-host. "In the event of a tie we have a number of procedures to work out who the true winner is. Isn't that right, Elina."

"Yes, Ruslan, it is. And to explain it all to us, here's our Executive Supervisor, Mr Filip Ivanović!" Filip flipped into TV mode and began to explain.

"Yes Elina, thank you. Because of this unprecedented six-way tie we've had to dig deep into our tie-break procedure to try to assess who has won this year's contest. In a normal year it would be the country who has gained the most points from the televote. But after the cancelation of yesterday's jury voting, the televote is all we have. So then it goes down to the song that received points from the most countries. This was a five way tie, as Australia, Belgium, Iceland, Kazakhstan and Moldova all had votes from 38 of the possible voting countries. Ukraine only received points from 36, so we must lose them at this stage."

Over in the green room, blue and gold Ukrainian flags could be seen to sink sadly onto the floor.

"So in the event of this tie, the next decider is the country that gained the most twelve point scores. Australia, Moldova and Kazakhstan each had six, Belgium had four, and Iceland only three. So we must say goodbye to Belgium and Iceland."

Now perched firmly at the front of his sofa again, Michi looked at Stefan with a confused and concerned look on his face.

"Does this mean that we can still win?" he asked, falteringly.

"Erm, I'm not 100% sure, but I think it possibly does," said Stefan, wondering quite what he was going to tell his bosses at Moldova Smash if his country took a second consecutive victory.

"So with the tally of twelve points out of the way, we now had to look at how many sets of ten points each song gained," Filip explained. "Two songs got ten points from six countries, and one got ten points from only the five. So I'm afraid that you have come third, Kazakstan. But what a brave attempt on your first try at the competition."

Michi and Stefan were now clasping each other tightly, as the picture on TV was now divided between the Moldovan and the Australian delegations. Over in the Australians seats, Space Truckers were still cracking beers open like they didn't have a care in the world. But the Moldovans were sat there absolutely terrified of what was about to happen. A second place would be fair but disappointing, but there was no way of knowing how a home audience would react at such news – especially given how volatile they had been throughout the night. But a win could plunge the finances of the Moldovan broadcaster into an absolute free-fall. They were in a lose/lose situation, whatever result transpired, and Stefan's head was absolutely spinning.

Filip continued.

"So lastly, we had to look at how many sets of eight points the two remaining countries received. One country got eight lots of eight point votes, while the other had seven. So we have a winner, and by the narrowest of margins, I can announce that this year's Eurovision Song Contest winners are..."

It seemed barely possible, but the Teapot fell even more silent than before. Audience members were anxiously grasping the nearest people to them, whether they knew them or not, and every single person who was watching, wherever they were on the planet, was hanging on the next word to fall from Filip's lips.

"AUSTRALIA!"

The whole arena exploded with confused release. No one could quite believe that the Australians had won it – let alone with such an uncharacteristic Eurovision song. Michi turned to Stefan with a worried look in his eye.

"That's... that's a good thing, right?" he asked, looking slightly tearful.

"It's a very good thing!" said Stefan. "You just got pretty much the greatest result that a runner-up has ever got in this contest. Your career is made, son. You can dine out on these stories for the rest of your life, and you'll always be our greatest underdog hero. And on top of all that, we don't have to go through the pain, headache and expense of holding this accursed thing again next year. Everyone's a winner!"

Out of nowhere, Tins, the lead singer of Space Truckers bounced over the back of the Moldovan sofas to give Michi an almighty hug.

"I thought you had us beat for sure there, mate!" he said, cheerfully. "And to be honest, I reckon you deserved to win tonight. We were all welling up as we watched you when we were waiting to go on. You were brilliant mate. Bloody brilliant! Now, if you don't mind, I've got to go down there and accept that bloody trophy. I've got no idea what to say, to be fair mate. I didn't expect that we were even going to be here in the final, let alone win the whole bastard thing! Keep it up, Michi. I can tell you're going to be a proper star!"

And with that he leapt back over the sofa, grabbed his fellow bandmates, and together they fought their way through the crowds to accept their hard won trophy.

"I did alright then?" said Michi, still unsure of himself.

"Look Michi," said Stefan warmly. "If a big burly old bloke like that said that he was close to tears watching your performance, well that's good enough for me. You're a winner, despite what the scoreboard says tonight. Good job, sir! Good job!"

Over on the stage, Space Truckers were accepting their big glass microphone from last year's winners, the Bessarabian Turbo Squad, and Elina approached Tins for a winner's interview.

"Well, how do you feel about that, Tins? Did you expect to win?"

"I can't bloody believe it, if I'm honest with you Elina! Fat old guys like us don't usually win in life, so it's like some kind of a weird dream."

"And where are you going to hold the competition next year?" Elina asked. "I understand that you can't hold it in Australia, so Berlin is the big rumour."

"Nah fuck that," said Tins, "if you pardon my French. We're dragging this thing back down under with us. We're going to hold it on the Gold Coast and you can all stay round my old Mum's farm just out of town. The whole thing is going to start at 7am on the Sunday morning, local time, and it's going to be the best Eurovision Song Contest ever – even better than this one! You heard it here first!"

Filip held his head in his hands in disbelief up on the balcony.

"I had a horrible feeling that he was going to say that?" he said. "The genii's out of the bottle now. It's going to be hard to go against them on that."

"Still, a nice little trip to Australia on expenses isn't one to be sniffed at," said Terry gleefully. "Even if it is off the back of that terrible, terrible song."

"Ah, don't knock it," said Filip, sagely. "They were the act that read the room best tonight, and so I reckon they thoroughly deserve it, how ever much of an old noise it is."

Back on the stage, the Australians were beginning their winning reprise. Bogrolls were flying everywhere, getting all tanged up in the celebratory tinsel and causing a right old mess on stage.

"I want every single person who performed tonight out of the green room and up on stage with us right now," Tins shouted as the intro began to kick in. "You all deserve it. Every one of you is a winner in my book!"

And soon the stage was absolutely groaning with the weight of disappointed pop stars from all around Europe, each wringing their last few seconds of glory out of what would be for many the biggest moment of their careers.

41

Once the crowd had all left the arena and the performers had got their slap off, a fleet of buses pulled up outside the artists entrance to ferry anybody who was still up for a shindig to the official after party a short drive away across the river at Tighina Castle. The beautiful old structure had sat there overlooking the Dniester since at least the fifteenth century, and was a glorious mash of architectural styles, from Moldavian to Bessarabian to Ottoman to Russian and all sorts in between, depending on which invading force had passed that way at any given point in history. At its heart lay a wide, ragged courtyard that had been dolled up for the party. The previously unkempt floor surface had been rather gracelessly tarmac'd from one end to the other, and food and drink stalls lined the two longest sides of the castle walls. At one end sat a large stage festooned with the flags of both Moldova and Transnistria, while at the other a handful of enormous spotlights etched their beams high into the night sky. And atop the walls around the courtyard's perimeter, big barrels of fire punctuated the darkness every ten feet or so. It promised to be a party that nobody was likely to forget in a hurry.

The place was already heaving with many of the event's volunteers who had descended onto the party en masse about an hour before the show had finished and hoovered up the best of the free food and drink like sparkly locusts. Although to be fair, after working two-and-a-bit weeks of very long hours for free they totally deserved it. This also meant that there was already quite the atmosphere going on by the time the delegations and officials began to arrive, so there was none of that awkward standing about waiting for something to happen that you get at a lot of parties. The Danish pop kids from Happy Band were the first to arrive and piled straight in to the party fun down the front. Despite their middling result and difficulties at the hands of the Norwegian black metallers they'd had the time of their lives and were relishing every last minute of this experience before they all went back to music college on Monday morning.

North Macedonia were next in, and they too had had a few sticky moments at the end of some baseless barbs from the EuroStorm website. But they just steamed in with the party kids and let all the aggravation of the past couple of weeks wash away from them in glorious abandon.

As more and more of the delegations started to arrive, the party notched up a couple more pegs each time, and when the place was finally packed to the ginnels, Lucian Dobre got up onto the stage to make a few remarks.

"Eeeeeeeuuuuurooooovisiooooon! Make some motherfucking noise, brothers and sisters!" he cried. And indeed the crowd did.

"What an amazing night we've all had," he continued, "and I'd like to thank each and every one of you for making it the greatest Eurovision of all times! I can see that not quite everybody from the show tonight has got here yet, so if you find them before I do, tell them I love them! Now to bring the party to an even higher level, let me introduce to you, Moldova's national heroes, The Bessarabian Turbo Squad!"

The local volunteers and workers went absolutely wild, and one end of the castle's courtyard turned into a seething mass of happy humanity bouncing about and carrying on. The BTS played for about twenty minutes before they stopped the show and went all serious for a moment. Their lead singer Skippz held his hand up to quieten the crowd. "Guys, guys, before we play our Eurovision winning smash hit, there's someone that I want to introduce. You all saw him up on stage tonight, bringing Moldova their second greatest result ever at this wild old contest – ladies and gentlemen, I give you my new hero, Michi Rotari!"

As Michi shuffled nervously onto the stage he was instantly buoyed by the huge friendly reception from the crowd.

"Come on Michi, don't be shy," said Skippz warmly. "You deserve your place on this stage, so come on over and take the applause!"

Michi walked towards the front of the stage and soaked up the acclaim – acclaim that he still didn't entirely believe he deserved. But when the crowd began to chant his name, quietly at first, but then in a loud wave that echoed around the castle grounds, he finally began to realise that he was not an imposter, that he thoroughly deserved to be there on his own merits, and that his life was about to change in ways that he couldn't yet anticipate.

"You'd better get used to that, Michi lad," Skippz laughed, "because you're going to be hearing it an awful lot over the next few weeks."

Again, Skippz held his hand into the air to calm the audience. "Now, I have one question for you, Michi..."

Michi looked puzzled. "What's that?" he asked.

"Do you know the words to our Eurovision-winning smash hit tune?"

"Are you crazy?" Michi laughed. "Every Moldovan knows every last word of it, whether they like the song or not!"

"Great, then you're going to sing it along with us, right now!"
"What...? Me?"

"Of course Michi! Grab a mic and let's get going! 1-2-3-4..."

The rest of the BTS struck up the intro, Skippz winked at Michi and then piled into the vocal. Michi just stood there stunned and wide-eyed for a second or two before he started to sing along – at first quietly, and then for everything he was worth. He thought back to his early gigs with Glory Of The Crow and Dirty Brew in those near-deserted basement bars up in Sectorul Ciocana, and how he'd always dreamed of moments like this. And now it was happening, right here, with his nation's biggest band in the most historic building in the country, and in front of a huge crowd of people from all over the world who all seemed to know his name. He knew there and then that this was where he was always meant to be, and he just couldn't believe his luck.

Meanwhile, back at the Teapot, Filip, Terry and the press crew were just finishing off the last few bits of business after the winner's press conference when Dumi and Stefan stuck their heads around the corner of their office to coax them all out to the after party.

"Lads, lads, put those papers down and come over to the castle to drink goodbye to this baby," said Dumi cheerfully, already fairly refreshed from his evening in the President's private bar.

"Yeah, all of that can wait until tomorrow," Stefan added. "Vasile the driver has sorted us out a luxury Marshrutka. He tells me it's 'full of disco' — so let's get down there!"

"What do you say, Filip?" said Terry hopefully. "Shall we go forth and get down?"

"Oh sod it, let's do it!" Filip replied with a beaming grin as Sunny, Jeff, Jan and Dean all let out a little cheer.

"The disco bus will take us, we're off to Bender Castle!" Sunny and Dean began to chant to the tune of the Vengaboys' biggest hit as they locked up the office and made their way to the transport.

"You've worked bloody hard for us this last few weeks, you lot." said Filip with an avuncular tone. "You all deserve to let your hair down and have a bit of a blow out!"

"I'll tell you what, Filip," said Jeff, "if anyone deserves a blow out tonight it's you. How you've managed to keep this whole thing together and get it all on stage on time and in reasonable order without losing all your hair I'll never know. We ought to carry you into that castle on a chair, because you bloody well merit it!"

"Well that really is terribly kind, Jeff, but there's no need. I absolutely love what I do, despite all the bumpy bits, and it's been an absolute honour to share it all with you."

As they came out of the bowels of the arena they saw Vasile waving, beckoning them towards the most splendid looking minibus you ever did see. Decorated in a shimmering gold wrap, and with colourful spotlights spinning around on its roof rack, the driver slid the side door open and a wall of sweet smelling smoke flowed out down the steps and onto the asphalt, while the pounding sounds of local turbo techno punctuated the air.

"He wasn't wrong when he said it was full of disco, was he now," laughed Terry.

"Yeah, that'll do wonders for my migraine," Filip replied with a smile.

When Vasile eventually picked his way through the traffic and pulled up at the castle gates, the eight of them piled out, then stood and gazed at the big building in utter wonder.

"You know, people are always asking me why I spend so much of my working life getting so involved in this silly little song contest," said Filip, his eyes filling with pride. "And it's for moments like this. Moments that you can't ever fully explain to people who haven't been through it themselves. It's for all the songs and the camaraderie and the nonsense and the total, total excess of it all."

As they walked through the gates they were greeted by a big gaggle of crew members all propped up at the nearest bar.

"Hey, Filip, boys! Come and have a drink with us!" shouted Håkan, now dressed in national costume from head to toe.

"He swapped it with one of the interval dancers for a handful of old heavy metal t-shirts," said Ice with a smile. "Unwashed, at that!"

"I'm not sure who got the worse end of the bargain there," Filip laughed, as everybody bundled up into a big group hug. In the background, Space Truckers were just getting up onto the stage to run through their winning song. Filip stepped back a couple of paces and addressed his friends and colleagues before things got too noisy.

"I just want to raise a toast to every one of you," he said proudly. "This year's contest has been the absolute biggest pain in the arse of my entire professional career. And you lot have given me nothing but stress and headaches from day one. Then there's all those bloody artists and their silly little egos, plus the local politicians sticking their noses in."

Filip could see the towering form of The Ox standing guard by the castle gate, and beckoned him over.

"Oxman!" he said warmly. "Oh behalf of all of us here I'd like to thank you and your team for looking after us over the last few weeks and keeping the show safe. There were times when we probably couldn't have gone any further without your assistance."

The big man looked genuinely moved by Filip's thanks. "It was nothing, sir. It is what we do. Thank you too for allowing us all to do our work here. It has been nothing but a pleasure!"
"Oh, one more thing, Ox!" said Terry, "Thank you so much for keeping Michael Storm out of our hair for the last few days. It's made our job in the press office much easier."

The Ox suddenly jolted rigid and his eyes snapped wide open.

"Oh shit," he said, looking concerned. "I forgot to tell my cousin to let him out of his pig shed! Lucky you reminded me!"

Everybody laughed that hearty kind of laugh that you only give out when you learn of the misfortune of somebody who perhaps kind of deserved it.

"That should teach him for being such an arse!" said Dean.

"I wouldn't bank on it," Terry chuckled. "But at least it gave him the chance to think about what he'd done at best, and probably really annoyed him at worst. And that's got to be a win in anyone's book!"

The ageing Aussie punks struck up the first few chords of their song on the big stage in the background and Filip raised his voice a little in order to be heard over the noise.

"And then there's this lot," he said, jabbing a thumb over his shoulder at the winning band. "Next year is going to be an absolute bloody logistic nightmare. But we got through this one, and this organisation will sure as dammit get through the next one! And do you know what? I couldn't have got through any of the endless barrage of problems and nonsense without you horrible lot. And for that I thank you all from the bottom of my cold, Serbian heart."

"Three cheers for Filip the Great!" bellowed Håkan from the top of a barrel. Once the cheers had subsided, Hanna walked up to Filip and gave him a most uncharacteristic hug.

"So I take it you won't be joining us in Australia next year, seeing as you had such a horrible time here in Moldova?" she said with a cheeky smile.

"Of course I bloody will," Filip replied. "I wouldn't miss it for the world!"

About Roy D Hacksaw

The Eurovision Song Contest might seem like an unlikely subject for a gnarly punk rocker to write about, but Roy D Hacksaw has surprising form in this field. Being a bit of an old fart, he grew up in a time where his main access to music on TV came as part of the many variety shows that littered the three available channels in the back end of the sixties and early seventies. All the cool music shows were on way after his bedtime, and his old man really couldn't stomach Top Of The Pops. So it was always a treat when on a Spring Saturday night every year his Dad would go out to play snooker and he could sit and watch Eurovision with his Mum. As the decades passed by and he got more involved in punk rock the old contest lost a little of its shine and he found himself watching it less frequently. But he still always kept an eye on the results. That was until in the early nineties when he found himself in Sweden on Eurovision night and he could see how differently the locals viewed the contest. It was more of a popular national passion than the mildly entertaining embarrassment that we Brits viewed it as, and this instantly rekindled his passion for the show.

A few years later, when Katrina & The Waves won the thing for the UK, he realised that he could finally achieve his long-held ambition to attend one Eurovision in his life, so when the next year's contest was held in Birmingham in 1998 he blagged his way in on a press ticket, and unbeknownst to him his life was never going to be quite the same again.

Since then he's travelled all over the continent covering the contest for an array of magazines and websites, including heat, BBC Online and Popbitch. In that time he's partied in palaces, shaken hands with Presidents, and been to places that he'd only previously dreamed of visiting. From bobbing about in the Dead Sea with a gaggle of sunburned Estonians to being jostled by Vladimir Putin's security in Moscow, and most unlikely of all, spending an incredibly strange afternoon with Engelbert Humperdinck and Jedward in a hotel room in Baku, the contest always has always offered way more than just a gaggle of silly songs if you know where to look, and shown him things he could never have imagined when he was sitting watching the contest with his Mum back in the mists of time.

He even had a stab at getting on the contest himself – the song Rush Goalie by his band the Cesspit Rebels got to the last 50 of the UK qualifying competition in 2001. On top of that he sat on the UK's shortlisting panel for the contest in 2017 ("Don't blame me," he says. "There was nothing even remotely noisy among the songs we had to chose from!"), helped translate the chorus of the

2000 Israel entry into English, and currently writes a blog called Eurovision Apocalypse that highlights all the weird and wonderful songs and performers that attempt to represent their nation each year. And usually fail.

Away from Eurovision, Roy is a professional writer, who edits magazines and creates questions for quiz shows. He also plays in horrible gnarly punk rock bands like Hacksaw, GlueHorse and Chaotic Dischord.

Oh, and before you ask, he asked us to tell you that the contest isn't all political and Europe doesn't actually hate us – the UK just sends boringly average songs, which is the only real reason why we get such terrible results these days. And if you want an argument about it he's got the stats to prove it!

Also by Roy D Hacksaw

Bugger Banksy

Did you ever wonder what happens to the inhabitants of a building after the artist known as Banksy leaves one of his artworks on their wall? Especially when there's something slightly less than legal going on inside? Join Glyn and Kevin as they desperately try to keep their clandestine business secret after the world's most famous graffiti artist makes his mark on the side of their old barn in the Valleys of South Wales, and their solitude is invaded by an endless parade of unlikely visitors...

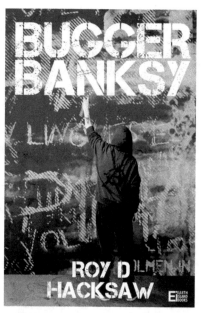

Available at www.earthislandbooks.com

CPSIA information can be obtained
at www.ICGtesting.com
Printed in the USA
BVHW030654240622
640577BV00018B/163